Where to Stash Your Cash Legally

Offshore Financial Centers of the World

Sixth Edition

Robert E. Bauman, JD

Sovereign Offshore Services LLC.
(The Sovereign Society)
98 S.E. Federal Highway, Suite 2
Delray Beach, FL 33483
Tel.: + 561-272-0413
Website: http://www.sovereignsociety.com
Email: info@sovereignsociety.com
ISBN 978-0-615-71732-6

Notice: This publication is designed to provide accurate and authoritative information in regard
to the subject matter covered. It is sold and distributed with the understanding that the author,
publisher and seller are not engaged in rendering legal, accounting or other professional advice
or service. If legal or other expert assistance is required, the services of a competent professional
advisor should be sought.

The information and recommendations contained herein have been compiled from sources considered reliable. Employees, officers and directors of The Sovereign Society do not receive fees or
commissions for any recommendations of services or products in this book. Investment and other
recommendations carry inherent risks. As no investment recommendation can be guaranteed, The
Sovereign Society takes no responsibility for any loss or inconvenience if one chooses to accept them.

The Sovereign Society advocates full compliance with applicable tax and financial reporting laws.
U.S. law requires income taxes to be paid on all worldwide income wherever a U.S. person (citizen
or resident alien) may live or have a residence. Each U.S. person who has a financial interest in
or signature authority over bank, securities, or other financial accounts in a foreign country that
exceeds $10,000 in aggregate value must report that fact on his or her annual federal income tax
return, IRS Form 1040. The Foreign Account Tax Compliance Act (FATCA) requires an annual
filing along with IRS Form 1040 IRS Form 8938 listing specified foreign assets. An additional
report must be filed by June 30th of each year on an information return (Form TDF 90 22.1)
with the U.S. Treasury. Willful noncompliance of reports may result in criminal prosecution. You
should consult a qualified attorney or accountant to ensure that you know, understand and comply
with these and any other U.S. reporting requirements.

Where to Stash Your Cash Legally

Offshore Financial Centers of the World

Sixth Edition

Robert E. Bauman, JD

About the Author

Robert E. Bauman, JD

Bob Bauman, legal counsel to The Sovereign Society, served as a member of the U.S. House of Representatives from 1973 to 1981 representing the First District of Maryland. He is an author and lecturer on many aspects of wealth protection, offshore residence and second citizenship.

A member of the District of Columbia Bar, he received his *juris doctor* degree from the Law Center of Georgetown University in 1964. He has a B.S. degree in International Relations from the Georgetown University School of Foreign Service (1959) and was honored with GU's Distinguished Alumni Award.

He is the author of *The Gentleman from Maryland* (Hearst Book Publishing, NY, 1985); and the following books, all published by The Sovereign Society: *The Complete Guide to Offshore Residency, Dual Citizenship and Second Passports* (10 editions, 2001- 2012); *The Offshore Money Manual* (2000); editor of *Forbidden Knowledge* (2009); *Panama Money Secrets* (2005); *Where to Stash Your Cash Legally: Offshore Financial Centers of the World* (6 editions through 2012), *Swiss Money Secrets* (2008); *How to Lawyer-Proof Your Life* (2009). His writings have appeared in *The Wall Street Journal*, *The New York Times*, *National Review*, and many other publications.

Author's Comment

For a quarter century, I have been researching and writing about offshore financial matters. That has included topics such as tax havens (more recently self-designated as "offshore financial centers"), asset havens, offshore banking, asset protection trusts, international business corporations, family foundations, limited liability companies, financial privacy and about the state of the offshore financial world in general.

Even though I had earned a degree in international relations, a law degree, and served eight years as a member of the U.S. House of Representatives, when I began this work I quickly discovered how little I knew about the real "offshore" world.

My early and limited acquaintance with "offshore" matters had created the erroneous impression that many retain after too many potboiler novels, Hollywood movies and TV shows. There, the offshore world was (and still is) depicted in the sensational shorthand of secret numbered bank accounts, sinister con men and fraudsters, money launderers, drug kingpins and corrupt foreign politicians taking bribes on tropical islands.

For 15 years or more, tax-hungry politicians from high-tax welfare states—including the U.S. government, together with their global leftist allies—have mounted a series of largely false attacks on the offshore financial world. They intentionally have smeared offshore financial centers as sinkholes of tax evasion, drug money and terrorist cash. At one point they even advanced the preposterous claim that tax havens caused the 2008–2012 global recession.

Their collective motive is obvious: the politicians want to tax more so they can spend more hoping to buy popular support, thus enabling continued power and the continuation of their failed past policies.

Then too, many American attorneys, accountants, insurance

agents and stock brokers have a vested interest in keeping their clients close to home, thus they warn against going offshore. They, like the U.S. Internal Revenue Service, want to keep you and your money where they can get to it.

Don't be fooled. It is fully legal for Americans to bank, invest, and purchase real estate, annuities and life insurance offshore. When this fog of manufactured lies is cleared away, the truth about "offshore" opportunities and profits is very impressive.

But finding the truth for the first-time offshore adventurer can be a frustrating, discouraging task and, if you get burnt, a very short and unpleasant journey.

The offshore world offers Americans few tax savings, certainly not as many as slick promoters claim. That's because American citizens and resident aliens are taxed on their worldwide income, while most other nations impose "territorial" taxes mainly on earnings within their own national borders. For those more sensible countries, taxes do end at the border.

But going offshore for Americans does offer some limited tax deferral and, most of all, in this lawsuit-happy age, it offers ironclad asset protection. It also guarantees far more financial privacy (and yes, secrecy) than now can be found in many other countries or in the United States, where the so-called PATRIOT Act has destroyed all financial privacy.

During the 12 years since the first edition of this book appeared, U.S. politicians and government bureaucrats have become an army of control freaks when it comes to Americans' offshore financial activity. They have imposed an entangling web of border controls, travel controls, currency controls, foreign investment and banking controls, all the while repeatedly implying that "going offshore" is somehow illegal (it is not) and even unpatriotic.

The politicians shamelessly used the New York City and Washington, D.C., terror attacks on September 11, 2001, as an excuse for even greater control. The continuing 2008 global financial crisis serves as yet another pretext not only to impose more financial controls, but to spend trillions of taxpayers' dollars to bail out banks and businesses, foreign and domestic, greatly increasing the ranks of those who are indebted the existing system of Big Brother government.

Counter-productive government controls and regulations stifling the American economy have grown exponentially. The invasion of law-abiding Americans' privacy is carried out in secret under the PATRIOT Act. The record of the FBI in the last decade is one long list of abused powers and unconstitutional acts, followed by apologies and promises to sin no more—but only when they were caught.

The U.S. Justice Department's Inspector General Report criticized the FBI abuse of "national security letters" (NSLs) in obtaining thousands of telephone, business and financial records without prior judicial approval. Although they cited the PATRIOT Act as their authority, the DOJ found the FBI illegally issued more than 20,000 NSLs, most having nothing to do with terrorism.

And government civil asset forfeiture seizures now total $2.5 billion annually, aimed mainly at innocent people never charged with a crime as state and federal police agencies seek easy sources of increased income.

So what does all this have to do with offshore financial havens and your ability to go offshore? If you cannot answer that question you may be in trouble already.

Wherever you live, thankfully "offshore" is a place well outside the immediate jurisdiction of your home country's government and its executive and judicial agencies.

When you move some or all of your cash, assets and investments offshore, you place them on the other side of a political and legal wall that stands as a formidable obstacle. Offshore serves as far more than a speed bump to lawsuits, claims, disgruntled business partners, a spouse, and family members, even to your government and its regulations or unexpected laws.

Asset protection planning means taking steps well in advance of potential trouble to protect your assets, property, savings, investments, stocks, businesses, retirement, and inheritances. Advance planning against unexpected threats takes on a new meaning considering the events in the U.S. and throughout the world today. History teaches that things can and do change quickly. Don't ever think you are immune.

That's what this book you're reading is all about—legal ways for you to protect your wealth, invest and increase your money, save on taxes, even making your home and finding financial privacy—and peace of mind—by "going offshore."

I will tell you the who, what, why, when and where of the offshore world—based on my personal experience, and that of the many experts with whom The Sovereign Society works across the globe; the same trusted professionals you'll find listed in these pages for your own personal use.

Welcome to the offshore world,

Bob Bauman

Robert E. Bauman, JD
Delray Beach, Florida
November 2012

Where to Stash Your Cash Legally
Offshore Financial Centers of the World

Chapter One

A Safe Haven Offshore = Peace of Mind

The reasons and uses of an offshore haven; the ways and means of moving your assets and wealth offshore to a tax-free or low-tax jurisdiction; strategies and the places where you can invest with maximum profitability, minimum taxes and greater financial privacy.

Fifteen years ago when I first began writing about the offshore world, the vast technological changes that now have created a new world economic structure were just taking hold.

I recall the late Bob Kephart, the founder of The Sovereign Society, returning from Switzerland in the late 1990s and saying with disgust, "Those Swiss banks don't even have email yet!"

Today, we have a technologically advanced global system that offers huge financial opportunities based on instant communications, interlinked databases, electronic commerce and digital cash flows. And, in many ways, this system has shifted power from the monopolistic policies of the high-tax nation state to the beleaguered individual citizen, greatly increasing personal financial freedom and the chance for profit.

In turn, this new global freedom has caused a reaction by grasping governments everywhere, trying desperately to keep control over their citizens and eager to know what they are doing, especially with their finances.

The technology that makes these global systems available for your use also are being used by government for constant surveillance in an attempt to track your every move, well beyond the official reports you are required by law to file with the government.

As part of Big Brother's plans to control its citizens and their money, political leaders in major nations will use almost any excuse to attack and curb offshore financial activity. They, along with their allies in the "news" media, have sought to portray "tax havens" as secretive places where crime and tax evasion is rampant. Even more ridiculous, they blamed offshore financial centers for somehow causing the 2008 global, four-year economic downturn that, in fact, was caused by their own unwise economic policies exploited by greedy bankers in New York and the City of London.

To a degree, these big government Big Brothers have succeeded. The political Left has so tarnished the phrase "tax haven" that these besieged offshore jurisdictions now prefer to be called "offshore financial centers."

Small wonder many people don't have a clue about what "offshore" actually means, while too many others have gained the worst possible impression of unjustifiably smeared tax havens.

A few clueless people even seem unaware of the major global financial revolution that has taken place. This book goes beyond the clues and reveals the secrets. It tells you the truth about offshore financial activity and tax havens, and how to profit offshore and what you can do personally to reap the benefits legally.

By now, most people understand the meaning of the huge advances in digital technology, satellite communications and the vast expansion of the Internet. With social networking, texting, smart phones, tweeting, iPads and iPhones, today's economic news travels fast.

Insider information is no longer confined to Wall Street and the City of London. Waves of news and rumors ripple daily through world time zones and stock markets as 24/7 media covers events live—an example of the irresistible technological advances that have forced a totally new operational reality on financial and banking systems — and on governments.

In many respects, all this constitutes a government bureaucrat's worst fear — hundreds of millions of instant communication devices and computers linked worldwide, electronic banking and online investment accounts, "smart card" money, easily available email encryption; free communications, much of it still unmediated by governments.

An astute observer put it this way: "You get untraceable banking and investment, a black hole where money can hide and be laundered, not just for conglomerates or drug cartels, but for anyone." (That may be true, but my advice is, "Don't try it," but more about that warning later.)

You can see why government bureaucrats, especially the tax collectors, are constantly in a frantic state. The freedom of this new world money system runs counter to all the Big Brother control freak, socialist policies that have bled taxpayers and crippled prosperity for most of the last 90 years. That official fear of losing control is what, in part, spurs the incessant attacks on offshore financial centers — and on those of us who use them legally to our advantage.

As the world now understands, the government is doing all it can to stifle these liberating trends. But I believe they will fail.

Why Go Offshore?

Until relatively recently, most people thought "personal finance" meant checking and savings accounts, home mortgages and auto loans. Even now, with available international offshore mutual and hedge funds — some of them successful even in the face of world economic turmoil — relatively few investors take advantage of available global diversification.

What follows are only some of the many reasons to "go offshore."

1. Investment diversification. Many of the world's best investments and money managers and bankers will not do business with U.S. citizens directly. This anti-American client attitude has stiffened in reaction to U.S. government policies since the 2008 UBS tax evasion scandal and the adoption by the U.S. Congress in 2010 of the *Foreign Account Tax Compliance Act (FATCA)*.

Foreigners, and many foreign banks, have made the choice that it is easier and less costly to do business with the rest of the world than it is to comply with the draconian rules of the U.S. government, especially those of the U.S. Internal Revenue Service (IRS), which now claims to have worldwide jurisdiction over every bank and financial institution that has American clients.

It is a fact that by going offshore, you can gain direct legal access to U.S.-restricted investments unavailable in the United States. Less than 2,000 foreign securities are traded on U.S. stock and other markets, representing a tiny percentage of the securities traded on world markets. The only practical way to buy these offshore shares is through a foreign bank or offshore stock broker. In these pages you will find the names and contact information for reliable banks, brokers, investment managers, insurance and annuity advisors and attorneys, all friendly to Americans.

2. Higher returns. There are opportunities in traditional foreign financial markets, such as stocks sold only on foreign exchanges that offer much higher returns than generally are available in U.S. markets. For example, through 2012 the Canadian-based Silver Wheaton (SLW), the largest metals streaming company in the world, has gained 746% in value since 2005 in Canadian dollars, or 952% in U.S. dollars.

3. Currency diversification. Investors wishing to stabilize their portfolios can protect their wealth against the fluctuating U.S. dollar simply by holding currencies the experts recommend, such as the Norwegian kroner, the Australian dollar and the Singapore dollar, all good long-term currencies, as long as stock markets remain soft. Past currency favorites such as the Swiss franc and the Japanese yen now pose more risk due to central bank intervention. For those interested in currency trading, consider the several Sovereign Society investment research newsletters.

While U.S. investors can purchase foreign currencies through a few U.S. banks, offshore banks generally offer higher yields, lower fees and lower minimums. Foreign currency opportunities are plentiful, such as earning nearly 13% on the declining U.S. dollar versus the euro in one recent year. For decades, the U.S. dollar has been losing value in relation to stronger currencies. In 1970, a U.S. dollar would purchase 4.5 Swiss francs but in 2012, the U.S. dollar equals less than one Swiss franc. Since 1971, the franc has appreciated nearly 330% against the U.S. dollar.

4. Safety and security. Starting in the 1980s, the United States experienced a wave of bank and savings and loans failures at a rate unmatched since the Great Depression. The underwriting of U.S. thrifts and S&Ls by the financial industry and the American taxpayer cost a staggering $153 billion. The disaster was a major threat to the U.S. financial system, and one of the most expensive financial sector crises the world had seen.

Beginning in 2008-2009, a government-prompted U.S. housing crisis in subprime mortgages and unregulated derivative investments augmented by Wall Street's reckless greed combined to produce another American banking crisis that again recalled the misery of that same Great Depression of the 1930s. Rescuing many of the major U.S. banks from themselves required trillions of taxpayer dollars in bailouts and even now, the end is not in sight.

In contrast, the offshore banks I recommend in these pages

were not, and are not, exposed to risky investments, such as sub-prime mortgages, Third World debt and highly leveraged derivative investments.

Indeed, we at The Sovereign Society take pride in the fact that for more than a decade we have warned against using certain offshore banks, including by name UBS and Credit Suisse. We have done our due diligence and the recommended banks in these pages are well-capitalized and conservatively managed—and they do welcome American clients at a time when many offshore banks do not. You can tell them The Sovereign Society sent you.

5. Asset protection. Lawsuits continue in epidemic proportions in America and tort reform gets nowhere in the U.S. Congress where millions of dollars in trial lawyer's political action committee contributions hold sway.

In America, if a creditor gets a judgment against you in the state where you live, that judgment may be easily enforced. In contrast, if you invest or bank in a suitable offshore jurisdiction, even Switzerland, you can be configured financially to be essentially judgment-proof.

The prudent use of offshore havens for safekeeping some of your cash and assets provides U.S. persons with a greatly enhanced ability to protect them from the threat of lawsuits, civil forfeiture, business failure, divorce, exchange controls, repressive U.S. legislation, lengthy probate and political instability. Going offshore where privacy laws are strict largely avoids the vast U.S. asset-tracking network, which permits private or official investigators to easily identify the unencumbered assets of a potential defendant.

6. Financial privacy. Let's face the truth: since the adoption of the so-called PATRIOT Act in 2001, in so far as the government is concerned, personal and financial privacy is dead in America.

Yet many people naturally want protection from the prying eyes of business partners, estranged family members and identity thieves surfing the Internet. Financial privacy can be the best protection against frivolous lawsuits that end with big judgments. If you don't appear to have enough assets to justify the time and expense of an attack, a plaintiff's attorney won't see you as an easy target.

Simply put, assets placed "offshore" are off the domestic asset-tracking "radar screen." The United States is one of the few nations lacking a federal law that protects bank or securities accounts from disclosure except under defined circumstances. Many disclosures that would be illegal in other countries, either under international agreements such as the European Privacy Directive, or under national laws guaranteeing financial secrecy, as in Switzerland or Panama, are commonplace in the United States. That fact makes "going offshore" even more important.

The six advantages I just described have especially strong application when it comes to placing your cash and other assets offshore.

Privacy as a Human Right

For citizens and foreign residents of the United States, discussion of the issue of personal and financial privacy must start with the fact that under the draconian terms of the 2001 PATRIOT Act, financial privacy in the United States is indeed dead and gone. The government now has the power to obtain financial information in secret about anyone—and to confiscate your wealth without notice. That questionable 2001 "law" is augmented by massive government police surveillance of all kinds, much of it of questionable legal authority.

Small wonder that many millions of Americans do business offshore to take advantage of still strong privacy laws in places such as Switzerland, Panama, Singapore, Austria and Luxembourg.

Of course, the usual cry by those who advocate ever-increased government surveillance of not just our finances, but every aspect of our lives, is that old saw: "If you aren't doing anything wrong, what do you have to hide?"

It is absolutely wrong to characterize this debate as "clean money versus dirty cash" or "security versus privacy" or, more recently, "the need for banking stability versus a global recession."

Privacy is an inherent human right, and a requirement for maintaining the human condition with dignity and respect. The real choices are personal freedom and liberty versus governmental control of our lives and fortunes.

Tyranny, whether it arises under the threat of terrorist attack, alleged solutions to banking problems, or under any form of unrelenting domestic official scrutiny, is still tyranny.

Liberty requires security without intrusion — security plus privacy. Widespread surveillance, whether by police or nosy bureaucrats, in whatever form it takes, is the very definition of a police state.

And that's why we should champion privacy, both personal and financial, even when we have nothing to hide.

Having said that, I must acknowledge that the world now lives in an era when terrorism is real, but also a convenient excuse for power hungry politicians in almost every nation. Official "anti-terrorism" policies are expressed in a host of national laws that severely curtail financial and personal privacy, assuming we are all terrorists. These so-called "anti-terrorist" laws were preceded by other broad U.S. laws that have failed originally premised on fighting drugs and combating money laundering and other crimes.

But in America, the combined effect of this onslaught of laws has all but abolished any personal or financial privacy — at least for those accused or suspected of crimes of any nature — and these days that can be anyone, with or without probable cause. Governments now have much greater powers in deciding who are "suspects" and the list of crimes alone based on paperwork or failure to report grows ever longer.

But please understand me: for the average offshore investor or person otherwise financially active offshore, there is little to fear from anti-crime laws that compromise privacy.

So long as you obey the financial reporting laws and tax obligations imposed on you by your home nation, you will remain in the clear. Professional advice will help and protect you in this essential education and in these pages we will tell you how to meet those obligations and who can assist you in doing so.

I will repeat in these pages an important reminder — the financial privacy and bank secrecy laws of many other nations are still very much stronger than those in the United States. In America, the PATRIOT Act and other draconian laws essentially have abolished the right to privacy. Privacy laws in other countries can be a definite advantage for you — and an added legal shield for your financial activities.

Offshore Legal Entities

By now the financially well-informed are comfortable with offshore bank accounts which they routinely use as investment vehicles. But the use of more complicated offshore techniques, such as the international business corporation (IBC), a foreign-based asset protection trust (APT), a private family foundation or a limited liability company (LLC) have seen far less use.

While using these legal methods takes a bit more time and effort, they can greatly enhance your choice of financial strategies and give you increased protection and investing effectiveness. In these pages I explain these proven strategies and show you how you to use them. You may find it difficult to believe, but each of these strategies in their basic form can cost less than $3,500 to implement, as I'll explain.

One more thought: perhaps you might consider relocating your personal residence offshore in a tax haven nation that welcomes foreigners with tax exemptions and special privileges that make life easier and less complicated. I will explain which nations, such as Panama, Uruguay and Singapore, offer such incentives and how you can take advantage of them.

Investment Profits Offshore

For the past two decades, the trend continues towards more foreign investment. In 1980, less than 1% of U.S. pension fund assets were invested abroad. By 2009, that figure had risen to 26%. In addition to pension funds, mutual funds and stock purchases, banks bought into emerging markets in a very big way, especially European and Japanese banks.

"When history books are written 200 years from now about the last two decades of the 20th Century," former U.S. Treasury secretary, Lawrence Summers, told *The New York Times*, "I am convinced that the end of the Cold War will be the second story. The first story will be about the appearance of emerging markets — about the fact that developing countries where more than three billion people live have moved toward the market and seen rapid growth in incomes."

Of course, that optimistic comment came well before the global recession of 2008 in which emerging market stock values sank along with those in other world markets. Even so, after bruising global downturns in past history, the U.S. economy usually has led the world back to growth, but developing countries could well be the engine that powers future recovery.

As of this writing, despite fears that they would be among the biggest victims of the financial crisis, emerging market giants like China, India and Brazil are rebounding, as the Organization for Economic Cooperation and Development (OECD) predicted, even as Europe, the United States and Japan lag behind in their recovery.

As historian and professor Niall Ferguson noted: "The globalization of finance played a crucial role in raising growth rates in emerging markets, particularly in Asia, propelling hundreds of millions of people out of poverty."

Cross-border investments have proven profitable, despite temporary setbacks. What used to be tagged "Third World" investment funds have become the more appealing "emerging market funds."

The global economy of today is very different from past times. As depressed as it may have been more recently, finance and technology still dominate the world economic scene. In 2010, average daily turnover in global foreign exchange markets was estimated at $3.98 trillion, a growth of approximately 20% over the $3.21 trillion daily volume of 2007. Some firms specializing on foreign exchange market put the average daily turnover in excess of US$4 trillion. That's more than 20 times the 1986 daily total of $270 billion. The volume of foreign exchange trade has increased by roughly 160 times in the last 30 years.

We all know that the fires of the global credit crisis that first appeared as a wisp of smoke in a corner of the U.S. mortgage market turned into a global firestorm that cut through the housing, bond, and stock markets. Between 2007 and mid-2011, U.S. households alone suffered a 29.5%, $10.06 trillion absolute drop in the value of housing assets. In those glory days before the crash, investment capital had exploded worldwide. In 2006, mutual funds, pension funds, and other institutional investors controlled over US$30 trillion, 15 times the comparable 1980 figure.

Boom and Bust

According to the U.S. Census Bureau's 2012 Statistical Abstract for Banking, Finance and Insurance, the U.S. mutual fund industry held more than $11.8 trillion in assets on January 1, 2011. Nevertheless, total net assets had still not returned to the January 1, 2009 level of $12.02 trillion, largely reflecting the sharp drop in equity prices experienced worldwide in 2008-2009.

Once autos, steel and grain dominated world markets, but more recently trade in stocks, bonds and currencies has replaced them. Notably, the World Trade Organization (WTO) reported in April 2012 that trade expansion in 2011 was up a mere 5%, which they called "a sharp deceleration" from a significant rebound in 2010 of 13.8%. Projects from the WTO expect more tapping of the brakes with just a 3.7% growth in 2012. Analysts for the WTO blame the lost momentum on the European debt crisis.

Those rosy numbers did not last. In 2008, total world trade dropped by almost 10%, the largest decrease in any year since World War II.

The global consulting firm McKinsey & Company produced some impressive numbers that tell us clearly where the action is today:

- The 2008 financial crisis and worldwide recession halted a three-decade expansion of global capital and banking markets. By 2012, growth had resumed, fueled by expansion in developing economies but also by a $4.4 trillion increase in sovereign debt. The total value of the world's financial stock, comprising equity market capitalization and outstanding bonds and loans, increased from $175 trillion in 2008 to $212 trillion at the start of 2011, surpassing the previous 2007 peak.

- The global stock of debt and equity grew by $11 trillion to 2011, the majority from a rebound in global stock market capitalization, mostly new equity issuance and stronger earnings expectations. Net new equity issuance in 2010 totaled $387 billion, and the majority of that came from emerging-market companies. Initial public offerings (IPOs) continued to grow in emerging-markets, with 60% of IPO volume occurring on stock exchanges in China and other emerging markets.

- The world's investors and companies continue to diversify their portfolios globally. The stock of foreign investment assets grew to over $100 trillion, hitting a historical high in 2011—a ten-fold increase since 1990. Over the past 25 years capital markets outside the U.S. have grown rapidly in size and importance. In 1970, non-U.S. stocks accounted for 32% of the world's US$935 billion total market capitalization. By 2011, foreign stocks represented over 60% of the total value of world stock market capitalization of over US$11 trillion.

- Cross-border investment is growing fastest outside of the old, traditional centers of financial wealth. In 1999, the web of cross-border investments centered on the United States, which was partner in 50% of all international financial positions. By 2009, the U.S. total cross-border investment share had shrunk to 32%. This reflected both a surge within Western Europe following creation of the euro, and phenomenal growth in the size of emerging markets. Prior to the 2008 financial crisis, cross-border investments between Latin America, emerging Asia, and the Middle East were growing at 39%, about twice as fast as these regions' investments with developed countries.

If you need more proof of the offshore investing trend, look at American over-the-counter (OTC) (off-exchange trading) last year. Foreign stocks' OTC trading in American Depository Receipts (ADRs) skyrocketed over 2010's trading of $102 billion to exceed $189 billion. Much of that staggering volume included shares of foreign companies, also known as "foreign ordinaries," which claimed approximately $120 billion of the OTC volume in 2011.

ADRs accounted for the rest. Most ordinaries are Canadian companies. U.S. domestic trading in foreign stocks has grown to represent the vast majority of the total dollar value traded over-the-counter. Securities garnered the lion's share at 80% of the $229 billion traded in 2011 — that's up from just 71% in 2010.

Regardless of boom or bust, what must be remembered is that wealth has become stateless, circulating wherever the owner finds the highest return and the greatest freedom. In other words, cash without a country.

From 1970 to 2010, spending by investors in industrialized nations on offshore stocks increased more than 200 times over while national capital markets merged into one global capital market. As stock markets close in London, they open in New York and as American exchanges end the day on the U.S. west coast, markets in Hong Kong, Singapore and Tokyo come to life.

Unfortunately, this same interconnected global market also helps to spread economic downturns faster than the speed of the bird flu virus.

In the global recession of 2008–2009, investors, banks and funds in many countries lost cash and value because of unwise foreign investments in so-called "toxic" unregulated subprime mortgages, stock swaps, derivatives and other esoteric investment vehicles, the shrunken value of which is a continuing problem.

Add to this world economic indigestion the problem of billions in sovereign debt of profligate spending by European countries such as Ireland, Greece, Spain, Italy and Portugal that owe the massive debts to shaky banks in France, Germany, and Luxembourg.

Avoiding Roadblocks to Prosperity

At a time when some politicians are demanding more government regulation such as the Foreign Account Tax Compliance Act of 2010 (FATCA), few realize that information about most offshore investments, profitable or otherwise, long has been denied to U.S. persons who want to invest offshore.

Cumbersome rules and regulations imposed years ago by the U.S. government on foreign investment funds and banks lock out foreign fund managers. Unwilling to waste time and money on bureaucratic registrations, until recently most offshore funds would not even do business with anyone who had a U.S. mailing address.

It is always convenient for America's political class to blame "deregulation" for every U.S. financial crisis and the excesses of the free market. Not only does that pass the buck, but it also creates a justification for still more regulation. The question is: Who regulates the regulators? Until that question is answered satisfactorily, calls for more regulation are symptoms of the very disease they claim to cure.

One of the main obstacles has been restrictive U.S. securities laws. Any "investment contract" for purchase of a security sold in the United States must be registered with the U.S. Securities & Exchange Commission (SEC) and often with similar state agencies. This is an expensive process. The U.S. also requires far more stock disclosure by sales entities than most foreign countries, burdening the process further with U.S. accounting practices that differ from those used abroad.

International fund managers are practical people who keep their eyes on the bottom line. Many correctly calculate that operating costs in the U.S. would wipe out any possibility of a profit margin.

Ironically, many mutual funds and hedge funds with top performance records are run from offices in the U.S. by U.S. residents, but do not accept investments from Americans. To avoid SEC red tape and registration costs, investment in these funds is available only to non-U.S. persons.

But all this is changing now as many foreign financial firms and banks are registering with the U.S. Securities and Exchange Commission in order to serve American clients. In these pages I will identify such firms that work with The Sovereign Society.

S.E.C. Goes Worldwide

In the UBS Swiss bank scandal that was exposed in 2007, the IRS played the major role in investigating U.S. clients who evaded taxes and this anti-tax evasion campaign got all the news coverage.

Much less notice was given to the fact that the U.S. Department of Justice charged that the services UBS rendered in Switzerland amounted to the bank's staff acting as unregistered investment advisers and broker-dealers in violation of the U.S. Investment Advisers Act of 1940 and of the U.S. Securities and Exchange Commission (SEC) rules.

Using this novel extraterritorial approach, the SEC sought to extend its jurisdiction to include any foreign person anywhere in the world who dares to advise Americans about investing.

The SEC claims that unless the adviser first qualifies and registers with that agency they are engaged in illegal, even criminal conduct.

In the final 2010 settlement, UBS paid a $718 million fine to the IRS on the tax evasion charges. It also paid $200 million to the U.S. based on the SEC charges. UBS was barred permanently from acting as investment advisers or broker-dealer for American clients in Switzerland.

As a result of the successful U.S. government attacks and the fines levied against UBS, a growing number of offshore banks have established special, separate SEC-qualified investment banking units for American clients only. Some independent offshore investment advisers also have registered with the SEC.

As part of your due diligence, check to see if the offshore bank you are considering is SEC registered. In the section on Offshore Banking (starting on page 70) I have listed foreign financial institutions (Jyske Bank and two independent Swiss investment advisers) that are now SEC registered.

Fortunately, there are ways for U.S. citizens to avoid these government obstacles. In these pages, I explain how you can access such offshore investments, legally and safely, using offshore entities such as a trust, a limited liability company, international business corporation, or even a private family foundation, located in a haven nation.

Or you may use the simple device of establishing a foreign trading account with an offshore broker. I'll have more to say about that in Chapter Two.

Exodus Offshore Grows

The revolutions within individual countries' economies include an increasing number of people escaping from leech-like national tax systems that financially prop up dying welfare states.

In the past, it was not uncommon for some of the wealthiest French or Americans to flee their homelands in an effort to escape excessive taxation — or even wealthy Russians and Chinese avoiding political instability. However, today's sovereign individual includes not just millionaires and billionaires, but those of more modest wealth who have joined this migratory exodus.

People in ever-greater numbers are seeking to start a new life in countries where hard work is rewarded, not punished by wealth confiscation — places where business is free to make its own decisions, without regulatory predators hovering over every attempt at free enterprise.

The numbers of U.S. citizens leaving the land of the free (and heavily taxed) is growing, according to U.S. Treasury figures. In 2011, more than 1,700 people renounced U.S. citizenship — a number than is more than twice the 2009 figures. *U.S. News & World Report* estimated that each year three million U.S. citizens and resident aliens simply leave America to make new homes in other nations. Admittedly, this surprising number of three million people leaving must be compared to the millions clamoring to get into the U.S. from even more restrictive nations.

But there's a huge difference in the economic status of these two groups. Those seeking admission are, by and large, poverty-stricken persons desperately trying to better their lot with new lives in what they see as the Promised Land. They'll settle for low paying jobs, welfare, free education for their kids and U.S. government-subsidized housing and health care.

Not all of these people are low income. Chinese millionaires and billionaires are flocking to the United States in record numbers. In 2011, "Investor Visa" was used by more than 2,000 Chinese citizens who sought entry and, ultimately, citizenship in the United States. In return for a modest investment of $500,000 to $1 million and the creation of a certain of number of jobs, this official U.S. program allows foreigners and their families permanent U.S. residence.

Those Americans seeking to escape the growing tyranny aimed right at them by the United States government are typically middle class and wealthier people. One estimate is that the loss of three million people annually equals a loss of 2% of the national workforce and $136 billion in income. And it is this gusher of fleeing Americans who take with them the lion's share of the U.S. tax base. These are among the very top 5% of the people who pay for all of those programs those new (and often illegal) immigrants covet.

Increasingly, the wealthy correctly perceive that they are under attack by their own government, so they take the only rational option left open to them. They're taking their wealth and leaving.

Look back on multiple government attacks on wealth during the last decade. What you will find is U.S. congressional legislation that has all but abolished domestic financial privacy and reversed the burden of proof forcing the accused to prove his innocence. These laws allowed billions of dollars of property confiscation by police under civil forfeiture fiat. Taken together they were all parts of the various failed wars against drugs, money laundering and anti-terrorism.

But, as they say, "Old habits die hard."

Despite the occasional financial excursion abroad, human nature dictates that most folks prefer to make and save money at home. We tend to be comfortable with the familiar and less-threatening domestic economy of our home nation.

Case-in-point: in 2011, only 30% of the more than 300 million Americans hold passports—that's half of Canada's rate at 60% and far less than the United Kingdom's 75%. The percentage of Americans with passports, a number that was in the teens just a few years ago, has spiked since the Western Hemisphere Travel Initiative was adopted in 2007. That requires American, Canadian and Mexican travelers to present documents showing citizenship when entering the United States. In 2009, only 74 million (about 26%) of Americans had passports—yet 30% is the highest percentage ever.

Taxes Drain Wealth

People who move some or all of their assets offshore simply recognize the present reality—that government at all levels is engaged in the systematic destruction of hard-earned wealth.

It's what I call the "*Nazification*" of the economy. That's certainly true in the United States, the United Kingdom and too many European Union (EU) nations. Sadly, in ever greater numbers, Americans must look to a select list of foreign lands for the kind of economic freedom once guaranteed by the U.S. Constitution—and these "tax havens" are under constant attack by major welfare state tax collectors.

All the warning flags of the approaching storm are flying: the odious Foreign Account Tax Compliance Act (FATCA), expanded Report of Foreign Bank and Financial Accounts (FBAR) reporting, tax information exchange treaties, offshore banks refusing U.S. clients, government confiscation of precious metals, police civil forfeiture of property and cash worth billions, exit taxes, passport restrictions, and still more depredations daily, as statist politicians fashion an American prison for its most productive citizens.

The tax collectors know that the most talented citizens of the U.S., U.K., EU and other welfare states are deserting, setting up financial shop where they and their capital are treated best. What has been called the "permeability of financial frontiers" now empowers investors instantly to shift vast sums of money from one nation to another and from one currency to another. Tyrannical politicians see these wealth shifts and are imposing multiple curbs on capital movements and financial freedoms.

Lovers of freedom see in these developments the potential for the liberation of "the sovereign individual"—the courageous person who declares independence from "decrepit and debilitating welfare states," as *The Wall Street Journal* described them. (See *The Sovereign Individual* by James Dale Davidson and Lord William Rees-Mogg [Simon & Shuster, 1997], an excellent book that explains the mass exodus of wealthy individuals from high-tax nations.)

No wonder the U.K. Revenue and Customs, the U.S. Internal Revenue Service and other tax hounds are worried. In Europe "undeclared" (and untaxed) income estimates range as high as 20% of Europe's combined gross domestic product (GDP), up from 5% in the 1970s. In the somewhat freer U.S., the underground "black market" economy accounts for over 8% of GDP. That means billions of dollars slipping through the eager hands of the taxman.

Why the growing black market? Confiscatory taxes, exorbitant labor costs, over-regulation, multiple reporting requirements with criminal penalties—all failures of big government. All things government bureaucrats love.

Diminished Privacy in the Digital Age

In many ways, life in modern America and the United Kingdom parallels the chilling description of life in the ultimate totalitarian state foretold in George Orwell's famous novel, *1984*. In part, we have ourselves to blame. Although we claim to value freedom and privacy, too many of us willingly surrender personal information piecemeal to all sorts of sources, until we stand exposed to the world.

Those who conduct their financial affairs with reckless openness make the work of government snoops easy. As you read this, corporate and government computers hum with detailed electronic facts about you and your family. Nothing is sacred: health, wealth, tax and marital status, credit history, employment, phone calls, faxes and email, travel, eating and reading habits, even individual preferences when cruising the Internet are recorded.

In an age of digital cash, interconnected databases, electronic commerce and instant worldwide communication, no area of financial activity offers more pitfalls than personal and commercial banking. Once considered discreet and honorable, banks and other financial institutions have been forced to become a U.S. version of Big Brother's Thought Police. This dubious role with American banks serving as spies was intensified in 2009 and later when the U.S. government handed them billions in bailout funds and took over what amounts to quasi-management.

Sadly, in today's world, you need to conduct your financial affairs with the utmost privacy, caution and discretion. In this book, I give you concrete legal and practical steps you can take to guard against being victimized by government run amok.

Action Summary

To protect your privacy and wealth, consider taking the following steps:

1. Establish an offshore bank account in a tax-free, privacy-oriented, financial-friendly nation. When done correctly, your cash will be

far more secure from almost all U.S.-based claims. But first, carefully investigate any foreign bank you consider using.

2. As part of your overall estate plan, create your own offshore asset protection trust, limited liability company or private family foundation to hold title to specific assets.

3. Precisely document all financial transactions so that you always have ready proof that your activities are legal.

4. Educate yourself about—and comply with—all laws, rules and regulations concerning reporting of your financial activities to government agencies.

5. Before you act, consult an experienced professional attorney and/or accountant and understand the U.S. and foreign tax implications of your plans.

6. Get a firm and reliable estimate of the cost of your plans, both at the start, upon implementation and for the first few years of operation.

Case in Point

The U.S. National Security Agency (NSA) operates America's largest-ever spy center. The NSA, the intelligence agency of U.S. Department of Defense, years ago secretly tried to impose on Americans the questionable ECHELON spy program. Now the "Utah Data Center," an ultra-secret project in the desert, is the latest government move to destroy all privacy. The heavily fortified, $2 billion secret center is part of a program codenamed Stellar Wind. The center intercepts, deciphers, analyzes and stores all the world's communications from satellites and underground and undersea cables from international, foreign and domestic networks. It stores all forms of communications, including contents of private e-mails, cell phone calls and Google searches, even personal data such as parking receipts, travel itineraries and so-called digital "pocket litter." This NSA project is the latest version of what the late columnist William Safire called "a super snoop's dream."

CHAPTER TWO

Creative Offshore Financial Strategies

In this chapter, you will learn specific personal and financial strategies for offshore living, residence, second citizenship, investing, bank accounts and conducting your business for maximum tax savings and the greatest profit. And I'll also explain U.S. government reporting requirements for offshore personal and financial activity.

Later in these pages, in chapters 4 through 11, I will describe the best jurisdictions and countries that qualify as tax and asset and banking havens; the ones best for achieving your personal wealth and estate management goals. (Note: I use the phrase *"jurisdictions and countries"* because some places are independent nations, while others are colonies of the United Kingdom.)

While reading later sections, keep in mind the strategies I describe in this chapter because I explain the individual types of offshore tax and asset havens where these strategies are best suited. Later you may want to match strategies to specific jurisdictions I describe.

Before I get to geography and specific places, first we will consider several personal, financial and business strategies you can employ offshore, even before you finally choose your own best tax or asset haven.

These varied strategies can be used individually or in combination, as your situation requires. But each one is fully legal and each has been used by many thousands of people worldwide — often with highly satisfactory results.

In later chapters when I discuss individual jurisdictions that qualify as international financial centers ("tax havens") and/or asset and banking havens, I'll suggest which havens are best suited for these strategies.

One or all of these may be just the financial strategies you need.

Part 1. Personal Strategies

Strategy 1:
Make Your Home Base in a Tax Haven

For those who choose to leave their home nation and live in a foreign country, places that qualify as tax havens can provide better living financially and greater profits.

While eventually you may consider obtaining citizenship in the foreign land of your choice, the first step is to qualify to become a *resident* officially approved by the government. (Keep in mind that once you become a citizen of a country, you are no longer an exempt "foreigner" and you may become subject to that country's taxes and other laws.)

Interestingly enough, for those who live in foreign countries for long periods, scientists have found a link between creativity and living abroad. *The Economist* magazine reported on a study by academics at the Kellogg School of Management that showed better problem-solving skills in 60% of students who were either living abroad or had spent some time doing so, whereas only 42% of those who had not lived abroad demonstrated such skills.

A second test found that those who had lived abroad were more creative negotiators, probably learned as coping strategy for foreign survival. And even when researchers discounted the possibility that creative people were more likely to choose to live abroad, the link between creativity and foreign life held true, "…indicating that it is something from the experience of living in foreign parts that helps foster creativity."

The authors of the report supplied no great detail as to why living abroad should stimulate the creative juices, but their conclusion contains the most likely rationale: it may be that those critical months or years of turning cultural bewilderment into personal concrete understanding may instill the ability to "think outside the box."

Lower Taxes

Even though U.S. persons (citizens and U.S. permanent resident aliens) are taxed on their worldwide income, there are many attractive places in which to live where taxes are reduced on business activities, or where business may be totally tax-exempt when conducted offshore. These hospitable places exempt foreigners who live there from taxes because they only levy taxes on income earned within their borders, under what is known as a "territorial" tax system.

Personal income tax rates in many major welfare states now equal 50% of income or even higher. This crushing burden of combined social security taxes, capital gains taxes, net worth taxes, wealth taxes and inheritance taxes, has prompted many to seek low or zero tax havens where they can make a new home tax-free.

Many countries provide tax incentives to qualified foreigners who become new residents. Residence qualifications include good health, a clean record with no past criminal acts, a guaranteed sufficient income and enough assets so that you won't need a job in the local market.

However, it isn't easy to find a haven offering both low taxes and an acceptable high quality of life that includes a wide range of amenities, excellent medical facilities, easy residence requirements and a warm climate, all within easy reach of major American or European cities.

But a few countries come fairly close to the ideal.

For instance, the Mediterranean island nation of **Malta** is one of the most attractive locations for foreigners looking for a warm climate, as well as low taxes. Permanent foreign residents enjoy a privileged tax status, with only a 15% tax charged on income remitted from outside to Malta, subject to a minimum tax liability of about US$5,000 per year. To obtain permanent residence, one must show proof of an annual income of about US$24,000 or capital of about US$360,000. Although a residence permit entitles you to live in Malta, you don't actually have to spend any minimum length of time there. This is particularly useful if you are away for long periods.

The **Republic of Panama** offers one of the most attractive locations for tax advantaged residence in the Americas. It has a special pensionado program for foreign retirees providing tax-free living with substantial discounts on the price of many goods and services. In 2012, Panama instituted a new, fast-track "Immediate Permanent Resident" visa for foreign nationals from 22 listed countries "that maintain friendly, professional, economic, and investment relationships with the Republic of Panama." Under its territorial tax system, all residents pay no tax on income earned outside Panama. Under several other immigration programs tailored to attract them, foreigners may acquire residence as a financially independent person/retiree or as an investor.

The Central American country of **Belize** also offers a special program for foreign retirees much like that in Panama, with zero taxes on offshore income and other incentives.

For people of great wealth, **Austria**, **Switzerland** and **Singapore** are among the nations with special immigration and tax arrangements for foreigners who wish to live or retire there. It's fair to say that there are countries in many parts of the world where individual arrangements can be made for tax-advantaged residence.

If you are looking for a place to do business offshore or to make a new home, the haven that will meet your needs can be found. It's out there waiting for you and I'll help you find it.

A word about personal security: Every country has safety and security issues, ranging from petty crime and scams to active terrorist groups and revolutionary movements. Each country's police and security forces operate differently—something a new resident must learn sometimes the "hard way."

For up-to-date security information on countries worldwide, check the websites listed below.

- US Department of State: Consular Information Sheets http://travel.state.gov/travel/cis_pa_tw/cis/cis_4965.html

- Overseas Security Advisory Council https://www.osac.gov/Pages/Home.aspx

- Australian Department of Foreign Affairs http://www.smarttraveller.gov.au/zw-cgi/view/Advice/

- International Crime Threat Assessment http://www.fas.org/irp/threat/pub45270index.html

- INTERPOL Country Profiles http://www.interpol.int/

- World Intelligence and Security Agencies http://www.fas.org/irp/world/

- NationMaster http://www.nationmaster.com/index.php/ (massive global database including crime and terrorism)

Strategy 2: Dual Citizenship

Let's say you have decided to establish a new residence in an offshore tax haven.

As a resident, you may want to consider acquiring citizenship there and, with it, a second passport. Dual citizenship simply means that a person is officially recognized as a citizen of more than one nation. Under U.S. law, this status is fully legal, and it is legal under the laws of many other nations, although not all.

The United States government had official recognition of dual citizenship forced upon it in 1967 by a U.S. Supreme Court ruling, *Afroyim v. Rusk*, 387 U.S. 253, when a U.S. citizen successfully argued that he had no intent to end his American citizenship when he acquired the citizenship of another country. The Court ruled that Afroyim's right to keep his citizenship was guaranteed by the Citizenship Clause of the 14th Amendment to the Constitution.

Prior to that ruling it was the U.S. government's legal position that whenever a U.S. citizen acquired citizenship of another country U.S. citizenship was automatically lost. Other acts held to end U.S. citizenship included voting in a foreign country's election or serving in an official position or in the military of a foreign government.

The *Afroyim* decision opened the way for a wider acceptance of multiple citizenships in U.S. law. A series of treaties in place between the U.S. and other nations which had limited dual citizenship following naturalization were abandoned after the U.S. government concluded *Afroyim* had rendered them unenforceable.

Since 1967, the official policy of the U.S. government is to presume a U.S. citizen does not wish to surrender their citizenship based on actions. Proof of intent is required before expatriation is officially recognized. The burden of proof is on the government to show intentional abandonment of U.S. citizenship.

This presumption is set forth in a 1990 U.S. Department of State publication. See http://travel.state.gov/law/citizenship/citizenship_778.html. Even though as a matter of policy the U.S. government now recognizes dual nationality, it still does not encourage it because of what the bureaucrats view as problems and conflicts that may result. Indeed, the U.S. Department of State website still fails to make clear that dual nationality is legal for Americans.

Although the U.S. government has been forced to accept dual citizenship, it still asserts legal control based on U.S. citizenship in numerous ways. For example, a dual citizen with a U.S. passport must use that passport to leave or enter the U.S. and is prohibited from travel to Cuba without prior U.S. State Department permission.

Perhaps the most onerous example of these U.S. controls is in the area of tax payments and tax reporting obligations. U.S. citizens are burdened with U.S. taxes no matter where in the world they live or where the income sources are located. Countries such as Panama with a more reasonable territorial system of taxation are taxed only on income earned within their country of citizenship, without regard to where they live or the income source.

Good Reasons

A second passport, quite literally, could save your life. History is littered with repressive instances when a government has blocked its citizens from traveling internationally. If it becomes necessary for you to leave and you have only your home country passport, you're stuck. That's because your passport is the property of your government and officials can seize a passport at any time.

At the very least, having a second nationality and passport is a hedge against unexpected political and economic events at home. The dual status gives you the option of residing in another country away from your home place, which may produce tax advantages as well. But remember these tax advantages are of limited benefit to U.S. citizens who are taxed on worldwide income, without regard to where they physically reside.

You may be able to acquire a second citizenship and passport based on your ancestry, by marriage or because of your religious affiliation. If you don't qualify on these grounds, your principle option for obtaining citizenship is through establishing residence in your chosen country for a required period of time (usually five years) or by obtaining citizenship by investment.

Citizenship by investment, also called "economic citizenship," describes the granting of citizenship by a sovereign country in exchange for a financial contribution to that country or for an investment in a business, real estate, or government-designated, job-producing project.

In recent years, the number of economic citizenship programs has dwindled down to only three. The several programs that did exist were criticized for allegedly offering to help international organized crime and terrorists. Such sensational charges were largely false, but they led to the termination of citizenship by investment former programs in Ireland, Belize, the Cape Verde Islands and Grenada.

St. Christopher & Nevis and the **Commonwealth of Dominica**, both small island nations in the eastern Caribbean (what used to be the British West Indies), are now the two major countries that promote legal citizenship by full-scale investment programs. In 2012, **Ireland** introduced a new economic citizenship program based on investing in that economically depressed country. In **Austria**, it is also possible, under certain limited conditions, to obtain citizenship without prior residence based on a substantial investment, but this is done on an individual basis and is rarely granted. Each of these programs requires that applicants pass a rigorous screening process.

St. Kitts & Nevis

The economic citizenship program of St. Kitts & Nevis (the nation's popular name) enjoys an excellent reputation and it offers visa-free travel to British Commonwealth and many other countries.

Under their current citizenship-by-investment rules, to qualify for St. Kitts & Nevis citizenship, an investment of at least

US$350,000 in designated real estate, plus additional government and due diligence fees are required. Alternatively, a cash contribution can be made to the Sugar Industry Diversification Foundation in the amount of US$200,000 (for a single applicant).

Using the charitable contribution is an easier route for most applicants because it provides a set cost and avoids further expenses associated with owning real estate in a foreign country. Plus, you don't have to live in St. Kitts & Nevis to secure your second citizenship, so buying real estate could just be an additional burden if you're not interested in spending time there.

Sugar Industry Diversification Foundation Option
Required contributions:
Single applicant: US$200,000
Applicant with up to 3 dependents (spouse, 2 children below the age of 18): US$250,000
Applicant with up to 5 dependents: US$300,000
Applicant with 6 or more dependents: US$400,000.
Each dependent child 18–25 years old and enrolled full-time as university undergraduate: US$35,000
Each dependent parent 62 years or older living with and supported by head of household: US$35,000

Registration, application, due diligence, and processing fees: application fee: US$250 per applicant plus 17% VAT; consulting fee, US$1,200 per application.

Investment in Designated Real Estate Option
Required investment:
Minimum US$350,000, plus approximately 7% in taxes, duties, and fees;
Alien land owner's tax, 10%–12% of purchase price, may apply;

Title insurance cost varies depending on the cost of the property. Registration, application, due diligence, and processing fees:

Application fee:

- US$250 per applicant plus 17% VAT
- security fee, US$3,500 per applicant
- processing fee, US$250 per applicant
- court fees, no additional charge
- consulting fee, $1,200 per application

Registration fee (after grant of approval):

- Head of household: US$35,000
- Spouse and each child under the age of 18 years: US$15,000
- Each dependent child 18-25 years enrolled full-time as university undergraduate: US$35,000
- Each dependent parent 62 years or older living with and supported by head of household: US$35,000

Depending on what an attorney or other professional may charge, usual legal fees can cost $20,000 for a single applicant or applicant and spouse; $25,000 for applicant, spouse, and up to two children; $5,000 for each additional dependent child. Also, 50% of the legal fee is refunded if the primary applicant is not approved. There is also a $500 escrow fee. Due diligence fees vary, from US$4,000 to US$8,000.

The real estate option requires the purchase of a condominium or villa from an approved list of developers with a minimum investment of US$350,000. Transaction costs add 10% to the purchase price (i.e., at least US$35,000, and likely US$50,000 or more) as real estate prices are now at a relatively high level in St. Kitts & Nevis.

Processing time for charitable contribution applications takes up to three months and dual citizenship is permitted, with no residency requirement. Using the real estate option lengthens the average processing time from four to 12 months or longer. The real estate cannot be re-sold until at least five years after purchase.

Commonwealth of Dominica

For now, and in the foreseeable future, there are two options to acquire citizenship:

1) Direct Family Cash Option: (family of 4, investor, spouse, 2 children under 18 years):
   Required contribution: US$100,000
   Children between 18 and 21 years: US$25,000 per child (up to 2 children)
   Additional children under the age of 18 years, US$15,000 per child

2) Direct Cash Single Option: Required contribution: US$75,000

For both options, the cash contribution is due only after the application has been provisionally approved by the government. Other government fees include:

- application fee US$1,000 per application (non-refundable);
- processing fee US$200 per applicant (non-refundable);
- naturalization fee US$550 per applicant; and
- stamp fee US$15 per applicant.

Depending on what an attorney or other professional may charge, usual legal fees can cost $20,000 for a single applicant or applicant and spouse; $25,000 for applicant, spouse, and up to two children; $5,000 for each additional dependent child. Again, 50% of the legal fee is refunded if the primary applicant is not approved. There is also a $500 escrow fee. Due diligence fees vary, from US$4,000 to US$8,000.

The government guarantees the return of all investment funds if an application is rejected for any reason or withdrawn, but US$2,200 in processing fees is non-refundable. Since granting citizenship is at the sole discretion of the government, there is no guarantee that applications will be approved. The government also has introduced more onerous due diligence requirements.

Republic of Austria

Investors of at least US$2 million in approved projects in Austria may be considered for immediate citizenship under an Austrian law seeking to attract extraordinary contributions to the nation.

This rarely granted Austrian passport offers the only possibility to obtain a "First World" (as compared to a "Third World") passport through investment, and one that offers the additional right to live, work and travel in 26 of the 27 countries of the European Union, because Austria is an EU member state. With Austrian residence, visa-free travel is possible throughout all Schengen countries.

Although Austria does not have an economic citizenship program *per se*, statutory law does allow the granting of citizenship to a foreign person if he or she is judged to contribute in some extraordinary way, including economic means, to the interests of Austria. However, this is not an easy way to acquire citizenship and the process may require a year or more to complete.

Applicants are approved on a case-by-case basis and must be willing to invest at least US$2 million in an approved project in Austria. Investment proposals are submitted to the Office of Economic Development. Those that provide export stimulation or local employment receive preference.

Representation by a knowledgeable (and well-connected) Austrian lawyer is essential, and is likely to cost considerably more than US$50,000. Fees of €250,000 (US$325,000) or more apply, depending on the case and the number of persons in an application, as each case is handled on an individual basis.

Persons of independent means with a proven minimum annual income of US$25,000 with an established home place in Austria and full health insurance coverage are eligible to apply for official Austrian residence. After five years and, in some cases, less, residents may apply for citizenship.

There are also citizenship opportunities for academics, such as university professors. Henley & Partners can provide details on these Austrian possibilities. In special circumstances, a person who can demonstrate that their proposed residence in Austria will make a unique scientific or technological contribution that benefits the public interest will be admitted with a tax-free status. This special status is reviewed annually by the Ministry of Finance.

Since citizenship by investment remains politically controversial within each of these three countries I, these programs could be changed, suspended or terminated at any time. In the event these programs are changed or abolished, those persons who already have acquired passports should be able to retain them but that is not guaranteed.

Republic of Ireland

In 2012, with its national economy in very bad shape, the Irish government started a new Immigrant Investor Program to attract both money and wealthy individuals from outside the EU. The program offers special immediate residence visas to foreign individuals willing to invest in Ireland.

This investment can eventually lead to full citizenship, and Irish citizenship opens the door to full personal and commercial access to all 27 countries in the European Union.

Under the new program, potential investor immigrants have these choices (all numbers are required minimums):

- Make a one-time payment of €500,000 ($666,000) to a public project benefiting the arts, sports, health or education.

- Make a €2 million (US$2.7 million) investment in a low-interest immigrant investor bond. The investment is to be held for a minimum of five years. The bond cannot be traded, it must be held to maturity.

- Invest €1 million (US$1.3 million) in venture capital funding in an Irish business for a minimum of three years.

- Make a €1 million mixed investment in 50% property and 50% government securities. Special consideration may be given to those purchasing property owned by the National Asset Management Agency (NAMA). In such cases, a single €1million (US$1.3 million) investment in property may be sufficient.

There is a separate Start-up Entrepreneur Program for foreigners with entrepreneurial abilities who wish to start a business in an innovation area of the economy with funding of at least €75,000 (US$99,000). They will be given a two-year residence for the purposes of developing the business.

Information is available at the Ministry of Justice webpage: http://www.inis.gov.ie/en/INIS/Pages/New%20Programmes%20 for%20Investors%20and%20Entrepreneurs

Emails can be directed to: investmentandstartup@justice.ie/.

For more information about these economic citizenship programs, contact:

Mark Nestmann, a senior member of The Sovereign Society Council of Experts, is a qualified professional who assists those interested in acquiring foreign residence and citizenship and is a recommended agent of the government.

The Nestmann Group, Ltd.
2303 N. 44th St. #14-1025
Phoenix, AZ 85008 USA

Tel./Fax (USA): +1 (602) 604-1524
Email: assetpro@nestmann.com
Website: http://www.nestmann.com/

Henley & Partners AG
Klosbachstrasse 110
8024 Zurich, Switzerland.
Tel.: +41 44 266 22 22 Fax: +41 44 266 22 23
Website: www.henleyglobal.com/austria
Contact: Ms. Maya Herzog
Email: maya.herzog@henleyglobal.com

Strategy 3:
Expatriation: The Ultimate Estate Plan

Heavily taxed Americans are renouncing their citizenship at record levels. Data from the U.S. government shows that renunciations of U.S. citizenship are expected to double in 2012, largely to avoid proposed tax increases. As many as 8,000 U.S. citizens are projected by immigration officials to renounce in 2012, about 154 per week, or 22 per day.

This compares to 3,805 in 2011 (about 73 per week), which was a previous record year. Many high net worth individuals have decided that having a U.S. passport just isn't worth the cost anymore.

Since its founding in 1997, The Sovereign Society has been almost alone in observing the accelerating trend of U.S. expatriation. State Department figures show that about 1,500 people formally ended their U.S. citizenship in 2010, compared with about half that figure in 2003. Last year, however, the number rose to 1,781, 16% more than 2010.

Number of U.S. Expatriates per Year

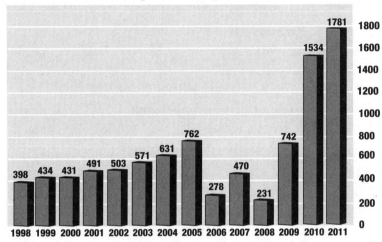

These are small numbers of course — with a 2012 population of 311,591,917 million Americans, these expatriates are a drop in the ocean. Yet the trend is clearly there.

Why is this happening?

Several lawyers told *The Wall Street Journal* that many expatriates are wealthy Americans who are leaving because of President Obama's policies and the general direction of the nation's political leaders.

"There is growing concern, particularly among the wealthy, about the future financial direction of the country," said Paul L. Caron, Professor of Law at the University of Cincinnati College of Law. "This President constantly demonizes the wealthy, who undoubtedly are concerned about the tax policy that would emerge in 2012, if a re-elected Barack Obama, unconstrained by re-election concerns, finally confronts the budgetary train wreck that he has done so much to cause."

The Saverin Case

If the last 30 years of accumulated assaults on the constitutional rights of U.S. citizens have not convinced you to make plans to escape America, perhaps the reactionary political demagoguery surrounding Eduardo Saverin will do the trick.

Saverin, the billionaire Facebook co-founder, in 2011 ended his U.S. citizenship as a legal means of avoiding U.S. taxes.

U.S. laws, unlike most nations, impose taxes on "U.S. persons" (citizens and resident aliens), no matter where in the world they live and without regard to their income sources. Terminating citizenship is the only way to avoid U.S. taxes.

The vast majority of other national tax systems impose taxes only on income earned within their borders. A Canadian or British citizen, for example, can move offshore and legally leave most domestic taxes behind. A Panamanian is taxed only on income earned within his country, none offshore.

In May 2012, the leading publicity hound in the U.S. Senate, Charles E. Schumer (D-NY), and his PR apparatchiks regarded the Saverin news as a great chance to make headlines and they pounced.

The "ultra-liberal" Schumer unveiled the Ex-PATRIOT Act (*Expatriation Prevention by Abolishing Tax-Related Incentives for Offshore Tenancy Act*). This legislative disaster would have imposed prospective 35% tax on U.S. earnings on anyone who ended U.S. citizenship during the last 10 years.

To add juice to the story, Saverin's 4% stake in the publicly traded Facebook was estimated to be worth $3 billion to $4 billion. This made him the perfect target for politicians—an ungrateful tax-dodging billionaire skipping out on America and its suffering taxpayers.

Indeed, by ending U.S. citizen status, Saverin probably saved hundreds of millions in eventual estate and gift taxes. If he remained a citizen, he would not have owed U.S. capital gains tax on his income until he sold his shares. Wealthy American shareholders often borrow against their shares and live tax-free off the unrealized appreciation for years.

Anyone in Saverin's position would be insane not to act legally to save all the taxes possible, and that's just what he did. As it is, he will probably pay $150 million because of the Exit Tax the U.S. imposes on expatriates.

Saverin, 30, who was born in Brazil, came to the U.S. as a teenager and became an American citizen, reportedly to avoid being kidnapped from his wealthy parents. Exercising his legal right as an American, he filed to surrender his U.S. citizenship in January 2011 and it became official last September. He also was among those 1,780 Americans who ended U.S. citizenship last year.

He now is a resident of Singapore, where, unlike the U.S., the government welcomes wealthy foreigners with low taxes and eventual citizenship. Saverin will benefit from major tax savings by becoming a permanent resident of Singapore, which imposes no capital gains taxes.

Perhaps the most atrocious part of Schumer's proposal is the attempt to bar re-entry into the U.S. forever. This ban would be retroactive and apply to anyone who ended citizenship during the 10-year period before 2012. Fortunately, once he got the publicity he wanted, Schumer's proposal died a well-deserved legislative death.

The Ultimate Plan

Indeed, expatriation has been called "the ultimate estate plan."

Expatriation is nothing less than a step-by-step process that can provide the legal right to stop paying U.S. income taxes for the U.S. person (citizen or resident alien) willing to terminate that status.

In sum, it requires professional consultations, careful planning, movement of assets offshore and most certainly, acquisition of a second citizenship. When that's done—and done exactly right—you can leave behind America as your home country and establish a new domicile, preferably in a low- or no-tax jurisdiction. And for U.S. citizens, this unusual plan requires, as a final step toward tax freedom, the formal relinquishment of citizenship.

Obviously expatriation is a drastic plan.

And in truth, there are many other perfectly suitable offshore strategies recommended in this book that can result in some tax savings and that don't require anything as dramatic as expatriation. These include purchase of international life insurance policies, annuities, and making offshore investments made through retirement plans, among others.

But for U.S. citizens and long-term U.S. resident aliens ("green card holders") seeking a permanent and legal way to end their obligation to pay U.S. taxes, expatriation is the only option.

Blueprint for Ultimate Tax Avoidance

Since the dawn of humankind, individuals have been migrating away from their native lands to seek better opportunities elsewhere. But since the development of the modern nation-state and the high taxation imposed by some nations on all the worldwide income of their citizen-residents, led by the United States, this process called "expatriation" has taken on significance because of the tax freedom it allows.

One of the first tax experts to appreciate the potential tax savings of expatriation was my friend and colleague, Marshall Langer, JD, a leading international tax attorney who practiced law in London and Miami.

Langer is the respected author of several major international tax treatises, but also the daring creator of a now out-of-print book, *The Tax Exile Report* (1992). This title gained international notoriety when the late U.S. Senator Daniel Patrick Moynihan (D-NY), red-faced and angry, waved a copy of the book at a televised U.S.

Senate hearing, denouncing it as "… a legal income tax avoidance plan." (Note that the senator said "legal"—and indeed, it is that.)

Compelling Numbers

In explaining why expatriation is so attractive to wealthy Americans (and others), a few years ago a *Forbes* magazine article gave the compelling arithmetic: "A very rich Bahamian citizen pays zero estate taxes; rich Americans—anyone with an estate worth US$3 million or more—could pay 55%. A fairly stiff 37% marginal rate kicks in for Americans leaving as little as US$600,000 to their children." Even though U.S. estate taxes at this writing have been temporarily reduced since then, an even more impressive part of the Langer plan is the ability to escape higher U.S. income, capital gains and other taxes.

When it comes to expatriation, however, Americans face a unique burden. Unlike almost every other nation, with one or two exceptions, U.S. citizens and long-term residents cannot escape home country taxes by moving their residences to another nation. The only way to leave U.S. taxes behind is to end U.S. citizenship or resident alien status.

New Refugees

Becoming a "tax exile" by choosing to expatriate is not without problems. In America, expatriation to avoid taxes has been a hot political issue for 25 years.

The original source of the expatriation controversy was a sensational article in the November 24, 1994 issue of *Forbes* magazine, entitled "The New Refugees." Filled with juicy details (famous names, luxury addresses, huge tax dollar savings), the story described how clever ex-Americans who became citizens of various foreign nations, legally paid little or no U.S. federal and state income, estate and capital gains taxes.

Ever since, expatriation has periodically been a "hot button" issue kicked around by the American news media and "soak-the-rich" politicians. Indeed, President Barack Obama repeatedly attacked offshore financial activity by U.S. individuals and companies during his 2008 presidential campaign.

It's understandable why politicians keep this political football in active play. To the average, uninformed U.S. taxpayer, expatriation seems like just another rich man's tax loophole. Before *Forbes* raised the issue, few people had even heard of the concept of formal surrender or loss of U.S. citizenship.

Taken together with the controversy over U.S. companies having offshore affiliates or re-incorporating offshore to avoid U.S. corporate taxes (both still legal at this writing), politicians have found in expatriation a convenient straw man that they can beat unmercifully.

Former President Bill Clinton's Treasury Secretary at the time, Lawrence Summers, later President Obama's top White House economic advisor, went so far as to call tax expatriates "traitors" to America. He was later forced to apologize for his hyperbole.

Right to End U.S. Citizenship

As a national political issue, expatriation is hardly new.

In the bitter aftermath of the U.S. Civil War (1860–1865), the U.S. Congress hotly debated the post-war status of the people in the southern states that had formed the Confederacy. Ultimately, Congress decided "rebels" who swore allegiance could again become U.S. citizens. The Expatriation Act of 1868 formally recognized that all Americans do have a right to give up their citizenship, if they so choose.

A century later, in the Foreign Investors Tax Act of 1966, Congress again decided to make an issue of expatriation. In that Act, lawmakers tried to impose onerous taxes on exiting wealthy

Americans who relinquished their U.S. citizenship "with the principal purpose of avoiding" U.S. taxes, a highly subjective intention that was virtually impossible to prove. This made for a good political issue, but the IRS couldn't prove such "intent" and didn't even try.

The lengths to which American politicians will go to penalize supposed tax expatriates is demonstrated by a never-enforced provision of U.S. law, sponsored by then-U.S. Representative (and later U.S. Senator) Jack Reid (D-RI) and enacted in 1996. The Reid Amendment permits the U.S. Attorney General to bar from returning to the United States anyone who renounces their U.S. citizenship to avoid taxes. Thus, Congress lumped together individuals exercising their legal right to avoid taxes by expatriating with narcotics traffickers and terrorists.

In a moment I will explain the 2008 U.S. Exit Tax imposed on expatriates, but consider the 2012 legislation proposed by Charles E. Schumer (D-NY), known as the Ex-PATRIOT Act (Expatriation Prevention by Abolishing Tax-Related Incentives for Offshore Tenancy Act). This legislative disaster would impose a retroactive 35% tax on U.S. earnings on anyone who ended U.S. citizenship during the last 10 years. The most atrocious part of Schumer's proposal was his attempt to bar re-entry into the U.S. forever for anyone who ended citizenship during the 10-year period before 2012.

The only other regimes that adopted similar punitive laws were Nazi Germany, the Soviet Union under Stalin and South Africa during apartheid.

Amidst the political furor, thoughtful experts question what they view as much broader and dangerous U.S. anti-expatriation precedents. They point out that these laws involve not only retaliatory government acts against resistance to high taxes, but pose possible human rights violations guaranteed by other American laws and even by the Human Rights Charter of the United Nations. It is worth noting that the U.S. Supreme Court has repeatedly affirmed the right of U.S. citizens to end their citizenship, as well as the right to enjoy dual citizenship.

In reality, this political frenzy probably reflects politics as usual and collective envy more than any sense of patriotism by Americans or their congressional representatives. Expatriation is not as serious a problem as some pretend since less than two thousand Americans, rich or poor, formally surrender their citizenship each year. Most expatriates give up their U.S. citizenship because they are returning to their native land or marrying a non-U.S. citizen, and not to avoid taxes.

Save Millions of Dollars, Legally

Amidst the controversy, until the 2008 Exit Tax there were very substantial tax savings for wealthy U.S. citizens who were prepared to end their citizenship. While only a handful of very rich Americans legally expatriated, the list included some prominent names:

In 1962, the late billionaire mutual fund founder Sir John Templeton (knighted by Queen Elizabeth in 1992), made a controversial decision. He decided to terminate his U.S. citizenship after moving his home to The Bahamas, where there were no estate, income or investment taxes. He became both a British citizen and a Bahamian citizen and lived tax-free in The Bahamas until his death in 2008. This move saved him more than US$100 million when he sold the well-known international investment fund that still bears his name, and many millions more in estate taxes when he died. Interestingly, Templeton's investment record improved markedly after he stopped worrying about the U.S. tax consequences of his investment decisions. As a result of tax-free compounding, Templeton was worth several billion dollars and when he died he was one of the world's wealthiest men. However, Sir John did not necessarily recommend that other investors follow his lead and switch allegiance to a tax haven such as The Bahamas. (It's almost impossible for an American to become a Bahamian citizen today.) But, Templeton strongly recommended that smart investors should take full advantage of tax-deferred vehicles such as life insurance, annuities, self-directed pension plans and off-shore business.

Other wealthy ex-Americans who took their formal leave from the U.S. included billionaire Campbell Soup heir John ("Ippy") Dorrance, III (Ireland); Michael Dingman, chairman of Abex and a Ford Motor director (The Bahamas); J. Mark Mobius, one of the leading emerging market investment fund managers (Germany); Kenneth Dart, heir to the billion dollar Dart container fortune (Belize); Ted Arison, head of Carnival Cruise Lines (Israel); and Fred Kreible, millionaire head of Locktite Corporation (Turks & Caicos Islands).

The Law Today—U.S. Exit Tax

While all those former U.S. citizens were able to escape American taxes, they did so in past years—but they probably could not do it again today.

That's because on June 17, 2008, President George W. Bush signed new anti-expatriation legislation, Public Law No. 110-245, unanimously passed by Congress under the misleading title of "The Heroes Earnings Assistance and Relief Tax Act of 2008," also called the "Heroes Act." (I'll just call it "the Act" from here on in.)

The Act dramatically changed the former income tax rules applicable to both U.S. citizens who expatriate and long-term U.S. residents (e.g., "green card holders") who decide to end their U.S. residence status. The Act refers to both groups collectively as "covered individuals." Much of this law has little to do with expatriation since it provided increased benefits for U.S. armed forces veterans. But because the rules of Congress require that all new spending programs be accompanied by a source of revenue to pay for them, the anti-expat tax crowd in Congress jumped at the chance to wrap their long-time anti-expatriate tax nostrums in the American flag.

The new expat tax was supposed to finance the hundreds of millions needed to pay for veteran's benefits, but few believed that to be true. A study by the Congressional Budget Office guessed that the law might net the government up to $286 million over five years.

This expat "exit tax"—because that indeed is what it amounts to—had been the devout wish of liberal, left-wing Democrats for a decade or more. In 2008, Democrat Rep. Charles Rangel of New York, then chairman of the powerful, tax-writing House Ways and Means Committee, slipped this horrendous tax restriction into a popular military pension/pay bill (without hearings or public notice). President George W. Bush, the great "tax cutter," signed it into law without so much as a whimper.

Rangel was later forced to resign as Ways and Means chairman when he was exposed as having failed for years to pay taxes on several sources of income, failed to report offshore real estate holdings and having traded special legislative favors in return for contributions.

Totalitarian Taxes on "Covered Individuals"

In advocating an exit tax Rep. Rangel and his political allies on the Left imposed expat exit restrictions very similar to those of Hitler's Nazis, apartheid South Africa and the Communist Soviet Union. Each of these totalitarian regimes in their despotic days fleeced persecuted departing citizens (Jews, gypsies, political dissidents) with similar confiscatory exit taxes.

In fact, the 2008 Act probably violates protections in the U.S. Constitution that guarantee the right to voluntarily end U.S. citizenship and the right to live and travel abroad freely, although I seriously doubt that any wealthy expatriate would ever waste money on a court challenge once they have escaped.

Under this law, a person who is a "covered individual" falls within the clutches of the Act if, on the date of expatriation or termination of U.S. residence, (i) the individual's average annual net U.S. income tax liability for the five-year period preceding that date is $145,000 or more (adjusted annually for inflation); (ii) the individual's net worth as of that date is $2 million or more; or (iii) the individual fails to certify under penalties of perjury that he or she has complied with all U.S. federal tax obligations for the preceding five years.

Of course, if you're lucky and don't now fit within the above definitions, this new law may offer a very real opportunity to escape U.S. taxes as you become more prosperous in the future. (More about that, and what might be a very good no-tax deal if you qualify later in this text.)

Exceptions

There is an exception in the Act for those who have dual citizenship and became U.S. citizens by accident of birth, either because they happened to be born in the U.S., or born to a U.S. parent and subsequently lived in the U.S. for only a limited time.

Covered individuals under items (i), (ii) or (iii) above, have two limited exceptions that avoid taxes under the Act. They won't be taxed if they certify compliance with all U.S. federal tax obligations and either: (i) were a citizen of the United States and another country at birth if, (a) they are still a citizen and tax resident of that other country and, (b) they resided in the U.S. for no more than 10 of the 15 taxable years prior to expatriation or giving up long-term residence; or (ii) they renounce U.S. citizenship before the age of 18-1/2 if they were not residing in the U.S. for more than 10 years before the renunciation or the termination of long-term residence.

In scanning random examples of the official U.S. State Department expatriate lists mentioned earlier, it seems that a large portion of those listed are probably green card holders of modest means who are returning to their country of birth. In other words, most persons who chose formally to end their American status are not very rich tax evaders, but rather folks whose assets and tax bills are well below the amounts the new Act states.

Of course, the official list of expatriates doesn't include those who simply move to another country and gradually sever their ties with the U.S. Technically, these people are still subject to U.S. taxes, but if they give up their claim to U.S. Social Security or federal pension benefits, it is difficult for the IRS to find them. This law may well increase that number.

Confiscation by Taxation

There was a time in the United States when tax rates on the top earning individuals approached 90% or more. The Reagan tax revolution brought those rates down to more reasonable, upper 30% levels.

But under the Exit Tax, covered individuals are taxed enormously under new Code Section 877A (called a "mark-to-market tax"). This vindictive tax taxes all assets as if the person's worldwide assets had been sold for their fair market value on the day before expatriation or residence termination. For 2012, the first $636,000 in unrealized gains from a covered expatriate isn't subject to the exit tax, a figure that is adjusted annually for inflation.

This phantom gain will presumably be taxed as ordinary income (at rates as high as 35%) or capital gains (at either a 15%, 25%, or 28% rate), as provided under current law. In addition, any assets held by any trust or portion of a trust that the covered individual was treated as owning for U.S. income tax purposes (i.e., a grantor trust) are also subject to the mark-to-market tax.

No doubt many people caught by this tax would have to sell their assets to pay the tax, leaving them with little or nothing.

Still More Taxes

Equally as bad, the stay-at-home relatives of rich expatriate Americans who remain behind as U.S. citizens could find themselves owing tax if they receive large gifts of money or property from their expat relatives.

The Act also imposes an additional tax of a potentially far-reaching scope: gifts and bequests to U.S. persons from "covered individuals" (beyond the annual 2012 gift tax exclusion of $13,000 per person) are subject to a U.S. "transfer tax" imposed on the U.S. transferee at the highest federal transfer tax rates then in effect (currently 45%).

Talk about highway robbery! Not only is wealth taxed away by the Exit Tax from a generous expatriate who gives a gift, the recipient of the gift is punished with a 45% tax on that gift.

Non-Grantor Trust Distributions

But as they say on those late night TV commercials, "But wait, there's more!" *Mucho más!*

The Act requires that trustees of certain "non-grantor" trusts (i.e., trusts of which covered individuals or others are not treated as the owners for income tax purposes) must withhold 30% of each distribution to a covered individual if that distribution would have been included in the gross income of the individual as if he or she were still a U.S. taxpayer.

Defying international law, the Act says no double taxation avoidance treaty of any country with the United States may be invoked to reduce this withholding requirement. Moreover, if the trustee distributes appreciated property to a covered individual, the trust will be treated as if it sold the property to the individual at its fair market value. This treatment of distributions applies to all future distributions with no time limitation.

Retirement Plans Cut in Half

Not content with all this tax persecution, the greedy congressional politicians went after expatriates' pensions as well.

The Act forces an expatriate to pay up to a 51% tax on distributions from retirement plans. The same goes for most other forms of deferred payments. If there's a small silver lining, it's that the tax isn't due until you actually receive payments from the plan. Plans covered by this provision include qualified pensions, profit sharing and stock bonus plans, annuity plans, federal pensions, simplified employee pension plans and retirement accounts.

Very Select Group

It is fairly clear that for anyone who falls within the definition of a "covered individual" under the 2008 expat tax law, the chance of legal avoidance of American taxes by ending citizenship is going to be a very costly endeavor. Indeed, under this confiscatory law, the richer you are, the more you stand to lose by leaving the U.S. behind.

But for those who are not "covered" by this punitive law, but who do have good prospects of amassing future wealth, this new law may well offer you a no-tax bonanza — if you are willing to reorder your life, acquire second citizenship, move to an offshore tax haven and turn in your U.S. passport. And in this era of economic globalization and instant international communications, many enterprising entrepreneurs are able to do business anywhere they desire.

Let's say you paid less than $145,000 in taxes for the last five years, your net worth is less than $2 million and you have no problem certifying that you complied with all U.S. federal tax obligations for the preceding five years. This law says you can leave home free!

No doubt there are many ways to rearrange your finances and title your property to avoid values being assigned to your balance sheet, keeping that net worth under $2 million. Indeed financial obligations might reduce your net worth. And once you have left the U.S. and have become a new citizen of a tax haven such as Panama, Uruguay, Singapore, Belize or Hong Kong, there is nothing to prevent assets being transferred to you.

In that case, it appears that the Exit Tax law allows you to end your citizenship and with that, also end your U.S. tax obligations. And the 2008 law also ended the former 10-year claim of IRS tax jurisdiction over an expats income and assets. In fact, as a foreigner, you too can enjoy the tax breaks American tax law affords to non-U.S. investors in America.

Something to think about in your estate planning!

Green Card Holders Get Stuck

The 2008 Act not only affects U.S. citizens who expatriate, but also can financially penalize "green card" holders who return to their home country.

If a foreigner living in the U.S. has a green card and has lived in the U.S. for eight out of the most recent 15 years, they are considered a long-term permanent resident, or "permanent resident alien" (so count your years here—you may have to leave soon to avoid the tax).

Most of these individuals never intended to make the U.S. their permanent home. Now, if and when they leave, if they have reached the asset/income tax threshold set in the 2008 Act, they too will be taxed as a "covered person." These people are not American tax dodgers but rather well-to-do Canadians, Britons, Indians, and other foreign residents perhaps concluding long-term business and professional assignments in the U.S.

When these foreign bankers, software engineers, chemists, teachers and others leave the U.S. to retire or transfer to a new post abroad, the Act will tax them on the unrealized capital gains of their total global assets. That includes supposedly tax-deferred U.S. retirement accounts, as well as assets like a cottage in Quebec, a share of a relative's business in Bangalore, or a great-grandmother's pearls kept in a London safe.

Here's one example: consider someone who paid $10,000 for a vacation home in France in 1980, came to the U.S. in 1990 when it was worth $100,000, and left the U.S. in 2008 when the French home was worth $1 million. That person would be subject to a capital gains tax of $135,000 on that one asset.

Only "permanent residents" ("green card holders") will be stung. As a result, wealthy persons considering moving to the United States may increasingly select long-term visas rather than formal residence status, potentially depriving the country of wealthy immigrants. Some developed countries have so-called "exit taxes" but critics say that the Act tarnishes the image of the U.S. as a friendly place for foreign talent and capital, at a time when America needs both.

Devastating for Foreign Workers

The U.S. National Association of Manufacturers described the proposal to tax expatriates as "potentially devastating" for American manufacturing's many long-term foreign workers. NAM argued that the rules should target U.S. citizens who expatriate to avoid taxes, not workers who return to their home countries for personal reasons and must, by U.S. law, eventually surrender their green cards. Previously, long-term residents who surrendered their green cards could avoid taxes on their unrealized gains by spending fewer than 30 days of any year in the United States for 10 years. Even then, only U.S., not worldwide, gains were subject to tax.

There is evidence that American companies have respond by

sponsoring fewer green cards or filling openings with workers on less attractive long-term visas, drawing a smaller and potentially less talented pool of workers to the U.S.

Green card holders now living abroad may consider immediately giving them up under a provision of the Act that allows retroactive dating for nonresidents. But green card holders now living in the United States have no way out, lawyers say.

Unwelcome Foreigners

One other point: there is still one more vindictive punishment for any "covered individual" who dares to end U.S. citizenship.

Once they are no longer U.S. citizens, they will be "foreigners" in the eyes of American immigration law. Generally, foreigners can apply for any of the many entry visas the U.S. issues. For example, foreign tourists entering the U.S. for visits usually are granted a 90-day visa that is renewable once for a total of 180 days. If a foreigner stays in the U.S. more than 180 days in one year, they run the risk of becoming a "U.S. person" liable for U.S. taxes.

However under the exit tax law, the IRS says: "...expatriated individuals will be subject to U.S. tax on their worldwide income for any of the 10 years following expatriation in which they are present in the U.S. for more than 30 days, or 60 days in the case of individuals working in the U.S. for an unrelated employer."

The tax-dodging U.S. Rep. Charlie Rangel and other politicians on the Far Left finally got their wish and enacted an exit tax on expatriates—much to the detriment of America, its economy and the nation's standing in the eyes of the world.

But don't let all this information about exit taxes scare you. If you don't come under the Act for net worth or other reasons, it means you can end your American tax liability by ending your citizenship and thus permanently detach yourself from the clutches of the IRS.

That possibility is something to seriously consider. If you need recommendations for professional tax advice, contact The Sovereign Society toll-free at 1-888-856-1412 or through the website at http:// sovereign-investor.com/contact-us/.

How it's Done

Long before anyone formally surrenders their U.S. citizenship, they should have reordered their financial affairs in such a way as to remove most, if not all, of their assets from possible government control and taxation.

Here are the recommended steps to take:

- Arrange affairs so that most or all income is derived from non-U.S. sources;

- Title property ownership so that any assets that remain in the United States are exempt from U.S. estate and gift taxes to the maximum extent;

- Move abroad and make a new home in a no-tax foreign country so that you are no longer a "resident" for U.S. income tax purposes;

- Obtain a new alternative citizenship and passport;

- Formally surrender U.S. citizenship and change your legal "domicile" to avoid U.S. estate taxes.

One of the most important decisions is the choice of your new second citizenship.

Millions of Americans already hold a second citizenship; millions more qualify almost instantly for dual citizenship by reason of birth, ancestry, or marriage. At this point you may wish to review the information described above in "Strategy 2 — Dual Citizenship" at the beginning of this chapter to see if any of these faster avenues are open to you.

Part 2: Financial Strategies

Strategy 1: An Offshore Bank Account

Until relatively recently, only the wealthiest investors could benefit from having an offshore bank account. In the days of snail mail and trans-Atlantic ocean travel, only the richest of the rich could afford the fees and legal advice associated with going offshore. Now, after dramatic changes in international travel, banking and communications, even a modest offshore account can be your quick, inexpensive entry into the world of foreign investment opportunities.

Put aside the erroneous popular notion that foreign bank accounts are designed for shady international drug kingpins and unscrupulous wheeler-dealers avoiding taxes. For some people, offshore accounts will always evoke images of cloak and dagger spies from the U.S. Central Intelligence Agency or the U.K.'s MI5, of shadowy clandestine operations and crooked officials in Third World nations.

Although these sinister images are entertaining, they hardly relate to your present practical purposes. What we want to do is build offshore financial structures that will increase your wealth legally and solidly protect your assets. Forget the intrigue and embrace the fact that an offshore bank account is a highly effective economic way to achieve your legitimate financial goals. There is nothing underhanded or sinister about protecting the wealth you have worked so hard to earn.

A foreign bank account can be employed as an integral tool in an aggressive, three-pronged offshore wealth strategy. One goal is to increase your asset value by cutting taxes and maximizing profits. The next is to build a strong defensive asset protection structure, and the third is using your account for profitable off-shore investments.

As I demonstrate in these pages, the possible variations on these important themes are nearly endless.

Offshore banking is big business worldwide. Estimates are that from US$3 trillion to US$5 trillion is stashed in nearly 40 offshore banking havens that impose no or low taxes, have less onerous regulations, guarantee privacy and welcome non-resident clients. Nearly a quarter of the entire world's private wealth is stashed in Switzerland alone!

High tax, deficit spending welfare system countries, led by the U.S., howl that tax havens are engaged in "unfair tax competition" but they never try to imitate tax havens by lowering their own high taxes or reducing spending.

Benefits of Offshore Banking

Let me be clear about one important fact up front.

An offshore bank account is not a tool to be used to illegally avoid taxes. As an American citizen or "green card" holder, the U.S. Internal Revenue Code taxes you on all your worldwide income. No matter where or how you earn your money, you'll owe some U.S. taxes and you must annually file with the IRS at least an IRS Form 1040 for income and related taxes.

What an offshore bank account does for you is provide a "safe haven" for your money. Many thousands of sovereign individuals already are using their offshore bank accounts for exactly that purpose.

The International Monetary Fund (IMF) recently confirmed that "stability reasons" — and not bank secrecy — helped foreign havens like Switzerland attract 27% (a total of $2.3 trillion) of the world's offshore wealth in 2011.

These smart people, just like savvy Argentineans and Russians, are using this simple, yet effective, tool to protect their wealth against a meddling government and their declining currency. You should consider doing the same.

Your offshore bank account is not just a place for safekeeping cash. One of the great advantages of an offshore bank account is it enhances your ability to trade freely and invest in foreign-issued stocks, bonds, mutual funds and national currencies that are not available in your home country.

Hedge Against Dollar Decline

Another major benefit of an offshore bank account is protection against the declining dollar.

Since the creation of the Federal Reserve in 1913, the value of U.S. currency has collapsed. What was worth $1 back then is worth less than 4.8 cents today. That is to say, the American dollar has lost more than 95% of its value. This trend continues almost daily. Clearly, having an offshore account is becoming a matter of some urgency while you still have assets to convert to more stable currencies. An offshore account has the power to help build your wealth through currency diversification.

From 1976 to 2009, the U.S. dollar lost an average of 73% of its purchasing power against most major currencies. That means $100,000 would only be worth $27,000 today. Yet, if you had held your "cash" portfolio in Swiss francs or Japanese yen during that time, your portfolio would be worth from $157,000 to $187,000 today.

Opening an offshore bank account makes it easy for you to access the power of currency appreciation. Unlike most U.S. banks, offshore banks offer "multi-currency functionality." That is, they give you the ability to invest and transact business in your choice of strong currencies, such as the Swiss franc—currencies that appreciate while the U.S. dollar sinks. That bank account also gives you a place to safely store gold, silver or other valuable investment items or documents offshore.

Investment Platform

An offshore account is an excellent platform from which to diversify investments. It gives instant access to the world's best investment opportunities, including currencies and precious metals, without concern about your home nation's legal restrictions that would otherwise apply if the bank account was located within your home country.

Offshore foreign stock, bond and mutual fund trading are not inhibited by restrictive laws such as the U.S. Securities and Exchange Act or the rules of its administrative agency, the U.S. Securities and Exchange Commission (SEC). An offshore bank allows the ready purchase of attractive insurance and annuity products not available in the U.S. and other nations. Tax savings may result from deferred investment earnings, capital gains, or appreciation, rather than receiving ordinary income that is not only taxed by the U.S. as current income, but at a higher tax rate.

An offshore bank account can provide opportunities to profit from currency fluctuations, the easy ability to purchase foreign real estate, and earnings from comparatively higher bank interest rates available only in foreign countries. You can also trade precious metals and other tangible personal assets through most foreign accounts.

Asset Protection

Another important benefit is the relatively strong asset protection foreign bank accounts provide. The existence of your offshore account is not readily known to a possible claimant considering a lawsuit or someone seeking to collect a judgment against your assets. The existence of the account must be revealed on your U.S. income tax return (IRS Form 1040), but that's not part of the public record.

At times in a judicial proceeding, you may have a legal obligation to reveal an offshore account in a full statement of your assets and liabilities. But there are times when it makes good financial sense to discourage a potential litigant and promote compromise by letting him know just how difficult it will be to reach your offshore assets.

Because of defendant-friendly local laws in asset protection haven nations, foreign judgment holders often have a very difficult time enforcing a judgment obtained in their own country. To reach your assets, a successful creditor must start all over using the foreign judicial process to press a claim against your offshore assets. To do that, they must bear the expense of hiring foreign lawyers and paying for travel and witness transportation.

Besides promoting compromise, the delay in such a strung-out process allows ample time for a defendant to fight the action, or simply move cash or assets to an account in another country. Because of such offshore local laws, courts in these countries rarely issue orders prohibiting such transfers (called "portability"), especially in civil cases.

Many of these nations have one- or two-year statutes of limitations accruing from the date an initial claim arises against the account holder. Since a U.S. lawsuit takes years to get through the courts, this means an American court judgment could be void under the foreign nation's one-year cutoff date. In fact, the U.S. judicial process often takes so long that time runs out in nations with five-year statutes of limitations.

Offshore Accounts More Accessible

A decade or more ago, only the wealthiest investors could benefit from any kind of offshore bank account. Now, after dramatic changes in international banking and communications, even a modest offshore account can be a quick, inexpensive entry into the world of foreign investment opportunities.

To open an offshore private investment account today, you do not always need a minimum deposit of US$1 million or more. Some banks with which The Sovereign Society has a relationship will open an account for as little as US$100,000 to US$250,000. But with lower minimums you don't get the individual service that comes with a deposit of US$1 million or more.

Five Steps to Choosing Your Offshore Bank

With all these potential benefits and lower barriers to entry, how do you go about choosing the right country and the right financial institution for your offshore bank account?

Step #1: Carefully examine and research established financial institutions in your country of choice. This allows you to gauge banking standards and it gives you a frame of reference with which to judge individual banks and their services.

Step #2: Check Google News and local newspapers and publications for any negative mentions about a specific bank you have in mind. Google can also provide the website of the country's official bank supervisory agency, which usually lists facts about each bank, its license, its current standing and any prior complaints or official actions.

Step #3: Beware of "banks" that only have an Internet presence. Most countries have outlawed "brass plate" banks that were little more than a name on a building or lawyer's office door. Absence of bank officials' names, a physical address, and phone numbers are almost always indications of fraud.

Step #4: Be wary of banks you find on the Internet that offer interest rates that are unreasonably high. If the offered deal appears too good to be true, it usually is.

Step #5: Find out which offshore private banks abide by, or exceed, the minimum standards set by the international Basel Accords, the banking supervision regulations issued by the Basel Committee on Banking Supervision (BCBS). These limit risk and require minimum capital, shareholder equity, disclosed reserves, and holdings in debt and equity instruments.

Here are seven preferred banking countries, in each of which we can recommend American-friendly banks:

1. Switzerland: historic banking center but high minimums to open accounts.

2. Denmark: innovative financial products and solid performance.

3. Austria: financial privacy and access to Eastern European investments.

4. Singapore: strong, Swiss-like privacy laws and a gateway to Asia.

5. Uruguay: American accounts welcome with strong privacy.

6. Hong Kong: Banking window to investment opportunities in China.

7. Liechtenstein: much like Switzerland, large minimums required here.

U.S. SEC Goes Offshore

One other important and relatively new consideration is an offshore bank's status when it comes to U.S. Securities and Exchange Commission (SEC) compliance and registration.

In the UBS Swiss tax evasion bank scandal (2008–2010), the U.S. Internal Revenue Service played the major role in investigating and prosecuting U.S. account holders who evaded taxes. This notorious aspect got most of the news media coverage.

Much less notice was given to the fact that the U.S. Department of Justice also charged that the services UBS rendered to U.S. clients amounted to the bank's staff acting as "unregistered investment advisers" and "broker-dealers" in violation of the U.S. Investment Advisers Act of 1940 and of the U.S. Securities and Exchange Commission (SEC) rules.

Using this novel extraterritorial approach, the SEC sought to extend its jurisdiction to include any foreign person anywhere in the world who dares to advise Americans about investments. The SEC claims that unless the adviser first qualifies and registers with that agency, then they are engaging in illegal, even criminal conduct in spite of the obvious fact that such activities are outside the United States.

In the final settlement, UBS paid $718 million to the IRS on the tax evasion charges. It also paid $200 million to the U.S. based on the SEC charges. UBS also was barred permanently from acting as investment advisers or broker-dealers for American clients in Switzerland.

As a result of the successful U.S. government attacks and the fines levied against UBS, a growing number of offshore banks have established special, separate SEC-qualified investment banking units for American clients only. Some independent offshore investment advisers also have registered with the SEC.

As part of your due diligence, check to see if the offshore bank you are considering is SEC registered. Below are four foreign financial entities that are SEC registered as of this date (2012). These two private banks and two Swiss-licensed independent investment managers, are recommended by The Sovereign Society and have undergone our due diligence investigation.

Valartis Bank (Austria) AG

Contact: **Patrick Doherty**, Senior Vice President
Address: Rathausstrasse 20, A-1010, Vienna, Austria
Tel.: + 43 (0) 577 89 186 Fax +43 (0) 577 89 150
Email: p.doherty@valartis.at / Website: www.valartis.at
Minimum Balance: US$100,000 or equivalent for a managed account.

Jyske Global Asset Management (JGAM) - Denmark

Contact: **Thomas Fischer**, Senior Vice President
Address: Vesterbrogade 9, DK-1780, Copenhagen V, Denmark
Tel.: +45 8989 5903 Fax: +45 8989 5901
Email: fischer@jgam.com / Website: http://jgam.com/
Minimum Balance: US$200,000 or equivalent for each of the
following accounts: a) personal investment account; b) managed
currency account or; c) IRA account. Minimum balance US$1
million or equivalent for a JGAM managed investment account.
Mr. Fischer is a member of The Sovereign Society Council of
Experts.

Weber, Hartmann, Vrijhof & Partners - Switzerland

Contact: **Robert Vrijhof**, Managing Partner
Address: Schaffhauserstrasse 418, CH-8050 Zürich, Switzerland
Tel.: +41-44-315-77-77 Fax: +41-44-315-77-78
Email: info@whvp.ch / Website: www.whvp.ch

Alpine Atlantic Asset Management AG - Switzerland

Contact: **Daniel Zurbrügg**, Managing Partner
Address: Usteristrasse 19, 8023, Zürich 1204 Geneva, Switzerland
Tel.: +41 44 200 7000 Fax: +41 44 200 7009
Email: info@alpineatlantic.com / Website: www.alpineatlantic.com
Minimum Balance: US$250,000 or equivalent

Choosing and Opening Your Offshore Bank Account

Before you choose a bank, you must pick the right haven nation where your banking needs will best be met. On the following pages, you will find information designed to help you make that decision. Different strategies offer unique benefits and I will show you what may work best to meet your specific needs

But first, ask yourself your true purposes for wanting an offshore bank account.

Do you want expanded investment opportunities? Increased privacy? Do you need asset protection from potential claims and creditors? All these worthy objectives can be accomplished offshore.

Once you know your objectives, your next step is to learn all about offshore banks that will fulfill your specific needs. For each bank you must determine the services it can provide. Check its reputation, financial condition and all associated costs and fees.

In many countries, banking fees are rather expensive, far more than Americans are used to paying. Often, the net benefits of an offshore account are diminished by high fees. Be practical and run a mathematical model and find out what your net profit (or loss) might be based on bank fees alone.

This is especially important for private investment accounts where not only set fees are charged but in some cases, percentage fees are levied. Few countries tax nonresident bank accounts per se, but some, like Switzerland, do collect withholding taxes on interest earnings. In the Swiss case, as with some other countries, these taxes may be credited against your U.S. tax liability under the existing double taxation treaties, but you must apply for this credit.

Maximum Privacy

If you want maximum privacy and strong protection from intrusive government officials, litigation and lawyers, avoid any offshore bank with established branches or subsidiaries located within your home country, especially if you live in the United States, its territories, possessions, or dependencies. American courts have been known to threaten the shutdown or confiscation of accounts in U.S. branches or subsidiaries when their offshore parent bank fails to comply with a U.S. court's orders, as in the recent UBS tax evasion scandal.

Never use your offshore account as a checking account for payment of home country bills. Bank fees for international check payments are costly and, what's worse, this creates recorded links that undermine the advantages of financial privacy. Offshore retail accounts are available in some offshore banks with which we work, even if you do not live or have a business there, but usually such accounts are allowed only for in-country foreigners who are residents.

On the other hand, if you're unconcerned about creditors or personal claims and you want ease and speed in setting up and managing an offshore account, head for the U.S. branch office of a foreign bank. You might also pick a major American bank such as Citibank that has many offices and subsidiaries overseas. This latter course allows you to use offshore bank outlets when you are abroad but realize that this option offers no asset protection and no real privacy.

A more convenient and more private course of action is to obtain a Barclays, Visa, MasterCard, or other international credit card from your offshore bank. While offshore cards are more expensive than their U.S. equivalents, the offshore bank can deduct your monthly charges from your account balance. This means you earn money offshore, incur bills offshore, make deposits into and pay with your offshore account, all outside your home country. As with offshore checks, never use that offshore credit card in your home country. Do that and your financial privacy is reduced and the cost is prohibitive.

Under no circumstances should you attempt to hide reportable income that is taxable in your home nation in your offshore bank account. Nor should you use an offshore bank credit card as an unreported piggy bank to conceal income or personal expenses. That sort of illegal activity is tax evasion and it can land you in jail. As part of their continuing anti-offshore campaign the IRS has a vigorous aversion to tax cheats who use offshore credit cards to hide income.

Source for Offshore Bank Information

U.S. laws force banks and financial institutions licensed to do business in the U.S. to disclose information about transactions in other branches even if their home office is in another country. Many nations have similar laws.

A bank's failure to disclose information can mean the bank and its officers may be held in contempt of court, fined and/or its managers imprisoned. Indeed, U.S. courts have imposed sanctions on the American branches of a foreign bank, even when refusal is based upon a foreign court order or law that forbids production of the requested data.

As I write this, more than a dozen offshore banks in Switzerland, Liechtenstein, and other countries are under investigation by the U.S. Department of Justice for allegedly assisting Americans to hide unreported funds or evade taxes.

Visit Your Local Library and Ask for...

To find basic information about an offshore bank, visit your local library and ask for the *Thomson/Polk World Bank Directory* (International Edition). This standard reference has a complete listing of banks in over 212 countries, including the U.S., with updated sections issued twice a year. It also analyzes a bank's financial size and strength, and it tells you how and whom to contact.

One of its five volumes is a 300-page reference that includes industry ranking tables for banks, including:

- worldwide and U.S. holding companies
- credit ratings
- international banking holidays
- central banks
- currency exchanges
- attorneys experienced in banking law
- regulatory agency contact information
- and trade association contact information

It also lists fund process information including ABA routing numbers and Federal Reserve telegraph names for U.S. banks, Canadian transit numbers for Canadian banks, and country routing or sort codes for international banks. The "Worldwide Correspondents Guide" section contains contact information for more than 12,500 banks worldwide and includes city locations, phone numbers, and routing numbers.

You can also consult a reliable local in-country professional with whom you have an established relationship. They are a valuable resource for banking advice and contacts. Once you have decided which offshore financial institution is best for you, the next step is to open the account.

Opening Your Account

Except for the geography involved, opening an offshore bank account differs little from starting a domestic, home country account. As would your local domestic banker, offshore bankers want to see you in person when your relationship begins.

Just as you need to do due diligence on your offshore bank, the due diligence that banks are required to conduct on potential clients has increased greatly under "know your customer" rules now in effect worldwide.

When you apply to open an offshore bank account you will be asked to provide some or all of the following:

1. A notarized copy of your **passport.** You may also be asked to provide a notarized copy of your birth certificate or driver's license. For the U.S. State Department procedure on how to obtain a notarized passport, see http://www.travel.state.gov/passport/npic/npic_872.html

2. A recent **utility bill** or equivalent document which confirms the details of your permanent home address. Make sure the bill you present is no older than three months.

3. A **bank reference letter** on your domestic bank's letterhead, or on a form provided by the offshore bank. Your domestic bank manager must sign this letter or form stating you are a reliable customer. Most offshore private banks prefer that this reference come from a bank with which you have had at least a two-year relationship.

4. A **professional letter of reference** from a doctor, lawyer, or accountant in your country of residence.

5. A **letter describing the specific source of funds** you will deposit initially and your subsequent projected banking patterns. The bank will use this "profile" information to measure your account activity to determine if there is suspicious or unusual behavior that the bank must investigate.

6. The **required minimum deposit**, which varies with each institution or type of account. The minimum starting point for some offshore private investment bank accounts is $100,000, though most require $500,000 to $1 million for full investment services. Retail accounts, where available, offshore usually require $5,000 as an initial deposit.

7. In some jurisdictions, such as the Republic of Panama, it is traditional that a **local professional introduce** a foreigner seeking a bank account. A member of our Council of Experts, Derek Sambrook of Trust Services Panama provides this service. (Contact information on page 95.)

8. Almost all offshore banks now require that U.S. clients complete **an IRS Form W-9** (Request for Taxpayer Identification Number and Certification) before they will agree to open your account. The form allows the bank to share information with the IRS and, in some cases, acts as a waiver of the foreign country's bank secrecy laws. This form is used by a U.S. person (including a resident alien) to give their correct U.S. Taxpayer Identification Number (TIN) and to certify the TIN is correct.

This one-on-one contact should be reciprocal. When you establish your account, immediately get to know your contact at the bank personally. That person should speak your language, understand your business and be totally reliable. Always have a "back-up" contact at the bank who knows who you are, in case your usual representative is unavailable.

While selecting an offshore bank may sound exotic or even difficult, it is actually not that different from picking a local domestic bank. It's important to examine closely the bank's reputation and financial condition, and to ask the right questions. What kind of fees does it require? What services does the bank provide? What do the services cost?

But with offshore banking there is one critical extra step. You must ensure the bank welcomes foreigners, especially those with U.S. passports. And you want to be sure they have experience with cumbersome U.S. tax reporting requirements. Plus, make sure they speak fluent English.

Offshore banking can be expensive so it is important to be sure you fully understand a bank's fee structure. Be sure to crunch the numbers to find out what your net profit (or loss) might be. And once you choose a potential offshore bank, get these questions answered before you transfer the first penny.

10 Questions to Ask Any Offshore Bank

1. What types of accounts are available to international investors?

2. Are there any restrictions on foreigners' investments, specifically on U.S. account holders?

3. What taxes, if any, will be withheld from my investment income?

4. What investments are considered part of the bank's balance sheet and available to the bank's creditors (including depositors) in the event of bank insolvency?

5. What are the fees for securities transactions and custody?

6. What other fees may apply to the account?

7. Is my account insured by law or otherwise against loss in the event of the bank's insolvency?

8. How do I transact business and with whom, and are telephone, fax, or e-mail orders accepted?

9. Is Internet banking available and secure? If so, is this service available in English?

10. Does the bank send U.S. clients a year-end statement showing any taxable interest paid?

Be sure you invest the time up front to check the bank's financial standing and perform due diligence. This is not always such an easy task. If you aren't sure where to start, first check out the bank's website to find their annual report or actually request a copy from the bank.

However, all the due diligence can't replace a personal visit. I recommend at least one face-to-face meeting at the bank when you open the account (often this is required by the bank) and a return visit at least every two years.

Out in the Open

Here's a tip that may help you avoid unwanted scrutiny while accomplishing your offshore financial goals in relative privacy and peace.

Let's be honest: many offshore jurisdictions known for no-tax, privacy and anti-creditor banking laws are also prime suspects for certain unsavory financial activities. When your name appears on a bank account in places such as The Bahamas or the Cayman Islands, it immediately raises red flags for suspicious U.S. government agents. (But then, so does the name of any tax haven.)

If privacy is your paramount goal, you do not need to use your own name when opening an offshore account. Instead, create a trust, family foundation, limited liability company or corporation under your direct or indirect control and open the account in its name. Many offshore banks in places such as Singapore and Hong Kong require American clients to have their accounts in the name of a legal entity. Even though this usually is not a matter of public record, all offshore banks require full disclosure of all beneficial owners of legal entities that open accounts and this information may be shared with your home government.

Still another way to obtain banking privacy is to "get lost in a crowd." You can establish your offshore account in a major banking nation where privacy is better protected than in the U.S. A good choice might be the United Kingdom or Switzerland where there are respected private investment banks. But accept the fact that IRS agents are suspicious of accounts held in any offshore financial institution.

You might choose a country where you have family ties, or one with an active international financial role, such as Hong Kong, Singapore, Ireland or Austria. In London, Vienna or Dublin, your bank dealings will not be deemed especially noteworthy, since thousands of Americans hold accounts in these places. If you create your own "privacy haven" out in the open, instead of going to a small bank in some exotic, far-flung locale, your money, and your privacy, usually will be somewhat more secure.

No Absolute Bank Secrecy

Let me make clear that banking secrecy does exist in many reputable haven jurisdictions.

Offshore financial centers ("tax havens") such as Panama, Nevis, Belize, Andorra, Singapore, the Cook Islands and Monaco officially impose banking privacy by law, waiving this protection only in criminal situations and usually only under court order.

Unlike the U.S., where bank employees have been turned into surrogate government spies, many offshore nations impose fines and prison sentences on bank employees for the unauthorized violation of the privacy of account holders. At this writing a former employee of Bank Julius Baer is serving time in a Swiss prison for just such a violation and an ex-employee of Liechtenstein *Landesbank* is on the Interpol international most wanted list.

But put one notion to rest right now—there is no such thing as a totally "secret" bank account anywhere in the world. And yes, there still are "numbered accounts" but not in the sense that the phrase used to designate an account with no name on it.

Even in nations with the strongest bank privacy laws, such as Switzerland or Austria, a bank account holder's true name is on record somewhere in an institution's files. Even if the account is in a corporate name, or the name of a trust or other legal entity, there's always a paper (or computer) trail to be traced, especially if government agents want to know about alleged criminals and their finances.

Tax Information Exchange Agreements

Almost all offshore banking jurisdictions now have numerous tax information exchange treaties (TIEAs) with the United States and other nations. These agreements allow the jurisdiction to share tax information with the U.S. or other governments upon a showing of probable cause that a tax violation may have occurred in the case of an account holder who is a citizen or resident of the requesting country.

Beginning in 2009, a major change in offshore banking privacy policies occurred under a coordinated threat of "blacklisting" from major nations. Abandoning decades of strict bank secrecy guaranteed by law, almost all tax havens have accepted foreign tax evasion or tax fraud as a valid basis for responding to foreign tax agency inquiries concerning their citizens with accounts in an offshore center.

The new standard for information exchange is that set by the Organization for Economic Cooperation and Development (OECD), based on Article 26 of the "OECD Model Tax Convention."

Under this OECD procedure, foreign tax authorities wishing to take advantage of tax information exchange agreements need to supply evidence of tax evasion (names, facts, alleged tax crimes) to the requested government. Supposedly, "fishing expeditions" are not allowed. In the absence of sufficient probable cause, the request may be denied by the foreign government, but each government varies in its policies on what constitutes probable cause.

At this time, the TIEA policy is now well established internationally. The OECD announced that by the end of 2011 governments had signed more than 700 TIEAs to exchange tax information. The OECD claimed that 20 countries already had collected "€14 billion

(US$19.9 billion) in additional revenues from more than 100,000 wealthy taxpayers who had hidden assets offshore."

The Imperial U.S. "External" Revenue Service

The Roman Empire's history of conquest for those countries and peoples who were conquered brought centralized control, the suppression of local laws, the imposition of a unified system of rules and general enslavement.

The question is whether the United States Internal Revenue Service has adopted the Imperial Romans as their model and as the inspiration for the Foreign Account Tax Compliance Act (FATCA). Are they now the External Revenue Service (ERS) an acronym which, come to think of it, sounds very much like the common British street word for a part of the human anatomy)? FATCA is a U.S. law that attempts to order all offshore banks and other foreign financial institutions to report directly to the IRS information about financial accounts held by U.S. taxpayers, or by trusts, corporations or other legal entities which have substantial U.S. ownership.

Failure to follow FATCA reporting rules will impose a 30% tax on all U.S.-based transactions with foreign banks that don't comply. It is no secret that offshore banks are furious at being deputized as IRS agents. But if they refuse to comply, the banks face a choice of paying that punitive 30% withholding tax or withdrawing completely from lucrative U.S. financial markets.

This unprecedented American law, adopted in 2010 with little public notice, follows the Imperial Roman model. It assumes that the jurisdiction of the U.S. government now extends to every bank and financial institution in the entire world. It also assumes that U.S. tax and reporting laws supersede the laws of every other nation, whether those countries like it or not.

FATCA is billed as an effort by a tax hungry Obama administration to combat tax evasion by U.S. persons holding cash or investments in offshore financial accounts.

As I have already noted, unlike most other countries, the U.S. government does not have a reasonable territorial tax system that ends at its borders. Americans are taxed on all their worldwide income without regard to where the individual lives or the sources of the income.

For many years, U.S. taxpayers with financial assets outside the United States have been required by law to report those assets to the IRS and to pay any taxes due—and most do so.

As successive big spending, budget deficit governments of both political parties have come and gone in Washington, D.C., politicians frantically have searched for more revenue. As part of this tax and spend policy, they assume that every American engaged in offshore banking or investing probably is engaged in tax evasion. Unfortunately, the UBS tax evasion scandal played right into IRS hands.

What FATCA means for you and me, is that starting in 2014 foreign financial institutions—including banks, investment brokerages and insurance companies—are going to be awash in new reporting regulations—if they agree to continue to welcome American clients once FATCA comes into force. And that is a very big "if."

In the face of massive protests from thousands of offshore banks, as well as official protests from governments in Canada, Panama, Switzerland, The Bahamas and many other countries, the IRS announced that the original January 1, 2013 FATCA effective date had been dropped.

Under this IRS schedule, offshore private banks, which face the most onerous FATCA requirements, will not be forced to provide details on U.S. clients with accounts with more than $50,000 until the middle of 2014. Lower value accounts at private banks won't need to be reported until 2015. Required personal reporting of offshore assets for American taxpayers began in April 2012 with the first filing of IRS Form 8938 (Statement of Specified Foreign Financial Assets).

Adhering to these complex IRS reporting regulations will cost offshore financial institutions hundreds of millions of dollars for greatly expanded compliance staffs, software programs, investigations of their U.S. clients and trying to understand and meet the IRS rules. Bank clients will pay the bill for this IRS mess in ever-higher bank fees.

Expat Americans Suffer

FATCA presents a special problem for millions of Americans who live and work offshore, each of whom suddenly is confronted with an obligation to file all sorts of new reports which carry penalties and possible criminal indictments. Many have had established bank accounts closed and been refused new ones as offshore banks have opted to stay out of this FATCA mess.

So if you ran a business, would you cater to clients that cost you more to serve and bring with them more risks? Or would you say, "Thanks, but no thanks" and focus your business elsewhere? It seems pretty simple. And, that is the exact decision thousands of foreign institutions are about to make—or already have made.

What the tax hungry U.S. politicians have ignored is that if FATCA ever comes into force it will cripple foreign investment in the U.S. at a time when the faltering economy needs all the foreign cash it can get.

There is some hope that after the 2012 U.S. elections a new president and majority in Congress will come to its senses and repeal FATCA.

But few are betting that the IRS, unless forced to, will abandon its Imperial Roman attitude—even as the American Empire it serves declines.

Fortunately for members of The Sovereign Society, over our

unique, 15-year existence The Society has established arrangements for bank accounts with numerous reputable and well capitalized offshore banks. Any bank mentioned in these pages is one that welcomes Americans clients, and will give a special welcome to Sovereign Society members.

Strategy 2:
The Offshore Asset
Protection Trust (APT)

To paraphrase that great old American TV show, *Gun Smoke*, "Get your assets out of Dodge."

Frivolous litigation, expensive legal defense costs, outrageous jury awards and government privacy invasions all combine to create an urgent need to protect your family and business wealth as well as your privacy.

What's the solution?

The offshore asset protection trust (APT)—a legal device that shields your wealth from lawsuits, creditors, an irate ex-spouse and even the government of your home country. One of the very best methods for asset protection is to create an APT located in an offshore haven jurisdiction.

Many offshore financial centers specialize in trust creation, including Bermuda, the Isle of Man, the Channel Islands of Jersey and Guernsey, Singapore and Hong Kong.

But I recommend the Republic of Panama. Only hours by air from the United States, Panama has a century-long history as a financial haven and a reputation for working closely with Americans.

The Republic of Panama, unlike the United States, has a sensible territorial tax system. It only taxes income produced within the borders of Panama. Thus, non-Panama trust or other income is exempt from local Panama taxes, but not U.S. taxes.

The first trust law in Panama was adopted in 1925 based on the British common law trust. In 1984 and again in 1995, the trust law was updated to include modern provisions specially designed to allow flexible operation and convenience for foreigners seeking offshore trusts.

Low Costs

Traditionally, the cost of creating a highly complex asset protection trust in a foreign nation has exceeded US$15,000, plus several thousand dollars in annual maintenance fees. Unless the total assets to be shielded justify such costs, a foreign APT may not be practical for you.

A few years ago, *Businessweek* estimated that "as a rule of thumb you should have a net worth of around $500,000" or more in order to justify a foreign asset protection trust. The magazine cited expert's fees for establishing and administering such trusts running as high as US$50,000, with some demanding a percentage of the total value of assets to be transferred.

While high cost once may have been the old rule, APT costs have changed for the better. These days, offshore trusts are not just for the very rich.

Panama is a good example of these lower costs. In the State of Delaware for trust creation and management some trust companies charge "basis points" on the net asset value of the trust assets. So, if you have a trust worth $500,000 and the trust company charges 2%, the fee would be $10,000. Others charge flat fees of $3,500 to $5,000 a year, regardless of the size of the trust estate.

In Panama, however, if your assets are valued at $400,000 or less, the initial cost to create an APT is $2,500 if you employ Trust Services Ltd., and this includes the first-year annual maintenance fee of $1,070. The trustee fee pays for keeping your trust compliant and covers the costs of administering the trust according to its stated goals.

Some people overlook annual maintenance fees, but a trust could be active for 20 to 30 years, or longer, so annual fees add up. A simple offshore APT holding title to less than $1 million in assets set up by Trust Services Ltd. in Panama (contact details below), for instance, charges $1,000 a year. Compared to a domestic U.S. trust structure which would charge $5,000, over a 25-year period that saves $100,000!

Trust Services SA
Derek Sambrook, Managing Director
Adam Carmody, Trust Officer
Suite 522, Balboa Plaza, Avenida Balboa
Panama, Republic of Panama
Tel.: +507 263-5252 / 269-2438
Email: sambrook@trustserv.com
Website: www.trustservices.net

But What is a Trust?

Most of us know the word "trust" but do we know what a trust is?

A trust is a formal legal arrangement voluntarily created and funded by a person (the grantor) that directs another person (the trustee) to take legal title and control of the grantor's donated property, to be used and managed for the benefit of one or more other persons the grantor designates (the beneficiaries).

The beneficiary receives income or distributions of assets from the trust and has an enforceable equitable title to the benefits, but does not control trust assets or manage trust operation. An offshore asset protection trust may also include another party to trust operation, the protector, a person vested with certain powers to monitor the performance of the trustee.

The creation of a trust arrangement is a planned, intentional act. A trust can serve a specific purpose or as part of a general estate plan. The trust grantor signs a written declaration describing his or her intentions, stating specific details of proposed trust operation, income distribution and the extent and limits of trustee powers.

A well-drafted trust document will reflect the grantor's precise intentions. Drafting a trust declaration as part of an overall estate plan requires expert advice based on a thorough examination of all existing arrangements that affect the grantor's estate.

To create a proper estate plan, the status of all other legal documents or devices, such as a will, or jointly owned assets, must be reviewed and coordinated with the trust. Conflicts must be resolved consistent with all applicable trust and tax laws. However, a targeted trust may be drafted only to accomplish limited or even single goals, such as asset protection.

Most offshore asset protection trusts are drafted as discretionary trusts, a form that allows greater planning flexibility. This means the trustee is given the power to decide how much will be distributed to beneficiaries and, in some cases, who qualifies as a beneficiary.

The trust declaration may vest a trustee with the right to make payments for purposes, at times and in amounts, the trustee decides. A trustee often is given the authority to recognize beneficiaries within named classes of persons ("my children and their heirs"), or the trust may contain a right known as a power of appointment allowing the trustee to choose beneficiaries from a class of eligible persons.

What a Trust Can Do

A trust may be created for any purpose that is not illegal or void as against public policy.

A trust can hold title to and invest in real estate, cash, stocks, bonds, negotiable instruments and personal property. Trusts can provide care for minor children or the elderly; or pay medical, educational or other expenses. A trust can provide financial support in an emergency, for retirement, during marriage or divorce, or even carry out premarital agreements.

To the uninformed, the trust process may seem complex and difficult, but, in fact, a trust is one of the most flexible yet efficient legal mechanisms recognized by law. Compared to the alternatives, it can provide superior asset protection and can assure that your bounty will be distributed exactly as you see fit.

The APT

In recent decades, asset protection using the trust format has gained wide popularity among people of wealth who are "in the know."

The foreign asset protection trust (APT) is any trust that helps individuals protect assets from attack by creditors. It is established in an offshore jurisdiction by a grantor resident in one nation under the laws of another nation where the trust operations are based and where trust laws offer greater protection,

Because the trust is governed by the laws of the nation where it is registered and administered, this "foreignness" serves as a shield for the grantor's business and personal assets, deflecting would-be creditors, litigation and potential financial liabilities, perhaps even an ex-spouse bent on revenge.

Here are a few reasons why an offshore APT can be so effective:

Judicial Obstacles: In many cases, the courts of asset haven nations often will not automatically recognize the validity of U.S. (or other nations') domestic court orders. A foreign judgment creditor seeking collection must re-litigate the original claim in the foreign court after hiring local lawyers. He may have to post a bond and pay legal expenses for all parties if he loses. The legal complexity and cost of such an international collection effort is likely to stop all but the most determined adversaries or, at the very least, to promote compromise.

Minimal Needs: An offshore APT need not be complex. Creation can be little more than the signing of formal documents and opening a trust account managed by your local trustee in a bank in the foreign country of your choice. Respected offshore multinational and local banks routinely provide experienced trust officers and staff to handle trust matters. Most international banks have U.S. dollar-denominated accounts, often with better interest rates than U.S. financial institutions offer.

Greater Protection: Under the laws of haven nations, assets placed in an offshore asset protection trust have far more protection than permitted under domestic U.S. trust law. The law in these countries is drafted specifically to provide an asset protection "safe harbor" that is unavailable in the U.S. and many other nations. With an offshore APT, foreign-held trust assets are not subject to the jurisdiction of your local or home country judicial system.

Fast Acting: Time under the statute of limitations for initiating a foreign creditor's suit varies. In many jurisdictions, the statute begins to run from the date the APT was established. Some haven nations, such as the Cook Islands, have a limit of one year for the initiation of claims. As a practical matter, it may take a creditor longer than that just to discover the existence of a foreign APT to which most assets have long since been transferred.

Better Investments: An offshore APT is an excellent platform for diversifying investments and benefitting from the global tax savings. An APT permits taking advantage of the world's best investment opportunities, without being blocked by your home nation's legal restrictions on foreign investments. As previously discussed, offshore foreign stock, bond and mutual fund trading are not covered by laws such as the U.S. Securities and Exchange Act or its administrative arm, the SEC. An offshore APT can also purchase attractive insurance and annuity products not available in the U.S. and some other nations. Tax savings may result from deferred investment earnings or capital gains, rather than ordinary income that will not only be taxed immediately but at a higher rate.

Confidentiality: The APT can provide far greater privacy and confidentiality, minimization of home country inheritance taxes and the avoidance of the probate process in case of death. It provides increased flexibility in conducting affairs in case of personal disability, allows easy transfer of asset titles and avoids domestic currency controls in your home nation. An APT is also a good substitute for, or supplement to, costly professional liability insurance or even a prenuptial agreement, offering strong protection for your heirs' inheritance.

Estate Planning: An offshore APT can serve the same traditional estate planning goals achieved by U.S. domestic strategies. These include using bypass trust provisions to minimize estate taxes for a husband and wife, trusts that allow maximum use of gift tax exemptions through planned giving and trusts that provide for maintenance and tax-free income for a surviving spouse.

Asset Transfer

As a practical matter, regardless of the time of APT creation, any assets physically remaining within your home country and its courts' jurisdiction generally are not protected from domestic judgment creditors.

Simply placing title to domestic property in the name of a foreign trust is paper-thin protection at best unless the property is actually moved offshore. When tangible assets actually are transferred to the foreign jurisdiction, as when funds, stock shares, precious metals or other tangible property is moved to an offshore trust account or the trustee's safe deposit box, a home country creditor will have great difficulty in reaching them, provided he even discovers the existence of the trust.

As a mandatory precaution, the APT and its trustee should always employ an offshore bank that is not a branch or affiliate of any bank within your home country. This helps insulate the offshore bank officials (and APT accounts) from foreign official or private pressure. It gives greater legitimate protection from home country pressures or just informational snooping — whether government or otherwise.

But consider this: even with this enhanced offshore financial privacy, in a given situation there can be great tactical advantage in letting a harassing party know your assets are securely placed well beyond their reach. The cost and difficulty of pursuit may well discourage any action on their part or result in a compromise.

Strategy 3:
Earn US$95,100 a Year —
U.S. Tax-Free

If you decide personally to follow your cash, assets and investments and go offshore yourself, there's a very useful provision of U.S. tax law about which you should know.

As I have noted, Americans and citizens of other nations move offshore for many reasons, to find a new or second home, to seek lower taxes, greater asset protection and more financial and personal privacy.

But there is an another group of international migrants, many of them educated and professional Americans who "go offshore" to find not only a better job, but to enjoy a major tax break that U.S. law grants to those who qualify — it's called the "foreign earned income exclusion."

If you are considering moving yourself or your family to a foreign country, or if you have an offer of employment abroad, here is a definite plus that may help you decide.

A few years ago *The New York Times* reported on a Louisiana professor with a PhD in economics who, despite being tenured at his prestigious Virginia university, left to teach at the American University in Dubai in the United Arab Emirates. Helping to tip the scales in favor of Dubai included great schools for his children, inexpensive house help, two top-of-the-line luxury imports he purchased without having to pay U.S. income tax.

The tax break to which the professor referred is known as the "foreign earned income exclusion."

Why is this important? Because no thanks to the U.S. Internal Revenue Code, along with a Supreme Court decision from the 1920s, U.S. citizens must pay tax on their worldwide income, no matter where they live and work. Most other countries allow their citizens who live abroad to avoid domestic taxes, but not the United States.

This foreign earned income exclusion is a legal tax break that allows a U.S. citizen who lives and works outside the U.S. to exclude up to $95,100 each year tax-free (the 2012 amount adjusted annually for inflation) of foreign earned income from U.S. income taxes.

If both a husband and wife work offshore it's possible that they could earn $190,200 tax free annually offshore, plus lower taxed housing allowances an offshore employer pays for you.

This is not a tax deduction, credit, or deferral. It's an outright exclusion of your offshore earnings from gross income, so you pay no U.S. income tax on that amount.

Qualifications

To qualify for these benefits you must: 1) establish a "tax home" in a foreign country; 2) pass either the "foreign residence test," or the "physical presence test"; 3) actually have earned income; 4) live in the U.S. for no more than one month during the year; 5) file a U.S. income tax return for each year you live abroad claiming the exclusion.

Usually your "tax home" is where your principal place of business is located, not where you live. The term "tax home" is broader when determining eligibility for the foreign earned income exclusion. Confusion over this point stings many Americans overseas. If you work overseas and still maintain a U.S. residence, your tax home remains in the U.S.

To qualify for the foreign earned income exclusion you must establish both your principal place of business and your actual residence outside the United States.

A complicated test that determines if you get this exclusion involves counting the maximum number of days you're in or out of the U.S.A. But the foreign residence test is easier for most taxpayers to pass. You must establish yourself as a bona fide resident of a foreign country for an uninterrupted period that includes an entire taxable year; and you must intend to stay there indefinitely. If you don't pass this test, you're considered a transient and won't qualify.

U.S. tax law defines your residence as a state of mind. It's where you intend to be domiciled indefinitely. To determine your state of mind, the IRS looks at the degree of your attachment to the country in question. A number of factors, none of them decisive are examined.

Your "tax home" is the location of your regular or principal place of business, not where you live. But the definition of "tax home" is broader when determining eligibility for the foreign earned income exclusion.

Confusion over this point snags many Americans overseas who think they are earning tax-free income. If you work overseas and maintain a U.S. residence, your tax home is not outside the U.S. In other words, to qualify for the foreign earned income exclusion, you must establish both your principal place of business and your residence outside the United States.

The bottom line is that you must establish yourself clearly as a member of a foreign community. This unusual tax break is only for those who actually live and earn offshore.

But think about this: suppose you have a legitimate business that can be based in an offshore tax haven such as Panama, where a territorial tax system only collects taxes on earnings from within Panama, and not from outside the country. And suppose the bulk of the income comes from worldwide sources, say, for consulting or professional advice. You could cut your U.S. ties, move to Panama and charter a Panama corporation (SA) for your business. You could then pay yourself (and perhaps your spouse or significant other) a salary for services rendered, plus housing and other expenses.

Needless to say, such an arrangement would have to be carefully planned with the advice of an expert U.S. tax attorney so that all requirements of the foreign earned income exclusion tests are met and you are certain to qualify.

Definitely something to factor into your planning if offshore beckons you.

For U.S. tax advice:

Josh N. Bennett JD
440 North Andrews Avenue
Fort Lauderdale, FL 33301
Tel.: (786)202-5674
Email: josh@joshbennett.com
Website: http://www.joshbennett.com/

Strategy 4:
Offshore Variable Annuities

Even though the U.S., the U.K. and the European Union continue to tighten the tax and financial reporting screws on wealth, there still remain private and profitable, yet strictly legal ways to protect and invest assets.

One of best of these is the offshore variable annuity because it allows you to avoid paying taxes until you actually withdraw funds. According to *The Wall Street Journal*, "Offshore annuities are becoming an investment vehicle of choice for those who have oodles of money they want to shelter from taxes."

This also is one of the easiest, least expensive methods to invest in offshore stocks and other funds. Another advantage is that annuity investments can be transferred from one fund manager to another with no immediate tax consequences. Plus, you achieve significant asset protection.

Annuities work very well for your children or grandchildren, because the earnings accumulated within the policy are tax-deferred until funds are paid out or withdrawn many years later when they are ready for retirement.

What really makes an offshore deferred variable annuity superior to its domestic U.S. brother is that it gives you access to a wide variety of international investment options, including foreign currencies, foreign investment funds and an entire host of offshore stocks and bonds.

Offshore variable annuity investments typically start around US$250,000, commonly exceeding US$1 million or more. In contrast, the average domestic U.S. annuity buyer's initial investment is only US$25,000 or less. The primary objectives in purchasing annuities and life insurance offshore are asset protection, greater wealth accumulation and access to international investment opportunities.

Because they are located offshore, away from restrictive U.S. laws, foreign insurance companies can be flexible in negotiating fees. But keep in mind that, unless eliminated by a tax treaty, a one-time 1% federal U.S. excise tax is levied on all life insurance and annuity contracts issued to U.S. persons by foreign insurers.

Good Income Play for Savvy Investors

A Swiss annuity, denominated in one of the world's most reliable currencies, the Swiss franc, is a good income play for savvy investors. That is because, as the dollar depreciates, your annuity income appreciates.

Example: Mr. Smith, age 64, invests 100,000 Swiss francs (CHF) in a Swiss annuity. Every year, for the rest of his life, this annuity will repay him a guaranteed 4,623 Swiss francs. His March 1, 2009 payment of 4,623 Swiss francs then would have converted into US$3,952.

Today, his 4,623 Swiss francs annuity payment would convert into US$5,173. That is $1,316 more cash earned with no added effort.

The Swiss franc appreciated 27% in two years against the faltering U.S. dollar, making Mr. Smith's investment more profitable for him.

The Swiss franc generally has reflected the state of Swiss banking, strong, valuable and unaffected by inflation and monetary fads. Since 1971, the franc has appreciated nearly 400% against the U.S. dollar.

Whatever the specific arithmetic, if you invest the usual minimum required, CHF100,000 (US$111,900) in a Swiss fixed annuity, with immediate payments over a 10-year term, inevitably if and when the dollar declines in value, you enjoy greater spendable income when you later convert Swiss francs back into the dollar at a much better exchange rate.

Annuity Mechanics

In this arrangement, the insurer is the legal owner of the annuity bank account and also is the investor.

The annuity purchaser has the right to choose initially and later change the overall investment strategy, but under U.S. law you cannot select the specific underlying investments or manage them yourself. The asset manager has the power to choose any investment he deems appropriate within the general instructions you have given, conservative, moderate or speculative.

He can pick from the entire global investment universe, without SEC restrictions or other rules that would otherwise apply to U.S. citizens. This allows him to place the deposit you made into your fixed annuity in all traded mutual funds, hedge funds, and stocks, bonds, structured products and the like.

Under this arrangement the insurer is the owner of the investments. You own an annuity policy with a value linked to the underlying portfolio of investments, but you don't own the individual investments.

Swiss and other foreign insurers have established special arrangements with the successful private banks and asset managers in Switzerland and throughout the European Union, giving you assurance that there is an investment strategy available to suit your needs.

You can be certain the insurer wants to make profitable investments as much as you do.

In the event of your death, the account funds will be paid to the beneficiaries according to your instructions.

Swiss Leader

History shows that Switzerland is the place for offshore annuities and life insurance.

While Swiss banking often gets the world's spotlight (for reasons both bad and good), Switzerland's other financial institutions and insurance companies offer a broad range of services that, in some cases, approach the flexibility of a bank account. Indeed, many Swiss residents use their insurance company as their only financial institution.

As for integrity, in the entire history of Swiss insurers, no life insurance company ever has failed to meet its obligations or been forced to close its doors.

And Swiss insurance policies—including annuities—have important advantages:

- Insurance and annuity accounts aren't subject to the Swiss 35% withholding tax on earned bank interest and are exempt from all other Swiss taxes, including on income, capital gains, and inheritance taxes.

- Swiss annuities generally offer higher interest rates than Swiss bank accounts.

- Swiss law gives annuities special asset protection including exemption from enforcement of foreign court judgments including bankruptcy.

However, all these special benefits are not limited to the Swiss people alone. You too can enjoy unequalled asset protection and guaranteed income at relatively low cost.

Deferred Taxes

An offshore variable annuity is a contract between you and a foreign insurance company that provides tax deferred savings. It can serve as a savings or retirement vehicle using investment structures similar to mutual funds, sometimes called "sub-accounts."

Here's how it works: you buy a variable annuity contract (policy) for an agreed-upon sum, often referred to as a "single premium." These monies are invested by the insurance company in one or more investments that you approve, such as an offshore hedge fund.

The annuity contract requires periodic payments by the insurance company to you representing the increased value of investments on which the annuity is based. The money compounds, tax deferred, until you withdraw part or all of it, at which time it is taxed as regular income.

This tax-deferred accumulation can continue until the contract maturity date, usually when you are 85 or older, a time when total income is lower. An annuity is not "life insurance," so you need not take a medical examination to determine "insurability."

In most cases when the annuity matures, it either must be surrendered or converted to a life annuity that pays out a specified sum, at least annually, for the rest of your life, or for some other agreed upon period of time. Because most investors buy variable annuities for their tax-deferred savings features, withdrawing funds as needed, most variable annuities never convert to a life annuity.

Strong Asset Protection

Variable insurance annuities offer significant asset protection, especially in Switzerland, shielding the cash invested and the annuity income from creditors and other claimants. Swiss law exempts annuities from foreign court judgments including bankruptcy.

Practical asset protection exists because: 1) the policies are issued by an offshore insurance company with no affiliates in the United States, and 2) the policy's underlying assets are held entirely outside your home jurisdiction. Any domestic investments are made in the name of the insurance company, not in your name.

The degree of asset protection afforded by Swiss insurance and annuities is unparalleled anywhere else in the world.

Swiss law holds that simply owning Swiss life insurance or, an annuity absent other evidence of business activity within the country, is not a sufficient basis for a Swiss court to honor a foreign legal judgment against you or your assets.

Swiss law offers significant asset protection for life insurance products including annuities. Neither is subject to collection remedies directed against the owner of the policy and the policies are not deemed to be a part of the bankruptcy estate of the policy owner.

If a U.S. or other foreign court authorizes the attachment or levy against a Swiss policy, whether in bankruptcy or otherwise, a Swiss court will not issue an order directing the assignment of the policy to the creditor or the bankruptcy trustee.

Because Swiss insurance companies are not subject to the jurisdiction of a U.S. court, without an order from a Swiss court the annuities are untouchable by creditors. Swiss courts repeatedly and strictly have upheld these protective rules. The law also offers special added protection for annuities naming spouses and children as beneficiaries.

Recognized by the Swiss Federal Office for Private Insurance Matters, these protections apply to all life insurance policies, including annuities and those linked to mutual funds and derivatives.

Company Protection

Statutory asset protection exists in other jurisdictions for annuity contracts as well. In the Isle of Man, a jurisdiction that is home to 192 insurance companies, claims by creditors can only be made through the local courts.

When a variable annuity is issued, the investment assets must be placed in this account and used only to satisfy the variable annuity obligation. If the company has financial problems, these segregated assets cannot be reached by insurance company creditors or creditors of other policyholders. The Cayman Islands, the home of many leading offshore insurance companies, has a similar "segregated accounts" law.

In Switzerland, according to Swiss attorney Urs Schenkero, "A life insurance policy...is protected from the policy owner's creditors if the policy owner has irrevocably designated a third party as beneficiary or if the policy owner has irrevocably or revocably designated his spouse and/or his descendant's beneficiaries."

The Swiss Insurance Act prevents a properly structured insurance contract from being included in a Swiss bankruptcy procedure. The law also protects the contract from foreign seizure orders or orders including them as part of foreign estate proceedings. Under Swiss law, if you are unable to pay your debts or file bankruptcy, all rights under the contract are assigned to the beneficiaries. Other offshore jurisdictions with a well-developed insurance sector provide statutory protection against creditor claims for insurance policies.

Offshore Variable Annuities and U.S. Taxes

Section 72 of the U.S. Internal Revenue Code treats both foreign and domestic variable annuities the same. But the IRS rules must be followed by an insurance company in drafting a policy in order for accumulations to qualify for tax deferral. Before you buy, always obtain a copy of a reliable written legal opinion issued by the insurance company that confirms the proper U.S. tax treatment of the company's annuities. Check the opinion and policy with your U.S. tax advisors if in doubt.

To the extent that the funds you withdraw from a variable annuity represent deferred income, they are taxed at ordinary U.S. income tax rates. A loan against a variable annuity from the issuing insurance company to the annuity buyer, or a third party loan secured by a pledge of the annuity, is a taxable distribution. Certain unsecured loans, however, may be tax-free. Also, borrowing against an annuity when it is first purchased is not taxable since no deferred income has accumulated.

Thus, you can acquire a US$2 million annuity contract and borrow up to US$1 million of the purchase price, pledging the annuity to secure the loan, with no adverse tax consequences.

Keep in mind this difference: tax deferral is available to variable annuities of U.S. investors but not to those who purchase foreign fixed annuities. A "fixed" annuity is an annuity contract guaranteeing a fixed income for a specified period of years or for life. A "variable" annuity income varies depending on the performance of the underlying investments.

Offshore Insurance is Reportable

U.S. reporting requirements relating to offshore insurance are similar to those the IRS imposed on offshore banks, such as filing the IRS Form W-9, as I discussed earlier under the offshore banking section.

The rules announced by the U.S. Treasury agency, the Financial Crimes Enforcement Network (FinCEN), greatly expanded the scope of investments that U.S. taxpayers must report annually. U.S. persons long have been required to submit the Foreign Bank Account Report (FBAR), U.S. Treasury Form TDF 90.22-1, by June 30th each year.

Current FBAR rules an expanded definition of the term "other financial accounts" includes reporting "an account that is an insurance or annuity policy with a cash value." This squarely targets U.S. investors holding non-U.S. life insurance or annuity contracts.

The obligation to file the FBAR in the case of life insurance or annuities rests with you as the policyholder, not with the beneficiary.

If you are interested in learning more about Swiss annuities, contact Marc-André Sola, a member of The Sovereign Society Council of Experts. Marc and his associates at NMG International in Zurich are experts in tailoring policies to each person's individual needs.

Marc-André Sola, Managing Partner
NMG International Financial Services Ltd.
Goethestrasse 22, 8001 Zurich, Switzerland
Phone: +41 44 266 21 41 Fax: +41 44 266 21 49

Email: info@nmg-ifs.com
Website: http://www.nmg-ifs.com/index.html

The Isle of Man is also a major center for offshore annuities and life insurance. Contact Colin Bowen, a member of The Sovereign Society Council of Experts:

Colin G. Bowen, Vice Chairman
Isle of Man Assurance Ltd.
Douglas, Isle of Man
Tel.: + 44 0 7740 651 664 (cell), + 44 1624 681 200
Email: colinb@ioma.co.im
Website: http://www.ioma.co.uk

Strategy 5:
Offshore Life Insurance

Despite all the talk of "tax reform" in the United States, when a death occurs without prior proper planning, the combination of income tax and estate tax can consume 50% or more of a U.S. person's estate.

Such ruinous consequences can be avoided with several planning techniques, but only life insurance provides these four key benefits: 1) tax-free buildup of cash value, including dividends, interest, capital gains; 2) tax-free borrowing against cash value; 3) tax-free receipt of the death benefit; and 4) freedom from estate and generation skipping taxes.

These benefits are available in any life insurance policy designed to comply with U.S. tax laws. However, for larger estates, a U.S.-tax-compliant life insurance policy issued by a carrier outside the U.S. offers these additional benefits:

- **Increased asset protection.** No protection for life insurance proceeds exists under federal laws. While many states have enacted laws that provide limited protection for life insurance policies, coverage varies from significant to non-existent. In contrast, many offshore jurisdictions provide statutory asset protection for the death benefit and investments held by an insurance policy. And, as a practical matter, it is much more expensive for a creditor to bring a claim before a foreign court than a domestic court.

- **Access to global investments.** Offshore insurance policies provide tax advantaged access to international asset managers and to offshore funds that are generally not accessible to U.S. investors.

- **Increased privacy.** Domestic assets, including life insurance policies, can easily be discovered by private investigators with access to any of the hundreds of "asset tracking" services now in existence in the U.S. In contrast, assets held offshore are off the domestic "radar screen" and cannot easily be identified in a routine asset search. The confidentiality statutes of some offshore jurisdictions are an additional barrier against frivolous claims and investigations.

- **Not reportable as a "foreign bank account."** A life insurance policy purchased from a non-U.S. carrier is not considered a "foreign bank, securities or other financial account." This means that there is no requirement to report the existence of the income derived from an offshore insurance policy to any U.S. government authority. However, depending on what country you purchase an offshore insurance policy from, it may be necessary to make a one-time excise tax payment to the IRS amounting to 1% of the policy premium.

- **Currency diversification.** Life insurance policies are free to make investments in non-U.S. dollar assets that may gain in the event of future declines in the value of the U.S. dollar.

Needless to say, the IRS is not pleased with a planning technique that simultaneously eliminates federal estate taxes, creates a situation where no U.S. person is subject to tax upon transfer of the assets to the beneficiaries and permits the policyholder to invest in highly lucrative offshore mutual funds without paying tax.

To this end, the IRS announced rules that would limit the tax benefits for investors in hedge funds that are setting up insurance companies in offshore jurisdictions, but that are not in fact operating as life insurance carriers. The IRS also is concerned with foreign insurance carriers that are investing in hedge funds and has promised to more aggressively enforce existing provisions in the U.S. Tax Code that prohibit life insurance investors from managing their own securities portfolio and that require adequate diversification within the policy.

However, these IRS policy changes have been "in the making" for several years. A properly planned and executed offshore insurance policy should not be affected. But, it is essential that you obtain expert tax advice when considering the purchase of an offshore insurance policy.

Life insurance remains one of few remaining opportunities for offshore estate tax planning combined with asset protection and tax deferral. And, without major changes in U.S. federal laws, these advantages will remain for the foreseeable future.

Isle of Man Assurance Ltd. specializes in tailored life insurance that can serve as a wrapper for all sorts of profitable investments. A member of The Sovereign Society Council of Experts, Colin Bowen is a veteran advisor on life insurance and related matters, including U.S. tax and reporting implications. Contact him at:

Colin G. Bowen, Vice Chairman
Isle of Man Assurance Ltd.
Douglas, Isle of Man
Tel.: + 44 0 7740 651 664 (cell), + 44 1624 681 200
Email: colinb@ioma.co.im
Website: http://www.ioma.co.uk

Strategy 6:
Offshore Investing

When it comes to profitable investing, too many Americans believe the U.S. sits at the economic and political center of the world, with other countries orbiting around us. And these misguided U.S. investors put the greatest share of their cash into domestic markets—a phenomenon known as "home-country bias"—but that's a big mistake.

More than a decade of impressively high foreign market returns should have convinced more American investors to trade offshore. Over-dependence on U.S. stocks is a weakness in any portfolio. Those who only invest in U.S. stocks are losing out on much larger profits abroad.

For smart investors everywhere, the message is clear: For solid profits, you must put some wealth to work in markets beyond America's borders. Since 2001, U.S. stocks have had seven winning years. In 2003, the S&P 500 gained almost 30%. That's huge by any yardstick.

Yet, even with that huge win, U.S. stocks never cracked the top 10 list of the world's best-performing stock markets—and given the U.S. financial situation these days don't expect America to move to the top of the list any time soon.

Until recently, putting money to work in overseas stock markets was largely the province of institutional investors and the super-rich, whose deep pockets attracted the interest of private bankers and exclusive U.S. brokerage firms that catered solely to the well-heeled.

That is no longer the case.

In 2007, there were approximately 1,500 emerging-market investment funds managing over US$200 billion in equities. In September 2012, ETFGI, an independent U.K. research and consultancy firm, said that global assets invested in Exchange Traded Funds (ETFs) and Exchange Traded Products (ETPs) hit an all-time high of over US$1.7 trillion at the end of August 2012. Over the past 10 years the compounded annual growth rate of these products globally has been 26.5%. In late 2012, there were 4,713 ETFs and ETPs, with 9,620 listings, assets of US$1,762 billion, from 204 providers on 56 world stock exchanges. Add to those figures the billions in multiple currencies denominated in other financial instruments and the total is overwhelming.

International and "emerging nation" mutual funds offer a simple way for American investors to profit from the growth of foreign companies. Such funds eliminate the inconvenience associated with direct ownership of foreign shares.

American investors can also profit from American Depository Receipts, or ADRs. These are listed securities traded on U.S. stock exchanges. ADRs represent shares of a foreign stock and are issued by U.S. banks that take possession of the securities. The banks convert dividend payments into dollars and deduct any foreign withholding taxes. ADRs give investors a greater guarantee of safety, as participating foreign companies have to meet certain U.S. Securities and Exchange Commission (SEC) accounting and disclosure standards.

Over the past 20 years, capital markets outside the U.S. have grown rapidly in size and importance. In 1970, non-U.S. stocks accounted for 32% of the world's US$935 billion total market capitalization. By 2011, foreign stocks represented over 65% of the total value of world stock market capitalization of over US$15 trillion.

Until the recent recession, leading U.S. stocks performed well over the years; but international stock markets historically have outperformed Wall Street as a whole. The rapid growth of capital markets around the world has also created abundant opportunities for fixed income investors. Worldwide bond market capitalization now exceeds worldwide equity capitalization. Non-U.S. bonds account for more than half of the world's bond market value. Non-

American investors have realized the enormous profit potential of cross-border investment.

Avoiding Roadblocks to Prosperity

International economic integration continues despite U.S. laws designed to hinder such activity.

One of the main obstacles remains restrictive U.S. securities legislation. Any "investment contract" for a security sold in the United States must be registered with the SEC and similar agencies in each of the states. This is a prohibitively expensive process. The U.S. also requires far more disclosure than most foreign countries and burdens the process with different accounting practices.

International fund managers are practical people who keep an eye on the bottom line. Many correctly calculate that operating costs in the U.S. would wipe out any profit margin they could achieve. Ironically, several mutual funds and hedge funds with top performance records are run from the U.S. by U.S. residents, but do not accept investments from Americans. To avoid SEC red tape and registration costs, investment in these funds is available only to foreigners.

Fortunately, there are ways for U.S. citizens to get around these obstacles. Although you're a U.S. citizen, you may be able to qualify under the law as an "accredited investor." As such, you will have a freer hand to buy non-SEC registered foreign stocks and mutual funds directly. An accredited investor is defined by SEC rules as an individual who has a net worth of US$1 million or more, or an annual income of at least US$250,000. In other words, you must have a lot of money.

You can also buy foreign securities through a trust, family foundation or corporation you have created offshore. Properly structured foreign legal entities—and I do mean properly structured—are not considered "U.S. residents, persons or citizens." These entities, therefore, have the unrestricted right to buy non-SEC registered securities.

Become Your Own Offshore Stock Trader

Traditionally, Americans used domestic brokers to invest in foreign markets, if the brokers offered these services. This required broker contact with a U.S.-based "market maker" or an affiliate firm located in the country where you wanted to buy shares. This was a slow, cumbersome route that didn't always guarantee timely access.

These types of opportunities, and many thousands more like them, are available right now on any number of stock exchanges around the world. And the best way to access them is through a foreign brokerage account or one of the relatively few brokerage firms here in the U.S. that provides direct access to overseas markets.

These firms offer American investors the opportunity to trade shares directly on foreign stock exchanges—in places like Hong Kong, Germany, Japan, Australia, and the United Kingdom. Some firms even offer access to smaller, emerging markets, such as Russia, South Africa and Turkey.

Forget about the big-name Wall Street brokerage firms. Merrill Lynch, Morgan Stanley and the like will not trade in overseas markets for individual investors, unless clients put at least $50,000 to $100,000 in their trading accounts.

Instead, consider the firms below. These are U.S.-based brokerage houses that not only cater to individual investors, they offer trading directly on foreign stock exchanges:

- **EverTrade**, the St. Louis brokerage unit of Jacksonville, Florida-based EverBank (www.evertrade.com)

- **E*TRADE**, the discount online brokerage firm (www.etrade.com)

- **Fidelity**, the online brokerage, mutual funds and retirement-services giant (www.fidelity.com)

- **Interactive Brokers**, an online brokerage firm (www.interactivebrokers.com)

- **Charles Schwab**, the original discount trading firm. (www.schwab.com)

Each of these firms offer varying degrees of access to overseas markets, and each has its pros and cons. For example, with an E*TRADE domestic brokerage account you can invest in international markets with ADRs, ETFs and mutual funds. You can upgrade to an E*TRADE Global Trading Account that allows you to trade foreign stocks directly online in six global markets in five local currencies, or in 77 international markets in 35 countries in U.S. dollars.

For investors, though, the fact that a variety of foreign markets are directly available through a stateside brokerage account dramatically changes the game. It opens up the world for you.

But there is another more direct route. One the easiest ways to buy and sell offshore securities is to establish your own foreign broker account. Start by investigating brokers in a country where you would like to make investments, a broker that you can use as your base for multi-country investments.

Go to the homepage of the foreign stock exchange of your choice. At the exchange find the web link labeled "local brokers/market makers." That will give you a list of licensed firms that trade securities for institutions and individuals in that local market.

Next, search Google for each firm's website. Then use the firm's "Contact Us" link to send an email, asking if they will accept U.S. investors as clients. You don't need to send your financial life. Just say: "I am a U.S. investor and want to invest in shares in (name your country of choice). Can I open an account at (name of firm you're contacting)? If so, please forward the necessary applications."

That will do the trick. You'll either receive "Sorry, no can do," or,

"Welcome to (name your country of choice)!" If you are accepted, you may want to use Google for due diligence to search for any news stories about the firm, either good or bad. You might also go to the country's official brokerage licensing agency to check the firm's status and past history.

The IRS has a web of rules and regulations that aim to wring maximum revenue from Americans who go offshore. These tax laws are extremely complex, so move cautiously and only with expert professional advice. At every step of the way, find out exactly what the U.S. tax and reporting consequences will be before you proceed.

Part 3: Offshore Business Strategies

Strategy 1:
An International Business Corporation (IBC)

One possible vehicle for offshore tax savings is an international business corporation (IBC). An IBC is simply a corporation registered in an offshore tax haven under its national laws. Since the IBC does business offshore but not in the nation where it is registered, it is exempt from most local corporate and other taxes under "territorial" tax systems that end at the border. Usually, there is an initial government incorporation fee and an annual maintenance fee.

An IBC can be used outside of the nation of incorporation for a variety of activities including consulting, investing, trading, finance, holding assets, or real estate ownership. In some cases, an IBC may confer a trade advantage under tax treaties or it may also be used as an integral part of a broader trust structure.

One of the main advantages of an IBC is that it can pay legitimate business expenses and it can be used to plough back profits for future business use. So long as these profits are used for business purposes, this avoids most immediate U.S. income tax liabilities. But even undistributed corporate income may be taxable to the IBC owner.

U.S. Tax Liabilities

U.S. court decisions strictly interpret tax and reporting obligations of a U.S. person actively involved in an offshore corporation. These cases attribute "constructive ownership" to the involved U.S. person as an individual, or they find actual control exists based on a chain of entities linking the U.S. person to the offshore corporation. The courts seek to identify the U.S. person with actual corporate control, as compared to stand-in paper nominees with only nominal control.

Decades ago, U.S. taxpayers, corporate or individual, could defer some taxes by establishing an offshore corporation. Back then, the foreign corporation was viewed under U.S. tax laws as a foreign entity and shareholders had to pay U.S. income taxes only on dividends.

Now the IRS "looks through" the corporate arrangement and taxes U.S. owners annually on the offshore company's earnings as well. If corporate income is primarily "passive" income, such as income from securities or interest, the IRS may impose penalty charges on the corporate shareholders.

There are some exceptions.

First, the "look through" rule only applies to controlled foreign corporations (CFCs) that have passive business activities. Thus, you can defer taxes on income from non-passive activities such as real estate management, international trade, manufacturing, banking, or insurance.

A second set of IRS rules that tax offshore corporate profits apply to what is called "passive foreign investment companies" (PFICs). In order to avoid a PFIC classification and tax penalties, at least 30% of the corporate income must be "active" income from the categories described above, plus management fees charged by the company.

The *Per Se* Rule

For U.S. persons who control shares in an offshore IBC, there are major limitations on U.S. tax benefits that would otherwise be available to a corporation formed within the United States. That is because the offshore corporation is probably listed on what is known as the IRS "per se" list of foreign corporations, which appears in IRS regulations, section 301.7701-2(b)(8)(i). The listed corporations are barred from numerous U.S. tax benefits.

This designation means that U.S. persons cannot file an IRS Form 8832 electing to treat the corporation as a "disregarded entity" or a foreign partnership, either of which is given much more favorable tax treatment.

Under IRS rules, the per se corporation that engages in passive investments is considered a "controlled foreign corporation," which requires the filing of IRS Form 5471 describing its operations. U.S. persons also must file IRS Form 926 reporting transfers of cash or assets to the corporation.

A U.S. person who controls a foreign financial account of any nature that has in it $10,000 or more at any time during a calendar year must report this to the IRS on Form TD F 90-22.1. There are serious fines and penalties for failure to file these IRS returns and criminal charges can also be imposed. As a general rule, U.S. persons can be guilty of the crime of "falsifying a federal income tax return" by failing to report offshore corporate holdings.

Any eventual capital gains earned by an IRS-*per se* listed corporation are not taxed in the U.S. under the more favorable CGT rate of 15%, but rather as ordinary income for the corporate owners, which can be much higher.

There is also the possibility of double taxation if the offshore IBC makes investments in the U.S., in which case there is a 30% U.S. withholding tax on the investment income. Under U.S. tax rules, no annual losses can be taken on corporate investments, which must be deferred by the U.S. owners until the IBC is liquidated.

However, compared to all these IRS restrictions, there may be offsetting considerations, such as complete exemption from foreign taxes, which may be more important in your financial planning.

As you can see, it is extremely important that U.S. persons obtain an authoritative review of the tax implications before forming an offshore international business corporation for any purpose, including holding title to personal or business real estate. A list of qualified U.S. tax attorneys and accountants can be found in the Appendix.

Certain tax havens, such as Panama, Hong Kong, the Isle of Man and the British Virgin Islands make it attractive to incorporate. When selecting a place to incorporate, here's what you need to consider:

- legal and political attitudes of the jurisdiction toward commercial activities

- corporate laws that facilitate incorporation and continuing management

- the level and speed of service obtainable

- the cost, both initially and for annual maintenance

All IBC-friendly jurisdictions have at least two requirements: l) maintaining an agent for the service of process, and; 2) payment of an annual franchise fee or tax.

Two of the best offshore financial centers for IBC incorporation that I recommend are Panama and the Isle of Man, with Hong Kong a close third.

Recommended for Incorporation

Rainelda Mata-Kelly, Esq.
Suite 406-407, Tower B, Torres de las Americas, Punta Pacifica
Panama City, Republic of Panama
Tel.: + (507) 216-9299 Fax: + (507) 216-9298
When calling from the USA or Canada, please dial: Tel (011 507) 216-9299
Website: http://www.mata-kelly.com
Email: rmk@mata-kelly.com
Ms. Mata-Kelly, a member of The Sovereign Society's Council of

Experts, specializes in Panamanian law in areas of commercial, immigration, real estate, contracts and incorporation.

OCRA (Isle of Man) Ltd.
Grosvenor Court, Tower St Ramsey, IM8 1JA
Tel.: 01624 811000
Email: ocra@ocra.com
Website: http://www.ocra.com/offices/isleofman.asp

Trident Corporate Services (Asia) Ltd.
18/F, Two Chinachem Plaza
68 Connaught Road Central Hong Kong
Main: (852) 2805 2000
Direct: (852) 3760 3760
Website: www.tridenttrust.com
Email: hongkong@tridenttrust.com

Strategy 2: Using Tax Treaties for Profit

There is at least one thing worse than paying taxes in your home country and that is paying taxes in two or more countries on the same income. In this case, "look before you leap" is very good advice. Careless offshore financial arrangements can result in redundant taxes that eat up most or all of the profits you might make.

Bilateral (two-country) tax treaties were developed to avoid these problems. Formally known as "double tax treaties," these agreements usually allow the source of income country to tax most of the income earned within its borders, while the taxpayer's home country agrees not to tax that income, usually by giving credit for foreign taxes paid against domestic taxes owed. Those are the basic principles, but the variations within each treaty are endless.

Current U.S. tax treaties were negotiated individually over the last half-century and usually remain in effect for set time periods (20 years or more), so re-negotiation is constantly ongoing. Most U.S. treaties are with industrialized countries or nations with major commercial and banking activities. Some European countries, especially the United Kingdom and the Netherlands, have their own network of tax treaties with an extensive list of nations, including many of their former colonial possessions.

There's little point in discussing the terms of each U.S. tax treaty in detail here, since they change periodically based on renegotiation or official reinterpretation. The information presented here is as current as possible. To be certain you are current, obtain professional advice on the status and impact of any tax treaty before investing offshore. U.S. treaties are available at http://www.irs.gov/publications/p901/index.html/.

Tax treaty strategies are less important to someone who simply wants to use an offshore bank or investment account as personal financial tools. But treaties can be of tremendous value when doing commercial business overseas in one or more nations. Depending on your business and the way a given tax treaty is structured, taxes can be significantly lowered or avoided completely.

Tax Treaty Loophole

In theory, bilateral tax treaties are supposed to remove or reduce the burden of double taxation. That's the theory, but not always the practical result. These agreements are designed to avoid or at least minimize double taxation.

However, they have another, less publicized function—that is to facilitate information exchange between countries that helps enforcement of domestic tax laws in instances where citizens have offshore financial activity. (More about privacy issues in Chapter 3.)

After World War II, with the British Empire crumbling, the United States routinely agreed to extend the terms of the existing U.S.-U.K. tax treaty to newly independent nations in the British Commonwealth. As the interdependent global economy began to grow, especially in the 1970s, these new countries and creative international tax planners found tremendous profits to be made under the terms of older, existing treaties.

Former British colonies became low- or no-tax havens for certain types of exempted income earned by foreign-resident persons, trusts and corporations. Liberal local tax laws combined with the tax treaties created a bonanza in tax-free transactions. Pick the right country, the right treaty, the right business and you could enjoy tax-free profits.

The good news for U.S. taxpayers considering going offshore is that these no-tax or low-tax countries have a significant financial interest in keeping these liberal tax treaty provisions available for foreign customers. In addition, many U.S.-based multinational corporations want these favorable offshore tax provisions continued in order to keep their capital costs in line with those of foreign competitors.

At this writing, one of President Obama's major tax increase proposals would abolish or seriously curtail the offshore tax advantages of U.S. corporations. But facing a tough re-election in 2012, and always in need of campaign contributions, it does not appear that the president or Democrats in the U.S. Congress are pushing this tax hike very hard, especially since a Republican-controlled House of Representatives would reject them.

If you are planning an offshore business, seek guidance from an attorney who knows international tax planning and tax treaties. Choosing the right country in which to incorporate your business could mean a dramatically reduced tax bill and better profits, so it's well worth checking out.

For U.S. corporate tax and reporting advice:

Josh N. Bennett, Esq.
440 North Andrews Avenue,
Fort Lauderdale, FL 33301
Tel.: (954) 779-1661
Fax: (954) 767-9989
Email: josh@joshbennett.com
Website: www.joshbennett.com

Strategy 3: Profitable "Stepping Stones"

Creative offshore tax planning often calls for business operations in more than one country.

That way, you can use the most advantageous combination of available tax treaties. International tax practitioners like to call this the "stepping stone" principle. The IRS derisively calls it "treaty shopping." Stepping stone transactions are most useful when passive interest or royalty income is involved, though some other commercial and service business structures can also be profitable.

The stepping stones work like this: a German investor naturally wants to earn the highest interest rates available. His tax advisor suggests investing through a Dutch company because the Netherlands has an extensive, ready-made tax treaty network with all other developed countries. The German could form his own Dutch corporation, but tax authorities prefer that he use an independent, pre-existing business. In effect, the German will invest money in an existing Dutch company that in turn will invest it elsewhere. The Dutch company will charge fees for its middleman role, receiving payments known as "the spread."

The tax treaty network allows a Dutch company to invest money virtually anywhere it wants. Under treaty terms, the interest it receives is not subject to withholding taxes in the countries where the money is invested. For example, the U.S.-Netherlands treaty provides for no withholding of tax by the U.S. on interest paid from the United States to a Dutch company. The Netherlands company is not required to withhold taxes when that interest, in turn, is paid to the German investor—so, no taxes all around.

The existing U.S. tax treaty network and the multiple "stepping stone" possibilities it offers to foreign investors, means the United States is a tax haven for the rest of the world, but not for its own citizens. Many foreign businesses and investors using U.S. tax treaties as part of careful structuring make money by basing their operations in America and legally paying little or no U.S. taxes.

Not surprisingly, the IRS disapproves of wholesale "treaty shopping" by Americans. In tax treaty renegotiations, the U.S. insists, not always successfully, on "anti-treaty shopping" provisions. The actual terms vary, but basically the IRS wants to re-write old treaties to limit tax benefits to those who are bona fide residents of the other bilateral treaty nation. In our example, that would have ruled out the German investor.

The Netherlands competes with Ireland in offering corporate tax haven facilities and the U.S. tech giants, Google and FaceBook, use the Dutch and Irish tax rules in their drive to minimize taxes through channeling of sales revenues from other countries into Ireland and the Netherlands. About 20,000 mailbox companies are hosted in Amsterdam and prominent musicians such as Bono of U2 and Mick Jagger of the Rolling Stones avail themselves of this system.

The IRS hates such arrangements. They see this as tax evasion using phony affiliates of businesses operating within the U.S. Fortunately for astute taxpayers, if it's done right, this system is completely legal and it works. The one key requirement is strict adherence to proper form and procedures and definitely no cutting corners.

The moral: there are ways to save taxes offshore, but do it right and be sure you know what you can and cannot do. To be safe, check with the experts recommended in these pages.

I repeat, tax treaties are changing constantly and that means the end of some formerly available tax saving strategies. Internal domestic tax laws change, too. What's here today is gone tomorrow. But serious international businesspeople must pay as much attention to tax treaty developments as they do to daily weather forecasts or stock market reports. It can be that essential.

Important Advice about U.S. Reporting

So you've gotten some or all of your assets located offshore. Now what? Do you have to tell the U.S. government that you have opened an offshore account? The answer is a very definite "yes."

1) IRS Form 1040 and U.S. Treasury Form TDF 90-22.1(FBAR)

The law says, "*Each United States person who has a financial interest in, or signature authority over bank, securities, or other financial accounts in a foreign country which exceeds US$10,000 in aggregate value, must report the relationship each calendar year by filing Treasury Department Form 90-22.1 before June 30 of the succeeding year.*"

If you're a U.S. citizen or permanent resident alien and hold US$10,000 or more in one or more foreign financial accounts, you must report the existence of your accounts each year, first on your federal income tax return, IRS Form 1040 (Schedule B). You must also file a separate information return (Form TD F 90-22.1, also known as FBAR), with the U.S. Treasury by June 30th each year.

The penalties for non-compliance are harsh; a fine of $10,000 for each unreported account for each year someone neglects to file the FBAR, although the sanction for a "negligent violation" is only a $500 fine. If one "willfully" fails to comply with this obligation, the fine is up to $500,000, imprisonment for up to five years, or both. Instructions for Treasury TD F 90-22.1 read, in part:

Financial Account. A financial account includes, but is not limited to, a securities, brokerage, savings, demand, checking, deposit, time deposit, or other account maintained with a financial institution (or other person performing the services of a financial institution). A financial account also includes a commodity futures or options account, an insurance policy with a cash value (such as a whole life insurance policy), an annuity policy with a cash value, and shares in a mutual fund or similar pooled fund (i.e., a fund that is available to the general public with a regular net asset value determination and regular redemptions).

Expanded reporting requirements are in effect for 2011 and apply to filing 2011 tax returns. These newly expanded U.S. Treasury rules cover offshore investments that and include:

- a foreign account that is an insurance policy with a cash value or an annuity policy;

- a foreign account with a person that acts as a broker or dealer for futures or options transactions in any commodity on or subject to the rules of a commodity exchange or association; and

- an account with a mutual fund or similar pooled fund which issues shares available to the general public that have a regular net asset value determination and regular redemptions

- holdings of "foreign financial assets" outside the U.S. valued at $50,000 or more

The rules also say U.S. persons must report *"an account with a person that is in the business of accepting deposits as a financial agency."* A financial agency is defined as *"a person acting for a person as a financial institution bailee, depository trustee, or agent, or acting in a similar way related to money, credit, securities, gold, or in a transaction in money, credit, securities, or gold."*

This means that if you entrust a foreign person or entity, not just a bank, with your money, securities, or gold, the U.S. Treasury wants to know about it. For instance, if you buy gold overseas and pay a custodian a fee for safekeeping it, that custodian could be acting as a financial agency. On the other hand, if you keep the gold in a safety deposit box at a private vault facility to which only you have access, the storage vault is not acting as a financial agency. This type of vault use is not reportable, but if the safe deposit box is provided by your offshore bank and is part of your bank's services, it is reportable.

With the official publication of expanded reporting rules in March 2011, hundreds of thousands of U.S. citizens and permanent residents previously not required to file FBARs now must file. For copies of the FBAR form, see http://www.irs.gov/pub/irs-pdf/f90221.pdf.

2) The Foreign Account Tax Compliance Act (FATCA) requires that along with annually filing IRS Form 1040, those with offshore accounts and other foreign property of a certain total values must file IRS Form 8938, "Statement of Specified Foreign Financial As-

sets." This form is in addition to the FBAR and does not replace it. Under this form, reportable assets include bank, brokerage or other financial accounts.

For advice concerning offshore reports contact:

Josh N. Bennett, Esq.
440 North Andrews Avenue
Fort Lauderdale, FL 33301
Tel.: (954) 779-1661
Fax: (954) 767-9989
Email: josh@joshbennett.com
Website: www.joshbennett.com

Foreign Citizens Included

The FBAR definition of "U.S. person" includes a citizen or resident of the U.S., or any person located "in and doing business in the U.S." This definition extends FBAR coverage to foreign citizens who are physically present and doing business in the United States.

Previously the definition of a "U.S. person" included only citizens and residents of the U.S., domestic partnerships, domestic corporations and domestic estates or trusts. Previously a foreign person physically present in the U.S. for less than 180 days each year, or not a U.S. resident by treaty definition, was exempt from FBAR requirements.

Trust Reporting

Accounts controlled by a trustee of an offshore trust must be reported by a trust beneficiary with a greater than 50% beneficial interest in the trust, but also by any person who "established" the trust and any "trust protector" that is appointed. A "trust protector" is defined as a person responsible for monitoring the activities of the trustee who has the authority to influence trustee decisions or to replace or recommend the replacement of the trustee.

The definition of trust "financial accounts" is also expanded to include, among others, trust owned foreign mutual funds, foreign hedge funds, foreign annuities, debit card accounts and prepaid credit card accounts.

The Qualified Intermediary (QI) Rule

The U.S. Internal Revenue Service has forced foreign banks and financial institutions into the unwelcome role of IRS informants, a.k.a. "qualified intermediaries" (QI). In effect, an agency of the U.S. government (the IRS) imposed extraterritorial tax enforcement burdens on foreign banks in this instance. The banks were forced to meet IRS established anti-money laundering and "know your customer" standards in order to get the "QI" stamp of approval.

Since 2001, U.S. persons holding U.S.-based investments purchased through offshore banks had a choice of either having the bank report the holdings to the IRS, or having the bank withhold a 30% tax on all interest and dividends paid. To avoid either, the U.S. investor could avoid buying U.S.-based investments through an offshore bank or financial institution.

In 2009, the U.S. Internal Revenue Service began to clamp down even further with greater long-distance oversight of foreign banks that provide accounts or sell offshore services to American clients. The professed IRS goal is thwarting what it claims to be rampant offshore tax evasion.

IRS Announcement #2008-98 proposed to toughen up existing IRS qualified intermediary rules that previously allowed participating foreign banks to maintain accounts on behalf of American clients without disclosing their names to the IRS. Until then, the IRS had allowed the banks to promise to identify clients, withhold any taxes due on U.S. securities in their accounts, typically 30%, and send the tax money owed to the IRS.

Under current and much tougher QI rules, foreign banks must actively investigate, determine and report to the IRS whether U.S. investors or legal entities the U.S. person controls are the holders of foreign accounts. (As I noted before, U.S. persons already are required by law to report offshore accounts on the annual IRS Form 1040.)

Under these rules the QI bank has a duty to investigate, determine and report to the IRS all accounts of U.S. persons or the legal entities they control to the same extent as that required of domestic U.S. bankers. They must also alert the IRS to any potential fraud detected, whether through their own internal controls, complaints from employees or investigations by foreign regulators.

In 2001, when the QI agreements were first imposed, offshore banks went along with the scheme because wanted continued access to U.S. financial markets and the U.S. banking system. Close to 100% of the offshore banks signed up. Many American clients at the time chose to have U.S. taxes withheld by their offshore bank. Others instructed their bank to not invest in any U.S. securities and some chose self-declaration to the IRS. No doubt, as in the 2008 UBS tax evasion scandal, some Americans defied U.S. reporting laws and simply did not report.

Americans Need Not Apply

In 2008, numerous offshore banks, wary of increasing IRS pressures, began refusing to accept any new American clients. The tougher QI rules only increased this unfortunate anti-American trend. (The Sovereign Society works with many American-friendly offshore banks that welcome U.S. clients.)

More than 7,000 foreign banks participate in the QI program with the supposed aim of helping the IRS keep track of American offshore investors. According to the IRS, foreign banks in the QI program hold more than $35 billion abroad in accounts for U.S. individual investors, partnerships, trusts, family foundations and corporations, but those banks withheld taxes of only 5% on that amount in 2003. The IRS argues entities receiving the offshore income claimed exemptions under foreign double taxation treaties with the United States, but if U.S. investors controlled those entities, some were not entitled to the tax exemptions.

The clear threat to offshore banks contained in the QI rules is the possibility that an uncooperative foreign bank could be denied access to the entire American banking system, meaning they and their clients could not do business within the major banking system of the world.

These tightened QI rules no doubt were in part the result of the tax evasion scandal at the world's largest private bank, the Swiss UBS that assisted an alleged 4,500 American account holders to evade U.S. taxes.

The IRS claims that since 2001 it has halted the participation in the QI program by about 100 foreign banks that were accused of violating QI rules. But in my observation, far fewer banks were embargoed and those tended to be banks located in backwater places such as Vanuatu and the Solomon Islands where Russian criminal elements had established a financial presence.

As I mentioned earlier, in 2009, a major change in the privacy policies of offshore banks occurred under the threat of "blacklisting" from major nations. Almost all tax havens accepted the addition of "tax evasion" as a valid basis for foreign tax agency inquiries concerning their citizens with accounts in an offshore financial center.

Tax Information Exchange

The current standard for tax information exchange is embodied in the Organization for Economic Cooperation and Development (OECD) Article 26 of the OECD Model Tax Convention.

Under this Article, countries that implement tax information exchange "consistent with OECD standards" agree to provide information upon request, but only if a specific person and bank are named, although Switzerland has interpreted this to mean identification by a bank account number. There must also be a prima face showing of tax evasion or tax fraud on the part of the subject of the request. Obviously, how much financial privacy is compromised will depend on the enforcement policies of each country.

These limits have not satisfied the more rabid advocates of full disclosure who are now loudly demanding mandatory "automatic" exchange of information between national tax agencies. They also demand that the beneficial owners of all legal entities be made a matter of accessible public record, a policy strongly resisted by all offshore financial centers.

Non-Reportable Foreign Investments

Here are three offshore investments that still are not reportable to the U.S. government.

1. Securities or precious metals purchased directly from an offshore bank, securities issuer, dealer, or individual. These are not reportable if purchased without your opening an account, so long as the total value of the foreign financial instruments or investment contracts doesn't exceed $50,000. If they are worth more, they are reportable on TDF 90-22.1. Gold and other precious metals if held as part of an "account" (as in a bank) are reportable.

2. Safekeeping arrangements. Valuables purchased outside the U.S. and placed directly into a non-U.S. safety deposit box or private vault to which only you have access are not reportable unless the value exceeds $50,000.

Many offshore banks offer safe deposit boxes for private custody of cash, securities, diamonds, gemstones, gold bullion and other precious metals. However this usually is as an associated service that is linked to a bank account. If that is the case, then it is reportable to the U.S. Treasury on the TDF 90-22.1, FBAR report discussed above.

Banks are not the only places that offer safe deposit boxes. Non-bank safekeeping is available through private vaults. Since private vaults are not financial institutions, they are subject to fewer recordkeeping and disclosure requirements. For added security and confidentiality, a box can be rented in the name of an offshore corporation. Because a vault safe deposit box is not associated with a bank account, it does not constitute a financial account and it is not FBAR reportable.

Here are two recommended foreign private storage vaults:

DAS SAFE, Auerspergstrasse 1, A-1080 Vienna, Austria. Tel.: +43-1-406 61 74, Email: info@dassafe.com Website: http://www.dassafe.com/ Established 1984.

Under the Austrian Banking Act, Das Safe, established in 1984, is supervised by the Financial Market Authority (FMA) and the Oesterreichische National Bank (OeNB).

Fees at Das Safe start at €330 ($462) a year for the smallest non-anonymous box. The annual fee for the smallest anonymous box is €420 ($588). There is a 20% tax on fees, and insurance is available. Much larger boxes and mini-vaults are also available. The rent includes $90,000 insurance coverage and additional coverage is available at €36 ($50) for each additional €70,000 ($98,000) of value insured.

As with banks, contents of a safe-deposit box or private vault are usually not insured against theft or loss. You can buy insurance, but you must disclose the assets and their location to the insurer. Both of the above vaults offer insurance. For this reason, you may wish to purchase insurance through Das Safe itself, rather than your domestic insurance carrier.

For the greatest privacy and the ability to move your valuables the furthest away from the grasp of those who covet them, a vault safe deposit box with Das Safe in Austria offers the maximum protection.

Mat Securitas Express AG
Steinackerstrasse 49 | CH-8302 Kloten, Switzerland
Tel.: +41 43 488 9000
Email: mse@viamat.com
Website: http://www.viamat.com/mse/en/index.php

Via Mat International is part of Mat Securitas Express, of Switzerland, one of Europe's largest and oldest armored transport and storage companies. For 60 years, Via Mat has specialized in international valuables logistics and storage, transport and insurance. Its Zurich Airport facility is in a tax-free zone and offers domicile-to-domicile deliveries to all important financial centers, storage for valuable goods in a customs-free warehouse, customs clearance of shipments and monitoring of transits.

Via Mat charges about $1,400 to transport $100,000 worth of gold coins from the west coast of the United States to the company's storage facility in Zurich. Extra charges apply for pickup and delivery to a non-Via Mat facility. They will also handle your customs declaration with customs authorities in both the United States and your destination country.

3. Real estate. Direct ownership in your own name of real property in a foreign country is not reportable. Income from real estate holdings, wherever located, is not reportable on Form TD F 90-22.1, but it is reportable as taxable income on IRS Form 1040.

However, real estate holdings are generally a matter of public record in the jurisdiction in which they are located and real estate cannot be liquidated easily. If you own the real estate through a holding company or trust, that entity may be required to file its own disclosure forms.

If you wish to purchase and hold real estate in a foreign country without disclosing your ownership, this can be accomplished by placing title in an international business corporation (IBC) located in a nation, such as Panama, where beneficial ownership does not have to be disclosed except to your attorney or by court order. Also an IBC that holds title does not have to be registered in the same nation where the real estate is located.

Avoiding Personal Double Taxation

Governments everywhere love taxes. The government in the nation in which an offshore bank account is located has the power to impose its own withholding taxes on any foreign owned assets and deposits and many countries do just that. For example, Switzerland levies a 35% tax on interest income.

In many nations, the law requires that taxes be withheld by the financial institution where the account is located. That's why it's important to check the potential tax liabilities beforehand, and then make certain to locate your account in a "no-tax" jurisdiction.

If you have a bank account in a country that has a "double taxation treaty" with your home country, you may qualify for a credit against your national income tax obligation in the amount of the foreign tax paid.

Average credits allowed vary from country to country according to the terms of the treaty in force at the time. In most cases, your home country tax authorities are unlikely to allow a credit of more than a fraction of the foreign tax withheld.

If you are concerned about tax treaty terms obtain a copy of the U.S. tax treaty with the nation you are considering for placement of your financial business. As I said earlier, treaties are published by the U.S. State Department in the Treaties in Force series, available in major libraries worldwide. U.S. treaties also are available online at: http://www.state.gov/s/l/treaty/tif/index.htm.

End Notes

In previous editions of this book, I listed contact information for offshore banks and financial institutions that I judged to be useful.

Because of the constantly changing policies of offshore banks and the refusal of some to accept U.S. clients, please contact The Sovereign Society at the address given on the first page of this book for information on currently recommended offshore banks.

Sovereign Society members have special access to offshore banking arrangements at banks we recommend in many nations, including Switzerland, Liechtenstein, Panama, Singapore, Hong Kong, Uruguay and other offshore financial centers.

One more word of caution: in several places in this chapter when describing the meaning and requirements of IRS reporting rules, I have used the phrase "appear to be." That's because IRS requirements change almost daily as the agency issues new rules and new interpretations and as courts rule on tax issues. You should always check with a qualified U.S. tax professional, an attorney or accountant, if you have any questions about IRS rules.

Throughout this book I also use the phrase "at this writing," which means that the statements I make were accurate at the time they were written. With the status of so many issues changing almost daily, you can keep up to date on all offshore matters with information from The Sovereign Investor and by subscribing to our several currency and investment newsletters.

CHAPTER THREE

What You Need to Know About Offshore Havens and Financial Centers

Here I explain tax havens and asset havens; their laws, procedures, how to use them and what methods give you maximum benefits. In addition, I predict the future of offshore havens and explain why attacks by Big Brother governments and their tax collectors have altered the character of tax havens considerably in recent years—for the better.

A *tax haven* can be defined as a country or other "jurisdiction" (some are colonial territories of other nations) that promotes and guarantees no taxes or low taxes for foreigners who choose to live or do business there.

To update the record, for reasons I will explain, those places that used to be proud to be known as "tax havens" now very definitely prefer to be called *"offshore financial centers"* or "OFCs" for short.

An asset haven describes a country or jurisdiction that has adopted special laws and established a judicial system that guarantees strong legal protection for wealth and assets placed there, plus a high degree of financial privacy.

The same jurisdiction can be both a tax and asset haven and usually they combine both functions. However, any given haven may qualify in just one or the other of these two categories.

In this chapter, I explain the differences and similarities of these havens, how to use them and where they are located. Specific, detailed treatment of our choices of the best haven nations can be found in Chapter 4.

Understanding Offshore Financial Centers

It may be surprising to the over-taxed citizens of the world to learn that some nations have the ability to finance the operation of their governments while imposing only low taxes, almost no taxes, or by offering special tax concessions to foreigners who bring in jobs, business and investments.

Seven American states have no state income tax: Alaska, Florida, Nevada, South Dakota, Texas, Washington and Wyoming. Two others, New Hampshire and Tennessee, tax only dividend and interest income. Just as these states offer their citizens a chance to escape from other states' income taxes, foreign tax havens may be the solution for offshore-minded people seeking national tax relief.

And you don't have to move your residence to these offshore havens in order to enjoy their promised benefits — only your cash and/or other assets.

But in spite of what you may have heard, know that for U.S. persons, tax haven nations offer only very minimal tax savings. And always keep this basic tax fact in mind: the U.S. government taxes all worldwide income wherever it is earned by Americans and wherever the U.S. person may live or have residence(s). This means U.S. citizens and resident aliens (both groups, remember, are known in tax law as "*U.S. persons*") must, by law, report all of their income to the IRS and pay U.S. taxes accordingly.

Unlike individual U.S. taxpayers, many American-owned businesses profit by establishing themselves as foreign corporations in tax havens, since a foreign company owned by Americans pays only limited U.S. taxes on certain types of investment income. If these corporate profits are kept offshore, reinvested or ploughed back into the business, some other U.S. taxes often can be deferred indefinitely. At this writing in late 2012, President Barack Obama has proposed to abolish these offshore tax breaks for American business but he is not pushing this very hard since he wants business campaign contributions for his re-election effort.

The U.S. Internal Revenue Code that applies to offshore business with U.S. ownership is highly complex (more about that in Chapter 11). The very best professional tax advice is needed to ensure you are in compliance with the law if you have ownership, partial or full, in an offshore business — and to make sure you are eligible for every tax break for which you may qualify.

Tax obligations differ in various nations according to their domestic laws, so before you go offshore, check the tax status of your intended country with advice from a competent professional you trust, one located in the intended country or a U.S. expert on foreign taxation.

Understanding Asset Havens

What characteristics qualify a given place as an "asset haven?"

Asset havens are countries or other jurisdictions with established laws that:

- offer legal entities that provide asset protection, such as trusts, family foundations, limited liability companies (LLCs) and international business corporations (IBCs);

- protect financial and personal privacy; and

- provide and support a judicial system that consistently favors asset protection.

Most asset havens also are tax havens — meaning they do not impose income, capital gains, estate, transfer or other taxes on foreigners who choose to open bank accounts or form LLCs, IBCs or trusts registered in the country.

However, not all asset havens are tax-free for foreigners or their business operations, an important factor you should consider and be certain of in each and every case.

Different Havens, Different Uses

Remember, an established tax haven jurisdiction does not necessarily qualify as an asset haven.

Most nations with favorable low tax laws do offer strong asset protection as an added incentive to attract foreign money and investments, but some do not. In these pages, I'll tell you which countries or jurisdictions offer the best deals and how you can use them to your benefit.

Not all tax havens are nations. Many are colonies or territorial possessions of other nations (e.g., Bermuda is a partial self-governing overseas territory of the United Kingdom). The Cayman Islands and the British Virgin Islands hold the same status. The Isle of Man and the Channel Islands are Crown Dependencies of the United Kingdom with a greater degree of independence.

Historically, many tax havens have spurred economic development by fashioning themselves into both tax and asset havens. Some of these countries have never imposed an income tax. Others are countries with special tax legislation or incentives favoring certain types of business over other types.

As I explain in detail in Chapter 11, the United States is one of the world's leading tax havens, giving special tax treatment to foreigners (but not to Americans), who invest in U.S. real estate and securities and commodities markets.

The United Kingdom also gives some tax breaks to foreigners, although former residential tax breaks were limited by the Labor Party government that had piled up huge budget deficits. In fact, the U.S. and U.K. are both leading world tax havens, if one bases that calculation on the total foreign-owned, tax-exempt cash and assets located and managed therein.

Tax Havens Come in Different "Flavors"

A tax haven is any country whose laws, regulations, policies and treaty arrangements make it possible for a foreign national who does business there to reduce or escape entirely personal and/or corporate tax burdens.

This is done by bringing yourself—or your trust, foundation, LLC or corporation—within the country's jurisdiction by registration there. This general definition covers all four major types of tax haven nations discussed below, each categorized by the degree and type of taxes imposed.

It's important to understand these tax haven differences. Not all foreign tax haven countries are created equal. You should fully understand the tax characteristics of each type before you make any decisions.

No-Tax Havens

In "no-tax" havens, sometimes called "true tax havens," foreign citizens who do business there pay no taxes—no income, capital gains, transfer or wealth taxes.

A foreign citizen can quickly and easily incorporate and/or form a trust or LLC and register to do business immediately. You can expect a few minor administrative taxes, like stamp duties on incorporation documents, charges on the value of corporate shares issued, annual maintenance registration fees, or other fees not levied directly as a tax on income. In addition, there will be the non-governmental costs of engaging a local agent and the filing of annual reports.

The government in a no-tax haven nation earns considerable revenue from the sheer volume of foreign corporations and trusts that are registered within its borders, even if these entities conduct most or all of their business elsewhere.

No-tax havens—all of which are located in the Atlantic Ocean or in or near the Caribbean basin—include Bermuda, The Bahamas, the Cayman Islands, St. Kitts & Nevis, the Turks & Caicos Islands, Belize and St. Vincent and the Grenadines.

Foreign-Source Income Havens

The second group includes "foreign-source income" tax havens.

These countries have a "territorial tax" system. They tax only income earned within the country's boundaries. Income earned from foreign sources is tax exempt, since it involves no in-country domestic business activities, apart from simple housekeeping chores. Often there is no income tax on profits from exports of local manufactured goods, although there may be a tax on domestic manufacturing itself.

These countries allow you or your corporation to conduct business both internally and externally, taxing only the income from in-country sources. These nations include Costa Rica, Ecuador, Guatemala, Honduras, Israel, The Philippines, Thailand and Sri Lanka. Since none of these nations qualify as full-fledged tax or asset havens, I won't discuss them further, but I encourage you to research them further if you find them of interest.

Others in this group are full-fledged tax havens. Some only tax domestic business activity and foreign business is tax-exempt. Others impose zero business taxes. These jurisdictions include Panama, Uruguay, the Channel Islands of Jersey and Guernsey, the Isle of Man and the United Arab Emirates.

Tax Treaty Nations

The third type of haven is called a "tax treaty nation."

While these nations impose taxes on worldwide corporate and trust income, their governments have reciprocal double taxation avoidance agreements with other nations—especially with major trading partners such as the U.S., France, Canada, Germany, and the U.K. These mutual agreements significantly reduce the withholding tax imposed on foreign income earned by domestic corporations and give credit against domestic tax liability for taxes paid by a local business to a foreign government.

Although these nations are less attractive for asset protection, they are suitable for lower taxed international corporate activity. Their main drawback is that international tax treaties permit the free exchange of information between national taxing authorities, allowing less privacy.

Among the leading tax treaty nations are Switzerland, Cyprus, The Netherlands, Belgium and Denmark. To review information on the use of tax treaties, see Chapter 2.

Special Use Tax Havens

The final category of havens features several countries that impose the kind of taxes Americans and citizens of the United Kingdom know and dislike — high taxes. However, these high taxes are tempered by a government policy of granting special tax holidays, concessions, or rebates to favored foreign business enterprises they want to attract and promote, usually as a means to increase local employment.

These concessions typically include:

- corporate tax credits for local job creation;

- tax exemptions for manufacturing and processing of exports; and

- tax benefits for international business or holding companies, offshore banks, or other selected industries.

In the U.S., critics call this kind of domestic business tax break "corporate welfare," but many nations (including the United States) offer these kinds of business inducements to foreigners. Among nations that offer generous special tax concessions to foreign-owned businesses are Chile, Portugal and Barbados.

For example, Barbados grants tax exemptions to retired foreigners who settle there. Living conditions are pleasant, with high literacy rates and educational levels. Special laws favor headquarters of international companies and major banks with income tax exemptions. The government also offers generous tax breaks and subsidies for foreign-owned local companies that increase employment. Cyprus offers similar benefits to retirees.

Fortunately for Chile, when the worldwide recession began to unfold in 2008, the South American country was in good shape to work for its own recovery. Part of the strength of the economy included bank and finance policies that meant the Chilean government did not have to spend a single peso on bank bailouts. Having paid down foreign debt during the fat years when copper prices were high, in 2009, Chile was one of the world's few creditor nations, with a debt rating that was upgraded by Moody's Investors Service.

Contacts

Chile — Pro Chile New York, 866 United Nations Plaza, Suite 603, New York, New York 10017; Tel.: 212-207-3266; Fax: 212-207-3649; Website: www.ProChile.cl, Contact web page: http://www.prochile.cl/importadores/en/apoyo-para-importadores/

National Chamber of Commerce of Chile, Santa Lucia 302, Piso 4, Santiago, Chile; Tel.: +562-639-6639 / -7694; Fax: +562-638-0234. Website: http://www.caccgp.com/

Portugal — Official government website: http://www.portugal.gov.pt/pt/GC19/Pages/Inicio.aspx or see http://www.portugal-info.net

Portuguese Foreign Trade Institute (ICEP), Avenida 5 de Outubro 101, 1016 Lisboa Codex, Portugal; Tel.: +351-1-793-0103; Fax: +351-1-793-5028.

Barbados — Barbados Government Information Service, Bay Street, St. Michael, Barbados, West Indies; Tel.: +246-426 2232; Fax: +246-436 1317; Website: http://gisbarbados.gov.bb/

Tax-Free Zones

Closely akin to "special use" tax havens are "tax-free zones" established in designated areas of some countries. Often these zones are used as trans-shipment points for finished goods, such as the Colón Duty Free Trade Zone in Panama (http://www.colonfreezone.com/) or the Hong Kong free zone. (For more about Panama and Hong Kong, see Chapters 8 and 9.)

Other tax-free zones, however, are major bases for industry, business and finance, complete with well-developed infrastructure and favorable laws to attract business to the zone. A good example is the Jebel Ali Free Trade Zone in the United Arab Emirates. The zone's website is at http://www.jafza.ae/en/.

Offshore Havens under Attack

To understand the position in which offshore financial centers (formerly known as tax havens) find themselves today, a review of the last decade of offshore financial and political events is in need. This historic background will help to explain the present state of affairs and how these past events may affect your rights and offshore financial activities.

Beginning in the early 1990s, there was coordinated criticism of tax havens from the governments of major high tax and big deficit nations and especially from their eager tax collectors, led by the U.S. Internal Revenue Service.

For years, the leading welfare states have run major budget deficits and have a constant need for ever-increasing revenues to finance their spendthrift ways. The 2008 global recession was the excuse for leftist politicians in many nations to hand out trillion-dollar bailouts/stimulus plans. This created an even greater need for tax revenues to finance the socialist plans and the resulting deficits.

This sort of fiscal insanity led to the European Union financial crisis involving budget deficit countries such as Greece, Ireland, Italy, Portugal and Spain needing bailouts of billions of euros to avoid debt defaults.

The big-spending political left especially hates legal tax competition from low-tax nations, which they insist is "harmful" to other high tax countries. Indeed, it is harmful—to their big spending and high tax plans.

They know that low-tax offshore financial centers attract smart investors. These high tax bureaucrats want to curb, if not abolish, tax havens. As part of their anti-tax haven crusade, they demand an end to financial privacy offshore, especially in nations that historically have had strict bank secrecy laws, such as Switzerland, Austria and Panama.

Governments of the major high tax, high deficit nations, especially the United States, Germany and France, along with a coterie of allied leftist groups, for the last two decades have aimed their political and economic guns directly at legitimate offshore tax, business and banking havens. Unfortunately these tax hungry bureaucrats have won many victories and as a result national sovereignty and independence have suffered along with the world economy.

The main antagonists and actors working against offshore financial centers (OFCs) have included the Democratic Party in the U.S., certainly including President Barack Obama, the United Kingdom's Labor Party in power from 1995 to 2010, the European Union, the Organization for Community and Economic Development (OECD) and its Financial Action Task Force (FATF), as well as the United Nations.

Each of these big spending, high taxing groups, for their own, and for common reasons, has joined in a coordinated attempt to crush OFCs which they insist are nothing more than centers for tax evasion.

OFCs were pressured to sign tax information exchange agreements (TIEAs) or face possible financial "sanctions" from major countries. For some unknown reason, the OECD, the research and propaganda arm of the high tax countries, initially set the signing of 12 tax information exchange treaties as a measure of whether or not an individual jurisdiction should be blacklisted as failing to adhere to "international standards." This set off a ridiculous scramble among tax havens rushing to sign their allotted 12 TIEAs in order to stay off the feared blacklist.

The next stage of political pressure for international information sharing on tax matters is already underway with demands for "automatic" tax information exchange between jurisdictions, which privacy advocates and OFCs strongly oppose.

Implementation of such expanded procedures may be challenging for some smaller offshore centers. At this writing, most offshore centers only disclose information on individual accounts when there is a specific request from another country with which the OFC has signed a tax information exchange agreement (TIEA). It remains to be seen how successful these radical forces arrayed against offshore havens may be. Politics and legislative changes eventually may lead to some additional restrictions on the use of tax and asset havens by citizens of certain nations, including the United States.

In my opinion, in the long run, tax havens and offshore financial centers will continue to play an important part in world finance and the financial activities of many astute people worldwide. They will survive because they efficiently serve important needs in the global financial system.

United Kingdom's Colonies

The U.K. Labor government officially announced an anti-tax haven campaign beginning as far back as 1999. This was significant because the British colonies (called by London "overseas territories") and the Crown dependencies of the United Kingdom include jurisdictions that were, and still are, some of the world's leading tax and asset protection havens.

London forced law reforms on the 13 U.K. overseas territories, which included many well-known tax havens, such as the Channel Islands (Jersey, Guernsey), the Isle of Man, the Cayman Islands, Bermuda, the Turks & Caicos Islands, the British Virgin Islands and Anguilla. The U.K. Labor government warned that each had to meet new "international standards" against money laundering and adopt "transparency" in their financial systems, including cooperation with U.K. and foreign law enforcement and tax authorities.

The Labor government claimed the power to act unilaterally to change laws within the colonies and threatened it would do so if necessary. London would use the arcane royal "Orders in Council" signed by the Queen, which in effect imposes the government's policies and rules on any overseas territory.

What British Labor really wanted was greatly reduced financial privacy, total bank and investment account surveillance and a general end to the financial freedom that allowed selected U.K. dependencies to prosper as tax and asset protection havens. And that is precisely what they got.

The U.K. Foreign Office bluntly pressured the Crown dependencies of Jersey, Guernsey and the Isle of Man into writing foreign tax evasion into their local laws as a criminal offense. Similarly, the U.K. government pushed Bermuda and the Cayman Islands into enacting "all crimes" money laundering laws that included criminalizing alleged foreign tax evasion. As London had ordered, these jurisdictions weakened their strict financial privacy laws under threat of being cut off from the U.K. financial and banking systems and from losing U.K. subsidies.

While London under the Labor party was demanding more openness and stricter regulation on the U.K. tax havens, the real reform work was done by the individual overseas territories and the three Crown dependencies — and these efforts were so successful that they created far better financial regulatory regimes than those in London or the United States — the two financial disaster centers where the colossal global financial mess that erupted in 2008 were allowed to fester.

Since the Conservative/Liberal Democratic Party coalition came to power in 2010, the new British government has been far more sympathetic to OFCs, including those under London's colonial dominion. This is a more sensible policy since the British offshore tax havens conduct a huge volume of financial business with firms in the City of London.

The United States

For many years, the U.S. Internal Revenue Service has officially viewed offshore financial activity by Americans as probable tax evasion.

This has been the IRS stance even though for Americans in offshore business and finance is fully legal under U.S. laws, so long as it is reported properly and taxes due are paid. The IRS claims that there are millions of alleged U.S. tax evaders whom it presumes guilty. The IRS also denounced the financial privacy traditionally provided by various legal tools, such as trusts and family foundations.

High on the IRS' annual "Dirty Dozen" target list are a certain segment of those who create and use offshore corporations, family foundations, trusts and bank accounts located in known tax havens — especially those havens where financial privacy laws are strict. If it's offshore, the IRS presumes guilt.

In October 2001, U.S. politicians took advantage of the widespread fear after the September 11, 2001 ("9/11") terrorist attacks to get their previously rejected anti-offshore proposals enacted into law. Their catch-all "anti-terrorist" legislation sailed through Congress with little debate just six weeks after the New York and Washington attacks. This law, known as the USA PATRIOT Act, all but ends Americans' personal and financial privacy.

Congress passed the PATRIOT Act without even knowing what was in it. Less than six weeks after 9/11, the Republican-controlled Congress rammed through a 362-page law, sight unseen, with few members having the courage to oppose one of the worst attacks on American liberties ever enacted into law. In spite of massive opposition to the law, it was extended and broadened in scope in 2006 and 2011, at the urging of both Presidents Bush and Obama with majority support from both political parties in the Congress.

The PATRIOT Act gives U.S. government financial police the power to confiscate funds and obtain financial information in secret. It even asserts U.S. police jurisdiction beyond the nation's borders by pressuring foreign banks that do business in America under threat of losing that access. (Refresh your memory about this by reviewing Chapter 2.) A few of these drastic police powers have been tempered slightly in the courts and some others remain under legal challenge.

Since its enactment, numerous abuses of this law have come to light, including extensive unauthorized wiretap surveillance and massive illegal issuance of tens of thousands of improperly authorized "security letters" by the FBI seeking personal and financial information without the approval of a judge or issuance of a search warrant. Although as a candidate in 2008, President Obama attacked the PATRIOT Act and its abuses, after he took office, he opposed weakening or reforming the law and adopted his own policies that go far beyond President George W. Bush's questionable surveillance policies.

United Nations

The United Nations for years has been trying to impose an expansive redefinition of "tax avoidance" on the world at large, fortunately without much success. A UN report argued that the common theme in financial crimes is the "enabling machinery" that exists in haven nations. The UN sees these OFCs as "an enormous hole in the international legal and financial system" that must be plugged tightly.

UN reports blatantly demand an end to what they call the "proliferation" of offshore trusts and international business corporations, curbs on attorney-client privilege, the use of free trade zones and the operation of gambling casinos. For good measure, the UN demanded an enforceable international financial reporting system in which all nations would be forced to participate. The UN has even laid plans for a global tax system, which it wants to operate, with each nation to be forced to pay taxes to the UN.

These UN demands, which have little chance of success, have served as a Greek chorus in the background as other groups described here have led the anti-haven battle.

OECD Blacklists Havens

The Organization for Economic Cooperation and Development (OECD) is a Paris-based research and propaganda group financed by major nations, including the U.S., Canada, the U.K., France and Germany, sometimes called the "G-20."

It is what is known as a "non-governmental organization" (NGO) and has no official standing in law. But it is an influential research and propaganda operation for the G-20's tax and economic policies. That influence has been built up over years by a large volume of OECD reports, conferences and press statements, almost all of which are presented from a leftist political and economic viewpoint. As their tax hungry G-20 sponsors have ordered, much of the OECD output has been aimed at the eventual abolition of offshore financial centers.

The OECD propaganda campaign began with the publication of a 1998 report entitled, *Harmful Tax Competition: An Emerging Global Issue*. In it, the OECD, for the first of many times, condemned the tax practices of more than 30 tax haven jurisdictions. The report was a skillful global public relations ploy on behalf of the G-20 high-tax welfare nations trying to stifle the drain of cash fleeing to tax havens.

The OECD always defines "harmful tax competition" as any nation that chooses to levy low or no taxes. The goal is to end the tax competition that draws billions in cash to OFCs from smart people, especially those citizens suffering in the high-tax G-20 nations.

A corollary of the OECD "harmful tax competition" theme has been the accusation that billions of dollars in needed revenue are lost to governments because of massive tax evasion by foreigners hiding their cash and assets behind tax haven bank secrecy laws.

The 1998 report suggested ways to combat this so-called "harmful tax competition" including levying a tax on all funds transferred into tax havens and sanctions that would block havens from the global electronic banking system. It demanded that tax collectors in OECD member nations be given access to financial records in haven jurisdictions, thus negating national statutory guarantees of bank secrecy in countries such as Switzerland and Panama.

In 2000, the OECD released its first "blacklist," one of several condemning alleged "harmful tax practices" in 35 nations. But with the 2000 election of President George W. Bush, the OECD lost the key backing of the United States. During the Clinton years, then U.S. Treasury Secretary Lawrence Summers (later in the White House as chief economic advisor to President Obama), was one of the strongest advocates of crushing tax havens and imposing high taxes worldwide.

The OECD asked tax havens for signed commitments pledging to weaken their tax and privacy laws, and as an inducement, explicitly stated the commitments were binding only if all 20 OECD nations agreed to abide by the same tax rules. This was advertised as the "level playing field" guarantee—all nations would agree to do so or none would be bound to end tax competition.

This "level playing field" promise soon caused a major problem for the OECD since some of its leading member nations, including the U.S., U.K., Luxembourg, Belgium and Austria, were tax havens then (and remain so to this day).

From the beginning, all of these OECD anti-tax haven campaigns were a publicity front to benefit tax collectors from the G-20 high-tax nations. With smoke and mirrors, it threw around, but never proved, numbers—hundreds of millions of tax evaders, billions of lost taxes.

The historic fact that reduced taxes are the best incentive to keep people at home and to expand the economy was ignored. It never occurred to the OECD that tax havens would be unnecessary if governments would cut spending and lower taxes.

American free market leaders, including The Sovereign Society, consistently mobilized in opposition to the OECD's proposed global network of tax police. The goal of that coalition was to convince the Bush Administration that tax competition should be encouraged, not condemned. When the U.S. government decided not to support the OECD, it was obvious that the initiative would collapse—and it did.

All that changed in 2008 when majority political control of the executive branch in Washington shifted to an avowed opponent of international tax competition, Barack Obama. As a junior senator from Illinois, Obama was a co-sponsor of the Levin-Obama Anti-Tax Haven Act, first introduced in 2005. The latest version of this bill is pending in Congress at this writing with the endorsement of President Obama, but thankfully the Republican House majority prevents its adoption.

OECD Finally Triumphs

Over the years, deceitful politicians have used any convenient and plausible sounding excuse in their anti-tax haven crusade to fool the public. A complacent and largely ignorant news media aided and abetted this deceit, repeating false charges and doing very little investigative reporting.

During this time these politicians' anti-tax haven themes have shifted to take advantage of current hot button issues. In the 1990s, the accusation was that offshore financial centers were secretly hiding billions in drug kingpin money gained from illicit drug sales around the world.

When investigations showed that most drug funds were laundered in the U.S. and the U.K., the politicians used anti-terrorism as an issue, charging that terrorist funds were concealed by tax haven banking secrecy laws. Once again, official investigations revealed that the cash that financed the 9/11 attacks in New York and Washington came through normal banking channels in the U.S. and Europe, and not in any tax haven.

Even so, the 2001 PATRIOT Act that was adopted by the U.S. Congress only six weeks after the 9/11 attacks contained numerous restrictions on Americans' right to conduct financial matters offshore, based on the false claim of offshore terror funds.

When the recession that began in 2008 descended on the world, the worst in 30 years, these same dishonest politicians were quick to blame tax havens. The recession clearly was the product of greed and idiocy on Wall Street, in the City of London and elsewhere, aided by politicians in many countries. But at an April 2009 meeting of the G-20, the blacklisting OECD finally came into its full glory. Meeting in London, G-20 leaders made tax havens their chosen bête noire.

Impotent to do much about the global recession for which their tax and spending policies were partially to blame, U.S. President

Barack Obama, U.K. prime minister Gordon Brown, French President Nicolas Sarkozy and Germany's chancellor Angela Merkel, joined in attacking offshore jurisdictions for imaginary sins — imaginary because tax havens had little or nothing to do with causing the global recession that originated in the G-20 nations themselves. The assembled G-20 hypocrites pledged, "To take action against non-cooperative jurisdictions, including tax havens. We stand ready to deploy sanctions to protect our public finances and financial systems" — as if tax havens were actually a threat!

The G-20 also adopted yet another OECD list (this time the color was gray, not black) naming 34 supposedly "bad" tax havens, the sole criterion for "bad" being their refusal automatically to surrender tax information about foreigners with bank or financial accounts in their countries.

The G-20 list's authors carefully excluded themselves, the United States and the United Kingdom among them, two of the leading tax havens in the world. In the G-20 statement, these hypocrites crowed: "The era of banking secrecy is over."

Tax Havens Conditional Surrender

Oligarchy is a form of government in which all power is vested in a few persons or in a dominant class or clique. It is government by the few over the many.

The 2009 G-20 London meeting established a new, international oligarchy in which a few left-wing politicians and their allied activists, representing major tax collecting countries in the world, imposed their tax policies on smaller nations and jurisdictions.

For the first time, using the global recession as their excuse, the G-20 moved to impose international banking sanctions and controls that had the potential to cripple the economies of any OFC that refused to submit. Yes, these G-20 threats violated national sovereignty and ran roughshod over the laws in these jurisdictions made little difference—but in global politics might makes right, as the strong always remind us.

To put this in perspective, consider how an American president (and 314 million Americans) would respond if the United States similarly was threatened with an organized global boycott, blacklisted as a financial pariah, subjected to trade and banking sanctions, and foreigners who dared to do business with America were threatened with higher taxes and punishment. Yet, that is what the President of the United States and the other G-20 countries decreed to be the fate of tax havens.

Faced with these real threats, the OECD's blacklisted OFCs agreed to abide by Article 26 of the "OECD Model Tax Convention." This article recognizes "tax evasion" as a valid basis for foreign tax agency inquiries concerning their citizens with accounts in an offshore center. Under this OECD procedure, foreign tax authorities wishing to take advantage of tax information exchange agreements need to supply evidence of their suspicions (names, facts, alleged tax crimes) to the requested government. If there is sufficient probable cause to believe tax evasion has occurred, the requested government must supply the information.

These exchanges now have been formalized in tax information exchange agreements (TIEAs) between many nations. These treaties are based on an OECD model treaty that repeatedly has been updated. Each successive model has given tax authorities greater powers to retrieve financial information from the other treaty signatory.

Under OECD Article 26, bank secrecy laws, dual criminality requirements, and domestic tax interest requirements could no longer be invoked to prevent information exchange. These far more expansive tax information sharing provisions have gradually made their way into the international network of tax treaties and could well be incorporated into the many TIEAs under negotiation at this writing.

If a country agrees to implement information exchange arrangements without any express limitations "consistent with OECD standards," the laws that might have prevented your financial information from being disclosed to your domestic tax authorities may no longer offer any privacy protection. If you are concerned, you should obtain the text of any TIEA that applies in the offshore jurisdiction where you have an interest.

Faced with sanctions, in 2009 OFCs that agreed to this OECD principle included Andorra, The Bahamas, Belize, Bermuda, British Virgin Islands, Cayman Islands, Gibraltar, Grenada, Liechtenstein, Monaco, Panama, St. Kitts & Nevis, St Vincent & the Grenadines, the Turks & Caicos Islands, Costa Rica, the Philippines and Uruguay, among others.

What This Means for You

For those with existing offshore investments and banking arrangements, and those considering going offshore, in the past the trend had favored expansion of traditional financial freedoms.

At this time those offshore freedoms remain in place for Americans, although President Obama and his congressional allies have done all they can legislatively to significantly curb offshore financial liberties. Similar plans have been adopted in the United Kingdom, Germany and other major high tax nations.

The current situation in America and other nations makes it imperative that you keep abreast of offshore developments. You can do that with information from The Sovereign Society.

There are still many attractive legal opportunities for offshore asset protection, business, investing, banking, currency trading, even making a new home offshore. At this writing:

• It is legal to have and use an offshore bank account.

- It is legal to invest offshore in stocks, bonds and other investment properties and have an offshore brokerage account.

- It is legal to create and donate assets to an offshore asset protection trust or family foundation.

- It is legal to form and operate an international business corporation (IBC).

- It is legal to purchase offshore life insurance and annuities that allow deferred taxes.

- It is legal to invest in offshore mutual and hedge funds, precious metals and real estate.

- It is legal to acquire dual citizenship and a second passport.

- It is legal to voluntarily end U.S. citizenship and thus remove oneself from the U.S. tax system.

The truth is that, with the continued political strangulation of financial and personal freedom in the United States and other nations, the time is getting late for offshore wealth preservation and prudent asset protection planning. That planning means the transfer of at least some cash and assets into the hands of offshore asset managers in jurisdictions that have established histories of sound investment and currency management. In these pages we will tell you who and where they are.

The USA PATRIOT Act

Congress passed the PATRIOT Act without even knowing what was in it. Less than six weeks after 9/11, the Republican-controlled Congress rammed through a 362-page law, sight unseen, with few members having the courage to oppose one of the worst attacks on American liberties ever enacted into law. In spite of massive public opposition to the law, it was extended in 2006 and 2011 at the urging of both Presidents George Bush and Barack Obama, respectively, with majority support from both political parties in the Congress. For those interested in ordering *The PATRIOT Report* which I updated in 2012, go to: http://www.sovereign-investor.com/pages/svs/SVS_Bundle_Video.php?pub=ERIKA_VID&code=WSVSNA00

Chapter Four

Leading Offshore Financial Centers

In prior editions of this book, my Sovereign Society colleagues and I designated what we believed to be the four leading offshore financial centers in the world.

However the veritable revolution in the laws, rules and policies governing what used to be called "tax havens," especially in the area of financial privacy and bank secrecy, dictates a different approach in this edition.

Here we analyze offshore financial centers based on their individual best uses for you, without attempting to rank them in any artificial numeric world order.

- For example, Switzerland and Denmark offer some of the best SEC-registered wealth management experts.

- For superior personal banking services add Austria to Switzerland, with the Swiss also offering a link to banks in neighboring Liechtenstein which uses the Swiss franc as it currency.

- If you want to open your own regional Asian brokerage/investment accounts, Singapore or Hong Kong is the place.

- Gibraltar is a good brokerage and investment base for European business.

- Both Panama and Uruguay specialize in immediate residence and eventual citizenship.

- For your offshore asset protection trust it's the Isle of Man or the Cook Islands.

- Nevis provides limited liability companies overnight.

As you read, you will discover how each offshore financial center can best fit your needs. Where appropriate, we provide professional and official contacts.

In considering the usefulness of individual offshore financial centers (OFCs), we constantly review the laws, political stability, economic climate, tax regime and the overall financial standing of each jurisdiction.

Applying these and other important criteria, we start with six selected leading offshore financial centers that stand out from all others — **Switzerland**, **Liechtenstein**, **Panama**, **Uruguay**, **Hong Kong** and **Singapore**.

As with all other jurisdictions, we evaluate five factors for each and rate each on a scale of 1 to 5 based on the following questions:

Government/political stability: How long has the current system of government been in place? Is the jurisdiction politically stable?

Favorable laws, judicial system: Is there a well-established legal tradition and judicial system with a solid reputation for "fair play" with regard to foreign investors?

Available legal entities: Does the jurisdiction offer a variety of legal entities that meet the needs of the average foreign person seeking estate planning, asset protection or business solutions?

Financial privacy/banking secrecy: Does the jurisdiction have and enforce financial privacy laws? How strictly are they applied? Are there exceptions to these laws and, if so, how extensive are they?

Taxes: Does the OFC impose taxes on foreigners that invest and do business there, and to what degree? Are there tax treaties or tax information exchange agreements in effect?

Switzerland

Historic World Leader

Even considering its many recent international difficulties, Switzerland remains as one of the best all-around asset and financial havens in the world.

For centuries, the Swiss have acted as banker to the world and in that role Switzerland has acquired a reputation for integrity and financial privacy, although both have been tarnished of late. It is also an attractive place for wealthy people to reside, which may explain why Switzerland is home to 9.5% of all world millionaires.

Switzerland may be neutral in politics, but it's far from flavorless. The fusion of German, French and Italian influence has formed a robust national culture, and the country's alpine landscapes have enough zing to reinvigorate even the most jaded traveler. Goethe summed up Switzerland succinctly as a combination of "the colossal and the well-ordered." You can be sure that your train will be on time.

The tidy, "just-so" precision of Swiss towns is tempered by the lofty splendor of the landscapes that surround them. There's a lot more here than just trillions of dollars and Euros.

A Reputation to Uphold

A global survey of private banks published by Pricewaterhouse-Coopers found that the major attraction for a bank's new customers is its reputation. Certainly, Switzerland's solid financial reputation is central to the claim that this alpine nation serves as "banker to the world." Indeed, these days, good judgment and reliability are banking traits more sought after than ever before.

For over 250 years, as European empires and nations rose and fell, Swiss topography and determination have combined to defend their mountainous redoubt. All the while, the Swiss people maintained a more or less neutral attitude and policies towards other nations.

Factor	Findings	Rating
Government/ political stability	The words 'Swiss' and 'stability' have long been synonymous	5
Favorable laws, judicial system	Highly protective of personal wealth	5
Available legal entities	All major legal entities may be formed or are recognized under the Swiss legal system	5
Taxes	35% on interest paid, which can be reduced under bilateral tax treaties; income taxes negotiable for resident foreigners	3.5
Financial privacy/ banking secrecy	One of the world's oldest bank secrecy laws, but now with significant compromises and liberal tax information sharing	4
Final Rating		22.5

In 1945, after the 20th Century's second "war to end all wars," Swiss voters overwhelmingly rejected membership in the United Nations. It was not until 2002 that a slim majority backed UN membership. In 1992 and 2001 national polls, Swiss voters also rejected membership in the European Union, rightly fearing EU bureaucratic interference with Swiss privacy and banking laws. A recent national ballot soundly rejected a proposal to ease Swiss bank secrecy laws and more recent polls reconfirm that position.

After each of these national plebiscites and during wars and world recessions, ever-greater amounts of foreign cash have flowed into Swiss banks, confirming the widespread notion that Switzerland is the place to safeguard cash and other personal assets in troubled times. It is estimated that Swiss banks currently manage at least one-third of all assets held offshore by the world's wealthy. As a safe haven for cash, Switzerland has become something of a modern cliché.

According to the Swiss Bankers Association, with 9.1% of global assets under management (AUM), Switzerland is among the world's leading trio of wealth management centers, alongside the U.S. and the U.K.

It is no accident that the governments of both of these competitors have been among Switzerland's chief critics, pushing for an end to Swiss bank secrecy laws. Switzerland is also the world's leader in offshore private banking, with a market share of 40% as estimated by *The Times* of London. In 2008, the value of AUM in Switzerland (securities holdings in bank custody accounts) reached CHF 5.4 trillion (US$5.6 trillion), many times the Swiss GDP of $340.5 billion in 2011.

At the end of 2008, due to the global recession and the bear market, this figure decreased to CHF 4.1 trillion (US$3.8 trillion). In 2009, Swiss private banks managed assets held by foreign account holders of CHF 2.15 trillion (US$1.988 trillion) according to the Swiss Bankers Association. This was roughly half of the country's private bank asset base of CHF 5.2 trillion (US$4.8 trillion) that in the past has helped the Swiss economy to remain strong.

Switzerland's GDP dropped 2.7% in 2009—the worst contraction since 1975. With the banking and financial services industry accounting for about 12% of GDP, the Swiss economy was more vulnerable to the global credit crisis than some others. Zurich-based UBS AG, the European bank with the largest losses from the world financial turmoil, cut almost 20% of its workforce. However, in 2012, Switzerland's adjusted unemployment rate was about 3.1%, at a time when the U.S. rate still was nearly 9%. The Swiss National Bank effectively has implemented a zero-interest rate policy to boost the economy as well as prevent appreciation of the Swiss franc, and the economy recovered in 2010 with 2.7% growth and 2.4% in 2011.

Switzerland has one of the highest per capita GDPs (US$43,400 in 2011) in the world with inflation rates below 1% in recent years Its location in the center of Europe, a favorable tax regime, high standard of living and low crime rate make Switzerland an attractive place to live and work for expatriates.

Reduce Financial Privacy

In recent years, Switzerland's image as bankers to the world's rich has taken some serious hits. Disturbing to financial privacy seekers more than a decade ago was the major Swiss banks' surrender under pressure to demands of the U.S. Federal Reserve System.

In 1998, Swiss Bank Corporation and Union Bank of Switzerland merged creating UBS AG. The U.S. Federal Reserve approved UBS to do business in the U.S., but only after the banking giant agreed to provide U.S. regulators all information *"necessary to determine and enforce compliance with [U.S.] federal law."*

As events have shown, that meant U.S. tax laws, too. In 1998, U.S. regulators had threatened to shut down UBS's extensive U.S. operations. (In 2008, UBS had about 80,000 employees worldwide, 30,000 in the United States.) In 1998, rather than defend their U.S. clients' privacy rights, the bank compromised with the Fed. As a result, in 2008 and repeatedly afterward, The Sovereign Society, as advocates of maximum legal financial privacy, advised U.S. depositors considering Swiss banks to avoid UBS AG and any other Swiss bank with U.S.-based branches, affiliates or banking operations, other than a mere "representative office."

The U.S. government did not know then that over a period of years after the Fed's 1998 approval, UBS secretly assisted an estimated 4,500 American clients to engage in illegal evasion of U.S. taxes. UBS admitted its private banking managers conspired from 2001 to 2006 to defraud the IRS and the bank paid US$780 million to settle a federal investigation. A suit by the U.S. Department of Justice (DOJ) against UBS seeking the names of an alleged 55,000 Americans that had UBS accounts was settled in 2010 with the UBS surrender of 4,500 names.

Surrender to IRS Ends 78 Years of Bank Secrecy

The Swiss Bank Secrecy Law of 1934 was enacted to protect the assets of Jews and other persecuted Germans from Adolf Hitler's Nazi henchmen. The law made it a crime punishable with jail to reveal financial information about bank clients.

There is no dispute that the 1934 Bank Secrecy Law always and to this day has had solid majority support among the Swiss — and the privacy it afforded has been a major attraction for the trillions of dollars Switzerland holds and manages for the world.

In June 2012, the Swiss government did the once-inconceivable —they repealed the 1934 Bank Secrecy Law as it applied to U.S. persons with Swiss financial accounts.

A respected law that defeated the Nazis could not stop the combined political power of the seemingly disparate interests of tax-hungry U.S. IRS and profit-hungry Swiss bankers.

This radical departure from the Swiss undoubtedly was a result of immense political and financial pressure from 11 Swiss banks being investigated for helping Americans evade taxes — assertions leveled by the U.S. Department of Justice and the IRS. The Swiss government desperately had been trying to get the U.S. to drop tax investigations against 11 banks, including Credit Suisse and Julius

Baer, in exchange for a general amnesty and payment of fines and surrender of U.S. client names. The politicians also wanted to shield the rest of the 300-plus Swiss banks and financial institutions from U.S. prosecution.

Such a deal would be a shameful replay of 2009 when UBS was forced to pay the U.S. a $780 million fine and release the names of 4,500 clients to the IRS to settle a lawsuit that threatened to shut down UBS American operations with more than 30,000 employees. That deal was the first major crack in the 1934 Bank Secrecy Law.

In 2009, the Swiss government was forced to seek, and got, parliamentary approval for the UBS-IRS settlement after the **Swiss Federal Administrative Court** twice ruled that the deal was illegal because it violated the 1934 Bank Secrecy Law.

The June announcement cited the U.S. Foreign Account Tax Compliance Act, (FATCA) as the reason for the Swiss-IRS agreement. Switzerland's State Secretariat for International Financial Matters claimed in a questionable statement that a Swiss refusal to implement FATCA would cause "major disadvantages" for Swiss banks.

The Swiss bureaucrats suggested that the world financial community would stop doing business with a country that controls as estimated one-third of all the world's private assets, over $6 trillion, if it did not surrender to IRS and its FATCA demands.

According to *Forbes* magazine: "The prohibitive withholding tax of 30% on all payments from the U.S. and the likely consequence that foreign financial institutions would terminate their business relationships with Swiss financial institutions in the medium term would result in exclusion from the world's largest capital market," the Swiss bureaucrats added, presumably with a straight face.

The ever-efficient Swiss opted for a streamlined deal with the U.S. government that allows Swiss banks to hand over data about American clients directly to the IRS.

This compared to passing information through the Swiss government as a conduit as is the procedure in pending FATCA agreements between the IRS and the governments of the U.K., France, Germany, Spain and Italy.

The New York Times reported: "This better takes into account the particular characteristics of the Swiss financial center, crowed the Swiss Bankers Association that welcomed the sellout of traditional Swiss bank secrecy."

In the famous legend of William Tell that every Swiss knows and respects, Tell represents the common man, who respects authority but is quick to fight for his rights once authority turns despotic. Thus a modest peasant became a national hero.

Swiss Finance Minister Eveline Widmer-Schlumpf and her wimpy colleagues on the governing Swiss Federal Counsel don't even rise to the modest peasant level. They apparently forgot the noble example of William Tell. But they certainly did not forget their friends at UBS and Credit Suisse.

That the Swiss government would adopt such a drastic policy change on bank secrecy indicates that in the future any official guarantees of financial privacy should be regarded with suspicion.

Bank Secrecy No More

The first inclination upon reading the news that the Swiss Parliament had surrendered to the bullying of the U.S. government and demands of the U.S. IRS by approving the first major breach in that nation's once strict bank secrecy law, is to say the politicians sold out Switzerland and the Swiss.

Certainly there is no dispute that since the enactment of the 1934 Bank Secrecy Law, that law always, and to this day, has had solid majority support among the Swiss—and it has been a major attraction for the trillions of dollars Switzerland holds and manages for the world.

That is because the Swiss people really do believe in financial privacy and bank secrecy, unlike most of the brainwashing leftist tax collecting governments and their cowed subjects.

Then things began to change in 2010. Switzerland and its historic reputation for strict financial privacy were compromised seriously. The Swiss Parliament endorsed the waiving of Swiss bank secrecy law and allowed UBS to surrender U.S. client names to the IRS of American bank clients suspected of tax evasion.

With this drawing of Swiss bank secrecy blood by the U.S., Germany, France, and other big deficit, big spending welfare states queued up for the kill.

At the same time both chambers, in a very un-Swiss, undemocratic move, refused to submit the U.S. tax treaty to a nationwide vote, denying Swiss voters a chance to register what most observers predicted would be certain rejection. It says something about a majority of Swiss politicians when they are more afraid of the U.S. IRS and UBS than they are of their own citizens.

But the applicable explanation here, as it often is the United States, is: *"Follow the money!"*

It can be argued that over time Swiss bank secrecy would have been relaxed to some degree anyway — but the villain in this historic defeat was, of course — UBS — that mismanaged, greedy, tax evading behemoth bank that demanded and got a multi-billion bailout package by the Swiss government, when it posted record losses in 2008 and 2009.

While the U.S. government was threatening to shut down UBS in the United States (with its 30,000 employees), thousands of account holders took their billions in cash and left UBS. Many Americans clients that did not leave voluntarily were dumped by UBS, under IRS pressure.

UBS is the world's number two wealth manager measured by assets and Switzerland's largest bank. When push came to shove, UBS, and other nervous Swiss banks persuaded not only parliament but the governing Federal Council and a majority of Swiss legislative political parties as well to save their hides by sacrificing Swiss bank secrecy.

Traditional strict Swiss bank secrecy can no longer be counted on. But where in the world, as changed as this world is, can anyone find anything like what used to be known as "Swiss bank secrecy?"

A Swiss bank account has always been a red flag of possible tax evasion for foreign tax collectors, especially those in neighboring high-tax EU countries. French plainclothes tax police have stalked the streets of Geneva, recording French auto license plates. They then called ahead to have the cars stopped and searched at the French border. France also systematically screens mail to and from Switzerland for magnetically striped checks. German tax collectors apply similar surveillance methods.

In an effort to track down their nationals engaged in possible tax evasion, revenue-hungry tax collectors in both Germany and France have paid millions in ransoms to bank employee thieves who stole client computer records from banks in Switzerland and Liechtenstein.

EU bureaucrats continually have attacked Switzerland on a related tax issue. They claim low corporate tax rates in the Swiss cantons amount to a tax subsidy for the many foreign-owned corporations registered there. One Swiss official put it succinctly: low tax rates are not a subsidy and Switzerland will not raises corporate taxes to satisfy the tax-hungry EU.

For the usual anti-privacy, anti-tax haven crowd who habitually bash any offshore financial activity, Switzerland has always been a special target and the UBS-IRS scandal was a godsend for them. These leftists hated the Swiss Bank Secrecy Law because they believe that the privacy rights of the individual must be subordinated to government and that all offshore accounts probably are used for tax evasion.

Beginning in 2005, the EU began an anti-Swiss campaign demanding that banking secrecy, written into Swiss law in 1934, be abolished. The French and German governments even went so far as to call for a financial boycott of Switzerland unless they surrendered on bank secrecy. The Swiss said "no" and they meant it -- at the time.

When the Swiss finally agreed to collect taxes under the "EU tax directive," it was without revealing the names of any foreign person with a Swiss bank account. The Swiss stand was supported by the refusal of the EU's own members, Austria, Belgium and Luxembourg, to weaken their own bank secrecy laws. In 2011, Switzerland reached agreements with Germany and the United Kingdom to collect taxes on Swiss bank deposits held by German and British citizens. A similar deal with the French is pending at this time.

Rob Vrijhof, a leading Zurich investment manager who has been a trusted partner of The Sovereign Society since 1999 and who has spoken at our offshore events for more than a decade points out: "Many of the attacks on Swiss bank secrecy in the name of 'justice' are, in truth, attempts to eliminate cross-border banking competition, to impose an international tax cartel, or to undermine Switzerland's recognized status as a world financial center that easily competes with the City of London and with Wall Street." (See "Contacts" below for Mr. Vrijhof's information.)

Very Special Swiss Franc

The Swiss franc is a so-called "safe haven" currency, which means that investors and speculators buy it when other currencies, including the euro and the dollar, are under pressure. A "safe haven currency" is backed by a robust economy, a stable political framework and enough liquidity to deal with strong bouts of international trading. Neutral Switzerland, with its conservative economic policy and a strong financial sector, has been a classic safe haven currency for many decades, especially during the two World Wars as it is again today.

Switzerland's currency, the Swiss franc, generally has reflected the state of Swiss banking—strong, valuable and unaffected by inflation and stylish monetary fads. Since 1971, the franc has appreciated nearly 330% against the U.S. dollar. U.S. owners of Swiss franc-denominated assets usually have profited as a result. That profit came despite traditionally low Swiss interest rates and the bothersome 35% withholding tax on bank interest.

The 2012 sovereign debt crises in Greece and other euro-zone countries posed a significant risk to Switzerland's financial stability and drove up demand for the Swiss franc by foreign investors seeking a safe haven currency. The independent Swiss National Bank upheld its zero-interest rate policy and conducted major market interventions to prevent further appreciation of the Swiss franc. The franc's strength had driven up real estate prices, made Swiss exports less competitive and weakened the country's economic growth outlook, which is one reason the GDP growth slipped to 2.1% in 2011.

In spite of its reputation for bank secrecy, in 1990, Switzerland was one of the first European countries to make money laundering a criminal offense. That law resulted in the demise of the famous Swiss *compte anonyme*, as the French-speaking Swiss termed it—universally known as a "numbered account." Previously, it was possible to open a nominee account in which the identity of the account holder could be concealed from almost everyone except the highest bank officials.

Since 1994, a central office in Bern has been devoted exclusively to fighting organized crime. Mandatory "know your customer" guidelines are used by Swiss banks to investigate potential clients. This strict anti-money laundering law has transformed Swiss banking in a fundamental way. Previously, bankers had the option of reporting suspicious transactions to police authorities. Now, under pressure from world governments pursuing corruption, drug cartels and organized crime, the government requires banks to report suspicious transactions. Failure to report is a crime and bankers can now go to prison for keeping secret the names and records of suspected clients. Not so long ago, they faced imprisonment for failing to reveal such information.

The Swiss government also has proven willing to freeze assets before an individual is even charged with a crime if a foreign government can demonstrate "reasonable suspicion" that the accused engaged in criminal conduct. This is especially the case in high-profile drug or political corruption cases, such as those involving Swiss bank accounts of someone like the late dictator of the Philippines, Ferdinand Marcos.

World-Class Banking System

Although Swiss banking privacy once was legendary, secrecy is not the most important reason for Switzerland's success. Of far greater significance are the country's political, financial and economic stability and strength. Most of the world's largest companies and hundreds of thousands of honest, law-abiding foreigners bank with the Swiss. Traditionally, Swiss banks have managed close to 40% of the world's private wealth, or more than US$3 trillion in assets.

It is no coincidence that the official international intermediary banking institution, the Bank for International Settlements, is located in Switzerland at Basle.

Switzerland is home to several hundred banks ranging from small private and regional banks to the two giants, UBS AG and Crédit Suisse. These major Swiss banks have branch offices in most of the world's financial centers, from New York to Panama to Singapore.

Swiss banks combine traditional banking with international brokerage and financial management. To guard against inflation or devaluation, Swiss bank accounts can be denominated in the currency you choose — Swiss francs, U.S. dollars, Euros or any other major currency. An account opened in one currency can be switched to another denomination when the time is right for short-term profits or long-term gains and safety.

You can invest in certificates of deposit, U.S. and other national stocks, bonds, mutual funds and commodities; buy, store and sell gold, silver and other precious metals; and buy insurance and annuities. Swiss banks can act as your agent to buy and hold other types of assets. Of course, Swiss banks also issue international credit and ATM bank cards. Bank officers speak English as well as many other languages. Swiss banks are equipped for fax, wire, email, or telex and instructions are carried out immediately. Or, just phone your own personal banker who handles your account.

To some extent, "know your customer" rules have complicated the process of opening a bank account in Switzerland and proof of identity and references are required. But, the biggest downside is the high minimum deposit required by most Swiss private investment banks.

A few years ago many banks were content with initial deposits of only a few thousand dollars. Now Switzerland's popularity with foreign investors, along with the cost of administering "know your customer" laws, has led to sharp increases in deposit minimums, the lowest now being about US$250,000. Most private investment accounts require a minimum of US$1 million.

An alternative can be found in banks run by the various Swiss "cantons," as the largely self-governing provinces are called. These banks offer full services, have relatively lower minimum deposits and each cantonal government insures the deposits. Swiss banks usually require that foreigners applying to open a new account do so in person.

Because of U.S. government lawsuits against Swiss banks and onerous U.S. government regulations and reporting requirements involving Americans, such as that imposed by the U.S. Foreign Account Tax Compliance Act (FATCA), many Swiss banks now refuse to do business with U.S. persons.

The Sovereign Society can assist in making appropriate contacts with reliable Swiss or other offshore banks that have passed our due diligence tests and that welcome American or other foreign clients. If you wish to open a Swiss account, contact The Sovereign Society at 98 S.E. Federal Highway, Suite 2, Delray Beach, FL 33483. Tel.: 561-272-0413, Website: http://www.sovereignsociety.com, or Email: info@sovereignsociety.com.

Strict Control, High Quality

Swiss banks have attained their unique position with financial expertise, global capabilities and the high percentage and quality of their reserves, much of it in gold and Swiss francs. The Swiss financial industry is tightly regulated, with banks strictly supervised by the Federal Banking Commission (FBC).

Swiss law imposes stiff liquidity and capital requirements on banks. The complicated official liquidity formula results in some private banks maintaining liquidity at or near 100%, unheard of in other national banking systems. The Swiss reputation also rests on the fact that banks traditionally hold substantial unreported, hidden reserves. Every month, Swiss banks with securities investments must write the value of their holdings to current market price or actual cost, whichever is lower. This assures no Swiss banks will have unrealized paper losses, as often happens in other countries.

Swiss banks are also subject to two regular audits. The first audit is to ensure compliance with Swiss corporate law. The second is the banking audit, conducted by one of 17 audit firms specially approved by the FBC. These exacting audits provide the primary guarantee for Swiss bank depositors. Supervision and regulation of Swiss banking surpasses that of any other nation. Plus, the banks have comprehensive insurance to cover deposits, transfers, theft, or abnormal losses. This means that your funds are insured in the event of a bank failure—but that hasn't happened in Switzerland in many decades.

Fiduciary Investment Account

One popular Swiss account for foreign investors is the fiduciary account. A Swiss bank investment manager oversees the account, but all its investments are placed outside Switzerland, as the account holder directs. Funds that pass through the account are therefore not subject to Swiss taxes.

The fiduciary account comes in two forms: (1) an investment account and (2) a fiduciary loan account. With the investment account, the bank places the client's funds as loans to foreign banks in the form of fixed-term deposits. In the loan account, the customer designates the commercial borrower. Although the bank assumes no risk, it provides an important service by conducting a thorough investigation of the prospective borrower's credit credentials.

Many international companies use fiduciary loans to finance subsidiaries. There is an element of risk in making such loans, though. In the event of currency devaluation, or the bankruptcy of the borrower, the lender can lose.

Discretionary Accounts

With more than 250 years in the international portfolio management business, Swiss banks are among the world leaders in investment management. Experienced money managers constantly analyze world markets, choosing investments with the greatest potential and minimal risk. Swiss banks offer a broad selection of investment plans diversified by industry, country, international, or emerging markets. Outside financial managers can be employed to invest deposited funds and bank loans can be arranged for investment purposes.

These accounts are best managed by a private Swiss bank or by an independent Swiss portfolio manager. The Swiss invented what has come to be called "private banking." They honed private banking to a fine edge centuries before U.S. "cookie cutter" banks discovered the concept. With a private bank, you get personal contact and individual service. However, most private banks require a high initial minimum investment and a personal introduction from a well-known source.

Swiss Alternative: Insurance

Switzerland is also a world-renowned center for insurance and reinsurance. Many Swiss insurance companies offer a broad range of financial services that, in some cases, approach the flexibility of a bank account. Indeed, many Swiss residents use their insurance company as their only financial institution.

Swiss insurance policies offer other important advantages, including:

- Generally higher interest rates than bank accounts.

- They may be configured to offer significant asset protection, unlike a bank account.

- Insurance accounts aren't subject to the Swiss 35% withholding tax on earned bank interest.

U.S. tax law ended the tax deferral previously allowed on fixed annuity contracts issued by foreign insurance companies. All such annuity income must now be reported as part of taxable annual income. However, income from properly structured foreign variable annuities and life insurance contracts generally remains U.S. tax deferred.

Taxes

Switzerland is not a low-tax country for Swiss residents or companies, although tax rates are lower than in the surrounding EU nations. But foreign investors can avoid many local taxes by choosing certain types of investments that avoid taxes.

By law, Swiss banks collect a withholding tax of 35% on all interest and dividends paid by Swiss companies, banks, the government or other sources. Foreign investors to whom this tax applies may be eligible for refunds of all or part of the tax under the terms of Switzerland's network of more than 70 tax treaties with other nations.

In addition, there are many legal ways to avoid Swiss taxes by investing in accounts especially structured for foreign investors. These include non-Swiss money market and bond funds, fiduciary precious metal accounts and other instruments. For instance, Switzerland imposes no taxes on dividends or interest from securities that originate outside Switzerland. For this reason, many Swiss banks offer investment funds with at least 80% of earnings in foreign investments or, even better, in money market funds located in Luxembourg or Ireland where they are tax exempt.

Companies are welcome in Switzerland and are established in the form of a corporation (Aktiengesellschaft; AG). Shareholders are not personally liable for company debts and a corporation can be formed by one or more individuals or legal entities. Nominees may act as founders. There are no restrictions as to the nationality or the domicile of the founders or the shareholders.

The effective income tax rate for holding companies amounts to 7.83%. Dividend income is virtually tax exempt. Other attractive tax regimes for IP companies, financing and international trading activities as well as for principal companies are available that result in effective tax rates between 8% and 11%. Operating companies in other sectors pay income taxes at an overall effective tax rate of 12.6% to 24%. These are federal taxes and there may be additional cantonal taxes.

Tax Treaties Abound

To reduce the possibility that Swiss citizens or companies might be subject to double taxation, the Swiss government has entered into a global network of about 70 tax treaties.

Tax treaties, however, have the unfortunate side effect of eroding financial secrecy. It is not possible to claim a tax credit under a tax treaty without also revealing the income that was taxed. In addition, tax treaties have a second underlying purpose: they exist not only to help individuals and companies investing or doing business internationally to avoid double taxation, but also to facilitate information exchange between tax authorities.

The 1997 U.S.-Swiss tax treaty, still in effect, is a case in point.

While non-payment of taxes is not a crime in Switzerland, Article 26 of the U.S.-Swiss treaty permits the two governments to exchange information about alleged "tax fraud and the like." It also allows authorities to transfer information that may help in the "prevention of tax fraud and the like in relation to taxes."

Tax-Advantaged Residency in Switzerland

For the very wealthy foreign immigrant, Switzerland's cantonal tax system allows a unique personalized income tax plan that calls for annual lump-sum tax payments.

Foreign citizens who fulfill certain requirements may be eligible for this special tax arrangement in which Swiss taxes are levied on the basis of a person's personal expenditures and standard of living in Switzerland, rather than on worldwide income and assets. This lump sum taxation (*forfait fiscal* in French, *Pauschalbesteuerung* in German) is available throughout the country, except in the canton of Zurich.

This unique lump-sum taxation effectively caps the income and net wealth tax for qualifying foreign citizens. Switzerland is also attractive because it imposes no federal inheritance or gift taxes. But the cantons do levy inheritance and gift taxes, which means that there are 25 different inheritance and gift tax regimes. In the 26th canton, Schwyz, there is neither inheritance nor gift taxes.

The number of foreigners in the *forfeit fiscal* program climbed 31% between 2006 and 2010. The system was originally introduced by the canton of Vaud in the 1860s to get wealthy British residents to pay for local services.

Switzerland, a haven for refugees since Jean Calvin arrived in Geneva in the 16th Century, had 5,450 people in the *forfeit* system at the end of 2010 and more than 33% of those were French. Of the 300 richest people and families in Switzerland, 43 are French and include designer Daniel Hechter and the Peugeot family.

Under the *forfeit* deal, foreigners pay an average 75,000 Swiss francs (US$78,400) in annual taxes, earning over US$710 million per year in revenue. The system allows resident foreign citizens to negotiate a fixed tax rate based on their Swiss property factors, excluding income earned outside Switzerland.

Under the *forfeit*, expenditure is calculated at not less than five times the annual rental value of the individual's home in Switzerland and that is taxed at 30%. Ordinary federal and cantonal tax rates are applied to this figure and there is no obligation to declare worldwide income or assets, and no tax is paid on income from securities holdings. Deals vary widely among the 26 cantons that still allow it. (By comparison, many nations entice foreigners as individual or corporate residents by exempting them from all or most taxes, including the United Kingdom, Monaco, Luxembourg, Austria and Ireland.)

Forfeits have caused resentment among Swiss because top rates of income tax exceed 40% in cantons such as Geneva. Since 2009, five of the 26 Swiss cantons have repealed the scheme, while another five have kept the tax break but raised the bar for beneficiaries. The calculation rate was increased to up to ten times the annual rental value of the residence, instead of the former five, and the minimum level of income for beneficiaries was set at CHF600,000 (US$630,700) a year in some cantons. The Swiss Parliament increased the *forfeit* to seven times the rental value of a residence and set the minimum taxable income at CHF 400,000 (US$424,000).

The Swiss may be conservative in many ways, but they do welcome foreigners. Swiss voters rejected a proposal to impose a constitutional limit on the percentage of foreigners in their country. The proposal would have set a ceiling of 18% on the number of foreigners in this country of 7.6 million people. According to the Swiss Federal Statistical Office, 21.6% of the total population—and around 25% of the work force (some commute)—in Switzerland are foreigners.

People come from all over the world to live here. In fact, 86.5% of Switzerland's permanent foreign resident population is of European origin, two-thirds of whom are nationals of an EU country.

Private Banks

The Sovereign Society has arrangements with several leading Swiss banks to accommodate our members. Contact our office for information at 98 S.E. Federal Highway, Delray Beach, FL 33483; Tel.: 561-272-0413; Fax: 561-272-5427; Website: http://www.sovereignsociety.com Email: info@sovereignsociety.com.

Contacts

Embassy of Switzerland

2900 Cathedral Avenue, N.W.
Washington, D.C. 20008
Tel.: (202) 745-7900, Fax: (202) 387-2564
Email: was.vertretung@eda.admin.ch
Website: http://www.swissemb.org
  Consulates General are in Atlanta, Chicago, Los Angeles, New York, and San Francisco. Consulates are in Boston, Buffalo, Charlotte, Cleveland, Dallas, Denver, Detroit, Honolulu, Houston, Indianapolis, Kansas City, Las Vegas, Miami, Minneapolis, New Orleans, Oklahoma City, Orlando, Philadelphia, Phoenix, Pittsburg, Salt Lake City, San Juan, and Seattle.

United States Embassy

Sulgeneckstrasse 19, CH 3007 Bern, Switzerland
Tel.: + (41) 31-357-7011
Emergency: + (41) 31-357-7777
Fax: + (41) 31-357-7280
Email: bernacs@state.gov
Website: http://bern.usembassy.gov

U.S. Consular Agency

Dufourstrasse 101 3rd floor, Zurich, Switzerland
Mailing Address: Dufourstrasse 101
CH-8008 Zurich, Switzerland
Tel.: + (043) 499-2960, Fax: + (043) 499-2961
Email: Zurich-CA@state.gov

Recommended US SEC-Registered Investment Advisors

Weber, Hartmann, Vrijhof & Partners
Robert Vrijhof, Managing Partner
Schaffhauserstrasse 418, CH-8050 Zürich
Tel.: +41-44-315-77-77 Fax: +41-44-315-77-78
Email: info@whvp.ch
Website: www.whvp.ch
Contact: Ms. Julia Fernandez *
*Mr. Vrijhof and his staff can arrange Swiss bank accounts for Sovereign Society members.

Alpine Atlantic Asset Management AG
Contact: **Daniel Zurbrügg**, Managing Partner
Usteristrasse 19, 8023 Zürich 1204 Geneva, Switzerland
Tel.: +41 44 200 7000 Fax: +41 44 200 7009
Email: info@alpineatlantic.com
Website: www.alpineatlantic.com
Minimum Balance: US$250,000 or equivalent

Residence & citizenship assistance:

Henley & Partners AG
Klosbachstrasse 110, 8024 Zurich, Switzerland
Tel.: +41 44 266 22 22 Fax: +41 44 266 22 23
Websites: http://www.henleyglobal.com/switzerland
https://www.henleyglobal.com/countries/campione

The Principality of Liechtenstein

Major Changes in Oldest Tax Haven

This tiny principality, the world's 6th smallest country, is a constitutional monarchy that has graced the map of Europe since 1719. More recently it has transformed itself into a major offshore financial center. Among all the world's OFCs, Liechtenstein has adopted some of the most drastic recent changes, abolishing near absolute financial privacy and ending their past refusal to share client information with any other government.

Tiny Liechtenstein (16 miles long and 3.5 miles wide with a population of 36,700) is nestled in the mountains between Switzerland and Austria. It has existed in its present form since January 23, 1719, when the Holy Roman Emperor, Charles VI, granted it independent status.

In the past, the world's wealthy could do business here quietly, protected by strict secrecy and financial privacy laws. It also offered global banking and investment direct access through its cooperative neighbor, Switzerland.

With asset protection laws dating from the 1920s, a host of excellent legal entities designed for wealth preservation and bank secrecy guaranteed by law, at one time this tiny principality had it all. But that secrecy made it a prime target for outside pressure from the OECD, the U.S. and other major high tax countries. Under pressure, Liechtenstein more than blinked.

In the not too distant past, one had to be a philatelist to know the Principality of Liechtenstein even existed. In those days, the nation's major export was exquisitely produced postage stamps, highly prized by collectors. Until the 1960s, the tiny principality subsisted on income from tourism, postage stamp sales and the export of false teeth.

In the last 60 years, its tax free financial privacy propelled Liechtenstein to top ranking among the world's wealthiest nations. This historic Rhine Valley principality grew into a major world tax and asset haven, posting per capita income levels (US$141,000 in 2012) — higher than Germany, France and the United Kingdom.

Factor	Finding	Rating
Government/ political stability	A popular absolute monarchy, whose dictates are subject only to national referenda	3.5
Favorable laws, judicial system	Well-established and respected rule of law	5
Available legal entities	All major legal entities may be formed or are recognized under the legal system	5
Taxes	Foreign-owned entities are mostly tax-exempt, but there are TIEAs with the UK and others	4
Financial privacy/ banking secrecy	Weakened by legislation and TIEAs	3
Final Rating		20.5

Absolute Monarchy

The government is a constitutional monarchy, with the Prince of Liechtenstein (currently Hans-Adam II) as head of state. Until 2003, His Highness' power only extended to sanctioning laws passed by the popularly elected unicameral legislature, the Diet. For the most part, the Diet made the laws, negotiated treaties, approved or vetoed taxes and supervised government affairs. Proposed legislation was frequently submitted directly to citizen referendum.

This system changed on March 16, 2003, when Hans-Adam II won an overwhelming majority in favor of overhauling the constitution to give him more powers than any other European monarch. Liechtenstein's ruling Prince now has the right to dismiss governments and approve judicial nominees. The Prince may also veto laws simply by refusing to sign them within a six-month period. Tempering this authority is the fact that the signature of 1,500 Liechtenstein citizens on a petition is sufficient to force a referendum on the abolition of the monarchy, or any other change in the law.

In 2004, Prince Hans-Adam II ceded day-to-day rule of the country to his son, Prince Alois, now 45, while he remains the official head of state. This was seen as the first step towards the eventual full succession of power to Prince Alois.

Financial Center

Liechtenstein's economy is well diversified and it is, for its small size, one of the most heavily industrialized countries in Europe. Still, financial services provide a third of GDP. Its 16 locally owned banks, 60 law firms and 250 trust companies employ 16% of the workforce. Its licensed fiduciary companies and lawyers serve as nominees for, or manage, more than 80,000 legal entities, most of them owned and controlled by nonresidents of Liechtenstein.

Although only 16% of workers are in the financial sector, financial services account for 30% of the gross national product, with industry and manufacturing trade (4%), general services (25%) and agriculture and households (5%). Forty-six percent of the workforce is employed in the industrial sector and 40% of employees work in other service activities, such as trade, hotels and restaurants, transport and public administration. About 12,000 workers commute daily from Austria and Switzerland. GDP has grown as much as 10% annually in recent years and unemployment stays below 2%.

Today, Liechtenstein has positioned itself as "an oasis of political and economic stability" amidst the chaos of European debt crisis and despite significant pressure to tighten control over tax evaders. Leaders of this nation are distancing themselves from the tax haven label.

Liechtenstein was one of the first nations in the world to adopt specific offshore asset protection laws, as far back as the 1920s. Indeed, Liechtenstein's unique role in international circles was not so much as a banking center, but as—that hated phrase—a tax haven. The nation still acts as a base of operations for foreign holding companies, private foundations, family foundations and a unique entity called the Anstalt (i.e., establishment).

The banks and a host of specialized trust companies provide management services for thousands of such entities. Personal and company tax rates are low, generally under 12% for local residents. Any company domiciled in Liechtenstein is granted total exemption from income tax if it generates no income from local sources.

Liechtenstein is independent, but closely tied to Switzerland. The Swiss franc is the local currency and, in many respects, except for political independence, Liechtenstein's status is that of a de facto province integrated within Switzerland. Liechtenstein banks are integrated into Switzerland's banking system and capital markets. Many cross-border investments clear in or through Swiss banks. Foreign-owned holding companies are a major presence in Liechtenstein, with many maintaining their accounts in Swiss banks. It is currently trying to promote itself as a base for hedge funds.

Reputation

For the most part, Liechtenstein had an impeccable reputation with government regulators stressing the professional qualifications and local accountability of its well-trained financial managers. Liechtenstein's reaction to outside demands for stronger anti-money laundering laws has been very much in keeping with its conservative history.

In 2001, Liechtenstein was removed from the Financial Action Task Force (FATF) blacklist. In 2000, it adopted tough new anti-money laundering laws that covered "all crimes;" created a Financial Intelligence Unit (FIU); imposed much stricter "know-your-customer" and suspicious activity reporting laws; eased its historic, strict financial secrecy; and abolished the rights of trustees and lawyers not to disclose the identity of their clients to banks where funds are invested.

Liechtenstein's longstanding tax haven status was the source of criticism by the OECD, which placed the principality on its questionable, 41 nation FATF "harmful tax practices" blacklist because of its low taxes.

Stolen Names

Until early 2008, Liechtenstein managed to stay on the good side of the self-appointed international busybodies who make it their duty to attack tax havens and, most especially, banking secrecy.

It was then revealed that the German government illegally had bribed a disgruntled former Liechtenstein bank employee, Heinrich Kieber, to gain confidential bank information he had stolen from LGT Bank in Liechtenstein.

Herr Kieber worked for the LGT Group at LGT Treuhand (Bank) AG, in Vaduz until 2002. A man of questionable background, he had an outstanding 1997 international arrest warrant for a fraudulent real estate deal. He left Liechtenstein in 2002, after stealing confidential data from his employer, LGT Bank, and making copies of over a thousand names of foreigners with LGT accounts.

The German secret police paid Kieber €5 million (US$7.9 million) for the stolen data. The data, containing about 1,400 "client relationships," 600 of them Germans, was a major haul for German tax collectors. Germany shared the information with the governments of Britain, France, Italy, Spain, Norway, Ireland, Netherlands, Sweden, Canada, the USA, Australia and New Zealand.

Liechtenstein's billionaire royal family manages and controls LGT Bank and LGT Group. Banking secrecy and the government's refusal to share financial information, except in criminal cases, had been one of Liechtenstein's leading selling points. LGT Bank and Liechtenstein authorities rightfully advanced the theory that high-tax governments were using the stolen DVD and misinformation to scare people away from the principality and from its banks, which is what indeed happened.

After this highly publicized incident, the high tax governments of the G-20, assisted by the OECD, began a coordinated yearlong "surrender now" phase in their decade long anti-tax haven campaign.

To say the least, the worldwide publicity about the stolen bank list and the pressure from neighboring Germany, the G-20 countries and the OECD, hurt the principality's financial bottom line. Liechtenstein's banking industry suffered a 60% drop in profits in 2009, in part due to the global economic downturn, but also because of questions about its future as a leading tax haven. Assets under management by the principality's 15 banks were down 22%. Unlike most other countries, Switzerland included, Liechtenstein's banks did not ask for or require any government bailout support.

Liechtenstein was removed from the OECD black list of uncooperative tax havens in 2009 after it agreed to reveal foreign tax dodgers after bank data stolen in 2008 revealed hundreds of wealthy Germans and others had hidden assets in its banks.

That scandal plus tough markets and a rise in value of the Swiss franc (Liechtenstein's official currency since 1924) slashed assets managed in the country from a 2007 peak of CHF 153 billion (US$162 billion) to CHF 109 billion (US$115 billion) at the start of 2012. In 2012, ratings agency Standard & Poor's confirmed its AAA rating for Liechtenstein, citing "stable and conservative policies...which we expect to continue."

Secrecy Still Guaranteed By Law

Until 2009, there was a near-total absence of any international treaties governing double taxation or exchange of information with the one exception of a double tax agreement with neighboring Austria, primarily to cover taxes on people who commute across the border for work.

In 2009, Liechtenstein was one of the first acknowledged tax havens to adopt OECD tax information exchange standards that cover alleged foreign income tax evasion. As part of that major change in policy, the principality began negotiating tax information exchange treaties with other nations.

Liechtenstein's financial secrecy statutes historically were considered even stronger than those in Switzerland. The 2009 adoption of the OECD tax information exchange standard ended that claim. Nevertheless, Liechtenstein claimed that it still would enforce its strict confidentiality law with criminal penalties for unauthorized information release.

In 2008, Liechtenstein and the United States signed a tax information exchange treaty that provides for direct cooperation between the two countries' tax and judicial authorities. Enforcement of that treaty has called into serious question the good faith of the government's guarantee of the bank secrecy law.

In 2012, court records in a New York tax case revealed that on March 21, 2012, the Liechtenstein Parliament passed an internal law that amended the 2008 U.S. treaty allowing the Liechtenstein Tax Administration to broaden their responses to IRS information requests concerning U.S. persons with accounts in the principality. Instead of requiring specific names and account numbers as in the past, the change allowed responses based on descriptions of classes of U.S. taxpayers, in effect allowing "fishing expeditions" that Liechtenstein had guaranteed they would not permit.

Soon after the 2012 treaty change, the U.S. Department of Justice filed "Requests for Administrative Assistance in Tax Matters" with the Liechtenstein Tax Administration. The U.S. asked the Liechtenstein Landesbank to surrender documents dating back to January 2004 related to all accounts valued in excess of $500,000 held in the names of U.S. beneficial owners. The DOJ wanted to know whether "U.S. persons violated criminal laws of the United States by...not declaring their non-declared accounts to the IRS and failing to pay taxes on income gained on such accounts."

Banks now keep "know your customers" records of clients' identities, but these may not be made public except by judicial or official government order. Financial secrecy also extends to trustees, lawyers, accountants and to anyone connected to the banking industry. All involved are subject to the disciplinary powers of Liechtenstein's Upper Court. A court order or an officially approved request showing cause from a foreign government is required to release an account holder's bank records. Creditors seeking bank records face a time-consuming and costly process.

Big Bucks Banking

Liechtenstein's banks have no official minimum deposit requirements, but their stated goal is to lure high net-worth individuals as clients. Opening a discretionary portfolio management account generally requires a minimum of CHF 1 million (US$1.05 million). Trusts and limited companies registered here must pay an annual government fee of 0.1% of capital. Most banks also charge an annual management fee of 0.5% of total assets under their supervision. Bank, investment and professional fees here are at the top of the world scale.

If you're considering opening an offshore bank or investment account, Liechtenstein may be worth a comparative look if the level of your wealth permits it. The principality has benefits many other OFCs lack, including a strong economy, rock-solid (Swiss) currency, political stability and ease of access, plus a few added attractions of its own. The government guarantees all bank deposits against loss, regardless of the amount involved, even though there have been no recent bank failures.

In 2003, bowing to U.S. pressure, Liechtenstein signed a mutual legal assistance treaty (MLAT) with the United States covering a broad range of mutually recognized crimes. The treaty gave Liechtenstein the right to refuse to disclose information unless a request is authorized by a U.S. court order.

Rob Vrijhof, senior partner in a leading Swiss investment firm and a senior member of The Sovereign Society's Council of Experts, for years has done considerable business in Liechtenstein on behalf of international investors. He has witnessed a noticeable cleaning up of suspect practices, together with a new willingness to accommodate legitimate foreign banking and investment. He says, "I recommend Liechtenstein unreservedly—if you can afford it."

Foundation/Trust/Corporation Options

Liechtenstein is known worldwide among lawyers for its highly original and innovative legal entities created by statute, some of them copies of other countries' laws.

Liechtenstein law allows limited liability companies (LLCs), but does not provide for formation of international business corporations (IBCs) as they are known elsewhere. Over the years, the country's legislators have been highly inventive when it comes to unusual and useful legal entities fashioned to serve special financial needs.

Government regulation of the *Anstalt* (see below), foundations, companies and trusts is extremely strict. This is primarily accomplished through training and regulation of managers, not by prying into the internal affairs of the entity or its holdings. As a result, business management services available in Liechtenstein are excellent in terms of quality, if somewhat slow in execution.

The *Anstalt*

Liechtenstein is perhaps best known for the *Anstalt*, sometimes described in English as an "establishment" (the German word's closest English equivalent). The *Anstalt* is a legal entity unique to Liechtenstein and is something of a hybrid somewhere between the trust and the corporation with which Americans are familiar.

The *Anstalt* may or may not have member shares. Control usually rests solely with the founder, or with surviving members of his or her family. Both have the power to allocate the profits as they see fit. The law regulating *Anstalt* formation is extremely flexible, allowing nearly any kind of charter to be drafted. Depending on the desired result, *Anstalts* can take on any number of trust or corporation characteristics. They can be tailored to meet specific U.S. tax criteria, the basis for an IRS private letter ruling recognizing your Anstalt as either a trust or corporation.

Only limited information about those involved with an individual *Anstalt* or company appears on public records. The beneficial owners of a company do not appear by name in any register and their identity need not be disclosed to the Liechtenstein authorities. On the other hand, diligent inquisitors may discover members of the board of directors by searching the Commercial Register. At least one member of the board must reside in Liechtenstein. Unlike U.S. corporations, the shares of a Liechtenstein company do not have to disclose the names of shareholders.

The Family Foundation

Liechtenstein's concept of a "foundation" is unique. Although Americans associate a foundation with a non-profit, tax-exempt organization, in Liechtenstein a foundation is an autonomous fund consisting of assets endowed by its founder for a specific, non-commercial purpose. The purpose can be very broad in scope, including religious and charitable goals.

One of the more common uses is as a so-called "pure family foundation." These vehicles are dedicated to the financial management and personal welfare of one or more particular families as beneficiaries.

The foundation has no shareholders, partners, owners, or members — only beneficiaries. It can be either limited in time or perpetual. The foundation and a beneficiary's interest therein cannot be assigned, sold, or attached by personal creditors.

Only foundation assets are liable for its debts. If engaged in commercial activities, the foundation's activities must support noncommercial purposes, such as support of the family. Unless the foundation is active commercially, it can be created through an intermediary. The founder's name need not be made public. Foundations may be created by deed, under the terms of a will, or by a common agreement among family members.

A family foundation can sometimes be more useful than a trust, since it avoids many restrictive trust rules that limit control by the trust creator. On the issue of cost, a simple family foundation located here may cost US$30,000, while the same entity in Panama, where the law was copied in 1995, can cost as little as $15,000.

If you are interested in exploring the creation of a foundation, I recommend you obtain top quality tax and legal advice, both in your home country and in Liechtenstein.

Hybrid Trusts

You can use a Liechtenstein trust to control a family fortune, with the trust assets represented as shares in holding companies that control each of the relevant businesses that may be owned by the family. This legal strategy brings together various family holdings under one trust umbrella, which, in turn, serves as a legal conduit for wealth transfer to named heirs and beneficiaries.

Liechtenstein's trust laws are practical and interesting due to the country's unusual combination of civil law and common-law concepts.

In 1926, the Liechtenstein Diet adopted a statutory reproduction of the English-American trust system. They even allow trust grantors to choose governing law from any common law country. This places the Liechtenstein judiciary in the unique position of applying trust law from England, Bermuda, or Delaware (U.S.A.) when addressing a controversy regarding a particular trust instrument.

Even though it is a civil law nation, a trust located in Liechtenstein can be useful in lowering taxes, sheltering foreign income and safeguarding assets from American estate taxes. The law allows quick portability of trusts to another jurisdiction and accepts foreign trusts that wish to re-register as local entities. The trust instrument must be deposited with the Commercial Registry, but is not subject to public examination.

In 2009, revisions and updates of existing 70-year-old statutes by Parliament produced a new Foundation Act and amendments to the Law on Persons and Companies.

Taxes

In 2011, Liechtenstein adopted a first ever flat annual tax of 12.5% on the net earnings, including earnings from interest, of family foundations, trusts and corporations. The result of this new tax has been the re-domiciling of a number of Liechtenstein trusts, foundations and companies to Panama and other financial centers where no tax is imposed.

Low business taxes — the maximum tax rate is 20% — and easy incorporation rules have induced many holding or so-called letter box companies to establish nominal offices in Liechtenstein, providing 30% of state revenues.

The principality participates in a customs union with Switzerland and uses the Swiss franc as its national currency. It imports more than 90% of its energy requirements. Liechtenstein is a member of the European Economic Area, an organization that serves as a bridge between the European Free Trade Association and the EU.

Official Contacts

Liechtenstein Embassy

2900 K Street, NW, Washington, D.C. 20007
Tel.: (202) 331-0590 Fax: (202) 331-3221
Email: tamara.brunhart@was.rep.llv.li
Website: www.liechtensteinusa.org/
The U.S. has no Embassy in Liechtenstein; the U.S. Ambassador to Switzerland is accredited to Liechtenstein.

United States Embassy

Sulgeneckstrasse 19, CH-3007 Bern, Switzerland
Tel.: + (031) 357-7011, Fax: + (031) 357-7398
Email: bernacs@state.gov
Website: http://bern.usembassy.gov

U.S. Consular Agency Zurich

Dufourstrasse 101 3rd floor, Zurich, Switzerland
Mailing Address: Dufourstrasse 101
CH-8008 Zurich, Switzerland
Tel.: + (043) 499-2960, Fax: + (043) 499-2961
Email: Zurich-CA@state.gov

Recommended Attorneys & Trust Company

First Advisory Group

Aeulestrasse 74, Vaduz 9490, Liechtenstein
Tel.: + (423) 236-0404, Fax: + (423) 236-0405
Website: http://www.firstadvisory.li

Recommended US SEC-registered financial advisor:

Robert Vrijhof, Managing Partner
Weber, Hartmann, Vrijhof & Partners,
Schaffhauserstrasse 418, CH-8050 Zürich, Switzerland
Contact: Ms. Julia Fernandez *
Tel. 01141-44-315 77 77, Fax. 01141-44-315 77 78
Email: info@whvp.ch
Website: http://www.whvp.ch/index.htm
* Mr. Vrijhof and his staff can arrange Liechtenstein bank accounts for Sovereign Society members.

Available banks in Liechtenstein:

Bank Pasche (Liechtenstein) AG
Austrasse 61, 9490 Vaduz, Liechtenstein
Tel.: (+423) 239 33 33 Fax: (+423) 239 33 00
Swiss Clearing Number: 8814
Postal Account: 90-25494-7
Email: pasche.liechtenstein@pasche.li
Website: www.swissfirst.li

Neue Bank AG
Marktgass 20. Postfach 1533
9490 Vaduz Liechtenstein
Tel.: (+423) 236 08 08
Fax: (+423) 232 92 60
Swiss Clearing Number: 8802
Postal Account: 90-151

Panama

We recommend the Republic of Panama as one of the leading offshore financial centers. In an unusual intentional triple play among countries, Panama combines no taxes on offshore income, strong asset protection laws and quick residential programs that welcome foreigners.

Only hours by air from the United States, Panama offers a variety of lifestyles and geographic diversity with a century-long history of working with Americans. The real estate boom of a few years ago has cooled, but it has been replaced by an infrastructure boom spurred by the hyper-expansionist policies of current (2012) President Ricardo Martinelli.

A $5.2 billion modernization of the century-old Panama Canal, a long-thriving banking and offshore sector, plus capital flight driven by Venezuela's erratic, leftist Hugo Chavez, has helped provide Panama with the highest economic growth rate in all of Latin America. In 2011, growth hit 10.6%, an expansion that even outpaced China.

Alone among current offshore financial centers, Panama combines maximum financial privacy, a long history of judicial enforcement of asset protection-friendly laws, a strong anti-money laundering law, plus tax exemptions for foreigners. Thanks to its unique historic and often contentious relationship with the United States, it also exercises a high degree of independence from outside pressures, including those from Washington.

Factor	Findings	Rating
Government/ political stability	Although Panamanian politics remains volatile, it is now a stable democracy	3.5
Favorable laws, judicial system	Panama's modernized offshore laws date from the 1920s, but significant judicial corruption exists	3.5
Available legal entities	All major legal entities may be formed or are recognized under the legal system	5
Taxes	All residents and investors are exempt from taxes on all income earned outside Panama	5
Financial privacy/ banking secrecy	Strong, but TIEAs signed with US and other nations	5
Final Rating		22

Panama Revisited

To appreciate where Modern Panama stands today, historic perspective helps to understand the 50-year economic and political revolution that has occurred there.

In 1999, I returned to Panama for the first time in 20 years. Since then, I have visited many times.

Panama is a very different place than in the 1970s when I served in the U.S. House of Representatives as the ranking Republican on the Panama Canal Subcommittee. My visits then were made during U.S. legislative implementation of the Carter-Torrijos treaty negotiations, at a time when Panama was still little more than an American colony where widespread domestic poverty contrasted with the wealth of the U.S. government-run Panama Canal Zone.

A visitor to Panama City in 2012 finds a city in transition; roads torn up, excavators digging subway metro tunnels and huge cranes topping off more new high-rise condominiums, office towers, banks and hotels. The city's new *Cinta Costera* highway has also helped reduce downtown traffic bottlenecks.

On the south side of the Panama Canal, just across the Bridge of the Americas, the former Howard U.S. Air Force Base is being converted into a mixed-use residential, corporate and industrial park, called *Panama Pacifico*. Leading international firms, including Dell, 3M, Procter & Gamble and Caterpillar, are moving in. And another new shopping mall is going up, the fourth in recent years. Meanwhile, more than 10,000 new hotel rooms are under construction or in the planning stages.

Modern Panama has excellent digital Internet and other international communications. Downtown Panama City, the balmy, tropical capital on the southern, Pacific end of the Canal, suggests Los Angeles or Miami, except arguably more locals speak English here than in some parts of South Florida.

Panama City also offers first-class hotels and restaurants, including the inevitable Trump Tower. Night clubbing and fine dining can be local delights. For first time visitors, the Panama Canal is a must-see tour. For those who want to combine business with pleasure, there are multiple retirement and vacation retreats on the Pacific side, Bocas del Toro on the Atlantic side and the cooler, less humid Boquete in the western mountains on the Costa Rican border.

Image of Panama

When most people think of "Panama," they think—Panama Canal!

But the country is less well-known for what it has become in the last 50 years—second only to Miami, serving as Latin America's major international banking and business center, with strong ties to

Asia and Europe and a special relationship with the United States that, however contentious, serves both countries well.

Panama's historic change came at midnight, December 31, 1999, when 96 years of official United States presence in the Republic of Panama ended. Panama finally got what its nationalistic politicians had demanded for much of the last century—full Panamanian control over its famous inter-oceanic canal.

A New Era?

Indeed, in many respects—financial privacy, solid asset protection and freedom from outside political pressures—Panama has moved to the head of the OFC class.

There are historic reasons for Panama's enviable tax haven standing, including:

• A territorial tax system that taxes only earnings from within the country;

• Continuously modernized asset protection laws, dating from the 1920s;

• An array of useful legal entities (trusts, corporations, private foundations);

• A community of qualified offshore professionals and bankers;

• Some of the strongest financial privacy laws anywhere; and

• Considering its past history, a remarkable degree of political stability in a viable democratic system that works fairly well.

That stability was thought to be re-confirmed in 2009 with the election for a five-year term of supermarket tycoon Ricardo Martinelli as president. In an unheard-of landslide victory of more than 60%, Martinelli and his conservative coalition party bucked a trend of radical left-wing leadership in Central and South America.

The president pledged to bring foreign investors into tourism projects, cruise ports and airports, and direct more government spending to public infrastructure, such as a subway in Panama City, the capital.

He also promised much-needed fiscal discipline and an end to corruption, but it appears Martinelli has abandoned those pledges. New infrastructure is being built, but as deficits mount, fiscal discipline is in serious question, with cronyism and dictatorial actions under attack.

Indeed Nomura (http://www.nomura.com/), a major investment advisory newsletter in June 2012 had this warning: "We recommend zero exposure to Panamanian sovereign bonds. While this positioning might be relatively premature, we prefer to recommend it now in expectation of a sharp rise in fiscal spending for electoral reasons next year. For those that are currently involved in this credit, we think it may be opportune to begin executing an exit strategy." (The next elections are in May 2014.) Mary Ellen O'Grady, a respected conservative expert on Latin America affairs, writing in *The Wall Street Journal* (June 20, 2012) said there "...is a good reason to heed the warnings from a growing chorus of Panamanians that center-right President Ricardo Martinelli is moving the country toward authoritarianism."

"He is constructing public works but tearing down institutions," says Aurelio Barria, a Panamanian businessman and the leader of Civic Crusade, a nonpartisan movement famous for its democratic advocacy during the dictatorship of Gen. Manuel Noriega. As if to prove Mr. Barria's point, Mr. Martinelli went ahead with his plan to pack the Supreme Court by naming three new judges who will grow the bench to 12 from nine.

O'Grady added: "Even if, as critics contend, Mr. Martinelli is a power-hungry caudillo, some might be tempted to tolerate him because he is not left-wing. Importantly, he is not threatening property rights. But that ought to be little comfort. Once the institutional checks and balances that defend society against dangerous demagogues are destroyed, the door is open to candidates across the political spectrum. Just ask the Venezuelans."

Foreign Cash Welcome

The Martinelli administration has adopted an open-door policy for both foreign direct investment and skilled international professionals. The pro-growth policies are aimed at designated strategic sectors such as logistics, tourism, banking and Panama's role as a regional hub for multinational companies. New job creation has lowered unemployment down to 4.5% and economic growth up to 10.6% — the highest rate of growth in Latin America in 2011.

Panama is winning its struggle to emerge from the status as a "Third World" country where much of its population lived in poverty. It is in much better shape financially than its Central American neighbors to the north, or Colombia to the south. Although economic growth slowed for a time after the 2008 world recession, Panama still receives more than US$2 billion annually in direct foreign investments. Since the 1990s, inflation barely has exceeded 1% per year. Annual inflation has averaged 1.4% for the past 30 years, much lower than in the United States.

Then, there is the enormous wealth represented by the canal, generating over US$1 billion in annual revenues. While much of this income must be plowed back into maintenance, profits from the canal represent Panama's largest single source of income. And in a move that will increase the current flow of 14,000 annual ship transits, the Panama Canal is undergoing a complete modernization at an estimated cost of US$6 billion financed by the Canal and foreign investors.

The world famous waterway is getting wider locks that will accommodate the largest ships now afloat, such as oil supertankers.

The work, due for completion in 2014, the centenary year of the canal's opening, is providing a major boost to Panama's already thriving national economy.

The thousands of acres of land from former U.S. military installations, prized real estate with an estimated value of US$4 billion is being distributed and privatized. Development of this property already is bringing significant benefits to Panama.

Privacy, Profits and No Taxes

The Republic of Panama is ideally suited for the foreign offshore investor who wants to enjoy the increasingly rare privilege of guaranteed financial privacy and no taxes on offshore corporate or personal income.

According to the annual Economic Freedom of the World ratings that measure countries' economic freedom, co-published by the Cato Institute, the Fraser Institute in Canada and more than 70 think tanks around the world, Panama ranks 27th among over 200 countries.

Panama has adopted more than 40 laws protecting foreigners' financial and investment rights, including the Investments Stability Law (Law No. 54), that guarantees foreign and local investors equal rights. The country's central, world crossroads location makes it a natural base for global business operations. Importantly, Panama isn't directly under the political thumb of the United States. And unlike the British overseas territories of Bermuda and the Cayman Islands, London has no control here.

Among the 90 licensed banks in Panama, the major players are the 58 multinational banks representing 30 countries that primarily conduct offshore business. Panamanian banks held an official US$82.7 billion in total assets, with liquidity impressively high at an average 30% as required by law. The banks had virtually no exposure to the kinds of bad investments that undermined U.S., U.K. and other national banking systems. Banking accounts for about 11% of Panama's GNP. Nearly every one of the world's major banks has a full-service branch office in Panama, with representation from Japan, Germany, Brazil and the United States.

Financial Privacy

Panama also is one of the world's oldest offshore financial centers, with legislation recognizing foreign corporations with tax advantages dating back to the 1920s.

Central to this tax haven tradition has been statutory guarantees of financial privacy and confidentiality. Violators can suffer civil and criminal penalties for unauthorized disclosure. In the past, Panama pointedly refused to commit to exchanging information with tax authorities in other countries.

But in late 2010, the Martinelli administration signed a tax information agreement with the U.S. government—an act that prior Panama leaders had resisted for at least 20 years. It followed a Panama-Mexico TIEA and many more TIEAs other countries have followed since 2010.

Although critics claimed Panama had surrendered to the demands of Washington and the Organization for Economic and Community Development (OECD) in deciding to weaken its previously strict bank secrecy, others said it was an inevitable move, given the state of international financial and taxation policies.

Panama has a sensible "territorial tax system" that does not tax earnings outside its borders, so its tax collectors had no need to know what Panamanians or foreign nationals earn elsewhere in the world. All information under the U.S. treaty will flow one way, from Panama to the United States, negating benefits for foreigners from the country's financial privacy laws.

Speculation at the time said that the U.S. forced Panama to agree to the tax treaty in order for the Obama administration to submit a 2007 Bush free trade agreement (FTA) with Panama to the U.S. Senate, where it was opposed by U.S. labor unions.

In a meeting at the time I had with Frank DeLima, Panama's Minister of Economy and Finance, he defended the TIEA and told me: "I do not think that anyone in Panama who is obliged to comply with U.S. tax laws and who has done so has anything to worry about with this treaty and the way in which we will enforce it."

Asked if the TIEA was in fact a "one-sided deal" that benefited only the U.S., the Minister admitted that the IRS had more to gain since Panama's territorial tax system does not tax offshore earnings. He insisted that the increased world standing that Panama would achieve, together with the approval of the U.S.-Panama trade agreement, was worth abandoning strict bank secrecy.

"The only ones who should be disturbed are the law breakers," he insisted. He predicted no real economic harm to Panama from the TIEA. Events since then seem to support his estimate.

The Yankee Dollar

While "dollarization" has been debated as a novel concept elsewhere in Latin America, since 1904 the U.S. dollar has been Panama's official paper currency.

Panama has no central bank to print money. And as Juan Luis Moreno-Villalaz, former economic advisor to Panama's Ministry of Economy and Finance, noted, "In Panama... there has never been a systemic banking crisis; indeed, in several instances international banks have acted as the system's lender of last resort. The Panamanian system provides relatively low interest rates on mortgages and commercial loans. Credit is ample, with 30-year mortgages readily available. These are unusual conditions for a developing country and are largely achieved because there is no exchange rate risk, a low risk of financial crises and ample flow of funds from abroad."

I often have been asked whether Panama's use of the U.S. dollar as their currency means a declining dollar worldwide will hurt Panama's economy. The answer is that the health of Panama's economy depends on the same internal factors as any other nation, including unique GDP growth, employment and direct local and foreign investment, and not solely on its currency.

This separate and distinct economic existence has been demonstrated over decades as Panama has enjoyed very low inflation, while U.S. inflation at times soared to double digit levels. Should the dollar ever tank beyond repair, Panama can issue its own currency backed by its own strong domestic economic fundamentals.

Welcome Bankers

Panama grew as an international financial center after the enactment of Decree No. 238 of July 2, 1970, a liberal banking law that also abolished all currency controls. The law exempts offshore business in Panama from income tax and from taxes on interest earned in domestic savings accounts and offshore transactions.

Panama has adopted significant reforms in its banking system to minimize corruption and ensure that banking secrecy can be lifted in criminal investigations, especially when money laundering is alleged.

In 1999, a comprehensive new banking law was enacted that accelerated Panama's growth as a leading world offshore finance center. That law uses the guidelines of the Basle Committee on Banking Supervision, the international oversight group that sets banking standards, requiring all banks with unrestricted domestic or international commercial banking licenses to maintain currently (2012) capital equivalent to at least 30% of total assets. (In fact, Panama banks have far exceeded that minimal percentage requirement.)

Government investigative powers and tighter general controls bring Panama in line with regulatory standards found in European and North American banking centers. Under this law, a prima facie case of illicit financial conduct can launch an investigation of possible criminal conduct. The law also permits foreign bank regulators to make inspection visits to any of their domestic banks with branches in Panama.

Panamanian banks are very reluctant to open new accounts for Americans and other foreigners, unless the applicant has a home or an active business or investment in Panama. In most cases, foreigners need a personal introduction to a bank, and that can be obtained by arrangement with the professional contacts listed at the end of this section.

Panama's financial sector also includes an active, but fairly small, stock exchange, captive insurance and re-insurance companies and financial and leasing companies. Another major business and financial attraction at the Atlantic end of the canal is the booming Colón Free Zone (http://colonfreezone.com), a major tax-free transshipment facility, the second-largest free trade zone in the world, after Hong Kong, and currently (2012) scheduled for expansion.

IBCs and Foundations

Panama has liberal laws favoring trusts, international business companies and holding companies. Law No. 25 (1995), a private interest foundation statute as modeled after the popular Stiftung family wealth protection and estate planning vehicle long used in Liechtenstein.

Law 25 allows the tax-free family foundation to be used for investment, tax sheltering, ownership (but not management) of commercial businesses and private activity, with the founder retaining lifetime control. Foundation assets are not counted as part of the founder's estate for local death tax purposes and Panama does not recognize the often restrictive inheritance laws of other nations.

Some argue that the Panamanian private foundation law is only a clone of the Liechtenstein law. It is true that the Panamanian law is newer, but the costs of creating and operating a Panama foundation are far lower than in Liechtenstein where it can be as much as $30,000. For South American clients and others from civil law countries who are unfamiliar with the concept of an Anglo-American common law trust, a Panamanian private foundation often represents an ideal estate planning solution, even if just for the estate tax savings it may allow.

Panama's international business corporation (IBC) Law 32 (1927) was modeled after the U.S. state of Delaware's corporation-friendly statutes. There are about 350,000 IBCs registered in Panama, second only to Hong Kong's 400,000. A Panamanian IBC can maintain its own corporate bank account and credit cards for global management of investments, mutual funds, precious metals, real estate and trade. Non-Panama tax-free corporate income can be spent for business purposes worldwide and using the Panama IBC allows avoidance of home country zoning, labor, manufacturing, warranty, environmental and other restrictions.

Americans should consult a U.S. tax expert before forming a Panama IBC, since there can be some severe and costly U.S. tax consequences when using offshore corporations.

Leading Retirement Haven

Despite its relatively advanced industrial and financial infrastructure compared to other Latin nations, Panama remains an affordable place in which to live. A live-in maid earns about US$200 per month; first-run movies cost US$3.00. Unlike much of Central America, Panama boasts a first-class health care system with low costs compared to the United States—a doctor's office visit costs about US$45.

Because of Panama's geographical diversity, there is considerable variation in the climate. Panama City, the historical and financial center, has a year-round tropical climate, warm and humid. Yet, only a few hundred miles to the West near the Costa Rican border are sub-tropical forests, with cascading waterfalls, mountainsides covered with flowers and spring-like weather year-round. There are also many low-priced buys on condominiums and other real estate, particularly in Panama City and the surrounding areas, a byproduct of over-building during the now-slowed housing building boom.

There is a wide variety of programs in Panama for foreigners who wish to make a home there, the best known of these being the pensionado program. All resident visa applications must be made through a Panamanian attorney. There is no minimum or maximum age requirement, except that those less than 18 years old, the legal age of emancipation in Panama, will qualify as dependents of their parents. None of these visas automatically grants the right to work. Work permits must be applied for and obtained separately.

For many years the Republic of Panama deliberately has positioned itself as a first-class retirement haven, with some of the most appealing programs of special benefits for foreign residents and retirees anywhere in the world. In addition to the 2012 "Immediate Permanent Resident" visa, Panama also offers a variety of other visas for investors, persons of high net worth, wealthy retirees, small business and agricultural business investors and entrepreneurs, and those who simply want to immigrate and become Panamanian citizens.

The government makes retirement in Panama easy and laws provide important tax advantages for foreigners who wish to become residents. The only significant requirements are good health and a verifiable monthly income of at least US$500. There are no local taxes on foreign income and you can import your household goods tax-free.

Fast Track Residence

In a surprise policy move, in May 2012, President Martinelli signed an order that created a new category of "Immediate Permanent Resident" for foreign nationals.

Executive Order 343 created a new category for foreigners from what is now 24 listed countries "that maintain friendly, professional, economic, and investment relationships with the Republic of Panama." The list included the United States; the United Kingdom and South Korea were added later. A labor shortage, especially for skilled workers, was said to be a major reason for the new rules.

This new permit grants permanent residence immediately, unlike current investor visas that grant only temporary residence at first. There will be no need to renew the permit several times as current visas require.

In April 2012, when I met with the then Minister of the Presidency, Demetrio Papadimitriu, he emphasized Panama's need for thousands of better educated and trained workers. The Minister told me: "Martinelli's open-door policy seeks both foreign direct investment and skilled international professionals. We are looking for workers in growth sectors such as logistics, tourism, banking and those making Panama a regional hub for multinational companies." Prior to this rule, businesses were limited to hiring one foreigner for every nine Panamanian employees.

Under this new immediate immigration category, qualified applicants will be able to engage in professional and economic activities, establish businesses and have the right to work in Panama, permissions that in the past have been difficult to obtain. After five years they will be eligible to apply for full citizenship, as is the case with most of the country's visa programs.

The law grants immediate residence and a "cédula," the national identification card issued to all Panamanians, and will not only include qualified foreign individuals, but also dependent spouses, children under 18, family members with disabilities and dependent parents. Children aged 18 to 25 can be included if they are students.

In order to qualify for Immediate Permanent Resident status

the foreign applicant must submit one or more of the following: 1) proof of ownership of real estate in Panama; 2) an employment letter and work contract issued by a company registered in Panama; 3) evidence of ownership of a registered Panamanian corporation which has a valid business license.

Applications must be made to the National Immigration Service (NIS). Work permits are governed by Panamanian commercial and labor laws issued by the Ministry of Labor. Experience shows you will need to be represented by a qualified Panamanian attorney. Rainelda Mata-Kelly, JD, a leading Panama attorney and Sovereign Society associate, can assist applicants who qualify for this quick-residence category (see below).

Contacts

Embassy of Panama

2862 McGill Terrace, N.W., Washington, D.C. 20009
Tel.: (202) 483-1407
Consulates located in New York (212) 840-2450 or Philadelphia (215) 574-2994, Atlanta, Chicago, Houston, Los Angeles, Miami, New Orleans, and Tampa.
Website: www.embassyofpanama.org
Email: info@embassyofpanama.org

United States Embassy

Edificio 783, Avenida Demetrio Basilio Lakas, Clayton, Panama City, Panama
Tel.: +507-207-7000
Personal and official mail for the embassy and members of the mission may be sent to:
U.S. Embassy Panama, Unit 9100, DPO AA 34002
Email: Panamaweb@state.gov
Website: http://panama.usembassy.gov

Attorney

Rainelda Mata-Kelly, Esq.

Suite 406-407, Tower B, Torres de las Americas, Punta Pacifica
Panama City, Republic of Panama
Tel.: + 011 (507) 380-0606
Email: rmk@mata-kelly.com
Website: http://www.mata-kelly.com

Ms. Mata-Kelly specializes in administrative, commercial and maritime law and assists clients with immigration, real estate, contracts, incorporation, and other legal issues. She is a member of The Sovereign Society's Council of Experts.

Trust Company

Trust Services SA

Edificio Balboa Plaza, Oficina 522, Avenida Balboa
Panama, Republic of Panama
Mailing address: P.O. Box 0832 1630 World Trade Center
Panama, Republic of Panama
Tel.: +011 (507) 269 2438 / 263 5252
Email: marketing@trustserv.com
Website: http://www.trustserv.com

Licensed in Panama since 1981, this respected firm specializes in offshore corporations, trust and private foundation formation and maintenance. Derek Sambrook, a member of The Sovereign Society Council of Experts, is the Executive Director.

Uruguay

The Oriental Republic of Uruguay is one of the few remaining countries that still offer a sound banking system, welcomes Americans and their money, provides far greater financial privacy than the United States, as well as many attractive investment possibilities—and qualifies as a place where people seem genuinely happy. Spend a few days in Uruguay and you will be impressed by the friendly citizens, and soon you will realize that this is a place you might want to live.

Factor	Findings	Rating
Government/ political stability	Uruguay is a stable democracy with right of center politics	5
Favorable laws, judicial system	Modern offshore laws available with a clean judicial system and very little corruption	4
Available legal entities	All major legal entities may be formed or are recognized under the legal system	5
Taxes	All residents and investors are exempt from most taxes on income earned offshore	5
Financial privacy/ banking secrecy	Strong but honors TIEAs with other nations; it does not have a TIEA with the United States or Canada	5
Final Rating		24

Uruguay has escaped the rigid class society ("us vs. them") attitude that exists in most of South America. There are very few native groups that are targets of discrimination in other Latin America counties and there are no ethnically defined boundaries. An estimated 88% of the people here are of European descent, principally Italian and Spanish. Other immigrant groups include Portuguese, Armenians, Basque, Germans, and Irish, making the country somewhat like the ethnic melting pot the U.S. once was.

High Rankings and Happiness

The official name of the country is the Oriental Republic of Uruguay. "Oriental" in this case means "eastern" because all of Uruguay's territory (about the size of the American State of Washington) lies east of both the Uruguay River, separating it from Paraguay, and the huge, 137-miles wide estuary of the Río de la Plata, that meets the Atlantic here and forms the boundary with Argentina.

Uruguay had the 25th highest quality of life index in the world in 2012, and ranked first in quality of life/human development in Latin America. *The Economist* ranked it 17th out of 167 countries on the 2011 Democracy Index. *Reader's Digest* ranked Uruguay as the 9th "most livable and greenest" country in the world and first in all the Americas.

According to Transparency International, in 2011, out of 182 countries, Uruguay ranks 25th and is the second-least corrupt country in Latin America, behind Chile. It was the highest rated country in Latin America (and 26th in the world) on the Legatum 2011 Prosperity Index, based on factors that help drive economic growth and create happy citizens.

Besides all of these accolades, Uruguay has much more to make it what might be the best offshore residence for you. For one, it is still a tax haven…and in that sense Uruguay has now definitely earned its long-time nickname—the "Switzerland of Latin America," in the best sense of that title.

Investor-Friendly Country

Uruguay's economy is characterized by an export-oriented agricultural sector, a well-educated work force, and high levels of social spending. Political and labor conditions are among the freest in Latin America.

Foreign and local investors are treated equally under the law, there are no limitations on business ownership by foreigners and no currency exchange controls or forced currency conversion. Foreign currencies are used freely including dollars and Euros. There are no restrictions or taxes on transferring money into or out of the country. Most bank accounts are denominated in U.S. dollars, which are also used for pricing and in real estate and major business deals.

The Uruguayan economy is ideal for foreign expatriates even if they are retired. That is there are low levels of poverty, a relatively high standard of living and a large middle class. It has one of most equitable income distributions in Latin America. The result is lower crime rates and a very livable society. And if you do want to invest actively, start a company, or do business, Uruguay offers a very good environment.

If you had packed up and moved to Uruguay a decade ago you would have missed a lot—including the U.S. housing bubble and the property market crash—even as property values in Uruguay appreciated substantially, some even dramatically.

You also would have missed the world recession -- which mercifully passed Uruguay by, the only Latin American country that escaped unscathed.

Strong, Growing Economy

Unlike the faltering economic powerhouses of the America's, U.S., Brazil, Mexico, and Argentina, the Uruguayan economy expanded during the global recession. In 2011, Uruguay's gross domestic product (GDP) was $52.02 billion and the per capita GDP was $15,400, the highest in South America.

Uruguay is also South America's leader in direct foreign investment per capita, US$1.8 billion in 2011 for a total of over $10 billion DFI. Uruguay provides the perfect environment to invest or do business. An export-oriented agricultural sector, a well-educated workforce, and high levels of social spending define its strong economy. In 2009, Uruguay became the first nation in the world to provide every school child with a free laptop and wireless Internet access.

Uruguay is not a country where you should look for a cheap retirement. Its first world living standards come with first world prices. If you plan to be in Uruguay for a few months every year, the beauty and stability of the place make this requirement easy to meet, and one should consider investing in local property. Foreigners are not required be residents of the country in order to own real estate or to establish a corporation or to do business in Uruguay.

For this first-time visitor Montevideo, an attractive, modern capital city, among the safest in the World, impresses with its relatively clean, charming mix of old and new architecture, winding streets, busy people and leisurely traffic. The skyline is punctuated by a relatively few skyscrapers, and it has charming small shops, museums, and a lively *Ciudad Vieja* (Old City). There is much to be said for this city of 1.3 million souls—about half of Uruguay's total population.

South America's premier beach resort is here, the world famous Punta del Este, a town with miles of sandy beaches and blue Atlantic Ocean waters, along with the country's hottest nightclubs, the best casinos and shows, and the highest concentration of fine restaurants, not to mention its world-renowned property market.

And one other very important point: Uruguay offers not only financial, but also physical security—you feel and are safe walking the streets and byways in Montevideo, Punta del Este or anywhere else in this unusual country.

Investing

Among the many profitable investment opportunities offshore

real estate is a leader. Many foreigners purchase second or vacation homes that can return strong rental income when not in personal use. One of the easiest ways to invest directly for profit is farmland ownership, a safe, turnkey investment, easy to operate with appreciation potential and good returns.

Principal crops include soybeans, wheat, rice, cattle and sheep ranches and dairy farms. Forestry includes growing eucalyptus and pine and there are many vineyards, olive groves and fruit orchards. Foreign investors may farm the land directly or have a farm management company handle all aspects of operation. There is also an active market for cropland rental.

Banking

Sixty-one years ago, in the wake of World War II, Uruguay was described as the "Switzerland of the Americas" in a 1951 *New York Times* article. It earned that name because of its popularity as a haven for capital and precious metals fleeing Europe at the time, and for its adoption of Swiss-inspired banking laws and customs.

Uruguay's banking system is solid, appealing to investors and depositors from around the world who seek a safe haven that also offers tax advantages. Since January 1, 2008, almost 400 banks have failed in the U.S. Meanwhile, Uruguay's banks have operated without problems.

Unlike too many offshore banks in other parts of the world, many banks in Uruguay welcome American clients. Cities with main banking options available include Montevideo, Punta del Este and Colonia. Most of these banks offer e-banking.

Uruguay's financial reputation has made it an important regional financial center for the entire southern continent. There are 11 private banks, plus the government central bank, *Banco de la República* (BROU) that strictly supervises all the banks. BROU has a general policy against authorizing new banks.

The 11 private banks are totally or partially owned by leading American or European financial institutions. Banco Itau and Lloyds TSB in Montevideo usually will accept non-resident American clients in their retail banking branches. In addition, attesting to its regional banking role, there are over 30 representative offices of foreign banks.

Financial Privacy Guaranteed by Law

Unlike the United States, where the PATRIOT Act has destroyed financial privacy, Uruguay protection is based on a bank secrecy statute (Law #15,322, 1982) that forbids banks to share information with anyone; that includes the government of Uruguay and foreign governments.

The only exceptions are allowed in cases involving issues of alimony, child support, or alleged crimes, including foreign tax evasion and fraud; even then information can be shared only after obtaining a local court order.

The country does not exchange automatically tax or bank account information with the U.S. or Canada or any government. Uruguay does comply with Article 26 of the Organization for Economic and Community Development's (OECD) model standards for tax information exchange requests. That is, banks may exchange information upon proof of foreign tax evasion or tax fraud.

Uruguay limits such exchanges to countries with which it has signed tax information exchange agreements (TIEAs), specifically excluding both neighboring Brazil and Argentina. The Uruguayan government now has TIEAs with Germany, Mexico, Portugal, Spain, France, Korea, Finland, Malta, Switzerland, Liechtenstein, India, Belgium, Hungary, Malaysia, Chile and Luxembourg. It does not have a TIEA with either the United States or Canada.

One-third of all banks accounts in Uruguay are held by foreigners, including many thousands of Brazilians and Argentineans. The vast majority of accounts are denominated in U.S. dollars, which is also used for pricing and in real estate and major business deals. The local *Uy peso* and the euro are also available.

There are no exchange controls or capital restrictions and unlike neighboring Argentina, Uruguay has no political need for, and no history of, forced conversion of currencies or of freezing or confiscation of deposits. The government guarantees bank insurance on deposits only to a maximum of US$2,500 but bank failure is unknown here in recent years.

Bank financing is available to foreign residents, with proof of income. A first or second mortgage on U.S. property is often accepted to finance local bank loans. A bonus is the country's interest rates, which are around 7.5%. Banks offer up to 4.5% on various types of accounts. That means your money may earn 18 times more than it does sitting in a U.S. bank account where minimum interest is about 0.25%.

Still a Tax Haven

In keeping with current international "political correctness" Uruguay's government does not want the country labeled as a "tax haven." Nevertheless, Uruguay is, in fact, an offshore tax haven that imposes very few taxes on foreign residents living here.

Uruguay's has a territorial tax system; personal income tax only applies to Uruguayan-source income, including rental income of properties in Uruguay. There is a flat tax of 12% on interest and dividend income from abroad, which may apply to both Uruguayan citizens and foreign residents living in Uruguay. However, resident foreigners are credited with any income tax paid to other countries. Otherwise, income from abroad is not taxed, even if the foreign-source money is received by a bank in Uruguay.

However, if a resident foreigner already pays tax on income in another country, which Americans must do, Uruguay does not impose double taxation and credit is given on taxes already paid to the IRS or to other national tax collectors.

Free Trade Zones

Uruguay has several free trade zones in the country where foreign companies operate free of corporate and import taxes. In our recent tour, we visited Uruguay's main free zone, Zonamerica, near Montevideo's international airport. It is an impressive, privately owned modern commercial home to 7,000 workers including many global companies, such as Sabre, RCI, Tata, Merk, with extensive global and regional offices.

These areas are used for imported product storage, assembly and distribution for introduction into Uruguay or for export to other regional countries. These zones also are home to financial services, such as Merrill Lynch, KPMG, Deloitte, as well as many other types of services, all tax free.

Quick, Easy Residence

The immigration law of Uruguay states that residence is granted to those "who show intent to reside in Uruguay." That intent is evidence in the first instance by coming to the country and establishing a new home there.

Uruguay has a foreigner-friendly, open immigration policy, although, as with any official bureaucracy, it takes time—usually 12 to 18 months on average to obtain permanent resident status after coming to the country and applying. After 3 to 5 years, one can apply for citizenship and a passport.

Most foreigners enter Uruguay as a tourist for 90 days (extendable for another 90 days), find a living place and later a permanent home. Official residence status is not required to own real estate. Once you file for residence status with the National Migration Office you receive a temporary identity card, the cédula de identidad.

From that time forward you are considered a temporary "resident in process" and can stay in Uruguay indefinitely.

When permanent residence is granted you receive a new *cédula* that enables you to travel within the Mercosur countries, Argentina, Paraguay and Uruguay (except Brazil) without using your U.S. or other national passport.

The government requires that a temporary resident working towards citizenship must log a significant amount of physical presence time within Uruguay, at least six months during each year.

Citizenship

The law in Uruguay, as in the United States, allows its citizens to hold dual or multiple citizenships. New citizens are not required to surrender their home country passport and no notice is sent to the home country government.

While all this appears to be complicated, professional assistance will handle all these matters making certain you meet the legal requirements. We recommend Fischer & Schickendantz, a full service law firm that specializes in immigration law.

Juan Federico Fischer, Esq.
Fischer & Schickendantz
Rincón 487, Piso 4
Montevideo 11000, Uruguay
Tel.: + (598) 2 915-7468, ext. 130
Email: jfischer@fs.com.uy
Website: www.fs.com.uy

Contacts

Embassy of Uruguay
1913 I (Eye) Street, NW, Washington, D.C. 20006

Tel.: (202) 331-1313 / Fax: (202) 331-8142
Email: uruwashi@uruwashi.org
Website: http://www.uruwashi.org
Uruguayan Consulates: Chicago, Miami, Los Angeles, New York, and San Juan, Puerto Rico.

United States Embassy
Lauro Muller 1776, Montevideo 11200
Uruguay Mailing Address: UNIT 4500, APO AA 3403
Tel.: + (598) 2-418-7777 Fax: + (598) 2-410-0022
Website: http://montevideo.usembassy.gov

Hong Kong

Special Administrative Region of the People's Republic of China

Hong Kong remains one of the freest economies in the world, as well as a major offshore financial center with strong common law-based laws governing banking and finance, even though it is controlled, ultimately, by a Communist Party government in Beijing.

In the 2011 *Economic Freedom of the World Index*, published by the libertarian Cato Institute, among all other places in the world, Hong Kong retains the highest rating for economic freedom at 9.01 out of a possible 10 — a rating it has held for several years.

Beijing's Communists began their control in 1997 with the end of British colonial rule. The Communists have imposed restrictions, but on balance, the economy of semi-democratic Hong Kong remains remarkably free, a reflection of Beijing's need for this historic city-state as a financial conduit for China's business with the world.

Proof of this continued freedom again came in September 2012 with massive street demonstrations against a Beijing-backed plan for "moral and national education" that opponents said amounted to brainwashing and political indoctrination. A very large crowd, estimated at 120,000 by organizers besieged his headquarters and caused Hong Kong's chief executive, Leung Chun-ying, to back down and revoke a 2015 deadline for every school to start teaching the subjects.

The protests in Hong Kong were similar to the much larger Tiananmen Square protests in Beijing in 1989: for months large numbers of Hong Kong students had gathered in front of government buildings, staging sit-ins and hunger strikes.

Also like the Tiananmen Square protesters, the Hong Kong students were protesting corruption, a widespread perception that government officials have become too close to the city's business tycoons by accepting yacht trips while in office and discounted apartments and highly paid jobs after retirement. The Hong Kong protesters even put up a "goddess of democracy" statue that resembled the Statue of Liberty, much like that used by students during the Tiananmen Square demonstrations that were violently suppressed by the Communist controlled military.

Although the students were not satisfied with Leung's announcement, it represented a concession that could be seen as weakness by the Beijing officials who appointed him after his rigged selection by a committee of 1,200 prominent Hong Kong residents that included many handpicked Beijing allies.

The proposed national education curriculum, Beijing's version of contemporary Chinese history with a heavy dose of nationalism and favorable to the Communist Party's role, was originally to start with the academic year that began in early September, but few schools had begun teaching the subject.

In the September 2012 elections for the HK governing council, the back down by HK chief executive, Leung Chun-ying, on the indoctrination courses probably saved pro-Beijing candidates from a disastrous showing, but the controversy still helped pro-democracy candidates win 27 out of 70 seats in the legislature.

They wanted more but the complicated electoral system is rigged against pro-democracy candidates. They did get almost 60% of the popular vote, up from 57% in 2008, and won 39% of the seats. Most importantly, they have enough votes to block any plans from Beijing to curtail civil liberties. Many of the new lawmakers are more radically anti-Beijing than their predecessors.

Leading World Financial Center

By almost any measure, Hong Kong is one of the world's leading financial and economic powerhouses. In total cash and assets, it is the world's third wealthiest financial center, after New York and London. It has a very strong banking, business and investment infrastructure that rivals any place in the world.

Although it offers no natural resources with the notable exception of a world-renown deep-water port, Hong Kong is considered a world-class city. It also boasts a highly educated population of more than 7 million and is highly regarded for its productivity and creativity. There is a Chinese phrase that describes Hong Kong well, *Zhong Si He Bing*, literally meaning "combination of East and West."

Factor	Findings	Rating
Government/ political stability	Political freedom somewhat diminished but limited autonomy and free market economics are the rule	3.5
Favorable laws, judicial system	Rule of law respected but courts susceptible to pressure from Beijing	3.5
Available legal entities	All major legal entities can be formed and are recognized	5
Taxes	Foreign investors based here can avoid local taxes and corporate taxes relatively low	3.5
Financial privacy/ banking secrecy	Traditional financial secrecy strong, but no specific statutory guarantee	4
Final Rating		19.5

Gateway to China

If you're doing business in China (or anywhere in Asia) you

should consider Hong Kong as your base of operations. It's a place where you can obtain financing, do your banking, create the corporate or trust entities you may need to succeed in a very tough market—especially in China.

But keep in mind that Hong Kong has a major competitor for the role of leading Asian OFC236—Singapore. And both of these well-developed financial centers are competing against a growing mainland Chinese rival in Shanghai.

There is no question that China is an attractive market and Hong Kong is the gateway to the mainland.

The huge mass of 1.3 billion people in China are experiencing some of the most rapid, although highly uneven, economic growth in recent world history. For some, living standards have improved dramatically, yet political controls remain tight.

In addition to better living conditions, following restructuring of the economy, China boasted impressive results and efficiency that produced a tenfold increase in GDP since 1978. With a 2011 GDP of more than $11 trillion, this allowed China to become the second-largest economy in the world after the U.S. The dollar values of China's agricultural and industrial output each exceed those of the U.S. China is second to the U.S. in the value of services it produces. Still, per capita income is below the world average. In 2011, the per-capita GDP was only US$8,400.

But with only a rudimentary, struggling financial system consisting of banks, stock markets and financial exchanges controlled by the Communist government and the military, the Chinese domestic economy still lacks the experience and controls Western nations take for granted. Indeed, many of the existing financial institutions in China are loaded with billions in non-performing, politically allocated loans, thousands of shaky investments, permeated with official corruption.

To add to this certainty at present there is no "rule of law" or reliable judicial system in China, in the sense the Western world understands such basic safeguards. This means doing business in China lacks the legal protection foreign investors take for granted elsewhere.

This mainland financial situation has served to accentuate and expand the role that Hong Kong has played with great success since the Communist revolution took control of China in 1949 — that of China's financial window and conduit to the rest of world.

Hong Kong is situated ideally — legally part of, but also different and somewhat apart from, China. In Hong Kong, you can find what struggling mainland China sorely lacks — the legal, financial and investment expertise and experience that can provide you with a sensible approach to investing and doing business in China.

And that's where the profits will be — if you are prudent and careful in your approach. If you want to deal in China, unless you have longstanding family or business ties there, you are best served working with a Hong Kong-based partner who has firsthand knowledge of the Chinese market. The mainland has long been Hong Kong's largest trading partner, accounting for about half of Hong Kong's exports by value.

Hong Kong is a very easy place in which to reside and do business. It has easy access to China by train or ferry. If you become a Hong Kong resident, you can get a six-month, multiple-entry visa to China with little difficulty. From one of the most modern airports in the world there are multiple flights daily to all major centers in China, as well as in the U.S., Europe, the Middle East, Africa and Asia.

Hong Kong is proof that "money talks." China has too much invested in Hong Kong to destroy it all because of rigid political ideology. Today, 30% of Hong Kong's bank deposits are Chinese. China accounts for 22% of all Hong Kong foreign trade (including cross-border trade), 20% of the insurance business and over 12% of all construction. Hong Kong has also established itself as the premier stock market for Chinese firms seeking to list abroad.

In 2011, companies from mainland China accounted for approximately 43% of firms listed on the Hong Kong Stock Exchange, but was credited with 56% of the exchange market's capitalization. Hong Kong serves as the Chinese banker, investment broker and go-between in what is now a multi-billion annual trade flow. In the past 20 years, some US$300 billion of direct foreign investment has flooded into China—60% of which came from, or through, Hong Kong.

Since 1997 when China took over control from Britain, Hong Kong thrived under the Beijing promise of "one country, two systems" approach. The socialist economic policies of the mainland are not imposed on Hong Kong. Rather, Hong Kong has maintained its reputation for civil liberties, free press, a relatively independent judiciary and a usually reasonable system of government. Despite their fears regarding Hong Kong democracy, the leaders of the People's Republic of China seem to realize that they have an enormous stake in Hong Kong's economic health. They want Hong Kong to keep going, but on Beijing's terms.

As I found on my visits there, democracy advocates and civil libertarians in Hong Kong are continuously anxious about whether laissez-faire Hong Kong can maintain its independence from Beijing's authoritarian grip and keep its distinct identity as an amalgam of Western and Chinese sensibilities.

Beijing repeatedly has postponed promised direct elections for the chief executive and for the full legislature. Its critics say China is wielding an increasingly heavy hand in Hong Kong's affairs. Public mistrust of the Communist government in Beijing reached an all-time high, including during a visit in July 2012 by Chinese President Hu Jintao. More than 400,000 people marched in a protest against both Hu and the local Hong Kong government, one of the largest demonstrations ever in the city.

Fifteen years after the handover to Beijing no doubt the protest was inspired by Hong Kong's many challenges—political corruption, property prices at highest levels since 1997; the gap between rich and poor already the worst in Asia, the greatest in 40 years; air pollution continued to worsen; and there was no clear path to a system to allow the public to directly elect leaders as they repeatedly were promised. But the many street protests over the last 15 years have not affected Hong Kong's world business standing.

Prosperity, Low Taxes

In a strange twist of world economic fate, the clampdown by the European Union and the OECD on tax havens in the West created a benefit for far-removed offshore financial centers, such as Hong Kong and Singapore. Two factors caused wealthy people from the Middle East to shift cash towards Asia and away from Europe and the United States; first, the September 11, 2001 terror attacks in the U.S. and second, as a response to EU and U.S. tax evasion investigations and more stringent bank and financial reporting rules.

When much of the world was mired in a major recession beginning in 2008, Asian banks, many based In Hong Kong, were sitting on more than US$2 trillion of reserves. Funds had been continuously pouring money into emerging markets and Hong Kong has been a major beneficiary of this global trend. No leading Asian banks were caught in bank near-collapses so no bailouts were needed.

Economists attribute the strong Hong Kong economy to a series of factors: tight limits on senior citizen and other spending, no military spending and an economy that grew 5% last year, but mostly because Hong Kong has cashed in on China's economic boom.

Hong Kong weathered the world recession in good shape and its renewed prosperity is reflected in the government's tax receipts and cash on hand for the fiscal year that ended March 31, 2012. The budget surplus in cash reserves of HK$662 billion (US$85.3 billion) amounted to 3.5% of a 2011 GDP of US$350.4 billion, or 22 months' worth of expenditures. The government had US$12,150 in extra cash for every man, woman and child in the territory, and they rebated $6,000 to each citizen. The 2011 per capita GDP was $49,300. That impressive GDP figure is higher than that enjoyed by the citizens of Germany, Japan, the United Kingdom, Canada or Australia.

Hong Kong's total population of 7.1 million includes a workforce of 3.75 million. The unemployment rate was 3.2% in May 2012. Mainland Chinese real estate buyers have driven up housing prices as they seek political stability and, sometimes, safety from mainland tax collectors and fraud investigators. Rising apartment prices have pushed up government revenue from taxes on real estate transactions and from the sale of government land for further construction projects.

Retail sales surged 23% through November 2011, mostly because nearly 100,000 mainland visitors a day come to Hong Kong. Most of them head straight for the stores.

Tax breaks and allowances are so generous that only about 1.5 million people pay income tax. A single person starts paying income tax at HK$108,000 a year (US$14,000) and above. A married person with a dependent spouse can earn HK$216,000 (US$28,000) tax-free. The maximum income tax rate is 17% and most pay less. There are no sales or no capital gains taxes, no VAT and no tax on dividend income.

By comparison in mainland China, the top tax rate for high-income earners is 45%, though corporate taxes there are relatively low. Hong Kong's attraction also has been as a place to avoid the 17% value-added tax in mainland China, plus steep import and consumption taxes that can add another 10 to 50% to the price tags there. The tax savings on a single Louis Vuitton bag can cover round-trip airfare from practically any city in China to Hong Kong.

Business, Banking

It is relatively easy and quick to register a company and/or open bank accounts, although a local address is needed for either. This is simple to arrange with the help of any of the many businesses offering real or virtual offices for rent. However, most local banks reject accounts held directly in the name of American clients, although they may consider them if opened by a U.S.-person-owned trust, LLC or IBC.

Hong Kong maintains a three-tier system of deposit-taking institutions, namely licensed banks, restricted licensed banks and deposit-taking companies collectively known as authorized institutions. The territory has one of the highest concentrations of banking institutions in the world. More than 70 of the 100 largest world banks have an operation in Hong Kong.

The Hong Kong Monetary Authority actively supports policies for the maintenance and the development of the status of city-state as an international financial center and maintenance of the stability and integrity of the financial system

Hong Kong is the world's 9th largest banking center, 6th largest foreign exchange center, 11th largest trading economy, busiest container port and is Asia's second-biggest stock market. With low taxes and a usually trustworthy legal system, international banking and business flows in and out, assure of stability and a high degree of financial privacy.

Hong Kong is regarded by foreign firms as a highly advantageous regional location from which to do business. Almost 80% of foreign firms based in Hong Kong surveyed said they felt that it was the best location for them, due to advanced telecommunications networks, a free trade environment, low taxes and effective regulation. On an industry basis, according to the survey results, the financial services sector was the most positive overall.

Hong Kong's status as one of the world's top trading centers for stocks, bonds, commodities, metals, futures, currencies and personal and business financial operations long has meant that such transactions could be conducted there with a high degree of sophistication.

Business Tax

A major attraction for offshore business is Hong Kong's relatively low 17.5% business tax rate. Hong Kong has a territorial tax system that applies to "territoriality of profits." If profits originate in or are derived from Hong Kong, then they are subject to local tax.

Otherwise, they are tax-free, regardless of whether the company is incorporated or registered there. Interestingly, IBCs and all other foreign corporations generally may open a Hong Kong bank account without prior registration under the local business statute. This can save charges for auditing and annual report filing and removes the annoyance of having to argue with the Inland Revenue Department about the territoriality of the business.

On the other hand, one must be careful not to transact any taxable local business, because doing that without local registration is against the law. In cases where local business does occur, tax authorities generally are lenient, usually requiring local registration and payment of unpaid tax. But in some cases, IBCs have been forced to register as a listed public company at considerable expense.

Corporations

There are more companies—over 500,000—registered in Hong Kong than anywhere else in the world. (Here, they are called "private limited companies" and are identified with a "Ltd.," not an "Inc.") It is also home to the largest community of multinational firms in Asia. This is due, first, to the territory's colonial roots, which have for the past 150 years made it the natural hub in Asia for British companies and, second, to its consistent and longstanding reputation for openness, simplicity of operation and institutional familiarity.

In Hong Kong, there is no specific legal recognition of an international business company (IBC) per se, as there are in some offshore financial havens. The law recognizes only the one corporate "Ltd." form. Companies must have a minimum of one director and two shareholders. Shareholders or directors do not have to be residents of Hong Kong and they can be individual persons or corporations. Company incorporation does require a registered office in Hong Kong and a Hong Kong resident individual or Hong Kong corporation to act as the secretary. Hong Kong companies must be audited each year.

Hong Kong offshore companies require by law a local resident company secretary, who usually charges about US$500 per year for filing a few documents with the Company Registry. Annual auditing by a CPA starts from about US$500 for companies with few transactions and can easily reach ten times as much for a mid-size operational offshore trading company. (See the Contacts section for our recommended local service professionals.)

Financial Privacy

Until recently, Hong Kong's laws did not permit bank regulators to give information about an individual customer's affairs to foreign government authorities, except in cases involving fraud. Hong Kong never has had specific a banking secrecy laws as have many other OFCs such as Switzerland, Panama or Austria.

As a matter of local custom, rooted in British common law, Hong Kong banks always request a judicial warrant before disclosing records to any foreign government. Access is much easier for the HK local government. In 2010, Hong Kong changed its rules for exchanging tax information under income tax treaties. This allowed Hong Kong to adopt the latest OECD international standards and, in turn, to expand its network of income tax treaties from five treaties to 24, with an additional four treaties awaiting formal signature in 2012. Hong Kong's willingness to embrace greater transparency, after years of resistance, underscored their fear of being tarred as "bei sui tin tong" or "tax evasion havens," as tax havens are known in Cantonese.

Hong Kong also has a mutual legal assistance treaty MLAT with the United States. Anti-money laundering laws and "know-your-customer" rules have made the opening of bank accounts for IBCs more difficult, but no more so than other countries these days. Account applicants must declare to the bank the "true beneficial owner" of an IBC or a trust with supporting documentation. Proof must be shown for all corporate directors and shareholders of the registering entity and any other entities that share in the ownership.

Basics

If you intend to pursue business investments in Asia, keep in mind lessons other foreigners have learned the hard way. Pick your Asian business partners (and business investments) carefully, avoiding the inefficient mainland Chinese state-owned enterprises. Stick with solid basics like marketing, distribution and service. Be sure to carefully guard technology from theft.

And remember, a series of small ventures gets less government attention and red tape than big showcase projects that often produce demands for graft. Many foreign business investors have been burned by crooked bookkeeping, few shareholder controls, sudden government rule changes and systemic corruption.

Only recently as China's economy became more westernized did Beijing finally begin to address the need for laws guaranteeing the right for citizens and foreigners to own and transfer private property.

Most importantly, keep a sharp eye not on the Chinese government hype, but on what's really happening in China. Uncertainty means that offshore financial activities by foreign citizens can prosper, but without immediate assurance of success. Unless the "New China" is definitely your sphere of intended business activity, you may want to look elsewhere for your Asian financial base of operations in places such as Singapore or Malaysia.

On the Web:

Hong Kong Immigration: http://www.immd.gov.hk/ehtml/home.htm

Hong Kong Monetary Authority: www.hkma.gov.hk

Hong Kong Trade Development Council: http://www.tdc.org.hk

Official Contacts

Hong Kong Economic and Trade Offices

1520-18th Street, N.W., Washington, D.C. 20036
Tel.: (202) 331-8947 Fax: (202) 331-8958
Email: hketo@hketowashington.gov.hk
Website: http://www.hketowashington.gov.hk/dc/index.htm

(2) 115 East 54th Street, New York, NY 10022
Tel.: (212) 752-3320 Fax: (212) 752-3395
Website: http://www.hketony.gov.hk/ny/index.htm

(3) 130 Montgomery Street, San Francisco, CA 94104
Tel.: (415) 835-9300 Fax: (415) 421-0646
Website: http://www.hketosf.gov.hk/sf/index.htm

United States Consulate General

26 Garden Road, Hong Kong
Tel.: + (852) 2523-9011; Consular: + (852) 2147-5790
Fax: + (852) 2845-1598
Email for American Citizen Services: acshk@state.gov
Email: information_resource_center_hk@yahoo.com
(For visa inquiries, please use the Visa Inquiry Form)
Website: http://hongkong.usconsulate.gov/

Immigration & Residence Services:
Henley & Partners Hong Kong Ltd.
33rd Floor, Office Tower
Convention Plaza, 1 Harbor Road
Wanchai, Hong Kong
Tel.: + 852 3101 4100 Fax: +52 3101 4101
Website: www.henleyglobal.com/hongkong

Singapore

Singapore has become a major international financial center—but it's not exactly an offshore tax haven. It has traded its ancient Oriental image for towers of concrete and glass and rickshaws have been replaced by high-tech industry. Singapore appears shockingly modern, but this is an Asian city with Chinese, Malay and Indian traditions from feng shui to ancestor worship as part of daily life. These contrasts bring the city to life, but foreigners may want to avoid talking about local politics.

The Republic of Singapore (population 5.4 million) has the distinction of being a small island, a state and a city—all in one. Located just a few steamy miles north of the Equator, it has Malaysia and Indonesia as close and sometimes uneasy neighbors. The climate is hot and very humid, with rainfall of over two meters (about seven feet) annually.

Colonial Singapore gained its independence from Great Britain in 1965. Lee Kuan Yew became its autocratic leader and served until 1990, when his son, now in office, replaced him in his official capacities. The father remains the power behind his son's throne and his one-party state still does not tolerate dissent or opposition. There are no jury trials. Civil matters, such as alleged libel or slander, can escalate into criminal issues with serious consequences, especially for political opponents.

Draconian laws keep crime (and freedom) to a minimum, but the enforced stability attracts massive foreign investment. Moreover, as I can attest, the streets are very clean, since spitting or littering can land you in jail. Clean streets are a tradeoff for individual political freedom. And as local election results suggest, opposition to such restrictions is increasing.

Factor	Findings	Rating
Government/ political stability	Stabile but highly restrictive towards political opposition; strict libel laws, Draconian punishments	3
Favorable laws, judicial system	Protective of personal wealth, rule of law tempered by executive policies	4
Available legal entities	All major legal entities may be formed or are recognized	5
Taxes	17% corporate tax rate, 15% on interest; 20% maximum income tax; no tax on offshore income under a territorial tax system.	5
Financial privacy/ banking secrecy	Swiss-like bank secrecy but with compromises and liberal tax information sharing under TIEAs	4
Final Rating		21

Offshore Financial Center

Singapore has grown into a world offshore financial haven, certainly comparable to Hong Kong and way ahead of its neighbor, fledgling Labuan in nearby Malaysia. Singapore has cultivated a sophisticated private banking sector, offering discreet financial services aimed at luring wealthy clients. Along with Hong Kong, it sees itself as a second financial gateway to expanding China, the eventual colossus of the East.

In recent years, Singapore has emerged as the financial service center for African and Middle Eastern sovereign wealth funds wanting to put oil and natural resource money to work in Asia, as well as for Western money seeking investments in Southeast Asia.

A good example of the pro-Singapore trend occurred in 2012 when the world's number three commodities trader, Trafigura, moved its trading center to this city-state from Switzerland. One of Singapore's attractions is that, unlike land-locked Switzerland, it sits at the center of Asia's booming demand for raw materials and close to many key physical markets. But Singapore is also beating Switzerland on taxes. Official corporate tax rates in Singapore have fallen by 3% to 17% over the past five years but held steady at just above 21% in Switzerland.

Modern infrastructure, developed capital markets, an educated workforce, comparatively stable political institutions and a low crime rate are added attractions. Singapore is viewed as highly developed with some of the best investment potential in Asia and with some of the lowest levels of economic corruption. It has attracted investors seeking profits as well as those seeking safety outside the U.S. dollar.

Singapore is reportedly the world's fourth-largest foreign exchange center after London, New York and Tokyo, and is home to many businesses, multinational corporations, banks and financial investment companies. It holds the world's ninth-largest foreign exchange reserves, impressive for a small country. The currency is the Singapore dollar and it has become a safe haven currency, similar to the Swiss franc.

Singapore also provides investors the ability to access other regional markets. A number of companies with direct ties to Myanmar, Vietnam, Thailand and other neighboring economies are listed on the Singapore Exchange, providing a convenient way to invest in regional growth.

Singapore has become a financial melting pot attracting foreign corporate foot soldiers and investors. That benefits key Singapore industries such as banking as well as tourism and real estate. Regional business travelers and tourists now visit for shopping, casinos and finance. Singapore has attracted major investments in pharmaceuticals and medical technology production and actively seeks to establish itself as Southeast Asia's financial and high-tech hub.

Singapore has a highly developed and successful free-market economy. It enjoys a remarkably open and corruption-free environment, stable prices, and a per capita GDP ($59,900 in 2011) higher than most developed countries. The economy depends heavily on exports, particularly in consumer electronics, information technology products, pharmaceuticals, and on a growing financial services sector.

Although Singapore's economy declined 1% in 2009 during the global recession, its GDP maintained a healthy 8.6% growth average from 2004 through 2007. Notably, in 2010, Singapore saw a rebound of 14.8%, followed by a reasonable increase of 4.9% in 2011 based on the strength of growing exports.

The common language is English. Most Singaporeans are Asian, with commerce dominated by ethnic Chinese. Malays make up 15%, with a mix of Indians, Thais, Vietnamese, Laotians and a very small number of Europeans. Europeans hold most management positions and are generally well regarded. In Singapore, state regulation has created a paradise if you like high-rise buildings, crass materialism and minimal personal freedom.

Many Swiss banks, such as Bank Julius Baer, have expanded their operations in Singapore to capitalize on the new business opportunities. The number of private banks operating in Singapore has nearly doubled to 35 in the past six years, according to officials. The Singapore Monetary Authority estimates that assets held by banks in Singapore has grown 20% each year since 2000 to nearly US$700 billion in 2012.

Taxes

Singapore is not necessarily a tax haven. The government supports welfare state programs of free schools, low-fee universities, childcare, socialized medicine and subsidized housing.

But as competitors, the two Asian financial hubs of Singapore and Hong Kong have kept personal and corporate taxes among the lowest in the world to attract more foreign investment. Top individual income tax rates are 20% in Singapore and 17% in Hong Kong, compared with 35% at the federal level in the United States.

The two Asian financial centers also have simpler taxation systems than the U.S. and other countries. Businesses make an average of three tax payments per year in Hong Kong and five in Singapore, compared with 11 in the U.S. and a global average of 28.5 per year. The tax codes are also more transparent so that many small businesses don't require a tax consultant or adviser.

The corporate tax rate in Singapore is 17% and the GST (goods and services or VAT) tax applies only when annual sales exceed S$1 million (US$782,000). Dividends and capital gains earned from foreign subsidiaries/branches are tax exempt. There is no withholding tax on dividend distribution by Singapore based companies. The withholding tax on interest is 15 % and on royalties 10%.

Personal income tax rates are some of the lowest globally and based on residence. Tax rates are progressive beginning when income exceeds S$22,000 (US$17,200). The maximum rate is 20% on income over S$320,000 (US$250,000) per annum. There are no capital gains or inheritance taxes. Under a territorial tax system income from offshore sources are tax exempt; only income earned in Singapore is taxed. Non-residents are taxed on Singapore net income after expenses at 15% for employment income and 20% for director's and consultant fees.

Foreigners can incorporate with a single shareholder, one resident director with a local address, and a minimum paid up capital of S$1 within 48 hours. Self-registration isn't permitted but for foreign individuals or entities, professional firms provide company formation and local nominee directors. Work visas are available for foreigners for employment, entrepreneurs or short-term for attending to business.

Modern infrastructure, developed capital markets, an educated workforce, comparatively stable political institutions and a low crime rate are added attractions. Negatives are a high cost of living for employees, mandatory filing of audited accounts of a foreign parent company, and mandatory designation of an active local secretary.

I visited Singapore for a legal conference and personally saw how local trust laws have been updated on a par with leading offshore trust nations, such as Bermuda or Panama. Singapore strengthened its bank secrecy laws, originally patterned after the strict privacy laws in Switzerland, and more recently including Swiss-like compromises.

Under pressure from the G-20 major nations, the government joined other OFCs and adopted the OECD standards governing the exchange of tax information among nations. It honors bona fide requests for tax information. Instead of signing separate TIEAs, it amended existing double tax agreements with other countries to include information exchange provisions and by the end of 2009, when Singapore signed its twelfth protocol, it moved officially on to the OECD "white list."

Immigration

The government actively recruits wealthy businesspersons as residents. For those active in offshore finance, the island city-state wants to establish itself as Asia's newest private banking hub by luring the super-wealthy away from places such as Hong Kong and even Switzerland.

The government allows foreigners, especially Europeans, who meet its wealth requirements, to buy land and become permanent residents. The goal is to attract private wealth from across Asia, as well as riches that Europeans and other Westerners are moving out of Switzerland and European Union nations to avoid new tax and reporting laws there.

More than a third of Singapore's residents are now foreign-born with the majority of new citizens coming from countries other than China, nearly half from Southeast Asia. The surge of new arrivals from China was part of a government immigration push that almost doubled Singapore's population to 5.2 million since 1990.

Tensions over immigration are problems in many nations, but most of Singapore's population was already ethnic Chinese, many born of earlier Chinese immigrants. Some locals now blame mainland Chinese for driving up real-estate prices, stealing the best jobs and clogging the roads with flashy European sports cars.

The government has reacted by adjusting immigration downward. New permanent residents have decreased two-thirds since 2008, when 80,000 applications were accepted and the number of people granted citizenship has remained level at about 18,500 a year. But is spite of the growing complaints Singapore remains the third-most desirable immigration destination for affluent Chinese after the United States and Canada, according to a survey by the Bank of China

Political Change

The year 2012 saw an increased civic activism sweeping this highly politically controlled island. Many of the loudest vocal activists are young, wired and cynical about the government's argument that it alone can maintain the prosperity and social harmony that has transformed this resource-starved island into one of the most advanced economies.

Activists say some opposition started in the 1990s, but was seen in 2011 when the governing People's Action Party lost six seats in the 87-member Parliament. The PAP has dominated politics since 1959 and is headed by Prime Minister Lee Hsien Loong, the son of Lee Kuan Yew, Singapore's founding father. The PAP support in the May 2011 election dropped to a historic low of 60%, down 6 points from the previous election.

Public rallies have demanded repeal of the anti-subversion law coinciding with the 25th anniversary of Operation Spectrum, a crackdown on activists that led to the arrest of 22 student leaders, lawyers and teachers grabbed in nighttime raids and forced, in what they alleged were harsh interrogations, to confess to an anti-government plot.

Over the years, legal advocates here claim more than 2,600 people have been arrested under the Internal Security Act, which allows the authorities to imprison suspects without trial.

Based on the past 50 years of local history, no one is predicting any huge public agitation or the end of Singapore's one party rule, but political types do say increasingly people are dropping traditional reluctance to challenge Singapore's paternalistic leaders and their "autocratic light" style of governance.

Contacts

Government of Singapore: http://www.gov.sg

Monetary Authority of Singapore: http://www.mas.gov.sg

Embassy of the Republic of Singapore
3501 International Place, N.W., Washington, D.C. 20008
Tel.: (202) 537-3100 Fax: (202) 537-0876
Email: singemb_was@sgmfa.gov.sg
Website: http://www.mfa.gov.sg/washington

United States Embassy
27 Napier Road, Singapore 258508
Tel.: + (65) 6476-9100 Fax: + (65) 6476-9340

Email: singaporeacs@state.gov
Website: http://singapore.usembassy.gov

Professional Contacts

Singapore & Hong Kong

Sovereign Society recommended banks in Singapore & Hong Kong usually do not accept accounts directly from individual U.S. persons but require an intermediary to submit account applications. The banks do require account applicants to appear personally at their offices as part of the application process.

Below is contact information for our designated intermediary, Josh Bennett, JD, an expert attorney in offshore asset protection, U.S. offshore taxes and reporting requirements. He also acts as contact for Trident Corporate Services that provides incorporation, trust creation and related business and banking services in Hong Kong and Singapore and in many other OFCs worldwide.

Josh N. Bennett, Esq.
440 North Andrews Avenue
Fort Lauderdale, FL 33301
Tel.: 954 779 1661 Fax: 954 767 9989
Email: josh@joshbennett.com
Website: www.joshbennett.com

People's Republic of China
Jeffrey Y.F. Chen, Esq.
3A, Yunhai Garden Office Tower
118 Qinghai Road, Shanghai, 200041, China.
Tel.: (86) 21 52281952
Fax: (86) 21 52281957

Cell: (86) 13916089368
Email: lawyer_chen@lawyers.cn

Banks in mainland China do not accept account applications from foreign individuals nor from corporations unless the foreign company has registered subsidiaries located in China. Mr. Chen advises on investments, business or other legal matters concerning China.

CHAPTER FIVE

The United Kingdom

London remains one of the leading financial centers of the world, but the U.K. is not a tax haven in any sense. The "City of London," (the country's equivalent of Wall Street), is the world's second leading financial center, after New York City. The U.K. is home to a dwindling number of private banks and offers possibilities for careful investors. Despite its descent from empire status in the 20th Century, the U.K. still is home to a few service-oriented private financial institutions where private banking was perfected. These banks might be just what you seek.

I am not referring to the "nationalized" U.K. banks that were "rescued" from financial ruin, propped up by trillions of pounds sterling in Labor government bailouts at the taxpayers' considerable expense. An estimated £1.2 trillion (US$1.7 trillion) was spent bailing out the Royal Bank of Scotland, HBOS, Lloyds, and Northern Rock.

But for personal service and true privacy, there are a precious few remaining small British banking houses that have not been swallowed up in mergers and bailouts. Some that have been purchased by larger banks retain their historic separate identities and practices. A few of these banking survivors exceed in personal service anything in U.S. banks.

Traditionally the Bank of England, the nation's official central bank, for centuries has been a relative pillar of economic stability, although the continuing British economic downturn that began in 2009, plus years of government deficit-spending have weakened the powers of the "Old Lady of Threadneedle Street" (the central bank's London address since 1734).

For Americans, banking in the U.K. always has been just one step away from home. Since the founding of the Jamestown Colony in 1607, America has been linked inextricably with England—politically and financially. The shared experience of the colonial period, the American Revolution, two world wars, the Cold War and more recent military conflicts, formed bonds between America and its parent nation that remain strong to this day.

And while the United States clearly surpassed Mother England in both military and financial power, the U.K. remains a steadfast ally with which the United States continues to maintain its much-vaunted "special relationship."

The British Economy

Even in decline, the United Kingdom remains one of the world's great trading and financial powers and these are centered within the area known as "The City of London" or just "The City." In the medieval period. The City constituted most of what was then London, but is now only a small part of the metropolis, although a notable part of central London. It holds city status in its own right, and is a separate ceremonial county headed by the Lord Mayor.

With its relatively small size and limited resources, the U.K. economy still ranks among the four largest in Western Europe. During 18 years of Tory rule, ending in 1997, successive Conservative Party governments reversed the socialist trend that began in 1945, replaced nationalization with privatization and curbed the welfare state. State-owned sectors such as telephones, railways, airlines, power, water and gas were sold back to private concerns. The power of unions that held the nation captive with frequent, crippling strikes was greatly reduced.

Although the Labor Party returned to power in 1997, they did so by co-opting a large part of the Tory platform and emphasizing a need for political change. Labor control saw a return to their worst doctrinaire socialist tendencies, including massive deficit spending and corporate and individual taxes so high that individuals and companies fled for lower tax havens in Ireland and Switzerland.

In the May 2010 general election, Labor was ousted, but while the Conservative Party won the most seats in the House of Commons, it failed to gain an absolute majority. For the first time since World War II, a coalition government was formed. Conservative leader David Cameron became Prime Minister at the head of a coalition with the third-place Liberal Democrats. Since then the government has steered a more conservative course under difficult economic circumstances inherited from the Labor Party, but it has been at best a shaky coalition.

When the U.K. recovers from the continued recession, the major economic policy question is going to be: "On what terms will it participate in the financial and economic integration of the European Union?"

The current economic collapse of the EU, and with it the weakened Euro, has more or less answered that question for most Brits. The English always have viewed EU monetary union and other loss of sovereignty issues with extreme caution. Unlike the Labor Party, Cameron has made it clear he and the Conservatives will not surrender to the EU control over U.K. taxes and internal financial matters.

The British always have been reluctant to abandon the long-respected pound sterling in favor of the Euro—and now they are glad they did not. If an eventual euro acceptance depends on a national referendum, the outcome will probably decidedly be negative, based on national polls.

The United Kingdom enjoyed several years of controlled economic growth before the crash. For the most part, until the recession hit, the British remained loyal to the economic traditions that made them one of the most prosperous nations on earth. One of these traditions is a high level of service and privacy offered by their banks, financial and investment institutions.

U.K. Banks

For Americans one major advantage of banking in the United Kingdom is language. It is no exaggeration to say that English now has become the de facto international language of banking—and almost every other global endeavor. Language facility is certainly a big plus when banking offshore, where local customs and rules can be confusing enough without having to cultivate multilingual capabilities.

For those seeking an offshore bank account with a reasonable degree of privacy and freedom from U.S. withholding taxes, London may be the place.

In spite of growing government intervention and demands for financial information, as a foreigner, it is easy to get lost in the crowd of foreigners who bank in London. There is an advantage to banking in a major world financial capital where you are only one among many.

The IRS doesn't raise its eyebrows nearly as high when an American reports a London bank account, as it does for an account in the Cayman Islands or The Bahamas.

While confidence with your bank comes only after time, as a new U.K. client you can reap the considerable benefits of one of the oldest and, in many respects, one of the most efficient private banking systems in the world. The government guarantees bank accounts against losses of up to £85,000 (US$133,000).

U.K. Bank Privacy

A 1922 judicial decision declared four situations in which an

English banker could legally compromise a client's banking secrecy: 1) by an order pursuant to law; 2) when a duty to the public exists; 3) in the interests of the bank; and; 4) with a client's express or implied permission. Until a few years ago, these principles continued to guide the English banking system's privacy policies.

The general rule used to be that U.K. Custom and Revenue agents had no right to seek the identities of the true owners of shares of stock. In cases where a bank account holder was discovered not to be a British resident, agents ended their ownership inquiry as a matter of policy.

Today, anti-money laundering laws, tax reporting requirements and U.S. and other governments' pressures has seriously diminished banking privacy in England as they have everywhere else. The U.K. government, in partnership with the U.S., has been in the forefront pushing anti-money laundering "all crimes" laws on British overseas territories, Crown dependencies and British Commonwealth nations. "All crimes" refers to the expansion of the application of money laundering laws from their original anti-drug targets, to any type of financial offense, but especially including foreign tax evasion.

The Bank of England supervised all British banks until 1997 when the Labor government made sweeping changes and the Financial Services Agency (FSA). Many criticized the FSA as a muscle-bound giant with too many duties and not enough practical sense.

When the Conservative-Liberal coalition government took office in 2010, it abolished the FSA and moved its responsibilities to new agencies and back to the Bank of England. The Financial Conduct Authority is responsible for policing the City and the banking system. The Prudential Regulatory Authority regulates financial firms, including banks, investment banks, building societies and insurance companies. All other responsibilities are exercised by the Bank of England and its Financial Policy Committee.

Money Laundering Laws

The 2002 Proceeds of Crime Act gives the U.K. police plenary powers to seek financial information related to money laundering, terrorism and many other alleged crimes. It imposes a positive duty on bankers, solicitors (lawyers) and other professionals to report any financial "suspicious activities" to the police. This means that financial privacy is diminished to a great degree for anyone who is the subject of police interest.

As in the U.S., Britain's anti-money laundering laws place the burden of detection on individual banks, their managers and even clerks and tellers. If a bank fails to establish and carry out detection procedures, it may be fined, and uncooperative bank officials face a two-year prison sentence. British bankers are forced to spy on their own customers, just as their American counterparts are required to act as spies under the U.S. Bank Secrecy Act and the PATRIOT Act.

U.S.-Style Forfeiture

The Labor government gave the U.K. American-style civil forfeiture laws with broad police powers. HM Customs and Revenue and the National Criminal Investigation Service (NCIS) virtually have a free hand to rifle through tax files at will. The official line is that tax inspections are only targeted at individuals suspected of crimes.

However, this paves the way for police "fishing expeditions" looking for evidence to build civil forfeiture cases. An important House of Lords decision held that anyone investigated for suspected U.K. tax offenses at least must first be given a warning and explanation of their rights.

As in the U.S., U.K. government forfeiture policy calls for cash confiscation from individuals suspected of criminal activity, even if insufficient evidence exists to convict them in a court of law. In theory, if a suspect is judged to be "living beyond his visible means," the police can ask a court to freeze his or her assets immediately pending investigation.

Future of British Banking

Beyond the larger question of which banks may fail in the United Kingdom without continued government bailouts, financial privacy is an important issue.

The defeated Labor government was a leader in the global attack on tax havens mounted by the high-tax G-20 countries and the OECD. The major goal was to force all countries to agree to a system of automatic exchange of tax information between governments. Since 1975, a tax information exchange treaty between the U.K. and the U.S. has allowed great latitude in its application.

While British courts may legally compromise your financial privacy in response to a foreign judicial subpoena, in the past they did so only occasionally—and then under diplomatic pressure. But now it is likely that the British system will reveal your bank records if substantial probable cause is shown by your home government.

The U.S. Treasury and the IRS maintain large staffs at the American Embassy in London's Grosvenor Square. All things considered, your money may be only marginally safer in England than in the U.S. if the Feds come knocking.

Home of Private Banking

Many English "private banks" offer a measure of discretion that American institutions will not (or cannot) approach. But some added privacy is not the only advantage of private banking in the U.K. English bankers work hard to provide excellent service in addition to financial security.

Americans love convenience and speed, usually at the expense of civility and dignity in everyday life. The British are more willing to provide personalized and traditional services. And while it's not easy to find such care, banking with small, private British banks provides a welcome reminder of gentler, more civilized times. Of course, such service does not come cheap.

There are some trade-offs involved to obtain this kind of personal service. First, without a formal introduction from a prominent British person or a respected American bank manager, you won't be able to open an account with C. Hoare & Co. or Child & Co. or at Rothschild's, for instance.

- **C. Hoare & Co.** is England's oldest, privately owned banking house. Founded in 1672 by Sir Richard Hoare, it remains family owned and is currently managed by the 11th generation of direct descendants. It provides private banking, financial planning and investment management services that include loans, mortgages, savings accounts and investment advisory services as well as tax and estate planning services. The bank's clients typically are high-net-worth individuals and families. 37 Fleet Street, EC4P 4DQ, London, Tel.: +44 (0)20 7353 4522. Website: http://www.hoaresbank.co.uk/, Contact: http://www. hoaresbank.co.uk/secondaryNav/talktous.php.

- **Child & Co.** (1 Fleet Street, City of London, Greater London EC4Y 1BD, U.K. Tel.: 020 7353 4080) was founded in 1664. It is now a subsidiary of Royal Bank of Scotland. It specializes in private banking and wealth management.

- **N M Rothschild & Sons** (known as Rothschild) is a private investment banking company owned by the Rothschild family. It was founded in the City of London in 1811 and is now a global firm with 50 offices around the world. Website: http:// www.rothschild.com/, Contact: http://www.rothschild.com/ contactus/.

In truth, these small, exclusive British private banks neither need nor want a large number of customers, so applicants are screened with particular care. To gain entry, it helps to have an existing relationship with a U.S. bank that's affiliated with an international private bank network (such as Harriman, J.P. Morgan, or the oldest privately owned bank in America, Brown Brothers,). Making the necessary connections might take some time and effort, but the rewards are worth it.

Non-Doms Lose Tax Haven

Nearly two million foreigners live in England and, until 2008, many were able to escape most of the terribly high income and other taxes that U.K. citizens are made to suffer.

What shielded foreigners from taxes was the so-called "non-dom" income tax exemption, a major tax break for wealthy foreigners who made their homes in the U.K. Under U.K. tax law (until the 2008 change) anyone living in Britain but not born there and who qualified, could choose what is known as "non-domiciled" tax status.

In essence, that meant they claimed a foreign country as their "tax domicile." The non-dom law made London a tax haven for many thousands, from Russian oil tycoons to international investment bankers and Saudi princes. In 2008, the country had 68 pre-global recession billionaires, three times as many as in 2004. Only three of the U.K.'s 10 richest people were born in Britain.

This law allowed thousands of wealthy foreigners who lived and worked in the U.K. to pay taxes on the relatively small amount of money they actually brought into the U.K. each year ("remittances") and on what they earned in the U.K. They paid no U.K. taxes on much larger offshore earnings. Importantly, it was argued, these foreigners enriched the U.K. by spending billions on real estate, goods and services and investments. According to British Treasury figures, about 112,000 people claimed non-domiciled status in 2006-07.

The British Left repeatedly attacked this non-dom tax arrangement. When Labor gained power in 1994, then-Chancellor of the Exchequer, Gordon Brown, pledged to close the "non-dom loophole," but did nothing.

Finally, in 2008, with the economy sinking, Brown, by then prime minister, adopted tough tax proposals on high-earning non-domiciled residents that included an annual levy of £30,000 (US$47,000) on those who had lived in Britain for at least seven years. This non-dom tax provoked a storm of criticism from business leaders who claimed it would drive well-paid foreign workers out of Britain, which appears to have happened to some extent.

The government also closed the loophole that allowed non-doms to bring assets purchased with foreign earnings into Britain without paying tax on them. Goods worth more than £1,000 kept in the U.K. for more than nine months became liable to tax. U.K. tax law still does not require payment of income taxes by non-doms on much foreign-source income, or estate taxes on foreign assets.

Income from U.K. sources generally is subject to U.K. taxation without regard to the citizenship or the place of residence of the individual or the place of registration of a company.

For individuals who are neither resident nor ordinarily resident in the U.K. this means they are liable for U.K. income tax liability in the form of taxes deducted by a U.K. income source, together with tax on income from a trade or profession carried on through a permanent establishment in the U.K. and tax on rental income from U.K. real estate.

Individuals who are both resident and domiciled in the UK are additionally liable to taxation on their worldwide income and gains.

If you are considering becoming a resident of the U.K. and think you can qualify legally as a "non-domiciled," be sure to check the current tax status and what benefits may still be available, if any.

Taxes on Former Residents

In the past, the U.K. might have been generous tax-wise to resident foreigners, but it definitely is not kind to its own citizens who go offshore (known as "expats"), many to avoid high U.K. taxes.

Until 1998, U.K. citizens who lived and worked outside the U.K. for more than a year were exempt from taxes on their earnings, if they were physically in the U.K. no longer than 62 days each year. The Labor government abolished this "foreign earnings deduction" in what it called "tax fairness." Now any U.K. citizen who earns any amount of U.K. source income while in the U.K. must pay taxes on their entire year's earnings, regardless of where in the world the rest of the income was earned.

The results were predictable and swift. In particular, nonresident U.K. athletes and entertainers were forced to modify their travel schedules to avoid earning even a single shilling of U.K. source income.

Case in Point: The Rolling Stones canceled the U.K. leg of their 1998 world tour as a direct result of tax law. The world's leading rock band claimed it would have lost over £12 million (US$23.7 million) if they played four concerts scheduled in 1998 in the U.K. Labor government spokespersons were quick to respond to the announcement of the cancellation as being driven by greed. But when the Stones offered to play the concerts for charity in return for a tax exemption, the government turned down the offer.

The bottom line: Great Britain is a great place to live, but a bad place to be tax domiciled. Just ask Mick Jagger.

Avoid U.K. Withholding Taxes

British bankers do not deduct withholding taxes on interest paid to nonresident accounts because the law imposes no taxes on a foreigner's account. When opening an account, a foreigner must state that he is a nonresident and show proof with a passport. What are by now traditional "know your customer" rules in most countries and in the U.K. impose broad information requirements on all persons opening new accounts.

If you decide to make a long-term home in the U.K., very careful tax plans must be made to avoid the possibility of U.K. estate taxes being imposed. British law treats a foreigner who is resident in the U.K. during 17 out of the 20 years prior to death for estate tax purposes, as having been domiciled in the U.K.

These U.K. death taxes can be avoided with the creation of a trust or IBC. When a foreigner purchases shares in a U.K. company, capital transfer taxes (estate taxes) may be payable to Customs and Revenue when the purchaser dies. But purchasing U.K. shares in the name of an IBC completely avoids U.K. death taxes.

I'll say it again: check with your tax professional before you do anything.

For tax and other legal information for foreign persons establishing residence in the U.K. contact solicitor: **James McNeile**, Withy King law firm, James Street West, Green Park, Bath, UK BA1 2BT Tel.: (01225) 489787 Email: james.mcneile@withyking.co.uk Website: http://www.chambersandpartners.com/uk/Firms/83987-45371/303640

For assistance in obtaining U.K. residence, contact:

Immigration Advice Service
Tel.: +0844 887 0111
Email info@iasservices.org.uk
Skype: immigrationadviceservice
Website: http://www.iasservices.org.uk/

U.K. Investment Trusts

In the U.K. an entity known is an "investment trust" is a closed-end financial fund that sells shares to individuals and invests in securities issued by other companies.

Initial purchase of British investment trust shares must be made through a brokerage house or bank. The shares are publicly traded on the London Stock Exchange, frequently at a 10% to 12% discount to net asset value. When you sell or switch between funds, you may face an even bigger discount. In the interim, you can have more money working for you than you are investing.

The accounts of investment trusts also are subject to regulation by the government. That means these funds are audited periodically by major international accounting firms, but even so, check the facts carefully before you buy.

The British and the Scots pioneered the development of investment trusts and the total number trading in London far exceeds closed-end funds trading in New York. Many specialize in investments in non-British markets, a painless indirect route into European equities for Americans operating offshore.

Unlike U.S. funds, a U.K. investment trust's total investments may exceed 100% of the value of invested shares. Borrowing to buy additional shares is allowed, increasing both leverage and risk. U.K. investment trusts do not pay tax on capital gains realized within the portfolio and most dividends are distributed to the trust shareholders. Management charges are low compared to those of unit trusts (mutual funds) in Britain.

For investment trusts, smaller is not necessarily better. It is difficult to withdraw money from smaller trusts that may require written withdrawal notices or impose "no withdrawal" time periods. A good source for up-to-date information is the *Financial Times* of London (www.ft.com), the respected journal that publishes weekly net asset value figures for all funds. Check before you invest.

City of London Investment Management Company Ltd. was founded in 1991 by Barry Olliff, the current CIO. City of London

(CoL) is an active emerging markets equity manager with offices in London, U.S., Singapore and Dubai. 7 Gracechurch Street, London EC3V 0AS Tel.: + 44 (0) 207 711 1566, Email: ukclientservicing@ citlon.co.uk; US Office: The Barn, 1125 Airport Road, Coatesville, PA 19320 Tel.: + 1 610 380 2110 Email: client.servicing@citlon. com, Website: http://www.citlon.co.uk/index.php.

U.K. Unit Trusts

In the United Kingdom, the "unit trust" is the equivalent of an open-ended mutual fund in the United States. Because of adverse U.S. tax consequences from such investments, check with your American tax advisor before investing.

British banks will hold stocks, bonds and unit trust shares and collect dividends and interest for foreign clients, with no withholding taxes levied on investment accounts. There is even a reimbursement of the 40% tax on corporate dividends when you file for relief from the U.K. Customs and Revenue. This unusual tax credit is payable to U.K. company shareholders as reimbursement for corporate taxes already paid by the company in which they own shares of stock. Customs and Revenue routinely informs U.S. authorities about U.K. tax payments made by Americans.

Communicating with Shareholders

British banks usually communicate well with unit trust shareholders on behalf of companies. In the U.K., official rolls of corporate shareholders are maintained either by the corporation, the unit trusts, or the bank that holds shares for nominee share purchasers. These institutions routinely keep shareholders up-to-date on any important developments.

Generally, U.K. investment and unit trust managers are more accessible than their American counterparts. In the U.S., heavy institutional investor involvement in the mutual funds market leaves fund managers with little time for small investors. In the U.K., firms customarily deal with masses of small investors and are significantly more forthcoming with information and help.

Profits from Interest Rate Differentials

Some British and continental banks allow overseas investors simultaneously to deposit assets in a high-yield currency then borrow the equivalent value or more in a low-yield currency, such as the dollar or the euro. The lending bank requires the borrower to deposit the loan with them.

The remaining difference between the yield and the fee the bank charges for the loan is credited to your account, which opens another possibility for high interest returns. Of course, the risk is yours; the interest rate is higher on the second currency precisely because there is a devaluation risk.

Gamblers who cover the exchange risk by buying currency "futures" may lose the interest advantage as well. That's because the price of futures reflects interest rate differentials and because significant transaction fees are charged for small sums. To beat the odds, you must predict currency trends more successfully than even the market can.

Jyske Global Asset Management (JGAM), part of **Jyske Bank**, offers the "invest loan" leverage to international clients. JGAM, a Jyske Bank subsidiary and is a U.S. SEC-registered investment adviser. Contact:

Thomas Fischer, Executive Vice President JGAM
Vesterbrogade 9, 1780, Copenhagen V, Denmark
Tel.: +45 8989 5901
Email: info@jgam.com
Website: http://www.jgam.com

Another popular U.K. bank plan (also available in other off-shore financial centers) enables business customers in good standing to borrow against their own deposits, effectively lowering taxable earnings and enabling a build-up in foreign exchange assets, even as loans are repaid. As a foreigner unfamiliar with local bank plans, get a second opinion from a U.S. accountant or tax attorney before you proceed with any plans offered.

CHAPTER SIX

United Kingdom's Offshore Financial Centers

Some of the world's leading offshore financial centers long have been (and still are) those known as "Crown dependencies" of the United Kingdom. Included are the Channel Islands and the Isle of Man. These unique jurisdictions have a well-developed regime of law that offers strong asset protection, solid investments and tax savings, including life insurance and annuity products that have the advantage of being U.S. tax-deferred investment vehicles.

Located not far off the southeast coast of the United Kingdom a group of islands offers even more sophisticated financial services than those found in the fabled City of London.

Located in the Bay of St. Malo in the English Channel, about 30 miles from the north coast of France and 70 miles from the south coast of England are the Channel Islands of **Jersey**, **Guernsey**, **Sark** and **Alderney**. To the west of the United Kingdom, between the U.K. and Ireland in the Irish Sea, is the **Isle of Man**.

So unique are all these financial centers that tens of thousands of investors and businesspersons worldwide use the services of investment houses, accountants, lawyers, insurance brokers and trust and corporation services located there.

While each of these semi-independent islands is associated constitutionally with the U.K. in their status as Crown dependencies, until recently each remained free of most of the U.K.'s tax and other financial restrictions. In the past, that broad financial freedom, coupled with determined self-promotion, made these islands important world business centers in miniature and in many respects they remain so.

After the end of World War II, the British government tolerated the offshore finance industry in these Crown dependencies because on balance it brought more expatriate and foreign wealth into the U.K. than was lost from the attractive tax avoidance mechanisms the islands offered.

When the Labor Party government regained a parliamentary majority in 1997, that tolerance turned into antagonism and attacks. Over the next decade various restrictions were imposed and by 2009, in the midst of the worst British recession in 30 years, Labor Prime Minister Gordon Brown demanded "the end of tax havens." He demagogically blamed these islands for the British economic downturn, which actually had its root causes in the City of London, Wall Street and elsewhere.

Second Dissolution of the British Empire

"I have not become the King's First Minister in order to preside over the liquidation of the British Empire." Winston Churchill's famous statement in November 1942, just as the tide of the Second World War was beginning to turn towards victory, pugnaciously affirmed that great British leader's loyalty to the global colonial institution he had served for most of his life.

Britain fought and sacrificed on a world scale to defeat Hitler and his allies—and won. Yet less than five years after Churchill's defiant speech, the British Empire effectively ended with India's 1947 independence and the 1948 termination of the British Mandate in Palestine.

Gordon Brown, Britain's Labor prime minister, seemed bent

on causing another major setting of the sun on what little then remained of Britain's truncated empire in 2009. Under pressure from British labor unions and a nose-diving economy, Brown suddenly began attacking Her Majesty's Crown dependencies as well as the U.K. overseas territories (OSTs). Most of these OSTs also were, then and now, leading tax havens nurtured as such by London for the last half century (and by Brown himself in his decade as Chancellor of the Exchequer).

Under heavy fire for deficit spending and £1.2 trillion (US$1.7 trillion) in bailouts for the Royal Bank of Scotland, HBOS, Lloyds, and Northern Rock, Brown latched on to the idea that blaming offshore tax havens for alleged lost tax revenues was good politics. One British newspaper headlined: "Brown does a U-turn on tax havens."

On Brown's blacklist were most of the U.K. overseas territories, including the Cayman Islands, Bermuda, the British Virgin Islands and the Turk & Caicos Islands. The Labor government also turned hostile to the Crown dependencies, Jersey, Guernsey and the Isle of Man—all the major offshore financial hubs that are closely tied to the City of London.

So unique had these offshore financial centers become that hundreds of thousands of investors and business persons worldwide use the services of their investment houses, banks, accountants, lawyers, insurance brokers, trust and corporation services.

Brown's move was a radical departure from past government's historic policy of protecting the pre-eminence of Britain's financial services industry, both in London and in the overseas territories. His move was also a crude political attempt to counter criticism and pressure from high tax nations France and Germany who charged that the U.K. tax havens, comparable to the villainous Switzerland, were obstacles to imposing a global "transparent financial system"—meaning an end to financial privacy everywhere as a means to collect more taxes.

OFCs Self-Regulate

Her Majesty's Labor government attacking the British offshore tax havens produced an ironic result. Over a decade as Labor governments in London demanded substantial reforms in all U.K. offshore financial centers, and that is just what they got. Reforms included statutory transparency, tax information sharing, and anti-money laundering laws, all important reforms Brown conveniently ignored when he attacked the overseas territories.

These offshore reforms are now written into local laws in these semi-independent islands and include:

- Much stricter anti-money laundering and foreign tax evasion statutes;

- Extensive banking client surveillance;

- Cooperation with foreign officials seeking tax and other information about persons and legal entities based on the islands;

- Major weakening of previously strict financial privacy laws and,

- Imposition of the EU savings tax directive, which all U.K. offshore centers now enforce and collect.

As part of the worldwide campaign to curb the use of tax havens described in Chapter 3, the U.K. Labor government concentrated on curtailing the strict financial privacy and bank secrecy formerly offered by these islands.

Of course, an honest foreign taxpayer who is active financially offshore, and who knows and abides by his own country's reporting rules, has little to fear from the reduced degree of privacy now available in the U.K. havens. It should be noted that the Isle of Man, Jersey and Guernsey each have existing tax information exchange agreements (TIEAs) with the United States.

When the pressure from London began 20 years ago, the Labor

government stated its willingness to precipitate a constitutional crisis by forcing these changes into law without the approval of the islands' governing bodies. No threats were needed. One by one, each island's politicians adopted the changes demanded with minimal protests.

Unique Status

These self-ruling British Crown dependencies have the power make their own laws and to set their own corporate and personal income tax rates. Through their constitutional association with the U.K., although they are not considered EU members, the islands enjoy some selected benefits of EU membership, such as the direct access to continental financial activities within all 27 EU countries.

The EU savings tax directive is an international procedure under which banks in the 27 EU member countries collect taxes from foreigners who have accounts there, then remit them to the persons home countries.

When the EU savings tax directive was proposed, the Labor government agreed with the EU demand that it force all the Crown dependencies to comply and collect taxes on foreigners. As a result, the Isle of Man, Jersey and Guernsey withhold tax but refused to provide names of account holders. The islands remit 75% of the withheld taxes to the EU countries of origin of the EU investors at a current tax rate of 35%. The tax applies only to citizens of the 27 EU nations and not to investment or interest earnings of U.S. persons.

Multiple Financial Services

For the potential foreign banking client or investor, the Channel Islands (Jersey and Guernsey) and the Isle of Man have a great deal to offer in the way of investments, banking, insurance and useful legal entities. The Channel Islands Stock Exchange, located in Guernsey, lists over 3,500 securities, and receives international recognition.

The Channel Islands enjoy high ratings as international finance centers. Surveys for the City of London Corporation rate Jersey in the top 20 of all world financial centers. A 2012 survey of the smaller, specialist financial centers by Banker magazine grouped Jersey and Guernsey in the top five. The islands also enjoy widespread international respectability for their level of financial regulation, and anti-money laundering measures.

The Channel Islands are the last remnants of the medieval Dukedom of Normandy founded in 911 AD which famously conquered Great Britain at the Battle of Hastings in 1066. Her Majesty, Queen Elizabeth II, is the official head of state, not as Queen, but in her separate role and title as "Duchess of Normandy." These islands were the only British soil occupied by German troops in World War II.

For the most part, both Jersey and Guernsey base their legal systems on the ancient customs and laws of the French province of Normandy, their near neighbor at the eastern edge of the English Channel. The Channel Islands have also incorporated many British common law features into their commercial code and legal activities, although with a French flavor.

In theory, the British parliament lacks power to enact laws for these islands. Technically, they are not considered a part of the United Kingdom. The special status of the Channel Islands and the Isle of Man in relation to the United Kingdom means that while they are not actually part of the U.K., the U.K. is responsible for their foreign relations and military defense.

In their internal domestic affairs, the islands govern themselves, although laws enacted by their legislative assemblies must be validated by "Royal Assent," until now a pro-forma procedure common to all British territories.

Jersey

Officially called the Bailiwick of Jersey (pop. 94,949 in 2011), it has developed into one of the world's leading offshore finance jurisdictions in the last half century. In volume of business and assets, it is much larger than Guernsey, its smaller neighbor.

Jersey draws on its political and economic stability, product innovation and the quality of its regulation and legal system to support the successful development of its offshore finance industry. It has attracted many of the world's leading financial groups to its shores and its workers have the experience to cater to the diverse needs of global investors. Jersey has thriving banking, mutual funds and trust sectors. While it is a leading center for private clients who want a safe, well-regulated home for their assets, it has also diversified to become a preferred jurisdiction for worldwide corporate and institutional business as well.

Jersey's economy is based on international financial services (43% of GDP in 2009), followed by agriculture, and tourism. Low taxes (20% on income and 5% on goods and services) and no death duties make the island a popular tax haven. Living standards are close to those of the UK.

Jersey's financial institutions are home to an astonishing amount of wealth and represent 50% of the island GDP. The estimated GDP was £3.70 billion (US$5.76 billion) in 2009 and the per capita GDP was US$45,000. By 2012, there were 55 banks representing many nations, although that number has been as high as 72. Jersey banks held a total of US$359.4 billion in assets at the end of Q1, 2012.

In March 2012, there were 14,563 clients who had a total of £20.962 billion (US$30.68 billion) under various forms of investment management. There were 1,412 registered funds in Jersey in the same month. (It's impossible to quantify the value of trust assets exactly since they don't have to be reported to authorities.) Individuals must be professionally qualified or have years of direct, hands-on experience to be licensed to set up and manage trust companies. Jersey provides financial services to customers worldwide with over 13,000 people employed full-time in this sector.

Jersey is innovative. It has developed financial alliances with the Gulf States and the United Arab Emirates. The finance industries in Jersey and the Gulf region see opportunities in jointly working to deliver financial services, including Muslim Shari'a law compliant products. There are firms in Jersey incorporating Islamic investment vehicles such as Sukuks, Islamic asset-backed investment certificates, certified as complying with the requirement of Shari'a law that is governed by the Islamic religion

Tourism accounts for one-quarter of GDP. In recent years, the government has encouraged light industry to locate in Jersey with the result that an electronics industry has developed, displacing more traditional industries.

Jersey companies may be freely incorporated with a share capital denominated in any currency and there are no restrictions on inward or outward investment or on the repatriation of dividends, interest and profits. Bank interest on deposits, payable to a nonresident, is exempt from Jersey income tax. Royalties are treated for the purposes of tax in the same way as interest.

The authorities deter "active" foreign investment (new businesses and permanent immigration) but welcome "passive" investment (purchase of real estate for investment purposes, or the purchase of existing business assets). This is part of the general policy of protecting the island›s scarce resources and thus the island does not offer investment incentives, other than its permissive low tax regime.

Banking

In recent years, there has been a consolidation of banks and banking staffs on the islands, a reflection of a world banking trends. Nevertheless, total assets under management in each of these islands have continued to increase to record levels, a testament to their standing among global investors. Very few companies operate on the Channel Islands of Alderney and Sark that have very sparse populations.

As do most offshore jurisdictions, Jersey's banking law has traditionally established the confidentiality of a bank account, but other laws provide a number of routes by which that confidentiality can be breached on application from other countries with a demonstrable case against a particular individual or company. Fishing expeditions are not entertained.

The history of the last 10 years concerning Jersey's banking secrecy is mainly a story of attempts by the OECD and the EU to impose extensive information-sharing requirements on the island's financial institutions. By 2010, Jersey had signed 16 TIEAs, including one with the United States.

There are more than 55 banks operating in Jersey including branches and subsidiaries of British clearing banks and international banks, offering a full range of services. (See http://www.offshore-library.com/banking/jersey/.)

Advantages of banking on the Island include confidentiality, freedom of currency exchange, tax deferral, tax reduction and low commercial and political risk. There are no exchange controls. In the event of a bank failure the government of both Jersey and Guernsey will pay up to £50,000 (US$78,000) per individual customer.

Banking operations in Jersey are governed by the Banking Business Law and the Banking Business Order both of 1991. The laws provide for the protection of Jersey as a financial center and for depositors. Operations are supervised by the Jersey Financial Commission (http://www.jerseyfsc.org/) which also issues banking licenses.

Jersey is regarded as one of the safest offshore jurisdictions in which to bank, invest or establish a trust because it is an economically and politically stable jurisdiction which employs the strict regulatory practices.

Opening an offshore bank account in Jersey is much the same as in any well-run jurisdiction with anti-money laundering and know your customer due diligence rules. Basic requirements are completion of an application form, with notarized copies of identification, proof of current address and citizenship and proof of fund sources presented in person.

Trusts, Corporations and Funds

Although Jersey law has its roots in the Norman law, which is a Roman or civil law code, the Trusts Law 1984 codified an entirely Anglo-Saxon body of trust law, resolving many uncertainties and increasing protection for beneficiaries. Subsequent amendments included the recognition of purpose trusts in 1996, although the usual Jersey trust form is discretionary. This has led to an increase in corporate use of Jersey trusts.

Companies that incorporate in Jersey are governed by the Companies Law 1991, which closely follows the English 1948 Companies Act. For private companies, beneficial ownership has to be disclosed but is not on the public record. Shelf companies are not available however the formation process is quick and inexpensive provided that a new company does not intend to carry on business on Jersey itself. There is an incorporation fee of £200 (US$312) and an annual return fee of £150 (US$234). A company must have a registered office in Jersey. Accounts need not be audited, but have to be filed with the Jersey revenue authorities. Partnerships of all types also are available and since 2009 foundations are also recognized.

Americans enjoy specific benefits when doing business through these islands, such as purchasing non-U.S. mutual funds that typically cannot sell shares in the United States because of SEC regulations. U.S. investors can invest in these funds by using an accommodation address on the islands, thus legally skirting the SEC rules that forbid offshore funds from sending materials or having direct contact with investors when physically located in America.

Taxes

The islands' tax systems have been remarkably free of political manipulation for many years. Successive legislatures have preserved the standard income tax rate at about 20% for more than half a century.

In answer to OECD complaints about the two-tax system formerly in place that exempted foreign-owned business but not locals, corporate taxes were reduced to zero for all businesses, with the exception of some banks and financial firms. There is no inheritance tax, gift tax, or other wealth taxes. The possibility of any increase in the income tax or the enactment of new taxes is remote because the islands want to continue to attract corporate business.

Nonresidents are subject to income tax only on locally earned income, and bank interest is exempt. A local trust is treated as a nonresident for tax purposes, provided none of the beneficiaries is an island resident.

Immigration

Jersey, the largest of the Channel Islands, is attractive for private residence or to establish an international business. The government of Jersey closely controls long-term residence and allows only rare exceptions for those who do own a residence. Very few wealthy new immigrants are accepted annually by Jersey—only about seven a year. The government favors those purchasing luxury and high end real estate because these individuals add to local tax coffers.

There are no corporate taxes other than on some trust and banking operations. The Jersey government usually grants residence to persons who qualify to purchase property. Applicants for residence permits are required to prove a net worth of at least £20 million

(US$32 million) and an income sufficient to produce an annual tax liability of at least £150,000 (US$234,000) at an income tax rate of 20% and to buy local real estate worth at least £1 million (US$1.6 million).

Guernsey is far less restrictive on newcomers who want to establish residence, but requires work permits for those who start any form of business. Establishing residency on the Isle of Man is simpler, mainly because it is comparatively spacious, with a land area more than seven times larger than Jersey and more than 10 times the size of Guernsey.

One of the lesser Channel Islands, Alderney, has a small number of financial service companies and places few restrictions on immigration by wealthy foreigners. Sark, an even smaller island, has few residents and tight property ownership restrictions, but no taxes.

British Expats Do Well

The Channel Islands are the preferred place for offshore money market funds sold to the British expatriate market. Because of a legal quirk, this once was the only place where a single corporate entity could offer money market funds in a variety of currencies, making it easier to offer free switching between currencies to customers investing only modest sums. Other offshore havens now offer streamlined transactions, but the Channel Islands remain the center for multi-currency money market and bond funds.

The range of business being conducted on the Channel Islands and the Isle of Man is highly diverse. Mutual funds offer shares that literally span the globe. Major corporate employee pension and benefits programs are headquartered in the islands.

Few Brits use the islands for tax avoidance or retirement these days as many did in the past, because of determined anti-tax avoidance campaigns by HM Customs and Revenue tax collectors and the broader investigative powers they now have.

Contacts

States of Jersey Government: http://www.gov.je

Jersey news: http://www.thisisjersey.com

One of the leading Jersey attorneys is **Mourant Ozannes**, reportedly the world's third-largest offshore law firms with 250 attorneys and offices in the Cayman Islands, Guernsey, Hong Kong, and London. Offices at 22 Grenville Street, St. Helier, JE4 8PX, Channel Islands, Tel.: 44 1534 609 000, Email: jersey@mourantozannes.com.

There are so many trust, banking, and investment companies in Jersey that it is difficult to know where to start.

There are 77 trust companies alone. **Atlas Trust Company (Jersey), Limited** is a small trust company founded by professionals, all of whom have considerable experience in the financial field. Atlas will put you in contact with other professionals on the island who might also be able to accommodate your financial goals. Contact Atlas at PO Box 246, 1 Brittania Place, Bath Street, St. Helier, JE4 5PP Tel.: +44 (0) 1534 608878. Ian R. Swindale is managing director.

There are a number of major stock brokerages in Jersey such as:

Citigroup Quilter, P.O. Box 276, 4th Floor, 28-30 The Parade, St Helier, Jersey JE4 8TE, Tel.: +44 (0)1534 506 070, Email: jersey@quilter.com, and;

James Capel Ltd., HSBC House, Esplanade, St Helier, JE4 8WP. Tel.: +44 (0) 1534 616 200.

Leading banks include:

Coutts & Co. Ltd., P.O. Box 6, 23/25 Broad Street, St. Helier, Jersey, JE4 8ND, Tel.: +44 (0) 1534 282 345l.

Lazard Brothers Co. Ltd., P.O. Box 108, 2/6 Church Street, St. Helier, Jersey JE4 8ND, Tel.: +44 (0) 1534 37361.

Investment managers include:
Coutts Offshore Europe Ltd., P.O. Box 6, 23-25 Broad Street, St Helier, JE4 0TF, Tel.: +44 (0) 1534 282345;
Kleinwort Benson (Channel Islands) Investment Management Ltd., PO Box 76, Kleinwort Benson House, West Centre, St Helier, JE4 8PQ, Telephone: +44 (0) 1534 613000.

Guernsey

The Bailiwick of Guernsey (population 65,608) embraces not only 10 parishes on the Island of Guernsey, but also the islands of Herm, Jethou, and Lihou, as well as Alderney and Sark, the latter two each with its own parliament.

Guernsey has a strong economy dominated by its financial sector. Financial services, such as banking, private equity fund management, and insurance, account for about 32% of total income. GDP is estimated to be over US$3 billion which averages at about US$45,000 GDP per capita.

Political stability and a history of low taxes and a respected international reputation as an important financial center make it an attractive place for foreign investors to conduct business. To protect the island's limited resources the government discourages labor-intensive local investment by non-residents. Other than low taxes there are no investment grants or incentives.

Guernsey has Europe's largest captive insurance sector, and also has strong banking, investment fund and trusts sectors, with very well-developed advisory and financial professionals. The Channel Islands Stock Exchange is based here. Most corporations are tax exempt except for certain finance companies taxed at 10%.

As with Jersey, Guernsey is not an EU member but both islands have come under much EU and OECD pressure in opposition to their low- or no-tax policies. Both islands formerly exempted only foreign owned corporations from taxes which the OECD attacked as discriminatory. Both islands responded by abolishing all corporate taxes other than those on selected finance companies, known as the Zero-Ten corporate tax system.

In 2011, the Guernsey government followed the example of the Isle of Man and switched from a withholding tax system under the EU tax directive to the automatic exchange of tax information. Guernsey signed a TIEA with the United States in 2006 and now has 32 TIEAs with other jurisdictions including most major countries.

An independent survey in 2012 found Guernsey to be the most popular place for fund management in the U.K. In September 2011, *The Banker* magazine ranked Guernsey as the number one specialist finance center in Europe and second in the world.

Contacts

Banking:
Royal Bank of Canada
P.O. Box 48, Canada Court
St. Peter Port, Guernsey, Channel Islands, GY1 3BQ
Tel.: +44 1481 744000

Investment:
Investec Asset Management
P.O. Box 250, Glategny Court
Glategny Esplanade, St Peter Port Guernsey GY1 3QH
Tel.: +44 (0)1481 710 404
Email: offshore.investor@investecmail.com

Attorney:
Collas Day, P.O. Box 140, Manor Place
St Peter Port, Guernsey, Channel Islands, GY1 4EW
Tel.: 44 1481 723191

Captive Insurance:
Aviation Insurance Brokers Ltd.,
Granary House, The Grange,
St Peter Port, Guernsey, Channel Islands GY1 2QQ
Tel.: 44 1481 724330

States of Guernsey Government: http://www.gov.gg/article/1582/ Home

Guernsey News: http://www.thisisguernsey.com/guernsey-press/

The Isle of Man

The Isle of Man's history and legal system differ from those of the Channel Islands, but its advantages for offshore business users are similar. Located in the Irish Sea just 30 miles from the U.K. mainland, the island is firmly established as an important international offshore financial center. Historically it has never been part of the U.K.

Its independent parliament, the Tynwald, claims to be the oldest in the world and traces its origins back over a thousand years. The Tynwald is responsible for all domestic legislation, including taxation for its 76,000 citizens.

Unlike the Channel Islands and their French civil law influence, the legal system is based on English common law, the currency is the pound sterling and social and economic links with the U.K. are strong; the island defense and foreign affairs are conducted by the

United Kingdom. The island is a member of the EU single market trade area and the value added tax (VAT) area, but is otherwise not part of the EU fiscal area. There are no exchange controls.

The economy has averaged over 6% growth in real terms over the past 27 years. The 2010 national income figures show real growth in nearly every sector of the economy. The GDP value for 2010 was £3.2 billion (US$4.98 billion).

The Isle of Man avoided recession and the latest economic figures are encouraging, with national income forecast to grow by 2.5% in 2010 and by 4% in 2011. The Island's per capita national income was £39,276 (US$61,400) that year.

An independent report published in early June 2012 provided evidence of the Isle of Man's positive contribution to the global economy. The Economic Research Report, produced by Ernst & Young LLP, describes the Island as a key commercial partner that delivers many benefits to the international community, to the U.K., and City of London in particular. The report showed that the Island provided US$38.9 billion in net financing to the UK in the second quarter of 2011, using Bank of England statistics.

Taxes

As with Jersey and Guernsey, under EU and OECD pressure over a period of years, the government gradually abolished corporate income tax altogether, and a 10% tax applies only to financial institution Income tax provides the major revenue at a maximum rate of 18%. The first £10,500 of personal income is taxed at 10%, rising to 18% on the balance up to £100,000 (US$156,000). Above that is tax exempt.

There is no capital transfer tax, no surtax and no corporation tax, no wealth tax, no death duty, no capital gains tax and no gift tax. Value added tax is collected by the Isle of Man Customs & Excise at the same rates which apply in the United Kingdom.

Opportunities

The Isle of Man has strong banking, investment fund and captive insurance sectors, with a well-developed advisory and financial infrastructure. There are a number of business formats, corporations, limited partnerships and limited liability companies (LLCs). There is an active trusts sector, and it offers on-line gambling licenses.

The Isle of Man offers tailored annuities and life insurance, international banking, trust and incorporation services, global investment funds, and pension funds.

And all of this activity is carefully regulated. The government fully supports the island's financial sector, yet maintains strict control through the Insurance and Pension Authority and a Financial Supervision Commission that licenses banks, trusts and investment advisors. Strict laws govern financial managers, investors' rights, outlaws money laundering and exclude undesirable elements.

This high level of compliance with global financial standards was confirmed by the International Monetary Fund (IMF) in a 2009 investigation and report. This tough supervision assures financial integrity and has earned the Isle of Man a reputation for what The Economist condescendingly described as "stuffed shirt probity."

Colin Bowen, Deputy Chairman of Isle of Man Assurance, Ltd. and a senior member of The Sovereign Society Council of Experts, explains that, unlike some offshore financial centers, Manx banks, investment funds, insurance companies and other professionals welcome American clients.

The Isle of Man offers an excellent communications network, modern business facilities and a highly skilled work force. The financial sector is the largest single contributor to GDP, employing more than 20% of the total work force of nearly 40,000.

Banking

More than 40 licensed banks (including many international banks) offer comprehensive, discreet and confidential services that compare favorably with the banks in Switzerland or Liechtenstein. In addition to banking, high-caliber legal, accounting, insurance and other financial services are available on the island.

Banking on the Isle of Man can take many forms, but often accounts opened by foreigners are associated with the trusts, corporations, insurance or pension plans they have set up on the island.

Under the Isle of Man Banking Act of 1975 as amended, all banks have to be licensed by the government. Banks on the Isle of Man are not directly supervised by the Bank of England, but they do apply its standards in practice.

Investor and depositor protection is strong and on a par with the UK. Individual depositors are protected up to a maximum of £50,000 (US$80,000) per depositor. Interest on deposits paid to nonresidents is free from withholding tax.

In spite of its ancient history, banking on the island is modern, sophisticated and user-friendly. Total deposits in the 28 banks on the Isle of Man banking system in 2011 exceeded £59 billion (US$95 billion).

There are more than 200 licensed corporate and trust service providers on the Isle of Man. There are also nearly 40,000 companies and partnerships and about 40,000 trusts under the administration of these local service providers.

Life Insurance and Annuities

One way to obtain maximum financial privacy is to purchase the products for which the Isle of Man is known worldwide—excellent insurance and annuity products carefully tailored to individual needs.

The usual minimum premium for these policies is US$250,000 but most are purchased for US$1 million or more. These policies are popular with Americans because, under U.S. tax law, this is one of the last investment areas that permit legal tax deferral. That's because life insurance allows four key tax free benefits:

1. Tax-free build-up of cash value, including dividends, interest and capital gains;

2. Tax-free borrowing against cash value;

3. Tax-free receipt of the death benefit; and

4. Freedom from estate and generation-skipping taxes.

These benefits are available in life insurance or annuity policies specifically designed to comply with U.S. tax laws. For a more detailed explanation of the many benefits of offshore life insurance and annuities, see the description in Chapter 2, under "Offshore Variable Annuities" and "Offshore Life Insurance."

Contacts

Banking:
HSBC Bank International Ltd.
P.O. Box 39, HSBC House, Ridgeway St, Douglas, IM99 1BU
Tel.: + 01624 684800
Email: offshore@hsbc.com

Trusts:
IOMA Fiduciary
IOMA House Hope Street Douglas IM1 1AP
Craig Brown, Managing Director,
Tel.: +44 (0) 1624 681207
Email: craig.brown@iomagroup.co.im

Company formation:
OCRA (Isle of Man) Ltd.
Grosvenor Court, Tower St Ramsey, IM8 1JA
Tel.: 01624 811000
Email: ocra@ocra.com
Website: http://www.ocra.com/offices/isleofman.asp

Insurance & annuities:
Colin Bowen, Deputy Chairman, IOMA
IOMA House, Hope Street, Douglas IM1 1AP
Tel.: +44 1624 681200
Email: colinb@iomagroup.co.im
Website: http://www.ioma.co.im/Fiduciary.aspx

The Channel Islands and the Isle of Man are well-established and regulated offshore financial centers you should consider. Each island has modernized its financial services regulatory laws and complies with international standards.

These islands do operate under anti-tax avoidance pressure but that comes mainly from the U.K. tax authorities directed at U.K. citizens doing business here. Each island does have a TIEA with the U.S. government.

These havens offer a solid tradition and much experience in the creation and management of asset protection trusts, international business corporations and with offshore finance, banking and insurance. They offer some of the best professional investment experts and fund managers anywhere.

Choose carefully and you can find some excellent offshore legal products, especially in mutual funds, annuities and life insurance as an investment and U.S. tax-deferred vehicles.

A Word about Americans Investing Offshore

Access to investment and mutual funds on the Channel Islands and the Isle of Man is certainly not limited to major corporations, insurance companies and wealthy investors.

Middle class, small-share investors are also welcome, certainly including foreigners, because volume makes profits. These funds typically allow free worldwide switching between funds that invest in the U.K., or in money market instruments denominated in sterling or foreign currencies.

Because of U.S. SEC restrictions most unit trust (mutual fund) groups will not respond to inquiries from a United States address because they are not registered with the SEC and therefore cannot solicit business from U.S. persons. One way in which U.S. persons can avoid legally these restrictions is by investing in the name of your own offshore trust, private foundation or international business corporation.

Traditionally, Americans have used domestic brokers to invest in foreign markets, if the brokers offered these services. It required broker contact with a U.S.-based "market maker" or an affiliate firm located in the country where you wanted to buy shares. This was a slow, cumbersome route that didn't always guarantee timely access.

As an alternative, as explained in Chapter Two, you can open an investment account with an offshore broker in London or on any of these islands in your own name and then purchase individual stocks in many offshore markets.

SEC rules do limit sharply the ability of foreign brokers to solicit business inside the U.S., unless they are registered with the SEC, a lengthy and costly procedure. However, the SEC does not prohibit U.S. citizens from opening offshore brokerage accounts to buy and sell foreign stocks so long as you, the investor, approach the foreign firm and the overseas firm doesn't approach you.

CHAPTER SEVEN

Special OFCs in Europe

*While it has no monopoly on jurisdictions that qualify as
low-tax or asset protection havens, economic and political
developments made Europe a financial center dating back
to the Middle Ages. In Chapter Four, I described two
European countries, Switzerland and Liechtenstein, which
are among the leading offshore financial centers.*

*Here some of the lesser-known European OFCs are
described. Some are best for tax-free residence, others for
banking, investment funds or as an international business base.*

*In considering European venues for your cash and
investments, keep in mind the continuing pressure from
high tax EU countries and the OECD to end all financial
privacy and to impose uniform high income and corporate
taxes on all of its EU member states, a trend these OFCs
continue to resist.*

Austria

The Austrian Republic is not a haven in the sense of low taxes,
but it is a "banking haven." That's because this nation has some
of the strongest financial privacy laws in the world. That privacy
guarantee has constitutional protection that can be changed only
by a national referendum of all voters.

For a very few select of the foreign wealthy, Austria also offers
low-tax residency for those who can qualify.

The Austrian Republic has long been a bastion of banking privacy
strategically located on what was once the eastern European border

of countries dominated by Communist Russia. From the end of World War II in 1945 to the collapse of Soviet Communism in 1992 with the Soviet Union and the United States locked in armed confrontation, Austria served as a willing Cold War financial and political go-between for both West and East.

With a population of 8.3 million, Austria covers approximately 75% of the eastern Alps. It has borders with Germany, Liechtenstein, Switzerland, Italy, Slovenia, Hungary, Slovakia and the Czech Republic. German is the official language.

Vienna was once the center of power for the Austro-Hungarian Empire but Austria was reduced to a small republic after its defeat in World War I. Following annexation by Nazi Germany in 1938 and occupation by the victorious Allies in 1945, Austria's status remained unclear for a decade. A 1955 treaty ended the Allied occupation, recognized Austria's independence, and forbade unification with Germany. Austria joined the European Union in 1995.

Austria, with its well-developed market economy, skilled labor force, and high standard of living, is closely tied to other EU economies, especially Germany's. Its economy features a large service sector, a sound industrial sector, and a small, but highly developed agricultural sector.

Following several years of solid foreign demand for Austrian exports and record employment growth, the international financial crisis of 2008 and subsequent global economic downturn led to a sharp, but brief, recession. Austrian GDP contracted 3.9% in 2009 but saw positive growth of about 2% in 2010 and 3% in 2011.

The international financial crisis of 2008 caused difficulties for Austria's largest banks whose extensive operations in central, eastern, and southeastern Europe faced large losses. The government provided bank support, including in some instances, nationalization, to stabilize the banking system. This high banking exposure to central and Eastern Europe continues as well as political and economic uncertainties caused by the European sovereign

Austria may be a good place for you to do business. It ranks among the 10 richest countries in the world on a per capita basis. The 2011 GDP was US$425.1 billion with a per capita GDP of about US$50,000. Its capital gold reserves rank third in the western world. It is industrialized and developed with a large service sector. Most people, especially the younger generation, speak English.

Austria always has had close links to eastern European countries and has benefited from these links since the collapse of the Soviet Union. Many businesses have relocated from Eastern Europe to Austria in recent years. Among the major Austrian companies is the Red Bull drinks label and Swarovski crystal. Worldwide, Austria has the highest number of graduates from secondary education; the workforce is reliable and highly motivated. Industrial labor problems are almost non-existent.

Secrecy: It's the Law

When Austrian national banking laws were officially re-codified in 1979, the well-established tradition of bank secrecy was already two centuries old. During that time, Austrian bank secrecy and privacy produced two major types of so-called "anonymous accounts." These accounts usually required no account holder identification, no mailing address and no personal references.

Just deposit funds and use the account as you pleased, all done anonymously. Both the Sparbuch bank account and the Wertpapierbuch securities account have been abolished, victims of the European Union's fixation with destroying financial privacy wherever possible.

Notwithstanding the demands of the EU, current Austrian bank secrecy laws forbid banks to "disclose secrets which have been entrusted to them solely due to business relationships with customers." The prohibition is waived only in criminal court proceedings involving fiscal crimes, with the exception of petty offenses. The prohibition does not apply "if the customer expressly and in writing consents to the disclosure of the secret."

As an additional layer of protection, Austrian law raises this guarantee of banking and financial privacy to a constitutional level, a special statute that can only be changed by a majority vote in a national referendum, a highly unlikely event. All major political parties support financial privacy as a longstanding national policy.

As a member EU country, until 2009 Austria strongly opposed EU demands for compulsory withholding taxes and financial information sharing. In 2009, in a change of policy under pressure from the G-20 countries and the EU, Austria agreed to apply Article 26 of the "OECD Model Tax Convention."

As discussed before, this article recognizes "tax evasion" as a valid basis for foreign tax agency inquiries concerning their citizens with accounts in an offshore center. Under the OECD procedure, foreign tax authorities wishing to take advantage of tax information exchange agreements must supply evidence of their suspicions (e.g., names, facts, alleged tax crimes) to the requested government. If there is sufficient probable cause to believe tax evasion has occurred, the requested government must supply the information.

Austria was one of three EU nations exempted from the 2005 EU tax directive information sharing plan (along with Belgium and Luxembourg). All three nations, joined by non-EU member Switzerland, declined to share tax information, but each collects the 35% EU withholding tax on interest paid to nationals of EU member states. Foreign nationals of non-EU nations, including U.S. persons, are not subject to this EU withholding tax.

Austria's opposition to weakening European bank secrecy laws was demonstrated again in 2012 when it joined with Luxembourg to block the European Commission's plans to negotiate new and stronger savings tax agreements with non-EU members Switzerland, Monaco, Liechtenstein, Andorra and San Marino. Austria's Finance Minister challenged the EU's motives, insisting that it was trying to abolish banking secrecy and ensure an automatic exchange of data rather than include non-EU countries.

Stocks and Bonds

Until the continuing world recession that began in 2008, the Austrian stock market had one of the world's best performance records in recent years. It benefited in part from the Eastern European expansion boom that began in the 1990s after the East-West Iron Curtain disintegrated and its formerly Communist-dominated Eastern European neighbors turned to free market polices.

Nonresidents are not subject to restrictions on securities purchased in Austria and they can be transferred abroad without restrictions or reporting. Nonresidents can purchase an unlimited amount of bonds and/or stocks on the condition that the money used for purchase is in either foreign currency or Euros. When securities are sold, the cash proceeds can be freely converted and exported without restrictions.

Taxes

Taxes are comparatively low; corporate income tax is 25% and has been since 2005. The highest personal income tax rate is 50%. All resident companies and permanent establishments of non-resident companies are subject to corporate income tax. Resident companies are liable for tax on their worldwide income. Non-resident businesses are taxed on their Austrian-sourced income only. Dividend income is exempt from corporate income tax when the shares are held by a private foundation. Income from interest and capital gains from the selling of shares are subject to an interim tax of 12.5%.

Austrian tax authorities found a way to profit from their attractive banking haven status—the government levies a 25% tax on the total bank interest earned. Foreigners can avoid the 25% tax on bond interest because no tax is withheld if a declared nonresident is the bank account holder. Interest paid on investments held in non-bearer form in Austrian banks, such as certificates of deposit, is also exempt from the withholding tax. Interest on convertible bonds, however, is subject to a withholding tax of 20% at the payment source.

Unfortunately, an American citizen bondholder is subject to capital gains tax in the U.S. on the full capital gain, despite the Austrian tax. A double taxation treaty between the U.S. and Austria eases this hardship. If you file a request with the IRS, the Austrian tax will be partly repaid, diminishing the net tax burden to 10%. The remaining 10% tax can offset part of the U.S. capital gains tax ordinarily imposed. The double taxation agreement does not apply to Austrian interest and dividends, which remain fully taxable in the U.S.

The Austrian government's decision to reduce the corporate tax rate from 34% to 25% in 2005 led to a 30% increase in new investment projects. In addition to cutting corporate taxes to one of the lowest levels in the EU, the reforms also reduced the tax burden on multinational firms using Austria as regional headquarters. Austria also offers significant tax concessions to holding companies, foundations and certain other investment incentives, all successfully designed to attract foreign capital.

Live in Austria Income Tax-Free

It is not widely known, but a wealthy foreigner who can qualify to become a resident of Austria also may qualify for a unique tax break—100% of annual income completely free of taxes! This preferential tax treatment, called a Zuzugsbegünstigung, used to be ready and waiting at the obliging Ministry of Finance. (My Vienna sources say that as a result of alleged abuse this program was quietly suspended in 2012.)

A foreigner who is a new Austrian resident can qualify if the person meets all the following requirements:

- had no residence in Austria during 10 years prior to application

- doesn't engage in any business activity within Austria

- can prove sufficient income from outside sources

- agrees to spend a minimum of US$70,000 in Austria each year

- has a place to live and intends to stay in Austria for at least six months (183 days) each year

When all those conditions are met, a foreigner may be able to live tax-free in Austria. All income from foreign pension or retirement funds, dividends and interest from foreign investments and securities or any offshore businesses outside Austria are tax exempt.

In most cases, officials grant a tax break of at least 75% of potential tax liability—but a good local lawyer may be able to negotiate a 100% reduction. If you have foreign income taxable in your home country and there is no double taxation agreement between Austria and your country, the Ministry of Finance may grant you a zero tax base, or a special circumstances ruling, but only after you establish your residence in Austria.

Is Austrian residence status for sale to the very rich? To be frank, yes. If you are a reputable and wealthy foreigner, there will be few obstacles to becoming a resident. Residency gives you the best of both worlds—life in an extremely desirable location, but without the high taxes Austrian citizens must pay.

Once in residence, you could apply for citizenship, but that would defeat the purpose. As an Austrian citizen, you'd be liable for full taxation. The only additional advantages would be having an Austrian passport and the right to purchase as much real property as you wish, which is otherwise very difficult for a foreigner merely residing in Austria.

Even with its agreement to share tax information using the OECD standard, Austria's financial and banking privacy laws provide much great security than most other countries. As a result, it's wise to keep Austria near the top of your potential banking list, especially if your major area of business interest lies in Eastern Europe or Russia.

Contacts

Ministry of Finance
Hintere Zollamtsstrasse 2b, 1030 Vienna, Austria
Tel.: +43-1-5143-33
Website: http://english.bmf.gv.at/Ministry/_start.htm

Recommended Bank:
Valartis Bank (Austria) AG
Contact: **Patrick Doherty**, Senior Vice President
Rathausstrasse 20, A-1010 Vienna, Austria
Tel.: + 43 (0) 577 89 186 Fax +43 (0) 577 89 150
Email: p.doherty@valartis.at
Website: www.valartis.at

Recommended offshore vault for storage of precious metals and other valuables:
DAS SAFE
Auerspergstrasse 1, A-1080, Vienna, Austria
Tel.: +43 1 406 61 74
Email: info@dassafe.com
Website: http://www.dassafe.com/

Recommended Consultant on Residence and Citizenship

The Nestmann Group
Hertha Firnbergstrasse 9/311, 1100 Vienna, Austria
Tel.: + (43) 1 587 57 95 60
Email: drkleeber@nestmann.com
Website: http://www.nestmann.com

Embassy of Austria
3524 International Court, N.W.,
Washington, D.C. 20008
Tel.: (202) 895-6700 Fax: (202) 895-6750
Email: austroinfo@austria.org

Website: http://www.austria.org

United States Embassy
Boltzmanngasse 16 1090, Vienna, Austria
Tel.: + (43-1) 313-390 Fax: + (43-1) 310-0682
Email: embassy@usembassy.at

U.S. Consular Section
Parkring 12a 1010, Vienna, Austria
Visa Information / Appointment Hotline: + (43-0900) 510-300
Fax: + (43-1) 512-5835Email: ConsulateVienna@state.gov
Website: http://vienna.usembassy.gov

Andorra

The Principality of Andorra, nestled high in the Pyrenees between Spain and France, is a low-tax jurisdiction for very wealthy foreigners who enjoy winter sports. It's difficult to become a citizen, but establishing residency is fairly easy. There are no income taxes (yet) and banking privacy still exists but is dwindling.

High and Jagged

Andorra is a tiny, mountainous country without many taxes, a military or poverty. It has only been accessible from France or Spain by motor vehicles over mountainous roads in long journeys, depending on weather conditions.

The country's standard of living is high, the cost of living relatively low but growing and the scenery delightful. According to legend, Charlemagne, Emperor of the Holy Roman Empire, in 748 gave Andorra its name and its independence. Gazing over the mountain region newly wrested from the Moors of Spain, he is said to have exclaimed, *"Wild valley of hell, I name you Endor!"* (The valley of Endor, at the foot of Mount Thabor in the Holy Land, was the campsite of the Israelites during the war against the Canaanites.)

With political and economic stability, no labor strikes, virtually no unemployment and the lowest crime rate in Europe, strict banking secrecy, remote Andorra could be your haven to get away from the modern world's problems.

Bargain Isolation

Until the end of World War II, Andorra was a time capsule of traditional European mountain life. Napoleon, declining to invade the diminutive joint principality, said, "Andorra is too amazing. Let it remain as a museum piece."

In the last three decades, the country has been transformed from a traditional pastoral and farming economy to one of commerce and year-round tourism. The population is increasing from 5,500 in 1945—the same as in the 1880s—to around 85,082 today. Only about 14,000 are citizens, the rest foreigners. Most of the others have moved there for work opportunities or to escape onerous taxes in their home countries. Andorra has an amazing 11.6 million visitors annually, many skiers, but many more bargain hunters for low tax discount goods and cigarettes.

Geography, Government

Andorra consists of 185 square miles, about one-fifth the size of the smallest American state, Rhode Island. Andorra's rugged terrain consists of gorges and narrow valleys surrounded by mountain peaks that rise higher than 9,500 feet above sea level.

It is an independent nation-state and is governed by 28 elected members of the General Council. Until 1993, the President of France and the Bishop of Seo d'Urgel (Spain), as co-princes, were responsible for Andorra's foreign affairs and judicial system. These "co-princes" could veto decisions by the General Council. They controlled the judiciary and police, but did not intrude into Andorra's affairs, except in 1933, when French gendarmes were sent in to maintain order after the judiciary dissolved the General Council. For the next 60 years, demands for independence were a repeated political refrain.

In 1993, Andorrans voted to sever their feudal links with France and Spain. The country subsequently gained a seat in the United Nations as the third-smallest member-state. While citizenship is a daunting prospect—it can only be attained by marrying an Andorran and by staying in the principality for at least 25 years—the number of resident foreigners in Andorra demonstrates just how attractive the country is as a tax haven. Seventy percent of the people who live in Andorra are resident foreigners and these immigrants are demanding more political rights.

Andorra established formal links with the European Union in 1991. After two years of tough negotiations, Andorra signed its first ever international treaty by joining the EU customs union, the first non-EU member country to do so. Andorra now applies the common EU external tariff and trade policy. This allows free transit of its goods (except for farm products) within the EU market. Andorra adopted the euro in 2002 and signed a monetary agreement with EU in 2011 making it effectively subject to the monetary policy of the European Central Bank.

Duty Free

Andorra's simple, pastoral life of a half century ago is gone. Instead, it became the shopping mall of the Pyrenees because of its duty-free tax status but that ended in 1993. The country still is exempt from the EU's value added taxes, making it a sort of "Mall of Europe." An estimated 11 million visitors a year — mostly day-trippers — invade Andorra. They pour over the border and head for shops along the central valley road. On weekends, traffic jams are a prelude to the jostling, shopping, crowd-packed streets of Andorra la Vella, the capital.

Until recently Andorra's citizens and residents paid no taxes on personal income, capital gains, capital transfers, inheritance, or profits. There is no sales tax or VAT. Until 2011 there were no taxes for resident companies or individuals other than modest annual registration fees, municipal rates, property transaction taxes, some minor sales taxes and a sliding scale capital gains tax introduced in 2007.

A law imposing a corporate income tax of 10%, initially on non-resident entities, came into force in 2011. Also in 2011, a new government introduced a 10% tax for non-residents on local-sourced income — so much for foreign investment. This tax is being extended to resident individuals who have incomes of €30,000 (US$42,000) or more per year. Since 84% of Andorrans earn less than that each year, this was a popular soak-the-rich measure.

There is also talk of the introduction of a value added tax to be followed by extension of the income tax non-resident individuals and corporations, but these plans have met with verbally violent opposition from the many foreigners residents here. Nominal local property taxes pay for municipal services—average annual rental property tax varies from around US$120 for an apartment to US$240 for a house of any size.

Little known outside of the skiing and financial communities, this small European tax haven saw some startling, double-digit rises in real property values in recent years, prior to the continuing 2008 global recession. Buyers come from an active local market, second homebuyers looking for ski condos and international buyers who want to establish residence in a leading tax haven. A 2-3 bedroom condo here can sell for US$500,000, approximately half the cost of similar digs in Monaco.

In 2009, for the first time in seven centuries, the government of Andorra opened up investment in resorts and other businesses to foreign investors. Along with lifting this curb on foreign investment, the government paid the usual lip service of now wanting to be seen as an "investment haven" and not a "tax haven."

Residents

A second residence in Andorra won't alter your domicile of origin for the purposes of home nation inheritance or estate taxes.

But if you're granted a passive residence in Andorra, you have the right to protection under the law, certain benefits from the health and social security systems, the right to a driver's license and the right to own and register resident-plate vehicles. Resident status does not confer the right to vote, nor does it allow local commercial activity, such as owning or running a business.

If you're looking for residence status, there are two categories of permits—both of which are difficult to obtain—those that give the holder the right to work in Andorra and those that don't allow employment.

To encourage immigration of high-net-worth individuals, often retired persons, the government grants "Passive Residence Permits" called residencias that are subject to a quota determined periodically according to the "economic and social needs of the Principality of Andorra."

Otherwise, long term residence is only possible to those with work permits, which are controlled by quotas. It is possible to get around this system by owning a nominee company, which is relatively expensive, but the government watches closely, and any kind of suspicious activity or competition against locals can bring rapid expulsion.

Due to the high ratio of foreigners to Andorrans in the Principality, the government uses selective methods of admitting new residents. Residence permits, residencias, are available to applicants, retired or otherwise, who have an address in the Principality and who genuinely wish to reside in Andorra and become an active community member.

The applicants must prove private income sufficient that he/she need not seek local employment. Once the applicant is accepted, a residencia is issued for one year, renewable after the first year for a period of three years. Applying for a residencia is a lengthy procedure and must be conducted in the official language, Catalan. Applications are handled by the Immigration Department of the Police. Tel.: + (376) 826-222).

Anyone in Andorra who is not a resident is considered a tourist—but there's no legal limit on the period of stay. Tourists can even rent or purchase a property for personal use for as long as they wish. So it's easy to live in Andorra, "perpetual traveler" style, without an official residence permit.

The annual quota for non-work permits in recent years has ranged from 200 to 500. The earlier you apply, the better your chance of success. Applicants must also show availability of sufficient economic means to permit residence in Andorra without having to work throughout the period of passive residence.

Bank Secrecy

Andorra has no exchange controls and bank secrecy is strict—but nowhere near as strict as it used to be.

In spite of claims by some offshore hucksters claiming inside contacts at Andorran banks, the government of Andorra no longer allows numbered and coded accounts without identifying and recording the true owners. Foreigners and their legal entities may open and operate bank accounts with fewer restrictions than imposed in Switzerland, for example, but the foreign party must justify the need for a local bank account by establishing residence in the country or buying a condominium.

Until 2009, bank secrecy laws prevented giving bank account information to foreign governments. Since then the Andorran government has applied the OECD standard for tax information exchange, providing information in individual cases where evidence of foreign tax evasion is alleged by a government with which Andorra has a tax treaty. Andorra now has 18 such treaties with other countries including neighboring France and Spain, as well as Monaco, Liechtenstein, Austria and the Netherlands, although none as yet with the United States or the United Kingdom.

Under pressure from the OECD, France and Spain, Andorra has adopted a broad definition of the crime of "money laundering." That includes having an account here that has not been declared to the tax authorities of the country where the account owner lives and is taxed. If an official foreign tax authority, such as the U.S. IRS, tells the Andorran government that one of its nationals is suspected of foreign tax evasion in Andorra, banking secrecy is automatically suspended.

The local Andorran judge orders the Anti-Money Laundering Police Unit to demand information about the person from all five banks in Andorra on all present and past accounts held in the banks or in money management or investment vehicles. That information is turned over to the foreign tax authorities before the suspect is ever charged or tried, much less convicted.

Locals quietly admit that, as deposits flee, the country is now financially bleeding to death. They predict that sooner or later most of the banks will disappear. No country with a population of 85,000 needs five banks. The banks here made all their profits from the business of nonresident clients, the vast majority being Spaniards. Now the bank secrecy is gone and foreigners are closing their accounts.

Interestingly, Andorra's two major banks, Andorra Credit Bank and Andbank (Andorra) have offices in Panama and other leading offshore financial centers. It appears that while these banks were founded in Andorra, they now look elsewhere for clients and funds, a trend that an Andbank official in Panama confirmed to me.

Andorra has been home to thousands of bank accounts belonging to prudent Spaniards. Annually, an estimated 10% of the billions of Euros that escape Spanish regulation and taxes are thought to be funneled through Andorran accounts. Perhaps 1,500 tax exiles from the U.K. have residences here also.

All five local banks have a worldwide network of foreign correspondents and some foreign branches. With no exchange controls, accounts can be held in up to 20 foreign currencies and traded in any quantity at the rate quoted in Zurich. Exchange rates for clients are some of the best in Europe.

A Local Opinion

A longtime American friend who has lived in Andorra for many years and himself is a former Swiss banker, tells me that "…the banks now require anyone opening an account here to appear in person. Lawyers can no longer open accounts for them. U.S. persons who reside here are not allowed to hold or buy any American securities in their local bank accounts. Since the adoption of strict American anti-money laundering and anti-terrorism laws, the banks here unanimously agreed to forbid any investments in, or holding of, U.S. securities. The banks are frank to say they don't want to waste excessive time and money in reporting to the IRS and the SEC. When the new U.S. laws took effect a few years ago the banks made resident Americans here sell all their U.S. investments or close their accounts."

My friend also observed that in his opinion all these recent taxes condemn Andorra to implode because "…two real attractions for foreigners—no income tax and banking secrecy—have been eliminated. What remains is a very ugly place to live with a proposed low initial tax rate that may not be low enough to attract a very appealing class of new residents."

The Economy

Slower growth in Spain and France has dimmed Andorra's current prospects. In 2010 and 2011, a drop in tourism contributed to a contraction in GDP and a deterioration of public finances, prompting the government to implement several austerity measures. The GDP in 2011 was US$3.169 billion with a per capita GDP of US$37,200.

The country has developed summer and winter tourist resorts, with more than 250 restaurants and over a thousand retail and wholesale shops. There are about 300 hotels, ranging from elegant to simple. Some have double rooms available for as low as US$50 per night. Tourism employs a large portion of the labor force.

During the winter, skiers flock to Andorra's slopes. High peaks separate six deep valleys and though the Pyrenees lack the famous Alpine altitudes, they are breathtakingly steep and far less expensive to visit. The Andorran government encourages upscale tourism at its popular ski resorts, attractive because of comparatively low prices. Ski areas are state of the art and bountiful snowfall guarantees weekend visitors from throughout Europe. Hikers use the lifts in the summer.

In the past, Andorra's thriving tourist industry hastened the country's economic transformation. Former shepherds—now wealthy investors—import cheap Spanish and Portuguese labor to supported a building boom, which transformed Andorra's central valley into a string of shops and condominiums. Don't get the idea, however, that all the land is developed. Only 8% of Andorra's land is both suitable and zoned for development. One can still find small villages in which to live. Many have less than 100 inhabitants and offer absolute peace and quiet.

Contacts

Andorran Tourism Board
http://www.andorra.ad/en-US/Pages/default.aspx
Andorra Government: Website: www.andorra.ad/
Embassy of Andorra
2 United Nations Plaza, 27th Floor, New York, NY 10017
Tel.: (212) 750-8064 Fax: (212) 750-6630
Email: andorra@un.int Website: http://www.andorra.be

The Andorran Permanent Representative to the United Nations is accredited as Andorra's ambassador to the United States. The U.S. Ambassador to Spain is also accredited as ambassador to Andorra. U.S. Consulate General officials in Barcelona are responsible for the conduct of relations with Andorra.

United States Embassy
Serrano 75, 28006, Madrid, Spain

Tel.: + (34) 91-587-2200
Fax: + (34) 91-587-2303
Website: http://madrid.usembassy.gov/
Email: amemb@embusa.es

U.S. Consulate General
Paseo Reina Elisenda de Montcada 23, 08034 Barcelona, Spain
Tel.: + (34) 93-280-2227, Fax: + (34) 93-205-5206
Website: http://madrid.usembassy.gov/
Email: amemb@embusa.es

Servissim, Head office
(Private Client services / property sales / rentals)
Carretera general, Edifici Areny, Baixos, Arinsal, La Massana, Principality of Andorra
Tel.: + (376) 737-900 Fax: + (376) 737-904
Email: headoffice@servissim.ad
Website: http://www.servissim.ad/

Banks in Andorra:
Andbank: http://www.andbank.com/
MoraBanc: http://www.morabanc.ad/
Banca Privada d'Andorra (BPA): https://www.bpa.ad/
Banc Sabadell d'Andorra ('A):https://www.bsandorra.com/
Crèdit Andorrà: http://www.creditandorra.ad/commercial_banking

Grand Duchy of Luxembourg

Luxembourg is primarily a business and banking haven rather than a personal tax haven. It is also a haven for international holding companies and investment funds. Its strong financial privacy laws, which have a long history, were weakened somewhat in 2009 when it adopted the OECD standard for tax information sharing.

Right in the Middle

Little Luxembourg (51 miles long by 34 miles wide) is a constitutional hereditary Grand Duchy. The House of Orange-Nassau and its branches have ruled here since 1815. The reign of the present ruler, Grand Duke Henri, began in 2000 and the Heir Apparent is Prince Guillaume, his son. Locals commonly speak French, German, English and their own peculiar version of German called Letzebürgesch or Luxemburgish. That's a dialect said to be incomprehensible even to those who have spoken "normal" German since birth.

Luxembourg City is a fortress, with a deep river valley surrounding the old city on three sides. From a castle built on its rocky promontory in 963, the strategic settlement grew, passed between Burgundian, French, Spanish, Austrian and Prussian control. Each conqueror strengthened the natural site, until at one point the defenses included three fortified rings, 24 forts, a 14-mile network of underground tunnels and more than 400,000 square feet of chambers carved into the sandstone for soldiers, animals and supplies. Even though a peace treaty in 1867 decreed that this "Gibraltar of the North" be destroyed, you can still see plenty of intriguing remains. In fact, the old town and the fortress walls constitute a UN World Heritage site.

The pie-shaped country, with a 2011 population of 509,074 shares borders with Germany to the east, Belgium to the west and France to the south. A charter member of the EU, Luxembourg is also a part of the Benelux group along with Belgium and the Netherlands, a three-country union that was a precursor to the EU. Since 1922, Luxembourg has had a fully integrated monetary and economic union with its larger neighbor, Belgium. The local currency was the Belgium-Luxembourg franc, now replaced by the euro. Today, Luxembourg City is the home of the European Court of Justice, the secretariat of the European Parliament, the European Investment Bank and European Court of Auditors.

Per capita, Luxembourg is the third-richest country in the world, with a national GDP in 2011 of US$62.9 billion. The country continues to enjoy an extraordinarily high standard of living; GDP per capita for 2011 was US$84,700 among the highest in the world, and the highest in the euro zone.

Luxembourg's economy was dominated by steel production, but since World War II the government successfully has encouraged development of a diversified financial sector. Tourism is also important.

In all of Europe, Luxembourg has the second-most extensive banking industry, after London, with over 150 banks. The private banking industry here possibly is Europe's largest in total assets. Most banks are foreign-owned and have extensive foreign dealings, but Luxembourg has lost some of its advantages as a tax haven because of OECD and EU pressure. The Stock Exchange specializes in collective investment funds and many of the several thousand Luxembourg-registered funds are listed there.

Offshore Haven

Although the nation's international banking activity dates back to the late 19th Century, Luxembourg did not hit its stride as an offshore haven until the 1980s. It was then that the Eurobond markets located there really put Luxembourg on the global financial map. Luxembourg is comfortably in the world's top 10 financial centers with a large accumulation of cash and a commanding presence in key areas such as holding companies, private banking, investment funds and reinsurance.

This growth process developed from forces over which Luxembourg had no control. Rather, growth came from foreign nationals seeking better profits and escape from their own governments' anti-free market policies, including:

- expanded foreign investment in European Common Market nations during the mid-1960s

- imposition by the U.S. Congress of a domestic interest equalization tax in the 1980s that drove American corporations to borrow funds abroad rather than at home

- German domestic capital flow restrictions and mandatory lending ratios

- the 35% Swiss withholding tax on bank account and other interest

- currency exchange controls in France

- stiff bank account reporting rules in neighboring Holland

To avoid these restrictive circumstances, astute western Europeans and Americans began searching for a safe place to invest their money. They also needed a convenient place to conduct business with maximum freedom and lower taxes. Right there in the middle of Europe, Luxembourg and its banks beckoned.

Microsoft, FedEx, AOL, iTunes and Skype are among companies with global or European headquarters—and big tax savings—in Luxembourg.

An example of Luxembourg's official willingness to cooperate with foreign business caused a political uproar in the United Kingdom in 2012. It was revealed that two major U.K. companies had agreed with the Luxembourg tax authorities to establish subsidiaries there that ultimately were taxed at a rate of 0.5% at a time when the U.K. corporate tax was 28%. One of the companies avoided £34 million (US$53 million) in UK taxes. All parties agreed the arrangement was legal but the usual anti-tax haven opponents screamed loudly.

Pressure from All Sides

Luxembourg's conservative nature is revealed in a still popular 19th Century local song lyric, "Wir welle bleiwen wat wir sin." This simply means, "We want to remain as we are"—a sentiment that easily could be the official national motto. This statement had special meaning while the European Union (especially neighboring Germany), pressured this tiny grand duchy for reforms of their banking and financial privacy laws for many years.

Unfamiliar to many Americans, Luxembourg is an established international financial and banking center. If you want a no-nonsense EU base for business operations and excellent private banking services, this is the place. Although this tiny country lacks the lure of the Swiss ski slopes or the white sands at Grand Cayman, it more than makes up for its lack of tourist attractions by offering possible tax-free operations and banking privacy.

Business Banking a National Passion

About 60% of all Luxembourg bank activity is now denominated in euros. Another one-third is in U.S. dollars. Roughly 24,000 people, 11% of the workforce, are employed directly or indirectly in the Grand Duchy's nearly 150 banks and financial groups and nearly 30% of the GDP flows from financial business.

German banks, in particular, operate here to escape domestic withholding taxes on interest and dividend loan limitations on corporate customers and they account for over 50% of all banking business. They also use the nation to deal in gold, as Luxembourg imposes no VAT. Luxembourg's authorities closely watch bank solvency and reserves. Bank accounts are insured against loss in an amount equivalent to about US$15,000 each.

Until 2009, the government did not believe it had a duty to ensure that a bank's foreign clients paid home country taxes. Tax evasion is not a crime here, although the government maintains tax treaties with many nations, including the U.S. and U.K. In 2009, Luxembourg joined other offshore financial centers in agreeing to apply the OECD standard allowing exchange of tax information in specific cases of alleged tax evasion by foreigners.

The government also began negotiating a round of tax information exchange treaties with other nations, including France and Germany, two major past antagonists on the issue of bank secrecy and it concluded a revised TIEA with the U.S. allowing information exchange in cases of alleged tax evasion.

Bank assets, liabilities and other operations must be reported to the Banking Commission. This enables the commission to maintain strict controls on the solidity and honesty of Luxembourg banks. Until the OECD 2009 agreement, the government provided information only when a crime was related to a bank account itself and the alleged offense was also a crime under local law.

Taxes

Keep in mind that Luxembourg is not a tax haven—it's an investment and banking center. The effective corporate tax rate is more than 30%. Personal income taxes can range up to 38%.

Resident companies are taxed on their world-wide income. Resident means that the business has its main establishment in Luxembourg from which it is managed, holds its general meetings and performs central administrative functions. Non-resident companies having a "permanent establishment" in Luxembourg (a place of business or fixed equipment including branches) pay income tax only on their income originating in Luxembourg.

The rate of tax on income less than €15,000 (US$18,750) is 20% and 21% for income above €15,000. There is a 5% employment fund surcharge and a charge of between 6% and 10.5% for municipal services depending on location.

World Connections

Luxembourg's financial picture depends on more than the solvency of its banks. The nation is a major transaction center and clearinghouse for international currency and bond markets. It is home to Clearstream Banking S.A., the clearing and settlement division of Deutsche Börse, based in Luxembourg and Frankfurt. It functions as International Central Securities Depository and clearing house for securities. As such it is one of the major custodians and clearers of the Eurobonds market.

This links Luxembourg's financial health to the state of the entire international banking system, especially the German and U.S. economies. Most banking clients in Luxembourg are multinational corporations, not individuals and their collective fortunes directly affect Luxembourg's financial stability.

In 2008, the financial turmoil and the worst global recession in 60 years posed daunting challenges to Luxembourg's small open economy. The financial sector, hosting a large number of foreign-owned subsidiary banks, Europe's largest investment fund industry and second-largest money market industry, was fully exposed to the turmoil. Besides financial service exports, the contraction in European demand also hurt the economy's traditional export sectors. As a result, Luxembourg faced its most severe recession since the steel crisis in the mid-1970s, but took credible steps to support and stimulate the economy and the financial sector.

Because of this tie to the prosperity of others, those seeking shockproof banking might do better with an account in Switzerland. This is particularly true if you possess sufficiently large deposit sums to command the personal attention of Swiss bankers. For those with less cash but who still desire privacy every bit as good as (or better) than Switzerland, by all means, try Luxembourg.

Virtual Tax Freedom for Holding Companies

Since 1929, Luxembourg has been a tax-free haven for holding companies and investment funds. Both are tax exempt except for a relatively small fee at initial registration (1% of subscribed capital) and an annual taxe d'abonnement, computed at about 0.2% of actual share value for holding companies and 0.06% for investment funds.

Holding companies, with their special status, escape most taxes, but a minimum tax of €1,575 was imposed in 2011. Holding companies are suited to holding international investments, but are not allowed to trade themselves.

Collective investment funds (UCIs) are also taxed on a low basis. Luxembourg has applied a withholding tax to non-residents' investment returns under the EU Savings Tax Directive since 2005. Income tax and municipal business tax on profits give a nearly 30% marginal corporation tax rate; rates for individuals are higher, and they pay a wealth tax in addition.

Holding companies typically own foreign company shares or bonds. They can manage these interests, but cannot engage in local business beyond operational maintenance and staffing. Holding companies are exempt from taxes on dividends, interest and royalties, bond interest, profits from securities sales, or purchases and capital gains taxes. Luxembourg is home to approximately 2,000 holding companies (which include many major multinational holding and finance corporations) and the number is steadily growing. Holding companies are exempt from taxes on dividends, interest, royalties, profits from securities sales and purchases and capital gains taxes.

The Grand Duchy's stock exchange is used extensively for issues of EU bonds, demonstrating Luxembourg's international importance. Numerous major banks operate there to handle this business. Luxembourg has also passed a series of new laws aimed at attracting mutual fund investment companies.

SICAV Investing

Luxembourg has its own mutual funds, known as Sociétés d'Investissement Collective à Capital Variable, or SICAVs. Each Luxembourg bank encourages clients to enroll in its SICAV, unless the investor has an unusually large sum to invest. Banks earn fees of between 1.5% to 3% annually for managing client mutual fund investments, plus commissions on sales of bonds or stocks in the fund.

The Luxembourg government also gets its slice from fees and taxes on the funds. There are more than 8,000 funds collectively with assets of more than one trillion Euros.

Luxembourg is the center of ready-made offshore private banking. Your banker alternates as broker and mutual fund salesperson. He or she can help you select one or more SICAV funds to meet your investment objectives, then complete all the necessary paperwork. SICAVs accept relatively modest initial deposits starting at a US$25,000 minimum at most local banks.

Contacts

Government of Luxembourg
Website: http://www.gouvernement.lu

Commission de Surveillance du Secteur Financier
L-2991 Luxembourg, 63 Avenue de la Liberté, Luxembourg
Tel.: +352-4292-9201
Website: http://www.cssf.lu/index.php

Ministry of the Economy and Foreign Trade
Boulevard Royal L - 2449 Luxembourg
Tel.: 352 24 78 1
Website: http://www.eco.public.lu/

Embassy of the Grand-Duchy of Luxembourg
2200 Massachusetts Avenue, N.W., Washington, D.C. 20008
Tel.: (202) 265-4171 Fax: (202) 328-8270
Email: washington.info@mae.etat.lu
Website: http://www.luxembourg-usa.org/

United States Embassy
22 Boulevard Emmanuel Servais, L-2535 Luxembourg
Grand-Duchy of Luxembourg
Tel.: + (352) 46-0123 Fax: + (352) 46-1401
Email: Luxembourgconsular@state.gov
Website: http://luxembourg.usembassy.gov

OCRA (Luxembourg) S.A.
P.O. Box 878, 19 Rue Aldringen
L-2018, Luxembourg
Tel.: +352 224 286
Email: luxembourg@ocra.lu
Website: www.ocra.lu
OCRA Worldwide is a leading independent corporate and trust
service provider.

Principality of Monaco

Monaco is a tax haven for the exceedingly wealthy—and great wealth is what it takes to afford living here. It is home to more millionaires and billionaires per capita than any place in the world, many retired and enjoying the very good life.

The 1.08 square miles of Monaco on the French Riviera is home to over 30,500 people, but this unique and ancient principality is not suitable for everyone. If you want to make this your permanent home, it helps to have more than a modest amount of money and an assured income for life. And it doesn't hurt to know the Prince and the royal family.

Monaco is for individuals who have already made their money—people who want to practice the art of living while others mind the store for them; people who want to spend time on the Riviera. If tax avoidance is the only goal, there are cheaper places to do that. Only 20% of Monaco's residents are Monégasque citizens, the rest are foreigners.

Many residents are just wealthy people who decided to retire in Monaco, drawn to the pleasant atmosphere, Mediterranean climate and leisure. It is also a popular resort, attracting tourists to its casino and beaches. Monaco has all the facilities that wealthy people consider necessary: country clubs, health clubs, and golf and tennis clubs. The second-0smallest country in the world also boasts the world's longest longevity for its citizens. Residents can expect to live to an average age of 89.68.

Indeed, Monaco may have a small population and area, but it has all the services and cultural activities of a city the size of San Francisco. Monaco's prices are expensive, but no worse than London, Paris, or Geneva. These days, there are as many Italian restaurants as there are French ones. Long before the euro, cash of any kind was the European common currency in this principality.

Some people may find Monaco's police presence a little severe. The principality has the lowest crime rate of any highly urbanized area in the world. This physical security is, of course, one of its great advantages.

Monaco is certainly what can be called "high profile."

The world remembers Grace Kelly, the Hollywood film star, who married Prince Rainier in 1956. The international spotlight followed her until she died in a tragic car accident in 1982. During his long rule, Prince Rainier III worked hard to expand the economic and professional scope of the country. Few recent monarchs can claim credit for extending their dominions by one-fifth without conquest. But, by land filling the sea, the Prince managed to expand his tiny principality by 23% in his long reign that began in 1949. This land expansion mirrored the late Prince Rainier's determination to make this a dynamic modern mini state.

In 1997, the Principality celebrated its 700th anniversary of life under the rule of the Grimaldi family. Three months after the death of his father, Prince Rainier III, on April 6, 2005, Prince Albert II formally acceded to the throne on July 12, 2005.

The Grimaldi children had wild personal reputations and the details of their private lives constantly appeared in the gossip columns of the European press. As they have aged, things have calmed down, although Prince Albert has acknowledged paternity of a child born to an African airline hostess and another born to California woman.

In July 2011, Prince Albert, 53, and Princess Charlene, 33, the former Charlene Wittstock of South Africa, were married in an elaborate wedding costing a reported US$70 million. A French newspaper claimed that a few days before the wedding, Charlene, was stopped at the Nice airport with a one-way ticket home to South

Africa following claims that her husband-to-be had fathered an il-
legitimate child during their relationship. The paper alleged that a
series of phone calls between the police and Palace officials followed
before Charlene's passport was confiscated.

Economy

Until the recession that began in 2008, Monaco had experienced
a remarkable economic development based on trading, tourism and
financial services in a tax-friendly environment. Until then Monaco
managed to generate annually over US$8 billion worth of business
and the state had an annual income of €593 million (US$800 mil-
lion), carried no debts and possesses unpublished liquid reserves of
at least US$1.8 billion.

In 2009, Monaco's GDP fell by 11.5% as the euro-zone crisis
caused a sharp drop in tourism, retail activity and real estate
sales. Although future growth is uncertain considering euro-zone
economic prospects, 2010 witnessed a reasonable recovery of
2.5% GDP growth. This modest growth, however, has dampened
public finances as Monaco registered a budget deficit of 1.9% of
GDP in 2010. Monaco's reliance on tourism and banking for its
economic growth has left it vulnerable to a downturn in France
and other European economies which are the principality's main
trade partners.

The principality is no longer just a frivolous playground for the
rich, although its government still is funded primarily through casino gambling proceeds. Ever since Monaco's famed casino opened
in 1856, the tourism industry has been an economic mainstay accounting for about 25% of annual revenue.

Tax Benefits for Residents

Undeniably, there are tax benefits to be gained from a move to
Monaco. The authorities no longer like the Principality to be known

as the tax haven that, in fact, it is. It's a low-tax area rather than a no-tax area, but still a haven.

Since 1869, there have been no income taxes for Monegasque nationals and resident foreigners—one of the main attractions for high net worth individuals. There are no direct withholding or capital gains taxes for foreign nationals, except for the French, who because of a bilateral tax treaty with Paris, cannot escape the clutches of the French tax collectors. There are first-time residential registration fees, but no ongoing real estate taxes, although foreign-owned real property is taxable when sold at 4.5% of the market value.

The state has no income tax and low business taxes and thrives as a tax haven both for individuals who have established residence and for foreign companies that have set up businesses and offices. Monaco, however, is not a tax-free shelter; it charges a nearly 20% value-added tax, collects stamp duties, and companies face a 33% tax on profits unless they can show that three-quarters of profits are generated within the principality.

Banking

The principality is a major banking center and has successfully sought to diversify into services and small, high-value-added, nonpolluting industries. There are corporate and banking advantages, too.

The Bank of France is responsible for the Monegasque banking system and carries out regular inspections. There is a strong anti-money laundering law. The banking services are not as comprehensive as they could be. The normal minimum for opening a bank account is €300,000, about US$375,000.

Confidentiality is good for business records and banking services. Banking secrecy is strict, but the government exchanges information about French citizens with neighboring France and it also abides by OECD Article 26 standards governing exchange of tax information in cases of alleged foreign tax evasion. Monaco was formally removed from the OECD's "grey list" of uncooperative tax juris-dictions but continues to face international pressure to loosen its banking secrecy laws and more actively help to combat tax evasion.

Residence and Citizenship

It is actually much easier to obtain a residence permit here than many might suppose. A clean record, solid bank references and a net worth of US$500,000 should do it. Fees for establishing residence are likely to cost in the US$10,000-$20,000 range.

The principality has offered financial and fiscal concessions to foreign nationals for a long time. These were restricted by 1963 Conventions with France and, more recent agreements with France. And herein lies a major concern. Monaco isn't likely to initiate changes in its tax haven status. But the rest of Europe, especially France, which has always exhibited a jealous dog-in-the-manger attitude towards the principality, might pressure it into getting into line.

If you're on the move already, stability may not be an impor-tant issue. However, you might be looking for a base and would do well to consider Monaco. The lifestyle is attractive but it's not everybody's cup of tea. If you are contemplating a move purely for financial or fiscal reasons, you might, depending on your specific requirements, do better elsewhere.

Once there, keep a low profile. Foreign nationals who are resi-dents do not make any public criticisms of the country. Why? If the authorities consider you a troublemaker, they can issue a 24-hour notice of expulsion. There's no one to appeal to and you'll be out the door.

Can we make any predictions about Monaco?

It's not going to become a ghost town. It is stable and any major changes are unlikely to come from inside. After 714 years under the rule of the Grimaldi family, Prince Albert, now in charge, definitely is far more liberal than his late father in many ways. He even has made noises about really cleaning up Monaco's reputation for alleged money laundering and tax evasion.

But the Monegasque financial and social establishment is not going to allow anything that hurts the financial bottom line. Welcome to Monaco.

Contacts

Government of Monaco: http://www.gouv.mc/

Department of Tourism and Conferences: http://visitmonaco.com/us

Embassy of Monaco
3400 International Drive, NW, Suite 2K—100
Washington, D.C. 20008-3006
Tel.: (202) 234-1530
Email: info@monacodc.org
Website: http://www.monaco-usa.org
U.S. diplomatic representation to Monaco is conducted by the U.S. Embassy in Paris. The U.S. Embassy in France is located at:

2 Avenue Gabriel, 75382 Paris Cedex 8, France
Tel.: + (33) 1-4312-2222
Website: http://france.usembassy.gov

U.S. Consulate General at Marseille is located at 12 Place Varian Fry, 13086 Marseille, France; Tel.: + (33) 4-9154-9200; Website: http://france.usembassy.gov/marseille

Monaco Real Estate Board: http://www.chambre-immo.monte-carlo.mc

List of Banks: http://www.yourmonaco.com/banks

Residence Assistance:
Henley & Partners AG
Klosbachstrasse 110
8024 Zurich, Switzerland
Tel.: +41 44 266 22 22
Fax: +41 44 266 22 23
Website: www.henleyglobal.com/monaco

Campione d'Italia

This little bit of northern Italy is completely surrounded by Switzerland and it's one of the least-known residential tax havens in the world. But you have to buy a condo or home to become a resident. Foreigners who can afford to live here and foreign-owned businesses used to pay few taxes. It may be Italian territory, but everything here is Swiss—license plates, currency, postage, communications and banking, but the taxes are Italian.

Commune di Campione, as the Italians call it, on the shores of beautiful Lake Lugano, is distinguished by its very uniqueness; a little plot of Italian soil, completely surrounded by Swiss territory. It is an Italian commune (municipality) of the Province of Como, an Italian enclave separated from the rest of Italy by Lake Lugano and mountains.

There are no border controls and complete freedom of travel. Home to less than 3,000 people (including about a thousand foreigners), in the southern Swiss canton of Ticino, it is about 16 miles north of the Italian border and five miles by road from Lugano, Switzerland—a beautiful scenic drive around the lake.

With no Campione border controls, there is complete freedom of transit. The village uses Swiss banks, currency, postal service, and telephone system. Even automobile license plates are Swiss. Strangely enough, because of ancient history and treaties, the enclave legally is considered part of the territory of Italy.

Campione is also a very pleasant place to live, located in the heart of one of the best Swiss and nearby Italian tourist areas of Lombardy. The region boasts lakes, winter sports, and the cultural activities of Milan, Italy, are only one hour away by auto.

All that's needed to become an official resident is to rent or buy property here, although formal registration is required. However, living here is very expensive; you might have to pay US$750,000 for a very small townhouse. Foreigners may buy real estate without restrictions, unlike in Switzerland.

But real estate prices are well above those in surrounding Ticino. Condominiums range from US$5,500 to $6,500 per square meter, and broker fees add a 3% commission. The real estate market is very small and prices are extremely high. The same apartment across the lake in Switzerland can easily cost half of what it costs in Campione.

This small market is served by a few local real estate agents, some of whom operate rather unprofessionally and some even without a license. A foreign buyer has to be very careful. If you are interested in establishing your residence in Campione and purchasing real estate there, you should be represented by a competent lawyer from the beginning. (See the end of this section for reliable professional contacts in the area we recommend.)

Corporations

Corporations registered in Campione have some advantages over Swiss companies. They use Swiss banking facilities and have a mailing address that appears to be Swiss, while escaping Switzerland's income and withholding taxes. Corporations are governed by Italian corporate law and can be formed with a minimum capitalization of about US$1,000.

Corporations can be owned and directed entirely by foreigners, a status Swiss law limits to some degree. Corporate registrations are usually handled by Italian lawyers in nearby Milan, and fees are modest. As part of Italy, EU business regulations do apply to Campione businesses, as do Italian corporate taxes, which can be high.

,The official currency is the Swiss franc, but the euro is accepted as well. All banking is done through Swiss banks, which gives its residents additional financial privacy. A famous casino did generate substantial revenue, which is among the reasons local residents enjoyed some special tax concessions.

Taxes

Until 2006, there were clear tax advantages to living in Campione. But when gambling was made legal in Switzerland, the casino, which was Campione's only major income source, declined. To make up the deficit some Italian personal income and corporate taxes were levied. But Campione still is exempt from Italian VAT. Tax advantages only apply to private persons residing in Campione, and not to companies domiciled or managed from there.

Residents of Campione do not pay the full Italian income tax. Based on a special provision in Italian law, the first CHF200'000 (US$225,000) of income are exchanged into euro, the official currency in Italy, at a special exchange rate. This results in a lower effective income and consequently a lower tax rate is applied. However, this only applies on the first CHF200'000 of income.

Besides this special concession, the usual Italian tax laws and tax rates apply. The 2012 Italian individual income tax rate is between 23%-43% and the corporate rate is 27.5%. As in Italy, there are no inheritance or gift taxes, and income from interest of foreign bonds paid through an Italian bank is taxed at a special, reduced rate of 12.5%. Capital gains taxes range from 12.5% to 27.5%

Inheritances of spouses and direct descendants or ascendants are subject to an Italian inheritance tax at a rate of 4% on the amount exceeding €1,000,000 per beneficiary. Transfers to brothers or sisters are taxed at 6% on the amount exceeding €100,000 per beneficiary. Transfers to relatives up to the fourth degree or relatives-in-law up to the third degree are taxed at 6% on the entire amount of their inheritance. Any other transfer is taxed at 8% on the entire amount.

To say that the Italian authorities are less than zealous in collecting taxes in Campione is an understatement. Unlike Switzerland or Italy, at this writing, Campione per se has no tax treaties but Italy has signed 95 double taxation treaties, but only three TIEAs.

Residence

To obtain a Campione residence permit, you must buy an apartment or a house. There is very rarely an opportunity to rent. Usual police clearance from the Italian authorities as well as approval by the local Campione authorities is also required. While residence permits are issued by Italian authorities, access to the territory of Campione is governed by Swiss visa regulations.

This means that the passport you hold should allow you to enter Switzerland without a visa otherwise you will have to apply for a Swiss visa beforehand. A passport is required for entry into Switzerland but a visa is not required for U.S. citizens for stays of up to 90 days.

Obtaining facts about Campione is much more difficult than for other tax havens because the enclave does not promote itself. There is no central office of information. Outsiders are not unwelcome, but no one readily volunteers news about this secret haven. A personal visit is mandatory for anyone seriously interested in making this their home.

Contacts

Government:

Amministrazione Comunale, Comune di Campione d'Italia
Tel.: 031 27 24 63.
Website: http://www.comune.campione-d-italia.co.it/

For information about Campione:

Dr. Ernst Zimmer
Consulting International, S.R.L.
Corso Italia 2, Campione d'Italia, 6911
Tel.: + 41 91 649 5244 Fax: + 41 91 649 4268
Email: capione@tele2.ch

Residence & citizenship assistance:

Henley & Partners AG

Klosbachstrasse 110, 8024 Zurich, Switzerland
Tel.: +41 44 266 22 22 Fax: +41 44 266 22 23
Websites: http://www.henleyglobal.com/switzerland
https://www.henleyglobal.com/countries/campione

Republic of Cyprus

This sunny island in the eastern Mediterranean Sea, politically divided between Greek and Turkish Cypriots, once was proud of its designation as a "tax haven." Since joining the EU in 2004, Cyprus has changed, raising corporate and individual taxes and sharing financial and tax information with other governments.

But it still offers attractive tax breaks for retired foreigners, especially if their income sources are offshore investments and royalties. Caution: the island government and its banks are in deep financial trouble.

Colorful History

Cyprus, a developed island nation south of Turkey, is the third-largest island in the Mediterranean Sea (after Sicily and Sardinia). It once billed itself as a "tax haven" but its membership in the EU has caused it to alter many of its low tax and financial privacy laws.

Over a 40-year period the government intentionally created a favorable offshore tax system while maintaining a normal domestic economy, although taxes were low by international standards.

The success of this program was confirmed by tens of thousands of offshore companies registered in Cyprus since 1975. After the island joined the EU in 2004, the offshore tax system was restructured. One result was that both domestic and offshore companies alike now pay a 10% tax.

Cyprus has double-tax treaties with more than 40 other countries, including most major Western countries, and most Central and Eastern European states. This is unusual for an offshore financial center making Cyprus a very effective location for holding and investment companies aimed at emerging markets.

With mild winters and dry summers (an average of 300 sunny days per year), Cyprus enjoys one of best climates in the Mediterranean. The population was 1,138,071 in 2012, with 80% Christian Greek Cypriots, 11% Turkish Cypriots and 9% foreign workers. Of these there are 210,000 displaced persons, both Turkish and Greek Cypriots, many refugees for more than 30 years.

Cyprus became an independent state in 1960, after 82 years of British rule. It has a system of democratic government based on human rights, political pluralism and respect for private property. Cyprus is a member of the United Nations and the British Commonwealth. The elected Cypriot president, Demetris Christofias, is the only Communist leader in the European Union.

Split Nation

After decades of conflict between Greek and Turkish Cypriots, violent hostilities in 1974 divided the island into two de facto autonomous entities, the internationally recognized Republic of Cypriot government in the south and a Turkish-Cypriot community (North Cyprus that governs about 37% of the land area). Yet another United Nations effort at reunification failed in 2004 when the Greek Cypriots rejected the plan. Cyprus for years has had a United Nations peacekeeping force on its territory.

With the fall of Communism in Soviet Russia in 1992, Cyprus became a financial (and literal) home away from home for Russian tycoons, bankers and businesspersons. Most of the country's 14,000 offshore companies are Russian-owned and there were more than 50,000 Russians living in the country as recently as 2010.

Shaky Banks, Government

In 2012, Cypriot banks were said to manage close to US$30 billion worth of assets.

But in June 2012, the Cypriot government joined five other

EU member countries asking the EU for a financial bailout. With empty public coffers and banks in decline, Cyprus needed as much as €10 billion, or US$12.5 billion, to restore these sectors. Cypriot officials also were seeking loans from Russia and China. In 2011, Cyprus got a €2.5 billion loan from Russia to cover its refinancing needs for 2012.

The crisis in Greece and a potential Greek exit from the euro affected the Cyprus economy whose banks were heavily exposed to Greece's debts.

In the past, the Cyprus' attraction was low taxes and lax government oversight of the financial sector, which may have contributed to its 2012 financial crisis. This made the island a hotspot for shady personal deals and "brass plate" firms—offshore entities that did no real work but raked in income earned abroad to avoid taxes. The island's economic prospects were lifted following the discovery of large reserves of natural gas in 2011, which eventually could bring a large injection of revenue.

The country has a "double-tax" treaty with Russia, which grants Cyprus-registered firms tax breaks on revenue earned in Russia. The use of Cypriot holding companies brings large amounts of foreign investment into Russia and facilitates investment worldwide by successful Russian businesses.

Under a 2012 revision of the Russian treaty, the rate of withholding tax on dividends paid from Russia to Cyprus remains at 5% if the investment in the Russian company amounts to €100,000 (US$128,000) or more and at 10% otherwise, giving considerable benefits compared with the general Russian withholding tax of 15% on dividends. It also provided for tax information exchange between the two countries using the OECD Article 26 procedures.

Island Changes

Once part of the Byzantine Empire, until recently Cyprus was a great place to make things disappear. This nation has long been a way station for international rogues and scoundrels, where officials traditionally were willing to look the other way. Just 150 miles from Beirut, closer to the Middle East than to Europe, Cyprus has been a Mecca for cigarette smuggling, money laundering, arms trading and the like. The site of secret meetings between Israelis and Palestinians, it has also been a refuge for the Russian mafia transporting wealth of immense size and dubious provenance.

Cyprus is also a popular low-tax haven for publicly traded companies, which can find significant advantages in the double taxation treaties network available to offshore companies. It is otherwise expensive and subject to significant disclosure requirements.

After joining the EU in 2004, it rapidly increased financial information sharing with other governments. The tax environment also became decidedly less friendly. The former 4.25% flat tax on offshore firms that attracted so many Russians in the 1990s has risen to 10%.

The offshore regime in Cyprus also has changed as part of the island's accession to the EU and as a result of agreements with the OECD. The 10% corporate tax gives Cyprus the lowest rate in the EU, after Ireland (12.5%), with the exception of the Isle of Man, Jersey and Guernsey, which have a zero rate. A "residence" based system of taxation is now in place.

Even before the G-20 and OECD attacks on offshore financial centers, Cyprus changed its laws to allow the exchange of tax and finance information, and also signed many double tax treaties. The island also now boasts one of the world's toughest anti-money laundering laws.

Cyprus plans to maintain its company and trust management regime, although the identity of the beneficiaries must be disclosed to the tax authorities when a company is registered or when a change of ownership takes place.

Retirement Tax Benefits

Cyprus usually does not offer citizenship to foreign nationals, but it may be a good place for a retirement home for some foreigners. Residence is fairly straightforward if you can demonstrate an annual income of as little as US$7,500 for one person or US$19,000 for a family of four.

Cyprus offers interesting tax benefits for a retired investor, author, musician or inventor if they come from the right nation. Cyprus is an attractive destination for a retired investor or anyone who receives substantial royalty income.

To obtain these tax benefits, one must become a resident, but not be domiciled in Cyprus. There are also certain residence programs for foreign nationals willing to make substantial investment in the island's economy. Foreigners who become residents are not allowed to carry on any local business unless granted permission, but they can conduct their business from their Cyprus base anywhere in the world.

Cyprus is a perennially popular location for international consultants and independent contractors and its burgeoning offshore sector accounts for the greatest percentage of expatriate workers. However, it is also a popular destination for active retirees (who are attracted not just by the lifestyle, but by the fact that the large number of double taxation treaties in place mean that retirement income from abroad will not usually be subject to withholding tax at source) and both of these groups are positively encouraged by the Cypriot government.

Residence & Taxation

Although residence for the purposes of taxation in Cyprus is defined as the "presence in the country for more than 183 days," calculation of tax liabilities is complex, because the country has several different levels of taxation for the various categories of persons living there.

However, as a basic guide, with the exception of foreign nationals working for offshore entities (for whom the rate of income tax is reduced by half), all groups are liable to pay the following taxes on income paid within Cyprus; income tax (at a progressive rate of up to 30%), capital gains tax (at a rate of 20%), estate duty (at between 20% and 45%) and real estate taxes.

Low Tax for Non-Domiciled Residents

A non-domiciled resident pays a flat tax of 5% on investment income received from abroad and remitted to Cyprus. The first US$4,000 of remitted investment income and all investment income that is not remitted to Cyprus is tax-free.

Royalties are treated as investment income. Foreign earned income can be remitted to Cyprus in order to reduce foreign withholding taxes under one of Cyprus' many tax treaties. When that is done, any foreign withholding tax paid can be credited against any Cyprus tax owed. That may well wipe out the 5% Cyprus tax obligation.

Unfortunately, these benefits are not available under the terms of either the Cyprus-U.K. or Cyprus-U.S. tax treaties, but nationals covered by most other Cyprus tax treaties can benefit. Cyprus has tax treaties with the United Kingdom, Denmark, Sweden, Ireland, Norway, Greece, Germany, Hungary, Italy, France, Russia, Romania, the United States, Canada and Bulgaria.

To qualify for local residence, an applicant must provide evidence of good character, show independent financial means and document income. The Cypriot Immigration Control Board also imposes minimum amounts of income that must be received by residents during a tax year. Foreigners allowed residence may purchase property in Cyprus, but only after obtaining a permit. Approval to buy real property is usually a formality for a house or apartment in which you plan to live.

Cyprus has ended almost all currency exchange controls, but new foreign residents were usually exempted in any case. Cyprus imposes death taxes, but the estates of non-domiciled residents are liable for taxes only on assets located in Cyprus at the time of death.

Contacts

Embassy of the Republic of Cyprus
2211 R Street, N.W., Washington, D.C. 20008
Tel.: (202) 462-5772 Fax: (202) 483-6710
Email: info@cyprusembassy.net
Website: http://www.cyprusembassy.net

Cyprus Trade Center
13 East 40th Street, New York, NY 10016
Tel.: (212) 686-6016
Turkish Cypriots maintain offices in Washington, Tel.: (202) 887-6198 and at the Republic of Turkey's Mission to the United Nations

United States Embassy
Metochiou & Ploutarchou Streets
2407, Engomi, Nicosia, Cyprus
P.O. Box 24536, 1385 Nicosia Cyprus
Tel.: + (357) 22-393-939
Fax: + (357) 22-780-944
Email: consularnicosia@state.gov
Website: http://nicosia.usembassy.gov

For information on residence applications, contact:

Chief Immigration Officer, Migration Department, Ministry of Interior Affairs, Nicosia 1457, Cyprus; Tel.: + (357) 22-804400;

Email: migration@crmd.moi.gov.cy
Website: http://www.mfa.gov.cy/mfa/mfa2006.nsf/index_en/index_en. General

Vassiliades & Co LLC is one of the leading law firms in Cyprus. Ledra House, 15 Agiou Pavlou Street, Agios Andreas, 1105 Nicosia, Cyprus Tel.: + 357 22 55 66 77
Email: cgv@vasslaw.net
Website: www.vasslaw.com
Offices also in Limassol, Athens, Moscow, Budapest, Seychelles and Belize City.

Kingdom of Denmark

Denmark occupies a peninsula north of Germany (Jutland) in northern Europe, bordering on the Baltic Sea and the North Sea and several major islands, Sjaelland, Fyn, and Bornholm. It is a member of the EU and its laws conform to the EU on most issues. While it qualified for the European Monetary Union (EMU), Denmark did not join, although the Danish kroner is pegged to the euro. It is a constitution monarchy with a unicameral legislature.

Danes enjoy among the highest standards of living in the world with a per capita GDP of US$40,200. The economy is characterized by extensive government welfare measures and an equitable distribution of income. Denmark's fiscal position remains among the strongest in the EU at 46.5% of GDP and a 2011 GDP of US$330.5 billion.

Denmark is not really an offshore financial center in the usual "tax haven" sense, but it does have two attractive features; a low-tax holding company regime and Jyske Bank.

Holding Companies

A holding company is a company that owns other companies' outstanding stock. The term usually refers to a company which does not produce goods or services itself; rather, its purpose is to own shares of other companies. Holding companies allow the reduction of risk for the owners and allow the ownership and control of many different companies (think Warren Buffet and Berkshire Hathaway). Under U.S. tax law 80% or more of stock in voting and value must be owned before tax consolidation benefits, such as tax-free dividends can be claimed as a holding company.

Denmark has high rates of personal income tax and is in the mid-range in terms of corporate tax, and has never been considered an offshore financial center. However, since 1999 its holding company law has provided outstanding opportunities for the international investor and subsequent adjustments to the law have increased its low tax attractiveness.

Historically, nine European countries (Austria, Belgium, France, Germany, Luxembourg, the Netherlands, Spain, Switzerland and the United Kingdom) have competed and continue to change their fiscal laws in attempts to make themselves the most attractive in which to locate a holding company.

However, the laws on Danish holding companies revolutionized the market and made it the most attractive location, with the result that the Netherlands' historic dominance of the holding company market was seriously threatened and other holding company jurisdictions slipped.

Denmark has about 80 double taxation treaties in place and this network of treaties offers greater leverage to reduce withholding taxes on incoming dividends. An elaborate network of double taxation treaties is a key factor for an attractive holding company jurisdiction and almost all dividend income received in Denmark is free of withholding tax.

Denmark's combined tax treaty network and its holding company regime means that about 35 major countries with proper structuring can route dividends through Denmark and not incur any withholding taxes. Among others these countries include Argentina, Austria, Belgium, Brazil, China, Cyprus, Finland, France, Germany, Greece, Iceland, India, Ireland, Italy, Luxembourg, Malaysia, Mexico, the Netherlands, Norway, Portugal, Singapore, Spain, Sweden, Switzerland, the U.K. and Malta.

In about 40 other countries withholding taxes are substantially reduced owing to this double taxation treaty network. This has proved lucrative for Denmark as corporations have set up hundreds of holding companies in the country.

Jyske Bank

I was first impressed with Denmark years ago when I first encountered one of their best known native sons, comedian-musician Victor Borge (1909–2000).

But again in 2008, when the government of Germany was engaged in bribery and paying for receiving stolen bank client names, most governments, including the United States, were happy to receive the stolen information—in this case, Denmark was a notable exception.

Its then tax minister, **Kristian Jensen**, described the case of stolen Liechtenstein bank names as an "advanced form of handling stolen goods." He added: "I think it's a moral problem to reward a criminal for information that he stole. I don't like this and I don't think this ethically is the best way to ensure that taxes are paid correctly." Here was a lone Danish voice in the tax collecting wilderness.

The French Revolutionary and Swiss philosopher Jean-Jacque Rousseau once wrote that happiness is "a good bank account, a good cook and good digestion." Sadly, if Mr. Rousseau were an American today, he wouldn't find much happiness outside of his kitchen.

He'd be tangled up in Washington's red tape, forced to undergo various invasions of privacy and he probably wouldn't be able to find a bank outside the U.S. that would accept him as a customer.

As of late, Americans who have lived abroad for years and have established lives, families and businesses overseas are now finding their bank accounts being closed. The simple reason: they hold U.S. citizenship.

It is not because foreign banks, particularly those in Europe, have a problem with Americans or their money. The guilty party is the Internal Revenue Service and its raft of new regulations, which now demand that overseas banks "fess up" on their U.S. customers' financial information or face a 30% withholding tax on the bank's U.S. business.

Consequently, many overseas banks are dropping their U.S. customers because they can service a German, Japanese or Moroccan client with much less hassle and less risk.

Thanks to the IRS, American citizenship overseas is no longer a privilege—it's a liability. But do not give up. There is a top notch group in Denmark who sees great value in U.S. clients and is catering to us.

In late 2001, Erika Nolan, the publisher of The Sovereign Society, had lunch in downtown Baltimore at a small Italian restaurant with a Forex trader turned private banker from Denmark. Thomas Fischer was representing a private bank in Copenhagen called Jyske Bank. Back then, Switzerland and Austria dominated the private banking scene in Europe, and the thought of banking in Denmark was akin to vacationing in Iowa—not bad, but definitely out of the ordinary.

We learned that Jyske Bank A/S is the second-largest Danish bank by of market share. The headquarters are located in Silkeborg, and the bank has offices, branches, and subsidiaries in Denmark, France, Germany, Gibraltar, the Netherlands, and Switzerland. The bank employs some 3,800 individuals.

However, Erika likes things that are out of the ordinary, because this is where she often finds the best opportunities. Thomas and his bank proved to be a rare find. Over the next eight years, she built a strong relationship between our two groups and many Sovereign Society members were able to gain valuable overseas exposure with complete peace of mind, thanks to Thomas.

In 2008, when many banks began to look negatively at their American customer base, Erika got a call from Thomas. Rather than walk away from U.S. business as we had feared, his bank committed itself to improving services and focused on catering exclusively to Americans. That's when Jyske Global Asset Management, or JGAM, was born.

JGAM

JGAM is not a bank. Rather, it is an asset management group that was created by Jyske Bank. After seeing the value in U.S. clients, the bank created this boutique subsidiary and worked through all the U.S. and Danish financial regulations.

JGAM is registered with the U.S. SEC so their relationship managers can legally visit clients in the United States and have open communication without any concerns. JGAM also issues straightforward end-of-year tax statements, which helps simplify the offshore U.S. tax-reporting requirements — thereby saving your accountant a great deal of time.

Boutique investment groups like JGAM are now much better alternatives to private banks. Everyone on the team is fluent in English and well-versed in the needs of an American client. They know our tax reporting issues, our currency concerns, our communication expectations and most of them know more about life in the U.S. than I do.

JGAM opens accounts starting at $100,000. This makes them the most affordable group of its kind, bar none. And their account-opening process is as straightforward as it gets.

You simply complete a detailed application with your name and address, the type of account you wish to open and the currency in which you want your funds to be denominated. (Please don't choose dollars.)

To meet all the "know your customer" rules, you must prove your identity and nationality by providing a notarized copy of your passport or certified birth certificate, as well as a utility bill to confirm your home address. You may also be asked to specify the source of your funds, and in some cases, obtain a reference letter from a bank in your home country to confirm the funds are legitimate.

Lastly, you will be asked to complete an investor profile so the folks at JGAM know your personal investment objectives, investment experience and your risk level. That's it.

Store Your Money Out of Harm's Way

Then, with the ease of a wire transfer, you can fund your account and have peace of mind that you have money out of harm's way in quiet and stable Denmark.

Erika opened her account with them in 2009 and Jeff Opdyke, The Sovereign Society investment director, became a client in 2011. The service both have experienced from Thomas and his team has been far superior to their prior experience with offshore banks. But it's not just them. We continue to receive positive emails from Sovereign Society members about JGAM's service.

If you are looking to diversify your wealth, Jeff Opdyke suggests you visit their website at www.jgam.com to learn about their full range of services. They also offer a free newsletter which shares their view on the markets. You can also email Thomas Fisher directly at fischer@jgam.com

JGAM has no offices in the U.S., but it is registered with the Securities and Exchange Commission to work with American clients, so you're not flouting any U.S. laws. And while JGAM has linked up with a U.S.-based IRA custodian in Texas, the firm holds the assets physically in Copenhagen. The process of opening an account at JGAM takes four to six weeks, which includes a 30-day "cooling off" period mandated by Danish authorities, just in case you change your mind.

JGAM requires a $200,000 minimum. All accounts below $1 million are discretionary, meaning JGAM's portfolio managers make all investment selections. But you can provide some level of input if you have certain requests, like you want none of your money held in U.S.-dollar assets.

Services are fee-based only, so JGAM will not load your portfolio with investments for which it receives incentive payments from third parties you don't know about. The annual fees charged are between 1% and 2% of the assets under management, depending on the size of the account.

You will also pay the trading costs imposed by the broker-dealers JGAM uses to place trades (Jyske Bank or Morgan Stanley), and that will add roughly an additional 1% on an annual basis.

Costs are a hurdle any money manager must clear to keep clients happy. And JGAM is doing a good job of that. JGAM's IRA accounts in 2010 gained between 7.5% and 9.1%, depending on whether you're looking at the low-, medium- or high-risk portfolio.

But I believe if you have a substantial nest egg in a 401(k), a 403(b) or an IRA, you should certainly think about the risks of keeping all your money within a deeply troubled financial system ruled by a fundamentally weak currency; sadly, that is America today.

Contacts

Jyske Global Asset Management (JGAM)
Contact: Thomas Fischer, Senior Vice President
Address: Vesterbrogade 9, DK-1780 Copenhagen V, Denmark
Tel.: +45 8989 5903 Fax: +45 8989 5901
Email: fischer@jgam.com Website: http://jgam.com/
Minimum Balance: US$200,000 or equivalent for each of the following accounts; a) personal investment account; b) managed currency account or; c) IRA account. Minimum balance $1 million or equivalent for a JGAM managed investment account.

Danish Government:
http://denmark.dk/en/society/government-and-politics

Invest in Denmark: http://www.investindk.com

Danish Ministry of Taxation: http://www.skm.dk/foreign

Tourism:
http://www.visitdenmark.us/en-us/denmark/tourist-frontpage-usa

Embassy of Denmark
3200 Whitehaven St. NW, Washington, D.C. 20008
Tel.: +1 (202) 234-4300
Email: wasamb@um.dk
Website: http://www.ambwashington.um.dk/en

United States Embassy
Dag Hammarskjolds Alle 24, 2100 Copenhagen Ø, Denmark
Tel.: +45 33-41-71-00
Emergency Tel.: + 45 33-41 7400.
Email: copenhagenirc@state.gov
Website: http://denmark.usembassy.gov

Gibraltar

The Rock, as it is known worldwide, is the United Kingdom's only continental European colonial possession, although it is a territory forcefully claimed by Spain. Gibraltar has fashioned itself into a dual-purpose residential tax haven for high net worth individuals from around the world and as a professional base for tax-free international banking, business corporations and trusts.

Colonial History

Gibraltar, a colonial possession of the United Kingdom, was ceded to England "forever" under the 1713 Treaty of Utrecht.

Neighboring Spain's 300 years of efforts to recover this British overseas territory, located on Spain's southern flank, have been rejected repeatedly by a large majority of the 29,000 citizens of Gibraltar, most recently by 99% in a 2002 referendum — and by successive British governments of both political parties.

Gibraltar residents voted overwhelmingly to reject any "shared sovereignty" arrangement and the government of Gibraltar insists on equal participation in talks between the U.K. and Spain. Spain strongly disapproves of U.K. plans to grant Gibraltar even greater autonomy.

In the 2011 elections, the Social Democrat Party (GSD) returned to power after 16 years in opposition. The new Chief Minister, Fabian Picardo, rejected any suggestion that his government even would be willing to engage Spain in sovereignty discussions including that of territorial waters. He said he felt an "enormous sense of responsibility" to defend Gibraltar against Spanish claims.

The colony's constitution grants local autonomy in many areas, but reserves strategic decisions to London. Its legal system is based on English common law. Gibraltar has been part of the European Union by its association through the U.K. since 1973. It does not come under the EU's VAT, *common agricultural policy* or external tariff regimes however Gibraltar has implemented much EU financial legislation and can apply common European passport rules for those in insurance, banking and fund management.

Constitutionally, Gibraltar is a Crown colony with internal self-government, the U.K. being responsible for defense, foreign affairs, financial stability and internal security. Gibraltar has its own House of Assembly with 15 elected members and two nominated members. There is a Council of Ministers, which consists of the Chief Minister and seven other Ministers.

Rock-Solid Economy

The famous Rock is tiny—only 2.5 square miles—but boasts a comprehensive banking and financial services industry. Gibraltar has no exchange controls and offers first-rate communications and infrastructure. The colony's financial services industry is the mainstay of the local economy, providing 30-35% of GDP, with 5,000 jobs that depend on the offshore finance center.

Self-sufficient Gibraltar benefits from an extensive shipping trade, offshore banking, and its position as an international conference center. Tax rates are low to attract foreign investment. The British military presence has been sharply reduced and now contributes about 7% to the local economy, compared with 60% in 1984.

The financial sector, tourism (almost 5 million visitors a year), gaming revenues, shipping services fees, and duties on consumer goods also generate revenue. Tourism and the shipping sector contribute 30% and 25%, respectively, of GDP. Telecommunications, e-commerce, and e-gaming account for the remaining 15%. The economy grew by 6.5% in 2010 to £G954m (US$1.5 million) and public debt fell to £G217m (US$340 million). The government had a budget surplus of £G31 million (US$48.5 million) or 8% of total revenue.

The currency is the Gibraltar pound (£G) = 100 pence and is at par with the British pound. There are no exchange controls in Gibraltar.

Offshore Leader

Gibraltar was one of the first of the British dependent territories to develop tax-exempt corporate forms for offshore business. It has high domestic income taxes, but offers low-tax regimes to companies and individuals, as well as incentives for incoming investment. It is probably the cheapest European offshore jurisdiction in which to operate but is smaller than many rivals.

There is a sophisticated business and professional infrastructure. Offshore business sectors include banking, insurance, investment fund management, trust management, shipping, and investment holding companies. In the past decade, there has been an influx of U.K. betting and gaming operations fleeing U.K. high taxes and using the very good telecommunications facilities to offer Internet betting services.

Under EU 'common passport' legislation any branch of an authorized EU bank may establish itself in Gibraltar subject only to notification procedures. Conversely, a Gibraltar-licensed bank may set up branches elsewhere in Europe.

Most of the 17 fully operational banks established in Gibraltar are branches of major U.K., U.S., Swiss or other European banks. Interestingly, Gibraltar has about 40 authorized banks entitled to accept deposits without establishing full branches in Gibraltar. At this writing, Gibraltar has 75 insurance companies, 43 trust companies and 551 licensed financial management companies managing over 3,745 registered trusts.

There are about 41,000 registered corporations. The banking

sector is well established in both the offshore and local market with assets of more than £G9.3bn (US$14.5 billion) Advantages of offshore banking in Gibraltar include its favorable tax status, lack of exchange controls, excellent communications, stable government, and EU membership.

Most Gibraltar banks offer special rates of interest to wealthier private depositors under the heading of private banking. Minimums are as low as US$10,000 in some cases, although some firms still maintain more traditional entry levels of US$100,000 or higher before offering special treatment to clients.

Gibraltar imposes no capital gains, wealth or estate taxes. The reopening of the border with Spain in 1985 enabled Gibraltar to expand its role as a major international finance center, against a background of political stability and administrative and legal systems derived from English common law and traditions. The absence of any exchange control restrictions together with exemptions and concessions from domestic taxes for certain categories of companies, high net worth and non-resident individuals and trusts administered for non-residents has created many opportunities for offshore investors and led to substantial growth in financial sector services.

Gibraltar, as do all U.K. overseas territories, applies Article 26 of the OECD tax information exchange model treaty. In 2009, it concluded a tax information exchange agreement with the U.S. allowing information exchange in cases of alleged tax evasion. It now has TIEAs with 20 countries including the U.K., France and Germany.

HNWI

Gibraltar is also home to many "tax exiles" from many nations, wealthy individuals who enjoy the local tax-free regime for foreign residents. Under Gibraltar tax law, the category known as "high net worth individuals" (HNWI) receives the biggest concessions.

Much banking activity is asset management for high-net-worth individuals because Gibraltar has made a special effort to attract such people with special tax rules. Under the high net worth individual (HNWI) tax scheme the minimum tax payable per annum to £G18,000 (US$28,000) and the taxable income level is £G60,000 (US$94,000) and up. Of special note is the fact that there is no capital gains tax or estate taxes in Gibraltar. The Gibraltar Deposit Protection Scheme covers 100% of a bank's total liability to a depositor or €100,000 (US$125,000), whichever is the lesser.

Autonomy Confirmed

Previously, when the OECD listed Gibraltar on its harmful tax competition "blacklist," the government countered with a cut in corporate tax rates across the board to zero. Both the OECD and the European Union attacked Gibraltar's tax haven status and Spain joined the critical chorus for its own purposes. The EU had ruled that Gibraltar's offshore favorable tax status was incompatible with EU regulations that apply to the United Kingdom and its colonial dominions.

Gibraltar appealed the EU ruling and in 2008 won a significant victory when the EU's highest court ruled that the Rock had "from a constitutional point of view, a political and administrative status separate from that of the central government of the United Kingdom." In effect, this affirmed the right of Gibraltar to set its own tax policies independent of the U.K., allowing its continuation as an offshore financial center in its own right.

The Future

Gibraltar may well be bothered by its somewhat uncertain political future. The former Labor Party government in London signaled willingness to "share sovereignty" with Spain, an arrangement that Rock residents strongly opposed.

More recently, the Conservative-Liberal coalition government in London said that any final agreement with Spain may be years, if not decades, away. London has pledged that no agreement with Spain will be made final unless the people of Gibraltar approve, which is highly unlikely.

Contacts

Government of Gibraltar: http://www.gibraltar.gov.uk

Financial Services Commission
P.O. Box 940, Suite 3, Ground Floor, Atlantic Suites
Europort Avenue, Gibraltar
Tel +350 200 40283
Web: www.fsc.gi
Email: info@fsc.gi

Gibraltar Tourists Board
Tel.: + (350) 74950 / 74982
Website: http://www.gibraltar.gi/home

Gibraltar Information Bureau
1156 Fifteenth Street NW, Suite 1100, Washington, D.C. 20005
Tel.: +1 202 452 1108
Email: gibinfobur@msn.com

Affairs for Gibraltar, a British overseas territory, are handled through the U.S. Embassy in London. The U.S. Embassy is located at:
24 Grosvenor Square, W1A 1AE London, United Kingdom
Tel.: + (44) 207-499-9000
Fax: + (44) 207-409-1637
Website: http://london.usembassy.gov

Gibraltar News: http://www.panorama.gi/
Gibraltar Asset Management Limited
One Irish Place, PO Box 166, Gibraltar
Tel.: +350 200 75181
Email: gam@gam.gi
Website: http://www.gam.gi/contact/

Banks in Gibraltar:
http://www.offshore-bank-list.com/offshore_banks_gibraltar.html

Republic of Malta

Malta offers an excellent deal in its special tax-free status for foreign retirees. It courts international business and financial firms with tax breaks and subsidies. But when it became a member of the EU, it revised its tax laws and no longer wants to be known as the tax haven that it still is.

South of the continent of Europe is Malta—a group of islands in the center of the Mediterranean Sea, south of the Italian island of Sicily and well positioned as a cultural and political stepping stone between Europe and North Africa.

About 95% of the nearly 400,000 islanders are natives, descendants of the ancient Carthaginians and Phoenicians that plied these waters. Malta offers an excellent climate and quality of life, modern health care and educational systems.

In 1530, the Holy Roman Emperor, Charles V, ceded Malta to the governance of the Knights of Malta. They built the fortifications in the harbor of Valetta, the capital, so well that in 1565 a Turkish siege was repelled largely due to the excellent defenses, which are still in existence today. In 1798, Napoleon invaded Malta and expelled the Knights.

At the Congress of Vienna in 1815, Britain was given possession of Malta. With the 1869 opening of the Suez Canal, Malta became an important strategic British base. During World War II, Malta was bombed heavily by the German Luftwaffe since it was a valuable Allied convoy port.

Great Britain formally acquired possession of Malta in 1814. The island staunchly supported the U.K. through both world wars and remained in the Commonwealth when it became independent in 1964. In 1947, Malta was granted self-government and in 1964, it became independent after being a British colony for more than 200 years. Malta has been a member of the European Union since 2005.

Almost entirely lacking energy or other natural resources and with a severe shortage of arable land, Malta is an import-hungry country. The government has tried with some success to create a high-technology manufacturing sector and to establish processing and distribution facilities around its rapidly growing Freeport.

There are extensive investment incentives and laws to increase the islands' role as a leader in international financial services. These provide a variety of tax and financial incentives to banks, insurance companies, fund management firms, trading companies, trusts and investment companies.

Business Incentives

While it is not a tax haven for individuals as such, Malta's government actively courts foreign capital with attractive incentives aimed at investors and entrepreneurs. These include generous tax incentives, soft loans, training grants and customized facilities at subsidized costs. This pro-business policy seeks to build on Malta's many existing strengths: favorable trade relations with countries around the world; a strategic location on world shipping lanes; and a high quality, productive, English-speaking workforce.

Economy

In the last decade, Malta's economy has averaged an annual growth rate of over 7%. The nation has maintained a surplus balance of payments, stable currency and low inflation (less than 1%) — all impressive numbers. These reflect the overall strength and diversity of the Maltese economy.

The British military and naval base once dominated Malta, but since 1979, when the British left, the excellent port facilities have been underutilized. Tourism is a major contributor to the economy, especially cruise ship visits. The Valetta airport has good connections to a wide range of European cities. Figures for 2011 show GDP of US$10.91 billion and a per capita GDP of US$25,700 which is low on the European scale.

Traditionally, agriculture was important, but the economy has undergone significant change. Manufacturing, especially high-tech industries, now accounts for over a quarter of Malta's GDP. About 26% of the labor force works in services, 22% in manufacturing, 37% in government, and 2% in agriculture. Major industries now include textiles, machinery, food and beverages, and high-tech products, especially electronics.

Tourism is also a growing and increasingly important sector. Key sectors that provide exceptional investment opportunities include trade, tourism, manufacturing, maintenance services, and international financial services.

Offshore Center

The Maltese government has enacted legislation to increase the islands' role as a leader in international finance services. It has intentionally moved away from the old "tax haven" model and refashioned itself as an international business center.

The government provides a variety of tax and financial incentives to banks, insurance companies, fund management firms, trading companies, trusts, and investment companies. These laws conform to the EU anti-tax haven requirements that Malta joined in 2004.

Malta's financial services industry has grown in recent years and it escaped significant damage from the international financial crisis that began in 2008, largely because it centered on the domestic real estate market and is not highly leveraged. Locally, little damage from the global financial crisis is attributed to the stability of the Maltese banking system and to its conservative risk-management practices.

The 2008 global economic downturn and high electricity and imported water prices did hurt Malta's real economy, which is dependent on foreign trade, manufacturing—especially electronics and pharmaceuticals—and tourism, but growth bounced back as the global economy recovered in 2010. Following a 1.2% contraction in 2009, GDP grew 2% in 2010.

Traditionally agriculture was important, but Malta's economy has changed significantly. Major industries now include high-tech manufacturing, food and beverages, tourism and international financial services.

The government actively seeks to attract foreign capital with generous tax breaks aimed at international investors. Malta is a good jurisdiction in which to establish low-tax international trading companies and treaty-protected international holding companies. Malta also has an important shipping register and is one of world's preferred jurisdictions for tax-free private yacht registrations.

In the last decade, Malta's economy has averaged an annual growth rate of more than 7%. The nation has maintained a surplus balance of payments, stable currency (now the euro) and inflation less than 1%. These factors reflect the overall strength and diversity of the economy.

Two unique factors have helped Malta's economy: online Internet gambling and generic pharmaceuticals. At a time when the United States and the U.K. both cracked down on online gaming, Malta welcomed the industry to its shores. Gaming companies are sanctioned by the Maltese government and courts. Leading online gaming companies have relocated to Malta, which has helped produce local jobs and bolster the already mature banking system.

The generic pharmaceutical industry has taken advantage of Malta's liberal patent laws that protect companies that do research and testing of generic drugs before a patent expires.

Taxes

Individuals who are domiciled and ordinarily resident in Malta pay income tax on their world-wide income. Individuals who are domiciled elsewhere, and who are resident but not ordinarily resident in Malta pay tax on their income arising in Malta, or remitted there but not capital gains, whether remitted or not. A six-month test is usually definitive in establishing residence.

Non-resident individuals pay tax on their Malta-source income only but local interest and royalty income are exempt from tax, as are capital gains on holdings in collective investment schemes or on securities as long as the underlying asset is not Maltese immovable property.

Returned migrants are offered a special tax regime: a person born in Malta who returns can elect to pay 15% income tax on local income only but there are various conditions. Highly qualified expatriate employees working in the financial services or online gaming industry are subject to a flat tax of 15%. The 15% flat tax incentive applies to highly skilled and qualified expatriates who are required for certain industrial sectors including individuals who do research or market an invention or technology in Malta and digital gaming professionals, such as game directors and game software designers.

Holders of Permanent Residence Permits issued under the Immigration Act 1970 pay tax at a reduced rate on income earned in Malta plus remittances of foreign income. Such individuals are considered to be non-resident for purposes of investments in offshore and non-resident companies.

There are no property taxes and permanent residents pay a 15% income tax on offshore income remitted into the country. Malta has three types of taxes: income, corporate and estate taxes — the latter applies only to property located on the island. Income tax rates for foreign residents range from 2% to 30%. A permanent resident is not taxed on capital gains paid from offshore, unless the person also is domiciled in Malta.

Residence, Not Citizenship

Malta is one of the most attractive locations in Europe for tax advantaged private residence. For non-Maltese persons, there is the possibility of acquiring permanent residence status through an attractive and efficient program. Persons of all nationalities are eligible to apply for residence permits without discrimination. These sunny Mediterranean islands especially cater to expatriates looking for a second or retirement home.

In late 2011, new rules aimed at attracting foreign high net worth individuals (HNWIs) took effect. They are aimed at not just those who want to invest in Maltese real property, but those who will contribute to the local economy.

There are two sets of rules, one applying to EU nationals (excluding nationals of Malta), European Economic Area (EEA) nationals and Swiss nationals. The other set applies to all other foreigners. Those admitted under the new rules are subject to a 15% tax on income received in Malta from foreign sources, but they have the right to request double taxation relief if the minimum amount of tax paid is €20,000 (US$25,500) for an annual of assessment.

A permanent residence permit entitles its holder to reside permanently in Malta with the freedom to come and go. As an EU member and of the Schengen Area agreement residents of Malta can travel within that area without obtaining a visa.

A permanent resident enjoys a privileged tax status, while at the same time benefiting from Malta's wide network of double taxation treaties. A further advantage of this status is that as long as the resident abides by the rules, they need not spend any particular time actually residing in Malta.

Foreign nationals are not eligible for immediate Maltese citizenship, but they are welcomed as residents. Maltese residency is of three types:

- Visitors staying less than three months are counted as non-residents
- Those remaining over three months are temporary residents
- Permanent residents are granted a permit entitling them to stay

Those in the latter category must own assets located outside Malta of at least US$360,000, or have a worldwide income of at least US$24,000 and demonstrate ability to remit to Malta a minimum annual income of US$14,400, plus US$2,400 for each dependent. A residence permit can be inherited by a surviving spouse, but not by other surviving descendants. Any person may apply for naturalization as a citizen of Malta after having resided there for at least five years.

Maltese citizenship law now allows second generation Maltese born abroad to become citizens of the island by registration and proof of lineage. The applicant must provide documentary evidence showing direct descent from an ancestor or a parent who was born in Malta. Documents required include birth, marriage and death certificates. The registration procedure can occur at any Maltese Embassy, High Commission, Consulate, or at the Department for Citizenship and Expatriate Affairs in Malta. Physical residence in Malta is not required to qualify. A passport is required for entry into Malta.

Contacts

Embassy of Malta
2017 Connecticut Avenue, N.W., Washington, D.C. 20008
Tel.: (202) 462-3611
Email: maltaembassy.washington@gov.mt
Website: http://www.foreign.gov.mt/pages/main.asp?sec=17

United States Embassy
Ta' Qali National Park, Attard, ATD 4000
Tel.: + (356) 2561-4000

Email: usembmalta@state.gov
Email for visa, consular inquiries: consularmalta@state.gov
Website: http://malta.usembassy.gov
Mailing address: P.O. Box 535
Valletta, Malta, CMR 01

Government of Malta: http://www.gov.mt/index.asp?l=2

Malta Tourism Board: http://www.visitmalta.com

Central Bank of Malta: http://www.centralbankmalta.com

Residence Assistance:
https://www.henleyglobal.com/countries/malta/residence/

Banks in Malta: http://www.europebanks.info/malta.php

Law Firm:
Chetcuti Cauchi, 20 St. Ursula Street, Valletta, VLT 1236, Malta
Tel.: + 356 22056230
Email: info@cc-advocates.com
Website: www.cc-advocates.com

CHAPTER EIGHT

Asia, Mid-East & Africa

The growth in Asian national economies, as well as those in the Middle East and Africa have spawned new offshore financial centers (Dubai, Labuan, and Samoa) and also transformed existing low-tax jurisdictions (Hong Kong, Singapore, both of which were discussed in Chapter Four). Here I describe the growing competition among these offshore centers and the struggle of the newer ones for acceptance in the offshore world.

The Cook Islands

Way out in the South Pacific (some say in the middle of nowhere) are the Cook Islands — home to a very modern code of offshore financial laws that may be just what you need: iron-clad asset protection trusts, IBCs, limited liability partnerships, global banking and a very strict financial privacy law that really does protect your personal business. Some folks don't like too much distance between themselves and their assets, yet distance provides greater protection — especially here.

Independent but Dependent

If you're researching the more esoteric parts of the world of offshore asset protection, you'll soon learn about the Cook Islands. Since 1981, when the government first began adopting (and later updating) a series of wealth and asset-friendly laws, the Cook Islands—though small in population and remote from the rest of the world—have come to play a definite role in offshore financial circles.

The Cook Islands are a self-governing parliamentary democracy in a loose constitutional association with New Zealand. As a Commonwealth member, Queen Elizabeth II is Head of State and New Zealand has a High Commissioner there. There is a Prime Minister and a cabinet appointed from among elected members of parliament. There is a written CI constitution with a Westminster-style parliament elected every four years by universal suffrage. The legal system is based on British common law and closely reflects that of New Zealand and other Commonwealth jurisdictions.

The people are ethnically similar to New Zealand Maoris and live in widely scattered islands in the South Pacific halfway between New Zealand and Hawaii, southwest of Tahiti. The capital, Avarua, on Raratonga Island, has direct flights to Los Angeles, Hawaii, and New Zealand. The climate is tropical with typhoons in summer.

A broad net of 15 coral islands in the central heart of the South Pacific, the Cook Islands are spread over 850,000 square miles. The islands occupy an area the size of India, with a declining population (10,777 in 2011) no larger than an American small town.

Local time is 10 hours behind GMT, with 9:00 am in Hong Kong being 3:00 pm the previous day in the Cook Islands. This geographic location gives the Cook Islands a strategic advantage in dealing with both the Asian and American markets.

Indirectly, the islands are part of the British Commonwealth by virtue of their unique association with nearby New Zealand. From 1901 to 1965, the Cook Islands were a colony of New Zealand and NZ still subsidizes the CI government. The New Zealand subsidy has become a sore point for both nations. The islanders even enjoy dual New Zealand and Cook Islands citizenship.

Like many other South Pacific island nations, CI economic development is hindered by isolation from foreign markets, limited domestic markets, lack of natural resources, periodic devastation from natural disasters, and inadequate infrastructure. Agriculture, employing more than one-quarter of the working population, provides the economic base with major exports made up of copra and citrus fruit. Beautiful black pearls are the Cook Islands' leading export.

The annual GDP is estimated at US$200 million with per capita GDP at less than US$10,000.

Planned Offshore Center

The Cook Islands' offshore industry was the result of the government's official collaboration with the local financial services industry. Financial services now rank second only to tourism in the economy. Despite some 50,000 visitors a year to the capital island, Rarotonga, the Cook Islands have remained largely unspoiled. Cook Islanders have their own language and enjoy a vigorous and diverse culture, though most speak English. The New Zealand dollar is the local currency, but most offshore transactions are in U.S. dollars.

This is a microstate with macro aspirations, but the grasp may have exceeded the reach. Their checkered history of high finance has been marked by some scandals, sponsored by fast-talking American, U.K. and New Zealand expatriates. It's no secret that certain American asset protection attorneys have played a large role in advising the government on asset protection issues, actually drafting statutes for the island's parliament.

Constantly teetering on the brink of bankruptcy, the CI government is chronically in debt, much of it a result of bad decisions. Two-thirds of the workforce is on the government payroll, financing an old-fashioned spoils and patronage system that would make an American big-city political boss blush. In the

1980s and 1990s, the country lived beyond its means, maintaining a bloated public service and accumulating a large foreign debt. Subsequent reforms, including the sale of state assets, the strengthening of economic management, the development of tourism, and a debt restructuring agreement, have rekindled investment and growth.

Local taxation includes a 20% corporation tax, and resident personal income tax at rates up to 30%. There is a VAT of 12.5% and stamp duties. Withholding tax on payments including interest to non-residents is 15%. The Cook Islands have no double taxation treaties, but 13 TIEAs have been signed since 2009, none with the U.S.

By locating Internet websites in the Cook Islands to carry out functions previously based in high-tax jurisdictions, such as sales and marketing, treasury management, supply of financial services, and most of all, the supply of digital goods such as music, video, training, and software, businesses can take advantage of low rates of taxation for substantial parts of their operations.

Tailored Wealth Protection

But don't let the deficits and the distance put you off. There is much here to cheer the hearts of knowledgeable offshore financial enthusiasts.

Existing statutes meticulously provide for the care and feeding of IBCs, limited liability companies (LLCs), as well as offshore banks, insurance companies and trusts. All offshore business conducted on the Cook Islands must be channeled through one of the six registered trustee companies. A comprehensive range of trustee and corporate services is offered for offshore investors. The government officially guarantees no taxes will be imposed on offshore entities.

Thousands of foreign trusts, corporations and partnerships are registered here, protected by an exceedingly strong financial privacy law, although that has been tempered somewhat by the adoption of OECD Article 26 standards for the exchange of tax information among governments. In 2009, the Cook Island's government welcomed the G-20's call for more transparency in tax information and adopted necessary amendments to its tax laws to conform to the new standard.

Strict Confidentiality

Strong financial and banking secrecy provisions apply in the offshore regime, requiring government officials as well as trustee company and bank employees to observe strict secrecy backed by criminal sanctions. The official registrar records of foreign companies and of international trusts are not open for general search, with defined exceptions under the Financial Transactions Reporting Act of 2004 and the Proceeds of Crimes Act of 2003.

In a major American legal case, the U.S. government tried to force the repatriation of funds under a Cook Island trust and lost, even though the Americans who created the trust for a time were jailed for contempt of court. Not even a federal court could crack the Cook Island trust laws. See the decision known as the "Anderson case" (*FTC vs. Affordable Media*, LLC, 179 F. 3rd 1228, U.S. Ct. of Appeals, 9th Cir. 1999).

In mid-2009, the OECD listed the Cook Islands as one of the tax havens committed to the internationally agreed tax information exchange standard but one that had not yet substantially implemented it. The CI government says it is committed to the OECD Article 26 standard and will implement it.

In 2012, the Cook Islands had signed TIEAs with Mexico, France, Denmark, Faros Islands, Finland, Greenland, Iceland, Norway, Ireland, Australia, Sweden, and New Zealand.

According to Puai Eickman, a leading CI trust officer, when the CI government receives a request for tax information from a foreign government with which it has signed a tax information exchange treaty (TIEA), (and none has been signed with the US), the standard of proof required of the alleged tax evasion or tax fraud is "beyond a reasonable doubt." (That is the highest standard of proof used in the US, usually for crimes such as murder).

Approval for release of requested tax, or any other information concerning foreign holdings, must be approved by a court applying this standard. No foreign government TIEA requests have been granted as yet and few have been received.

The CI Development Investment Act requires all foreign enterprises (those with more than one-third foreign ownership) to first obtain approval and register their planned activities with the Cook Islands Development Investment Board. There are various incentives and concessions for tariff protection; import duty and levy concessions; tax concessions by way of accelerated depreciation; allowance for counterpart training; and recruitment of Cook Islanders from overseas.

Updated Laws

The Cook Islands parliament systematically has adopted a series of anti-money laundering, financial reporting and anti-financial-crime laws. These laws were sufficient to get them removed from the Financial Action Task Force blacklist, which was their stated objective.

The laws liberalize the extent to which local financial institutions are obligated to disclose information and override all other laws, making compliance with anti-money-laundering laws and standards paramount, but only with court approval as stated above.

However, the law instituted a procedure that provides due process before any information can be released, including a formal request to the Financial Intelligence Unit showing reasonable grounds to believe that money laundering or criminal activities have taken place. This ensures that any information disclosed is done through proper channels with legal justification. This procedure is also used for tax information exchange requests from foreign governments.

International companies incorporated here have a great deal of flexibility in corporate structure with provisions for ease of administration and maximum benefit in global commercial transactions. Incorporation can be completed within 24 hours.

In 1989, by an amendment to the International Trusts Act 1984, the Cook Islands introduced the asset protection trust (APT). This legislation was considered cutting edge at the time and has since been copied and adopted by other offshore centers. The Cook Islands also has laws allowing international banking and insurance business to be conducted tax free, also with strong privacy protections. Both government and trust companies here constantly develop new products to meet the complexities of the offshore world.

Contacts:

Licensed Cook Islands Trust Companies

- AsiaCiti Trust Pacific Limited
- Cook Islands Trust Corporation Limited
- Global Consultants and Services (Cook Islands) Limited
- HSBC Trustee (Cook Islands) Limited
- Portcullis TrustNet (Cook Islands) Limited
- Southpac Trust Limited

Licensed Banks

Domestic Banks:

- ANZ Banking Group Limited
- Bank of the Cook Islands Limited
- Capital Security Bank Cook Islands Limited
- Westpac Banking Corporation

International Banks:

- ANZ Banking Group
- Capital Security Bank Ltd
- WSBC Bank

Recommended Bank:

Capital Security Bank Limited
P.O. Box 906, ANZ House
Rarotonga, Cook Islands
Tel.: + 682.22.505
Email: info@csb.co.ck
Web: www.capitalsecuritybank.com

Cook Islands Supervisory Commission
Email: Inquire@fsc.gov.ck
Telephone: (+682) 20798 Fax: (+682) 21798
P.O. Box 594, Avarua, Rarotonga, Cook Islands

Ministry of Finance & Economic Management
P.O. Box 120, Rarotonga, Cook Islands Tel.: 682 22878.

Recommended Trustee:
Puai T. Wichman, Esq. Managing Director

Ora Fiduciary (Cook Islands) Ltd.

Global House, P.O. Box 92, Avarua, Rarotonga, Cook Islands
Tel.: +682 27047 Dell: +682 55418
Email: puai@oratrust.com
Website: www.oratrust.com/

With 20 years of trust and company management experience, Puai Wichman heads Ora Fiduciary (Cook Islands) Ltd., one of six registered trustee companies in the Cook Islands. He describes Ora as "a boutique offshore financial services company that tailors its services to the particular needs of each of its clients." A native Cook Islander, Puai is a qualified attorney in both the Cook Islands and New Zealand and is a former president of the Cook Islands Trustee Companies Association. He holds a law degree from the University of Auckland, New Zealand, and is a member of the Asia Offshore Association. He welcomes inquiries from Sovereign Society members and assists in trust and corporate creation and in opening local bank accounts.

Malaysia (Labuan)

Malaysia is a pleasant, hassle-free county in Southeast Asia. It's wealthy and pluralist based on a fusion of Malay, Chinese, Indian and indigenous cultures. Malaysia's love of Western-style industrialization is seen in its big cities. Aside from gleaming modern glass towers, Malaysia has some of the best beaches, mountains and national parks in Asia. It is also home to an officially planned and promoted offshore financial center, called "Labuan" which aims to become the world's leading Islamic financial center.

History

Malaysia is a southeastern Asian peninsula bordering Thailand plus the northern one-third of the island of Borneo. It borders Indonesia, Brunei, and the South China Sea, south of Vietnam. The country exists under many different influences. It was ruled by the Portuguese, Dutch and British over five centuries. During the late 18th and 19th Centuries, Great Britain established colonies and protectorates in Malaysia, which were militarily occupied by Japan from 1942 to 1945. In 1948, the British-ruled territories on the Malay Peninsula formed the Federation of Malaya and gained independence in 1957.

Malaysia is really two countries in one, cut in half by the South China Sea. The peninsula is a multicultural mix of Malay, Chinese and Indian, while Borneo hosts a wild jungle of orangutans, granite peaks and remote native tribes. These two regions offer a stark contrast of state-of-the-art high rises in Kuala Lumpur compared to Sarawak's remote villages or the serene beaches of the Perhentian Islands.

Malaysia is comprised of three federal territories and 13 states.

It was first formed back in 1963 when former British colonies of Singapore, as well as Sabah and Sarawak (both East Malaysian states located on the northern tip of Borneo) joined the Federation Two years later, Singapore became independent in 1965.

In his 22-year tenure from 1981 to 2003, Prime Minister Mahathir bin Mohammad successfully helped diversify Malaysia's economy from its previous dependence on raw materials by expanding into tourism, manufacturing and services. His leadership converted the nation's plantation-based economy into what has been called an "Asian Tiger."

The western half of Malaysia is bustling and commercial, with urban centers sprinkled throughout the tropical vegetation of the country. Much of this development in the west is driven by the energy of its Chinese business community. In the east, Malays constitute the majority and agriculture, fishing and cottage industries predominate. Life in the east is quiet and laid back where one experiences the traditional Malay culture.

Boosted by economic diversity and a move away from raw materials, Malaysia also found economic success in large part due to a boom in electronic exports. Additionally, the country has benefitted from oil and gas exports, with big profits rolling in from worldwide high energy prices. Moreover, with healthy foreign exchange reserves, Malaysia has managed to keep Inflation and external debt low. The economy remains dependent on continued consumer growth in the U.S., China and Japan — all top export destinations and key sources of foreign investment.

Planned Islamic Financial Center

In the mid-1980s, Malaysian leaders, with British controlled Hong Kong about to be handed over to the Communist Chinese in 1997, decided to establish their own international offshore financial center (what used to be called a "tax haven"). They located it on Labuan, a small island off the coast of Borneo and formally launched it in 1990. Together with enactment of a series of offshore laws, the Malaysian government created the Labuan Offshore Financial Services Agency, although "offshore" was dropped from the title and it is now known as the Labuan International Business and Financial Center.

Labuan, a designated federal territory within Malaysia, is a group of islands located off the northwest coast of the island of Borneo facing the South China Sea. It is comprised of Pulau (a Malay word meaning "island"), Labuan and six smaller islands. Bahasa Melayu (Malay) is the native language, but English is widely spoken as well as Chinese dialects and Tamil. Labuan is 35.5 square miles in size, with a population of about 90,000, with a good harbor and airport. Islam is the official religion, but freedom of worship is guaranteed by law. Labuan, like the rest of Malaysia, has a parliamentary system of government based on the British common law.

Labuan offered then and now low-tax/no-tax corporate structures and provides a modern banking system that by 2012 had US$38.3 billion in total assets held by 57 banks.

There are two categories of companies, trading, and non-trading. A Labuan "trading" company is an operating business that sells products or services to customers. A Labuan "non-trading" company is a traditional holding company that owns assets or other companies that earns dividends, rents, and royalties. Labuan's offshore center offers services including banking, insurance, trust creation, international business corporations and investment fund management.

Offshore income is tax-free and there is no withholding, capital gains, or dividend tax. For trading companies that operate a business, there is an option to either pay 3% of their profits, or simply pay a flat tax of 20,000 Malaysian ringgits (US$6,300). Since Malaysia has double taxation treaties with many countries, foreigners whose business qualify under a tax treaty can operate a Labuan company and pay the low Malaysian tax instead of paying higher taxes in their home country.

Labuan offshore companies can make good use of Malaysia's double tax treaty network. This has made the island the preferred conduit for foreign direct investment in neighboring Asian countries including Korea and Malaysia itself. A stock exchange established in 2000, aiming particularly at the listing of Islamic financial debt issues, has had considerable success.

The main advantage Labuan enjoys is its role as a center for developing Islamic financial law. In 2011, the Labuan banking sector reported a rise in total assets of 13% to US$38.3 billion with the total number of Labuan banks at 57.

Islamic financial practices follow Shari'a, Islamic law based on the Koran. The law specifically prohibits the receipt or payment of interest and any transaction that involves gambling or speculation, a category that includes futures contracts, interest rate hedging and other financial arrangements common in the West.

In lieu of the payment of interest, Islamic institutions pay investors a share of their profits. Making a profit is not prohibited, but Muslims believe that financial relationships should be equal rather than hierarchical. Thus, profit sharing is preferable to interest, which implies the unequal relation of debtor to creditor.

The amount of wealth estimated to be under professional management in the world Islamic financial sector is about US$300 billion, a fairly small quantity in comparison with the global capital market, but still a significant and growing niche that Labuan seeks to serve.

Contacts

Labuan International Business and Financial Center
Suite 3A-2, Plaza Sentral, Jalan Stesen Sentral, KL Sentral, 50470

Kuala Lumpur, Malaysia
Tel.: + 603 2773 8977
Email: info@LabuanIBFC.my
Website: www.labuanibfc.my/

Malaysian Embassy
3516 International Court, N.W., Washington, D.C. 20008
Tel.: (202) 572-9700
Email: malwashdc@kln.gov.my
Website: http://www.kln.gov.my/perwakilan/washington

1) Consulate General, 550 South Hope Street, Suite 400,
Los Angeles, CA 90071
Tel.: (213) 892-1238;

2) Consulate General, 313 East 43rd Street
New York City, NY 10017
Tel.: (212) 490-2722/23

United States Embassy
376 Jalan Tun Razak, 50400 Kuala Lumpur, Malaysia
Mailing Address:
U.S. Embassy Kuala Lumpur, APO AP 96535-8152
Tel.: + (60) 3-2168-5000
Email: klacs@state.gov
Website: http://malaysia.usembassy.gov/

Republic of Mauritius

Mauritius is the most accessible island in the Indian Ocean, boasting a tropical paradise at bargain prices. Though geographically near South Africa, it's actually more influenced by its British and French ties and a predominantly Indian workforce. It is a favorite tax haven for wealthy Indians and a favorite target of India's tax collectors.

Mauritius is a volcanic island of lagoons and palm-fringed beaches in the Indian Ocean off the coast of Southern Africa and east of the island of Madagascar. It is strategically located between India, Africa and Asia.

It has a reputation for stability and racial harmony among its mixed population of 1.3 million Asians, Europeans and Africans. The island has maintained one of the developing world's most successful democracies and has enjoyed continued constitutional order.

Mauritius has been an independent member of the Commonwealth since 1968, and became a republic in 1992. The official language is English; the dominant ethnic group is Indo-Mauritian and the most popular religion is Hindu. The Government is presidential, with a single elected National Assembly and a Council of Ministers headed by a Prime Minister. The legal system reflects mixed French and British ancestry, and administration can be bureaucratic in the French style.

Mauritus' first explorers hailed from Portugal in the early 1500s (not counting Arab and Malay sailors in the 10th Century), but later claimed by the Dutch, French and then British in the 1800s before achieving independence from the U.K. in 1968. The Republic boasts a stable democracy with free elections and a laudable human rights record. As a result, it has attracted considerable foreign investment and garnered one of Africa's highest per capita incomes.

Since breaking free from the U.K. nearly 50 years ago, Mauritius has evolved from a low-income, agrarian economy to a highly diversified industrial, financial and tourism base. As a result, annual growth has remained steady at 5% to 6%. This has brought more equitable income distribution, greater life expectancy, lower infant mortality and better infrastructure.

The economic development policy of the Mauritian government has focused on nurturing offshore financial services through the expansion of local financial institutions, as well as supporting the domestic information telecommunications industry. At latest count Mauritius claims more than 9,000 offshore entities (IBCs, trusts), most of which are focused on the Indian and South African commerce, totaling a banking sector exceeding US$1 billion.

Moderate Tax Haven

The Mauritius offshore sector takes a cautious course. Until 1998, offshore laws allowed zero taxation across a range of offshore activities, including international business corporations (IBCs), banking, shipping, insurance and fund management, as well as in free trade zones. The legal system is a hybrid combination of both civil and common law practices.

With a strong anti-money laundering law, it has managed to avoid both the OECD and FATF blacklists. Offshore laws are continually modernized and are kept up to date and competitive.

Under a 2001 law, IBCs are known as "Global Business Licenses Categories 1 and 2." A GBL1 is used for international tax planning and structuring and is appropriate for investment funds or mutual funds seeking relief under double taxation agreements. A GBL2 is not considered as resident in Mauritius and is therefore exempt from local taxation, but it cannot access the benefits of the network of double tax agreements. It is primarily used for non-financial consultancy, trading, logistics, marketing or invoicing.

Mauritius has decided to be a "respectable" offshore financial center. Thus "tax free" is gone and there is now a tax rate of 15% in most areas, although corporate exemptions can reduce the tax considerably to as low as 3%. Mauritius has tax treaties with 30 countries that can be combined with offshore laws to produce profitable trade and investment, especially for the many thousands of wealthy Indian investors.

Conflict with India

Mauritius has been attacked by the government of India because of its role as a tax haven for wealthy Indians. But an official Indian survey showed that Mauritius accounted for 43% of cumulative foreign direct investment (FDI) that flowed into India. Of the total US$81 billion FDI that came in the last decade almost half (US$35.18 billion) was routed through Mauritius.

Mauritius has become a favorite of the Indian financial elite and a prime target of the Indian government seeking tax evaders. But in 2012 there was some very bad news for Mauritius and the tax-avoiding Indian elite.

Foreign institutional investors had invested over US$100 billion in Indian equities through 2012 and as much as 40% of that reached India through Mauritius holding companies. That was because the island's double tax avoidance treaty allowed investors to take advantage of much lower tax rates in Mauritius compared to India's higher taxes.

In 2012, a high court in India ruled that India's tax collectors had no power to collect taxes on transactions in Mauritius, saving the Indian Vodafone Company many millions. The Indian government promptly adopted a set of general anti-avoidance rules (GAAR) that empower revenue authorities to deny tax benefits without commercial substance.

Experts predicted this would hurt the flow of foreign investment funds into India, but they also said it would mean the end of Mauritius as a tax haven because it would negate the double tax avoidance treaty with India, on which the offshore haven depended for much of its business.

The response from the government of Mauritius and its nervous offshore sector has been to lobby the India government, asking for a "grandfather clause" as part of GAAR to exempt all existing investments from Indian capital gains tax and apply only to new cash and investment from Mauritius in India on and after the date the new Indian rules take effective force.

Contacts

Government of Mauritius
Module 05B4, 5th Floor, Cyber Tower
Ebene Cybercity, Rose Hill, Mauritius
Tel.: +230 454 9955
Email: portaladmin@mail.gov.mu
Website: http://www.gov.mu/

Embassy of Mauritius
1709 N Street N.W., Washington, D.C. 20036
Tel.: (202) 244-1491
Email: mauritius.embassy@verizon.net
Website: http://www.maurinet.com/embasydc.html

Mauritius Mission to the United Nations
211 East 43rd Street #1502, New York, N.Y. 10017
Tel.: (212) 949 0190/91 Email: mauritius@un.int

United States Embassy
Rogers House, Fourth Floor, John F. Kennedy Avenue
P.O. Box 544, Port Louis, Republic of Mauritius

Tel.: + (230) 202-4400
Email: usembass@intnet.mu
Website: http://mauritius.usembassy.gov/

Samoa

If you're looking for a tax haven that has an inside track with the People's Republic of China, or if you need to form a trust or corporation yesterday, this small Pacific island nation that sits on the other side of the International Dateline may be your best bet.

The few professionals who really know tax havens realize the relative importance of The Independent State of Samoa, a group of islands in the heart of the South Pacific Ocean, about halfway between Hawaii and New Zealand.

New Zealand occupied this former German protectorate then known as "Western Samoa" at the outbreak of World War I in 1914 (it later dropped "Western" from its name in 1997). It administered the islands as a UN mandate and then as a trust territory until 1962, when the islands became the first Polynesian nation to reestablish independence in the 20th Century. This small two-island country had an estimated population of 194,300 in 2012 as it celebrated the 50th anniversary of its independence.

In 1975, Samoa became one of the first countries in the South Pacific to recognize the People's Republic of China. That diplomatic recognition led to Samoa creating an Asian niche market for its offshore finance center targeting business in mainland China and the Far East. Because of massive amounts of aid from China, Samoa tends to be an offshore financial center especially for Chinese investors and caters to them.

Along with the Cook Islands, the strategic location of Samoa just east of the International Date Line in the South Pacific, allows an Asian investor the unusual ability to register a company yesterday. For those looking for legal entities to be used in the Asia in general or in China, Samoa is an interesting potential alternative to Hong Kong and Singapore.

The economy of Samoa traditionally depends on development aid and loans from other countries (China, Japan, Australia and New Zealand), family remittances from more than 100,000 Samoans who live abroad, agriculture and fishing. The country is vulnerable to devastating cyclones. Agriculture employs two-thirds of the labor force and furnishes 90% of exports, featuring coconut cream, coconut oil and copra. The manufacturing sector mainly processes agricultural products. Tourism is an expanding sector, accounting for 25% of GDP; about 122,000 tourists visited the islands in 2007.

In late 2009, an earthquake and the resulting tsunami severely damaged Samoa and nearby American Samoa, disrupting transportation and power generation, and resulting in 200 deaths.

Offshore Financial Center

The Samoan Government supports maximum deregulation of the financial sector, encourages investment and continued fiscal discipline. Foreign reserves are in a relatively healthy state, the external debt is stable and inflation is low. The government is a mix of parliamentary democracy and constitutional monarchy under a British common law legal system.

There are five major laws enabling Samoa's role as an international finance center:

- The International Companies Act of 1987 is the business corporation law;

- The International Banking Act of 2005 allows three types of bank licenses subject to the Basle international banking standards. All holders of international banking licenses must establish an office in Samoa, have at least two directors who must be individuals and employ at least one person.

- The International Trusts Act of 1987 governs the creation and registration of offshore asset protection trusts;

- The Trustee Companies Act of 1987 is the licensing law for trustee companies, which include corporate service providers, those who deal directly with clients. Only established professionals with international connections are accepted.

- The International Insurance Act of 1988 allows four categories of insurance licenses, general, long term, reinsurance and captive.

All entities established under the offshore laws, except for licensed trustee companies, are exempt from all local taxation, currency and exchange controls and stamp duties.

Fortunately for Samoa, out of concern for its offshore finance center it enacted the Money Laundering Prevention Act of 2000. Thus, the islands never appeared on the OECD and FATF blacklists. Samoa was among the first countries to commit to the OECD principles of transparency and tax exchange of information and it applies OECD Article 26 on official requests for tax information.

Contacts

Samoa International Finance Authority
Level 6, Development Bank of Samoa Bldg., Apia, Samoa
Tel.: 0685: 24071 / 66400
Email: offshore@lesamoa.net
Website: http://www.sifa.ws

Government of Samoa: http://www.govt.ws/

United States Embassy
5th Floor ACB Bldg.
Beach Rd, Apia, Samoa.
Mail: P.O. Box 3430, Apia
Tel.: + 685 21631

Email: AmEmbApia@state.gov
Website: http://samoa.usembassy.gov/

Independent Samoan Embassy
800 2nd Avenue, Suite 400D
New York, NY 10017
Tel.: 212-599-6196
Email: samoa@un.int

Republic of Seychelles

The 115 islands of the Seychelles are a tropical paradise. However seductive the travel brochure images, they simply can't compete with the real-life dazzling beaches and crystal-clear waters. All this and a fledgling tax haven that wants to serve your offshore needs quickly, efficiently and at a lower cost.

The Seychelles is an archipelago of 115 islands in the Indian Ocean off the east African coast about five degrees south of the Equator. It gained independence from the United Kingdom in 1976.

Most Seychellois are descendants of early French settlers and the African slaves brought to the islands in the 19th Century by the British, who freed them from slave ships on the East African coast. Indians and Chinese (1.1%) account for other permanent inhabitants. About 4,000 expatriates live and work in Seychelles.

Seychelles culture is a mixture of French and African (Creole) influences. Creole is the native language of 94% of the people; however, English and French are commonly used. English remains the language of government and commerce.

Frankly, I had never given a thought to the Seychelles, a remote country of 90,000 people that our publishing partner, *Lonely Planet,* describes as "115 islands scattered in the Indian Ocean… [with] exquisite ribbons of white sand lapped by topaz waters and backed by lush hills and big glacis boulders. And nary a crowd in sight."

Of course, when I consider recommending a country for my readers I consider its suitability as a place to live, the attractiveness of its tax and banking systems, the respect for the rule of law, individual freedom and the level at which it operates free market economic principles.

Alas, here is the lowdown on the Seychelles. After independence from the United Kingdom in 1976, socialist one-party rule bank-rupted this tiny country. The economy was saddled with price, trade and foreign exchange controls, government-owned companies, and state debt-funded development spending.

This caused rapid economic development, but also some seri-ous problems: large fiscal and external deficits and debts, persis-tent foreign exchange shortages and slow growth. Press reports indicated that high-level corruption contributed substantially to these problems.

Like a few other former British colonies, the Seychelles made an unsuccessful stab at becoming an offshore financial center with of-ficial encouragement of foreign investment in real estate and resort properties, with help from the World Bank.

This included the establishment of the Seychelles International Business Authority and legislation to encourage the development of offshore companies. For a time, there was an "economic citi-zenship" program aimed at foreigners—but that initiative died in 1997.

In 2008, facing the near-depletion of official foreign exchange reserves, Seychelles defaulted on interest payments due on a US$230 million Eurobond issued two years previously, severely damaging its credibility as a borrower.

Since 1976, the country has had a checkered history of coups and counter-coups by the military and rival parties, although it appears currently stable. President France-Albert Rene, who had served since 1977, was re-elected in 2001, but stepped down in 2004. Vice President James Michel took over the presidency and in 2006 and in 2011 was re-elected to successive five-year terms.

In 2008, the government signed a standby arrangement with the IMF that mandated floating the exchange rate, removing foreign exchange controls, cutting government spending, and tightening monetary policy. When this was done successfully, the IMF upgraded its assistance to Seychelles by US$31 million for three years. The economy recovered in 2010-11 after the reforms took hold and tourism increased. Seychelles is said to be trying to implement further reforms with a new tax system, reorganizing state owned enterprises, and deregulating finance and communications.

In 2012, one bright spot was the arrival of the Eastern Africa Submarine Cable System, an undersea fiber optic cable system connecting eastern Africa countries to the rest of the world. The system replaces an existing satellite connection. The increased bandwidth and stability is expected to significantly enhance the Seychelles offshore financial services and bring an influx of other businesses.

Planned Offshore Financial Center

Seychelles has comprehensive and modern international financial services laws adopted within the last decade. The legal system is based on a mixture of the English common law and French civil code. The company, banking, trust and other financial services laws are mainly based on English law and patterned after successful Caribbean offshore jurisdictions. Confidentiality is guaranteed by law and all civil proceedings concerning offshore entities may be held in closed session rather than in public.

The Seychelles International Business Authority (SIBA) regulates the offshore industry and registers offshore companies. SIBA also supervises the Seychelles International Trade Zone (SITZ), a development to encourage direct foreign investment which has been limited.

Over 25,000 IBCs have been registered in Seychelles, increasing 40% annually in recent years.

This increased demand is attributed to lower, competitive pricing, fast and efficient processing and turnaround for incorporation, acceptability to international banks, tax-free foreign investments, a high degree of privacy and asset protection and ease of administration.

In 2011 the estimated GDP was US$2.244 billion with a per capita GDP of US$24,700.

The commercial banking sector includes Barclays Bank PLC, Mauritius Commercial Bank, Bank of Baroda, Habib Bank and Seychelles International Mercantile Credit Banking Corporation (SIMBC) trading under the name "Nouvobanq." The first four are branches of foreign banks and the last is a joint venture between the Seychelles government and the Standard Chartered Bank African PLC. Commercial banks offer the full range of services.

Contacts

Seychelles International Business Authority (SIBA)
P.O. Box 991, Bois de Rose Avenue
Roche Caiman, Victoria, Mahe, Republic of Seychelles
Tel.: 248-380 800,
Email: siba@seychelles.net
Website: http://www.siba.net/

Permanent Mission of Seychelles to the UN
800 Second Ave., Suite 400,
New York, NY 10017
Tel.: (212) 972-1785
Email: seychelles@un.int
Website: http://www.un.int/wcm/content/site/seychelles.
The Seychelles ambassador resident in New York is accredited to the United Nations, the United States and Canada.

The U.S. Embassy in Mauritius also serves the Seychelles.

United States Embassy
Rogers House, Fourth Floor,

John F. Kennedy Avenue, P.O. Box 544
Port Louis, Mauritius
Tel.: + (230) 202-4400
Fax: +(230) 208-9534;
Email: usembass@intnet.mu
Website: http://mauritius.usembassy.gov/

United Arab Emirate: Dubai

*Dubai is one of the world's newer international financial
centers. It aimed to rival New York, London and Hong
Kong, and sought to serve the vast, oil-rich region between
Europe and Asia. When it began its campaign for world
recognition as an offshore financial center it attracted
leading Fortune 500 and regional firms, but the 2008
global financial recession and its aftermath slowed things
down to a Dubai crawl.*

The United Arab Emirates (UAE) are located in the Middle East,
bordering the Gulf of Oman and the Persian Gulf, between Oman
and Saudi Arabia.

The Trucial States of the Persian Gulf coast granted the United
Kingdom control of their defense and foreign affairs in 19th century
treaties. In 1971, six of these states, Abu Zaby, 'Ajman, Al Fujayrah,
Ash Shariqah, Dubayy, and Umm al Qaywayn, merged to form the
United Arab Emirates (UAE). They were joined in 1972 by Ra's al
Khaymah. The UAE's per capita GDP is on par with those of leading Western European nations. Its generosity with oil revenues and
its moderate foreign policy stance have allowed the UAE to play a
vital role in the affairs of the region.

The United Arab Emirates extend along the Arabian Gulf coast
bordering the Gulf of Oman and the Persian Gulf, between Oman
and Saudi Arabia With an area of 32.2 thousand square miles It
has a population of more than 5.3 million, according to 2012
figures, 50% Arab and 50% mixed. Arabic and English are the
dominant languages.

Jebel Ali, home of a huge man-made port, has the largest free-
trade zone in Arabia, housing an ever growing list of international
corporations which use the zone for both manufacturing and as

a redistribution point. Dubai international airport is second only to Tokyo in the number of daily transit passengers it handles and second only to Seattle as a sea-air transit hub. Dubai's harbor is the most important port in the Middle East and is ranked among the world's top 10 in terms of container traffic.

Petroleum has traditionally dominated the economy of the UAE. At one time an underdeveloped area, by 1985 the region had the highest per capita income in the world. This immense wealth has been invested in capital improvements and social services in all seven of the emirates. Petroleum production is centered in Abu Dhabi and Dubai. Industrial development is essentially petroleum related but is limited by a lack of trained personnel and raw materials.

Helped by the Jebel Ali Free Trade Zone home to 5,500 companies from 120 countries, the emirate's non-oil imports expanded by 200% from 1986 to 1994. In 2010, total non-oil imports stood at US$50,576,850 million. There are no foreign exchange controls, quotas or trade barriers. Import duties are extremely low, and many products are exempt. The UAE dirham is freely convertible and is linked to the US dollar.

Dubai Investment Park, also known as Dubai Internet City (DIC), has a highly developed technical infrastructure. By 2012 more than 1,400 companies had established themselves in the DIC, including almost all the big names in IT such as Microsoft, Oracle, HP, IBM, Compaq, Dell, Siemens, Canon, Logica, Sony Ericsson and Cisco. These companies represent a community of over 12,000 knowledge workers. The DIC occupies 3,200 hectares in the South of Dubai, near the Jebel Ali Free Zone, offering state of the art facilities and sites for manufacturing, offices, housing, and academic, research, distributions and logistics institutions.

Strategically located Dubai, one of the seven emirates, has become the leading UAE commercial gateway to nearly two billion consumers in Asia, Africa, Europe, India and the Middle East.

Fueled by billions of dollars in oil wealth, in the past construction was everywhere, but that has slowed noticeably. The emirate has worked to build a reputation as the Middle East regional business center. The Dubai government says that a quarter of all Fortune 500 global firms now service the Middle East and North Africa from a Dubai base.

Until recently, most Americans or people outside the Middle East had never heard of Dubai. This city-state first intruded on the consciousness of Americans in 2006 when a Dubai-based corporation planned to buy a company that managed several of America's major seaports. To listen to chauvinistic U.S. politicians at that time one would have thought Arab terrorists were about to invade America again.

The UAE is not considered a tax haven in the conventional sense but it comes within the type of country G-20 governments oppose because of its no-taxes regime. When the U.S. corporate giant Halliburton relocated its offices to Dubai there was a political outcry from the U.S. Left even though it was their legal right to do so.

Proud Tax Haven

Yes, Dubai is a tax-free offshore financial center and proud of it.

Jebel Ali, the first free trade zone in the UAE led the way in 2003 as a planned offshore financial center and as a major port. That was followed by a free trade zone at Ras Al Khaimah (RAK), another sheikdom, which also launched an offshore financial facility. RAK created an International Companies Registry, which allows foreign investors to register offshore companies without the need to establish a physical presence.

Jebel Ali and Dubai offshore centers have positioned themselves as a Middle East tax haven comparable to the Cayman Islands or Liechtenstein. Observers have predicted the UAE will become the world center for Islamic finance. With a GDP per capita in

2008 of US$40,000, it ranks with the U.S. and Liechtenstein in personal income.

Dubai's evolution has been dramatic, with modern skyscrapers and gleaming office blocks springing up on the banks of Dubai Creek. Development has been well managed and oil wealth well channeled. The rulers of Dubai have a penchant for grand projects—a new extension to port facilities, the world's tallest hotel, the Palm Islands, a massive project with 62 miles of new beachfront as well as hotels, villas, shopping malls, cinemas and Dubai's first marine park. However, the global recession has slowed much of this development.

Land-hungry Dubai is increasingly looking to the waters of the Arabian Gulf in search of new land on which to develop, as shown by yet another huge project, "The World," which plans to build 300 islands in the shape of the world's countries. Dubai signed a deal with the Louvre Museum in Paris to establish a branch of the museum there—a claim no other nation can make.

UAE Commercial Center

The United Arab Emirates (UAE) is a union of seven sovereign sheikdoms formed when the British withdrew from the Arabian Gulf in 1971. Dubai is located on the Eastern coast of the Arabian Peninsula, in the southwest corner of the Arabian Gulf. It boasts mountains, beaches, deserts, oases, camel racing, markets and the renowned duty-free shopping, all packed into a relatively small area. It is home to 1.7 million people, a majority of them foreigners, especially south Asians. Dubai was also home to some 100,000 British and other Western expatriates, with Brits as leaders in the offshore financial sector, many of whom moved here from banks and investment firms in the City of London. The global recession caused an exodus of expats in 2009. A quarter of the people trace their origins to neighboring Iran.

This diversity discourages any real ethnic tensions, and while conflict rages further north in Iraq, Dubai has remained trouble-free. The UAE government does not offer naturalization or permanent residence to expatriates. However, foreigners are permitted to purchase and own specifically designated property without a local partner or sponsor ("freeholds," as they are called).

While Dubai has emerged as a global economic player and a major tourist destination, less than a century ago it was little more than a desert settlement where Bedouin tribes roamed the sands and a huddle of settlers crowded around the banks of Dubai Creek. Only decades ago, Dubai had no running water, no roads and the main transport was the camel. But just before British colonial rule ended, oil was discovered in 1966 and Dubai blossomed.

Zero Taxes

Dubai also has one of the world's largest free trade zones and first-class Internet, media and communications infrastructure, much of it brand-new; all this and zero taxes. And Dubai has no Mutual Legal Assistance Treaties (MLATs) or tax information exchange agreements with the United States. Dubai stoutly resisted the Organization for Economic and Community Development's "harmful tax competition" initiative, preferring to keep its attractive zero-tax regime. In 2009, Dubai agreed to apply the OECD's Article 26 standards for tax information exchange, thus avoiding the G-20 blacklist.

Dubai is a good choice for companies setting up distribution channels in Europe, the Middle East, Africa and Asia. It's worth considering for a bank account, although the banks tend to cater to rich Arabs and Dubai's large expatriate community. Residence permits are easy to acquire, especially if you're hired by a local company.

Dubai seems to know no end to its ambition, nor does it have any inhibitions, with new plans, such as those for the Middle East's largest shopping mall, the new airport at Jebel Ali and the world's tallest tower in Burj Dubai on the drawing board.

Dubai might be just what you or your business needs as a base of tax-free operations in an important part of the world.

It is one free market Arab country that is friendly to America and the West and one that offers real possibilities for offshore investment, banking and commerce of all kinds. And it could very well offer you a firm basis for investment in real estate, stocks and as a base for your business in the Mid-East and worldwide.

DIFC

The Dubai International Financial Centre (DIFC) is the world's newest international financial center with an announced aim of rivaling New York, London and Hong Kong. It primarily serves the vast region of the Middle East between Western Europe and East Asia. Since it opened in 2004, the DIFC has attracted leading global firms as well as regional firms. A world-class stock exchange, the Dubai International Financial Exchange (DIFX), opened in 2005. The DIFC is a 110-acre free zone, part of the larger government vision of a free environment for progress and economic development in the UAE.

The DIFC opened in 2004. It had been hoped that the Center would double, to 20%, the financial sector's contribution to the GDP of the UAE by 2010; although this goal was not achieved DIFC continues to grow with an additional 64 companies joining in 2011. This brought the total of active companies located in the center to 813.

The DIFC focuses on several sectors of financial activity: 1) banking services, including investment, corporate and private banking; 2) capital markets, equity, debt instruments, derivatives and commodity trading; 3) asset management and fund registration; 4) insurance and reinsurance; 5) Islamic finance; 6) business processing operations and ancillary services.

Financial institutions may apply for licenses in these sectors. Firms operating in the DIFC are eligible for benefits such as a zero tax rate on profits, 100% foreign ownership, no restrictions on foreign exchange or repatriation of capital and full modern operational support and business facilities.

Contacts

U.A.E. Embassy
3522 International Court N.W.
Washington, D.C., 20008
Tel. (202) 243-2400
Website: http://www.uae-embassy.org/
Email: http://www.uae-embassy.org/contact-embassy/

U.A.E. Mission to the UN
747 3rd Avenue, 36th Floor
New York, NY 10017
Tel.: (212) 371-0480
Website: http://www.un.int/uae/

United States Embassy
Mailing address:
P.O. Box 4009, Abu Dhabi, UAE
Tel.: + (971) 2-414-2200
Email: abudhabiACS@state.gov
Website: http://abudhabi.usembassy.gov/

U.S. Consul General
Dubai World Trade Center
P.O. Box 9343, Dubai, UAE
Tel.: + (971) 4-311-6000
Commercial Office, Tel.: + (971) 4-311-6149

Website: http://dubai.usconsulate.gov/

Dubai International Financial Center Authority
The Gate, Level 14, P.O. Box 74777
Dubai, UAE Tel.: +971 4 362 2222
Website: http://www.difc.ae/
Email: http://www.difc.ae/contacts-0

Dubai Government: http://www.dubai.ae/en.portal

Dept. of Tourism & Marketing: http://www.dubaitourism.ae/.

Residence Assistance:
Henley & Partners Middle East JLT
P.O. Box 213626, Dubai
United Arab Emirates
Tel.: + 971 56 11 50 800

CHAPTER NINE

The Atlantic/Caribbean Financial Centers

The wide arc from Bermuda in the mid-Atlantic to Panama in Central America and the adjacent Caribbean is home to several historic offshore financial centers. Some are British overseas territories and, as such, had to yield to pressure from London to restrict their tax haven status, especially curtailing what was once strict financial privacy. In the past, these small jurisdictions built a reputation of protecting the wealth of offshore persons from many nations. But times have changed and you must check the current status of any OFC before you decide to do business there.

High finance generates far more money than agriculture, tourism and fisheries combined — especially among the Atlantic and Caribbean OFCs. Bananas don't outweigh billions in currency earnings.

After World War II ended in 1945, many of the sunny islands of the Caribbean realized this economic fact and purposefully transformed themselves into international tax and asset protection centers. Some of them as British colonies took these steps with encouragement from their colonial masters in London. At the time, the U.K. Foreign Office saw this transformation as a way to reduce the need for colonial cash subsidies from the British Treasury. In a far freer international atmosphere decades ago, London was not much bothered by far-off colonies where foreigners paid no taxes, arrived with briefcases full of cash and bank accounts could be opened in fictitious names.

Basic Change in Policy

By the end of the 20th Century, the tax collectors at the Her Majesty's Revenue and Customs began to imagine that vast sums of unpaid taxes were hidden in what London now officially calls "British overseas territories."

The socialist welfare states of Europe, joined by the United States, began to see "tax havens" (as they were then called) in general, as a vast sink hole of tax evasion and lost revenues. As explained in Chapter 3, tax havens came under siege from a diverse group of big government spending leftist antagonists including the European Union, the Organization for Economic Cooperation and Development (OECD), the Financial Action Task Force (FATF) and even the United Nations.

The U.S. "war on drugs" was a big boost for the U.S. Internal Revenue Service and other national tax collectors, since much of the illegal drug traffic originated in Latin America. Caribbean jurisdictions, where banking secrecy ("financial privacy") had always been a positive selling point, now were accused of hiding millions in illicit drug money.

Anti-money laundering laws became the new standard for international banking and finance. The major nations, especially the U.S. and the U.K., ignored the fact that their own domestic onshore banks laundered most of the criminal cash in the world. The drug war became a politically useful public relations ploy and an easy, shorthand way for politicians to accuse tax havens of being criminal cash conduits.

In most cases, a lazy news media cooperated in this tax haven smear with little concern for the truth. Besides, it made for a good story — drug kingpins stashing millions in illicit cash in secret bank accounts in little-known places with unfamiliar names that just looked shady.

This anti-tax haven campaign only intensified after the terrorist attacks in New York and Washington, D.C. on September 11, 2001. In the confused aftermath of these earthshaking 9/11 events, leftist politicians raised the false accusation that offshore financial centers had served as hiding places for terrorist cash.

That this later proved totally untrue, after extensive investigations, mattered little to the major nations who saw an opportunity to push their anti-tax evasion plans. These plans called for an end to financial privacy, automatic tax information exchange among nations and abolition of OFC tax exemptions for foreigners who dared still to do business with them.

The high-tax, big spending Labor government that took over in London in 1997 was among the strongest proponents of this new onslaught against tax havens, even though many of the leading havens were under British jurisdiction.

Labor had strong allies in the City of London, where many financial firms viewed far off tax havens as a drain on their business, preferring the familiar Isle of Man or the Channel Islands as business partners (see Chapter 6). This sharp reversal of U.K. offshore policy harmed the British overseas territories in the Atlantic and Caribbean for a time, but ultimately brought about needed reforms that produced net business gains in most jurisdictions.

The British Labor Party that viewed the U.K.'s colonial offshore tax havens with disfavor was defeated in the May 2010 general election. While the Conservative Party won the most seats in the House of Commons, it failed to gain an absolute majority. For the first time since World War II, a coalition government was formed. Conservative leader David Cameron became Prime Minister at the head of a coalition with the third-place Liberal Democrats. Since then the coalition government has steered a more conservative course and they have been far less opposed to the U.K. offshore financial centers than was the Labor Party.

To protect yourself, you must be knowledgeable when doing

business with any of these U.K. overseas territories (OSTs). In each of these jurisdictions, financial privacy and banking secrecy has been diminished. All now apply the OECD Article 26 standard for tax information exchange. In addition, in OSTs where foreign tax evasion was not formerly considered a crime it is now. All of these jurisdictions now have signed Tax Information Exchange Agreements with the United States, a step they had resisted for years.

In my opinion, several of these Atlantic, Caribbean and Central American OFCs remain well-developed offshore financial centers that continue to offer good professional, legal, banking, trust and corporate services. Insurance and annuities are also specialties. As an added attraction, some offer attractive, tax-free residential retirement programs for foreigners. But if maximum financial privacy is your major concern, move carefully in this area.

These definite pluses must be weighed against the rapidly changing political and legal climate in these OFCs, but I again remind you to obtain the current facts before you make decisions.

In a broad arc stretching southward from the mid-Atlantic to Central America are independent countries and some British overseas territories that specialize in offshore banking and finance. Each offers varying degrees of financial privacy and friendly, no-tax or low-tax special programs designed for foreigners.

Each of the sovereign nations in this group is a member of the United Nations and the more-or-less toothless Organization of American States (OAS). Some are also members of the British Commonwealth and others, by their U.K. association, enjoy special participation rights in the European Union.

Most are members of the Caribbean Community (CARICOM), an area-wide economic and trading group of 16 nations. Created in 1973, the CARICOM group includes Anguilla, Antigua and Barbuda, The Bahamas, Barbados, Belize, Dominica, Grenada, Guyana, Haiti, Jamaica, Montserrat, Saint Kitts & Nevis, Saint

Lucia, Saint Vincent & the Grenadines, Suriname and Trinidad and Tobago. Bermuda, the British Virgin Islands, the Cayman Islands and the Turks & Caicos Islands are associate members of CARICOM.

CARICOM members have developed the Single Market and Economy, a space within the community that exempts most goods and services from export and import duties applies a common external tariff. Revenues are shared among member states. It has free trade agreements with Cuba, the Dominican Republic, Costa Rica, the European Union, and is discussing further agreements with Canada, the Mercosur bloc (Argentina, Brazil, Paraguay, Uruguay, Venezuela), and the United States.

Anyone with investments, banking or offshore entities located in the United Kingdom's overseas territories, Bermuda, the British Virgin Islands, the Cayman Islands, Anguilla and the Turks & Caicos Islands, should keep abreast of the policies imposed on these OFCs by the British government in London.

When in power, the U.K. Labor Party aimed their attacks squarely at British people with offshore investments, banking, trusts and asset protection plans. U.K. banks were forced to reveal accounts of all U.K. residents with offshore financial activity. Tax collectors hounded those named. Indeed, her Majesty's Revenue and Customs (aping the U.S. IRS), seemed to assume that any Brit with offshore financial activity was evading taxes.

As expected, this dampened foreign interest in using some of these places as offshore financial centers. The resulting outflow of funds from places such as the Cayman Islands has benefited other haven nations such as Switzerland. Other major beneficiaries have been Middle and Far Eastern financial centers such as Hong Kong, Singapore and Dubai.

What London did not expect were the major "clean house" policy changes these U.K. offshore havens adopted on their own.

As did the U.K. havens in the Channel Islands and the Isle of Man, the Caribbean havens adopted stricter anti-money laundering, tough know-your-customer rules and much stronger criminal investigations aimed at financial fraud and terrorist cash. Indeed, some neutral observers judge that these jurisdictions now have tougher laws and better financial law enforcement than the U.K. itself.

The written constitutions that govern the overseas territories pursuant to the U.K.'s Statute of Westminster (1931) allow the British Crown (i.e., the government of the moment) to bypass local legislatures by declaring an emergency and imposing its own rules. These extraordinary powers were invoked in the Caribbean area dependent territories after they initially refused London's demand to enact "all crimes" anti-money laundering statutes that would enforce foreign tax claims. Until this threat loomed, these havens traditionally had imposed no taxes on income and did not recognize foreign tax avoidance or tax evasion as a criminal matter.

All four territories (Bermuda, the British Virgin Islands, Anguilla and the Turks & Caicos Islands) already had adopted tough money laundering laws that permitted enforcement of foreign confiscation orders in money laundering cases from "designated countries" — only the U.S. and the U.K. at the time. However, contrary to U.K. demands, they all included in their statutes a "fiscal offense" exemption that precluded enforcement in case of tax and customs violations alleged by a foreign government. In 1998, the Cayman Islands government was the first to remove the fiscal offense exemption. London said it expected all the territories to follow orders and each one did.

In the opinion of some once these anti-privacy demands of London were met, the U.K. overseas territories diminished their value as offshore financial centers. If the British Left had its way, the U.K. OSTs would be forced to repeal laws allowing a tax-free status for foreign investors and would have to reveal beneficial ownership of all trusts and international business corporations (IBCs). In spite of adopting increased transparency, the OSTs rightfully have refused to go that far.

These islands still offer superior financial services and investments in which you can have confidence without worrying about U.K. government intervention. What this U.K. history means to the average offshore investor is less financial privacy. For those trying to hide funds abroad, it means, as it should, an increased probability of discovery and prosecution.

The danger lies in a middle area in which foreign tax collectors try to conduct "fishing expeditions." They're looking for possible tax evasion simply because their citizens are financially active offshore. The TIEAs with the United States could lend themselves to just this sort of tax overreaching. But so far the way in which the island governments have administered the TIEAs with Washington have shown no evidence of allowing IRS fishing expeditions.

Anguilla

This luxury tourist destination has high-priced villas and upscale resorts. The most northerly of the British Leeward Islands, it retains the laid-back character of a sleepy backwater. Goats still wander the streets and reggae music blares from passing cars. However, it offers a unique electronic Internet system (ACORN) for instant registration of IBCs, trusts and other legal entities.

Anguilla (population 15,423) located in the Caribbean Sea between the Caribbean and North Atlantic Ocean is the northernmost island in the Leeward Island chain and is east of Puerto Rico. It was first colonized by English settlers from St. Kitts, beginning in 1650. The island was administered by England until the early 19th Century, when, against the wishes of the inhabitants, it was incorporated into a single British dependency along with St. Kitts & Nevis. After a 1967 rebellion and brief period as a self-declared independent republic, it became a separate British "dependency" (now termed a British overseas territory) in 1980.

Anguilla has few natural resources, and the economy depends heavily on luxury tourism, offshore banking, lobster fishing, and remittances from emigrants. Increased activity in the tourism industry has spurred the growth of the construction sector contributing to economic growth. Anguillan officials have put substantial effort into developing the offshore financial sector, which is small but growing. In the medium term, prospects for the economy will depend largely on the tourism sector and, therefore, on revived income growth in the industrialized nations as well as on favorable weather conditions.

Electronic Offshore

Since 1998, Anguilla's Commercial Online Registration Network (ACORN) has allowed for the filing of documents and signatures in electronic form. Today, 95% of all documents, including new registrations, are filed electronically by locally licensed service providers and their approved overseas agents, who are given direct access to ACORN. Using the latest technology, ACORN enables instant and secure electronic incorporation and registration of Anguillan domestic companies, IBCs, limited liability companies (LLCs), limited partnerships and trust companies. In addition to English, ACORN has been able electronically to incorporate companies with Chinese characters and in French, Spanish and Russian (Cyrillic).

Anguilla has enacted numerous laws authorizing offshore insurance, mutual funds, trusts and private interest foundations, but with a small professional sector and limited personnel, it will be a while before the island can compete fully with the established offshore big boys.

There is no income tax, capital gains, estate, profit or other forms of direct taxation on either individuals or corporations, whether resident or not, making it attractive for financial services. There are no exchange controls. Although the official currency is the Eastern Caribbean dollar, the U.S. dollar is commonly used. Anguilla is a common law jurisdiction. Its judicial system is administered by the Eastern Caribbean Supreme Court and the appeal process culminates with the Privy Council in London. There are several firms with experienced lawyers.

Contacts

Government of Anguilla: http://www.gov.ai/

Anguilla Financial Services Commission
PO Box 1575, The Valley, Anguilla
Tel.: + 1 264 497 5881

Email: info@fsc.org.ai
Website: http://www.fsc.org.ai

ACORN (Anguilla Online Commercial Registration Network)
P.O. Box 60, The Valley, Anguilla
Tel.: + 264497 588
Email: anguillafsd@anguilla.net
Website: http://www.axafsc.com/

There is no U.S. embassy in Anguilla. Relations are conducted through the U.S. Embassy in London and the Embassy of the United Kingdom, 3100 Massachusetts Avenue N.W., Washington, D.C. 20008; Tel.: 202-462-1340; Website: http://www.britainusa.com/.

Commonwealth of The Bahamas

During the 20th Century, these islands off the southeast coast of the U.S. blossomed into a major tax and asset protection haven, especially for nearby Americans offering tax exemption and well-crafted laws allowing IBCs, trusts, offshore banking and insurance—all wrapped in maximum financial privacy protected by law.

Because so many Americans used The Bahamas as their favorite offshore tax haven, the islands came under heavy pressure from the U.S. government and the IRS because of suspected tax evasion, drug smuggling and money laundering. In 2000, the government adopted U.S.-demanded laws that disrupted past cozy arrangements with Americans, but also diminished the islands role as an offshore financial center. The final act was a Tax Information Exchange Agreement with the United States.

It's still a nice place to retire, vacation, or have a second home, but more secure banking, investment, tax and asset havens can be found elsewhere.

Geography Determines History, Then and Now

Geography has always played a major part in determining Bahamian history. Located at the northern edge of the Caribbean, this chain of hundreds of islands lies in the North Atlantic Ocean, southeast of Florida and northeast of Cuba. The Bahamas archipelago at its nearest point is about 50 miles east of the United States.

Arawak Indians inhabited the islands in 1492 when Christopher Columbus made his first landfall in the New World on the island of San Salvador in the eastern Bahamas. After observing the shallow sea around the islands, it is reported that he said, "baja mar" (low water or sea) and thus named the area The Bahamas, or The Islands of the Shallow Sea.

English settlement began in 1647 and the islands became a British colony in 1783. Its population now is about 304,000. Since attaining independence from the U.K. in 1973, The Bahamas have prospered through tourism, international banking and investment management. But because of its geography, the country is a major transshipment point for illegal drugs to the U.S. and for smuggling illegal migrants into the U.S. And, as you will see, having the United States as your next-door neighbor has not been easy for The Bahamas. (By the way, the proper name is "The Bahamas" always used with a capitalized "The" by both the official Bahamian government and unofficial sources such as the BBC and the U.S. CIA.)

Offshore Powerhouse No More

The Bahamas grew from a tiny offshore tax haven comprising a few branches of foreign banks in the mid-1960s to a world banking powerhouse by the year 2000. The country's legislation and regulatory structure, comparatively highly skilled workforce and its friendly, pro-business government attracted some of the most prestigious financial institutions from around the globe.

The Bahamas is, and has been for several decades, home to a well-developed offshore financial center. Until a few years ago, it had more than 400 banks and trust companies, 580 mutual funds and 60 insurance companies operating here. It also had registered approximately 100,000 IBCs, mostly for nonresidents.

The asset base of The Bahamas' banking center was in excess of US$200 billion, positioning it among the top 10 countries in the world, behind Switzerland, the U.S., the U.K., Japan and the Cayman Islands, among others. Private banking, portfolio management and mutual fund administration are important. In those days, banks from 36 countries were licensed to conduct business within or from The Bahamas. Licensees included about 100 euro currency branches of international banks and trusts, as well as 168 Bahamian incorporated banking institutions. Sixty percent of all licensed banks offered trust services in addition to their regular banking operations.

The Bahamas is one of the wealthiest Caribbean countries with an economy heavily dependent on tourism and offshore banking. The 2011 GDP was US$10.81 billion and the per capita GDP was US$30,900. Tourism together with tourism-driven construction and manufacturing accounts for approximately 60% of GDP and directly or indirectly employs half of the archipelago's labor force. The Bahamian dollar is pegged to the U.S. dollar on a one-to-one basis.

Prior to 2006, a steady growth in tourism receipts and a boom in construction of new hotels, resorts, and residences led to solid GDP growth but since then tourism receipts have dropped off. The global recession in 2009 hurt The Bahamas, contracted GDP and widened the budget deficit. The decline was reversed in 2010-11 as tourism from the U.S. and investment returned. Manufacturing and agriculture combined contribute only one-tenth of GDP and show little growth, despite government incentives. Overall growth prospects in the short run rest heavily on the tourism sector and foreign investment in tourism infrastructure projects.

In 2012, the Progressive Labor Party Prime Minister, Perry Christie, defeated in 2007 by the Free National Movement Party, returned to power largely based on discontent with the economy. The debt burden had risen to 53% of GDP up from 31% in 2007 and the national debt was nearing US$5 billion.

After tourism, financial services constitute the second-most important sector of the Bahamian economy and, when combined with business services, account for about 36% of GDP. However, since 2000, when the government enacted new and stricter regulations on the financial sector, many international businesses abandon The

Bahamas and went elsewhere. Nevertheless, largely due to increased offshore financial activity, the GDP grew from US$3.2 billion in 1992 to US$10.8 billion in 2011.

And The Bahamas is still a tax haven. There are no business taxes or income taxes, although various registration and transfer fees amount to a tax estimated by some to approach 20%, depending on the nature of the transactions. But this may not last much longer. The PLP is talking about new taxes to plug the deficit and finance services including a VAT.

Since 2000 and the adoption of new, stricter laws, 200 of the 223 private banks in The Bahamas have closed and 30,000 international business companies have been stricken from the official register. The local news media attributed these departures, at least in part, to stricter money laundering legislation and a weakening of banking and financial secrecy.

Drastic, Unnecessary Changes

Until 2000, The Bahamas was one of the world's premier asset and tax haven nations.

But in the former Free National Movement (FNM) government (later defeated for re-election) systematically began to dismantle and dilute the islands' offshore legal framework that had been carefully designed to protect financial privacy and offshore wealth brought into the islands.

This signaled retreat from tax haven status by the FNM government was a defeatist response to the double "honor" of being listed on two tax haven blacklists issued by the FATF and the OECD. These outsiders charged The Bahamas with damaging "international financial stability," being uncooperative in combating money laundering and engaging in "harmful tax competition," meaning levying no taxes on foreigners. The Bahamas were threatened with undefined "stern countermeasures" if they failed to open bank and other financial records to foreign tax and criminal investigators and to make numerous other changes in their offshore laws.

Pressure from Washington

Instead of fighting back and telling these outsiders to "buzz off," the FNM government rapidly pushed through Parliament, over strong PLP minority opposition, a host of statutory changes that substantially weakened the very financial privacy and asset protection that had attracted to the islands tens of thousands of offshore bank accounts, international business companies and asset protection trusts. These new laws admittedly were drafted with the direct assistance of "financial experts" from London and Washington, D.C. The government also said it had accepted "a generous offer" of technical assistance from the U.S. Treasury Department, no doubt including IRS agents.

This capitulation to Washington's demands echoed a crisis in the early 1980s when the late Prime Minister, Lynden O. Pindling, accused of drug dealing, was confronted by an angry U.S. government that threatened sanctions against The Bahamas. Although Pindling was cleared of wrongdoing, he was forced to grant U.S. FBI and DEA enforcement officers' diplomatic immunity and free passage through the archipelago, plus limited access to secret offshore banks accounts of some accused criminals.

The Progressive Labor Party (PLP) parliamentary opposition argued that weakening the offshore laws that brought huge investments The Bahamas would result in capital flight and that is what happened. Many private banks and offshore financial firms departed citing the new laws as reason for the exodus.

PLP opposition members of parliament called on the government to resign over the OECD and FATF debacle, claiming that the blacklisting was directly related to the government's prolonged inability to deal with drug trafficking. Privately, Bahamian sources said government figures were implicated in numerous questionable, but highly profitable, financial activities, a situation the U.S. was holding over their heads unless they acted as Washington demanded.

In May 2002, the PLP opposition won control of parliament and a new PLP Prime Minister, Perry Christie, took office. All these new laws that were a major political issue that Perry and the PLP promised to reverse remained unchanged. Indeed, the PLP signed a U.S. Tax Information Exchange Agreement initiated by the defeated FNM government.

When the FNM in 2007 regained political control all the laws that drove away much of the offshore business remained in place. Both Bahamian parties caved in to the pressure from the U.S. government that had re-written the laws as it wanted them.

New Laws, Amendments to Old Laws

Among the many laws, the "Evidence Act 2000" removed the requirement that requested evidence could not be released to another country until a court proceeding had begun in the requesting nation. Evidence can now be released for foreign preliminary investigations. This law permits Bahamian enforcement of U.S. civil forfeiture orders. Another law allows confiscation of cash and assets under a U.S.-style civil forfeiture procedure that permits freezing of bank and other accounts. Still another law empowers Bahamian courts to extradite criminal suspects during investigations before trial. It should be noted that The Bahamas already had in force mutual legal assistance treaties with the U.S., U.K. and Canada.

Tougher Money Laundering Laws

Existing anti-money laundering laws were toughened to make violations punishable by a possible sentence of 20 years in jail and/or a US$100,000 fine for each instance. A "Currency Declaration Act" requires reporting of all cash or investment transfers, in or out of the islands in excess of US$10,000. The Central Bank also has broad powers to regulate offshore banks, their registration, operation and reporting. The law allows foreign bank inspectors to conduct on-site and offsite examinations of the accounts in bank branches or subsidiaries located in The Bahamas.

The Bahamas' "Financial Intelligence Unit" is modeled after the U.S. Treasury Financial Crimes Enforcement Network (FinCEN). Opposition members of parliament criticized the FIU's powers as far too broad, charging there are no provisions to prevent political "fishing trips" or "witch hunts" by government police. This unit can request ("order" might be a better word) a bank to freeze any funds suspected of being part of criminal activity for up to 72 hours, while a secret "monitoring order" is sought by police to confiscate money or block transactions. In such cases, all other financial confidentiality laws are waived. The FIU issued U.S.-style rules requiring "suspicious activity reporting" by all financial institutions.

Still other laws require all banks to verify the true identity of customers for whom Bahamian intermediaries open accounts. Bahamian banks now use special U.S. cash flow analysis software ("fishing expeditions") to detect possible money laundering. Offshore financial trustees and attorneys are required to maintain records of beneficial owners of offshore trusts and international business corporations. Previously, professional attorney-client privilege rules prevented revealing such information.

IBCs Under Fire

Until 2002, IBCs had not been required to disclose the identities of shareholders or other detailed business information unless under a court order. Now, the right of IBCs to issue and use bearer shares has been repealed and all IBCs are required to submit to the government the true identities and addresses of directors. There are currently more than 100,000 international business corporations in The Bahamas, with about 16,000 added each year. Secrecy of ownership undoubtedly was a large factor in attracting these IBCs and now that has ended.

Even though The Bahamas is still an offshore tax haven, it remains in considerable internal governmental and political turmoil. The mass exodus of so many Bahamian financial professionals speaks volumes about those who judge events first-hand. The best financial and investment climates are those that enjoy some degree of predictability and that's not The Bahamas.

My advice is to scratch The Bahamas off your list of offshore tax and asset haven nations. Things may change someday, but if you were thinking of using the islands as a base of offshore operations, forget it.

Contacts

Government of the Bahamas: http://www.bahamas.gov.bs/

Securities Commission of The Bahamas
Charlotte House, Charlotte Street,
P.O. Box N-8347, Nassau, The Bahamas
Tel.: +242-356-6291
Website: http://www.scb.gov.bs/

Central Bank of The Bahamas
P.O. Box N-4868, Nassau, The Bahamas
Tel.: +242-322-2193
Website: http://www.centralbankbahamas.com

Embassy of The Bahamas
2220 Massachusetts Ave., NW, Washington, D.C. 20008
Tel.: 202-319-2660

Consulates General:
231 East 46th Street, New York, NY 10017
Suite 818, Ingraham Building
25 SE Second Ave., Miami, FL 33131
Tel.: 305-373-6295

United States Embassy
42 Queen Street, Nassau, The Bahamas
Tel.: + (242) 322-1181 or after hours: + (242) 328-2206
Email: embnas@state.gov
Website: http://nassau.usembassy.gov

Barbados

This Caribbean island is not a full-fledged tax haven, but its low business and professional taxes, combined with a network of bilateral double tax treaties with major nations makes it a favorite for foreign investment, especially among Canadians.

Barbados is the most easterly of the Caribbean islands, northeast of Venezuela, 166 square miles in area, located 1,200 miles southeast of Miami, about four and a half hours by air from New York and eight hours from London. It is in the U.S. eastern time zone.

Although it only achieved independence in 1966, the country has one of the oldest Westminster-style parliaments in the western hemisphere in existence for 362 years. Ninety percent of the population of 288,000 is of African descent and more than 80% of the people live in urban areas. The education system is excellent with a literacy rate of almost 100% providing a highly trained workforce for both professional and skilled workers. English is the official language, which helps to make Barbados a good place to do business.

The island was uninhabited when first settled by the British in 1627. Slaves worked the sugar plantations established on the island until 1834 when slavery was abolished. The economy remained heavily dependent on sugar, rum and molasses production through most of the 20th Century. The gradual introduction of social and political reforms in the 1940s and 1950s led to complete independence from the U.K. in 1966. In the 1990s, tourism and manufacturing surpassed the sugar industry in economic importance.

Historically, the Barbadian economy had been dependent on sugarcane cultivation and related activities, but production in recent years has diversified into light industry and tourism.

Offshore Financial Center

Offshore finance and information services are important foreign exchange earners. International business and financial services employ about 3,000 Barbadians and, by some unofficial estimates, contribute 7.5% of the country's GDP. The major appeal as an offshore financial center is the country's low corporate and business taxes, plus a network of bilateral double tax treaties with major nations that allow tax credit for foreign taxes paid. Double taxation treaties exist with Canada, CARICOM, China, Cuba, Finland, Norway, Malta, Mauritius, Sweden, Switzerland, U.S., U.K., Venezuela, and Botswana.

While some neighboring nations are relatively impoverished, Barbados boasts one of the highest per capita area incomes at $23,600, from the booming offshore finance and information services sectors. Another advantage is sharing the same time zone as the eastern U.S. and Canadian financial centers and a highly educated workforce. However, in 2011, the debt-to-GDP ratio surpassed 100% as a direct result of the drop in tourism and financial services.

Barbados has avoided OECD and FATF blacklists by having low tax rates, double taxation agreements and exchange of information treaties as a way to attract business. It has a strict anti-money laundering law and is serious about applying "know your customer" and suspicious activity rules. Its no-nonsense, clean business image undoubtedly accounts for its popularity among foreign investors and businesses who choose to locate here.

The Barbados dollar has been pegged to the U.S. dollar since 1975 at a rate of two Barbados dollars to one US dollar and this stability has proven attractive to foreign business. The country has some exchange control regulations but international business corporations and financial services, including insurance companies, international banks and international trusts are exempted. A special tax break exempts from tax 35% of the paychecks of qualified foreign employees working in IBCs. There are 57 international banks; qualifying insurance companies and exempt insurance companies can make payments free of Barbadian income tax and in any foreign currency.

The government has established a separate ministry to facilitate the development of the international business sector. Some of the incentives include reduced tax rates between 1% and 2.5%, exemption from withholding tax on dividends, interest, royalties or other income paid to non-residents and freedom from exchange controls.

Contacts

Barbados Investment & Development Corp.
Pelican House Princess Alice Highway
Bridgetown, Barbados
Tel.: + 1 246 427 5350
Email: asobers@bidc.org
Website: www.bidc.com

Central Bank of Barbados
Tom Adams Financial Center, Spry Street,
Bridgetown, Barbados
Email: info@centralbank.org.bb
Website: http://www.centralbank.org.bb

Invest Barbados
Trident Insurance Financial Center
Hastings, Christ Church, BB15156, P.O. Box 1009
Bridgetown, St. Michael, BB11142
Tel.: (246) 626-2000
Email: info@investbarbados.org
Website: http://www.investbarbados.org/
(Offices in the U.S., U.K., China and Canada)

Official

Embassy of Barbados
2144 Wyoming Avenue, N.W.
Washington, D.C. 20008
Tel.: (202) 939-9200
Website: http://barbadosembassy.org
Email: washington@foreign.gov.bb

Consulate General
800 2nd Avenue, 18th Floor
New York, NY 10017
Tel.: (212) 867-8435

Consulate General
150 Alhambra Circle, Suite 1270
Coral Gables, FL 33134
Tel.: (305) 442-1994

U.S. Embassy in Bridgetown
Wildey Business Park
Wildey St. Michael, Barbados
Tel.: (246) 227-4399
Emergency after-hours telephone: (246) 227-4000
Fax: (246) 431-0179
Email: BridgetownACS@state.gov
Website: http://barbados.usembassy.gov

Belize

Belize, the only officially English-speaking nation in Central America, has had in place for over two decades a series of offshore laws allowing asset protection trusts, IBCs, maritime registration, insurance and banking—plus maximum financial privacy. Its parliament, courts and government support this offshore financial center and welcome foreign business and investment. An unusual feature is a special, tax-free retirement residence program for foreigners. But this is definitely a Third World country with all the problems that can present.

In the Caribbean region in third place, right after Panama and Nevis, stands Belize—offering banking privacy, low or no taxes and a business-friendly government. It should be on everyone's list of possible offshore financial bases, but its limitations need to be understood also.

Having visited Belize more than once I can attest that it's definitely "Third World," but people are very friendly and oceanfront real estate is still relatively cheap. Belize is one of the few remaining independent nations proud to hold itself out as a tax and asset protection haven.

Belize is the only English-speaking country in Central America, although half the people speak Spanish. Its mixed population of 327,719 includes descendants of native Mayans, Chinese, East Indians and Caucasians. Independent since 1981, its language came from its colonial days when it was known as "British Honduras." Situated south of Mexico, and to the east of Guatemala, with which it has a continuing border dispute. Belize is located on the Caribbean seaboard. It is home to the largest barrier reef in the Western Hemisphere and enjoys great deep-sea diving. To the east in the

Caribbean there's a sprinkle of tropical islands included within its national borders. A few years ago, American television viewers discovered Belize as the locale for one of the first reality TV shows called, "Temptation Island."

Belize retains many of the colonial customs and features familiar in places such as the Cayman Islands and Bermuda, although it is far less developed. The first settlers were probably British woodcutters, who in 1638, found the valuable commodity known as "Honduran mahogany." Bananas, sugar cane and citrus fruit are the principal crops. Like many small countries dependent on primary commodities, Belize more recently recognized the benefits of introducing offshore tax haven financial services to boost its income.

Clean Money

American government officials have had a case of nerves over Belize. Some feared that the sleepy little capital town of Belmopan would become a prime site for U.S. tax evasion and money laundering. But the Belizean government has cooperated with the U.S. in drug and money laundering cases, although extradition from Belize is still difficult. The nation's clean money reputation was also boosted by adoption of a strong anti-money laundering law that is enforced vigorously.

In 1992, the Belize National Assembly enacted modern legislation seeking to make the country a competitive offshore financial center. Drafters combed tax haven laws worldwide and came up with a series of minimal corporate and tax requirements that could well fit your business needs. The new laws include the Trust Act, which allows a high level of asset protection, great freedom of action by the trustee and no taxes on income earned outside Belize. There is also a statute allowing the creation of international business companies that can be formed in less than a day for less than

US$1,000. You only need one shareholder and/or director, whose name can be shielded from public view.

There are no local income taxes, personal or corporate and no currency exchange controls. Since 1990 when the International Business Companies Act became law, foreigners have registered about 5,000 IBCs. That's a small number compared to a place like the British Virgin Islands with over 400,000 IBCs, but the number is growing. Belize is also witnessing major growth in the shipping registry business. Other laws favor offshore insurance companies, limited liability partnerships and banking.

Over the last decade, the government of Belize has carefully and systematically established the nation as an offshore haven that welcomes foreign investment and foreign nationals. It has enacted a series of laws crafted to protect financial privacy and promote creation of offshore trusts and international business corporations (IBCs). It has an attractive special residency program aimed at retirement-bound foreign citizens.

London Pressures

A member of the Commonwealth and a former British colony, but independent since 1981, Belize still has strong ties with London and is thus susceptible to U.K. Foreign Office pressures. In 2000, shortly after the OECD "harmful tax competition" blacklisting of Belize, London made known that future aid of all kinds, including debt forgiveness, would depend in part on Belize's willingness to cooperate in modifying some of its tax-haven attractions. At one point, London suspended debt relief to Belize in response to alleged tax breaks for favored offshore investors in Belize.

Belize bowed to the pressure by promising to somewhat tighten its offshore regulations. This subsequently included repeal of the Belize instant economic citizenship program and limitations on the issuance and use of bearer shares.

Offshore Industry Expands

In spite of OECD's and London's carping, Belize's small offshore industry continues to grow, providing financial services to a largely nonresident clientele. These services include international business company and offshore trust formation and administration; international banking services, including foreign currency bank accounts and international VISA cards; fund management, accounting and secretarial services; captive insurance; and ship registration.

A sympathetic government continues to work closely with the Belize Offshore Practitioners Association in drafting future legislation covering offshore banking, captive insurance, limited duration companies, protected cell companies and limited partnerships. All professional trust providers now must register with, and be licensed by, the government.

The Belizean banking sector is small but secret by force of law. There are only five commercial banks. Privacy protection here is strong but Belize has fallen into line and adopted the OECD Article 26 exchange of tax information standards. It has now signed 13 TIEAs including ones with the United Kingdom and France, but not with the U.S. It does have a MLAT with the U.S. and an anti-money laundering law.

Some banking clients here have complained about a Third World attitude on the part of Belize bankers, with slow service and failure to protect client privacy due to sloppy work.

Third World

Richard W. Rahn, a respected fellow at the Cato Institute, in a 2012 article contrasting Belize with the Cayman Islands posed the question why one offshore financial center should be so spectacularly successful and the other so far behind when they were similar in some respects?

Rahn pointed out that the 2012 Index of Economic Freedom

ranks Belize as the 77th most economically free country in the world (out of 179). He said that if Cayman were large enough to be ranked, it almost certainly would be in the top 10. There is a very high correlation between economic freedom and per capita income. In poverty stricken Belize per capita GDP is $8,300; in the Cayman Islands it is $43,800. "Any country can decide to become freer," Rahn said. Belize ranks a miserable 93 out of 183 countries ranked by the World Bank's Best Places to Do Business project.

Rahn wrote: "It is obvious why Cayman is rich and Belize is poor, and it comes down to one word: governance. If Belize would clean up its courts, fully protect property rights and adopt the best economic practices of its competitors, it could quickly become rich. For instance, it takes an average of 44 days to get all of the required permits to open a new business in Belize. In some countries, such as Estonia, Singapore and even the Commonwealth of Virginia in the U.S., the required paperwork to open a business can be done online. Thus, days have been reduced to just a few hours."

Tax Free Residency

But Belize is trying. A good example of a Belize welcome of offshore persons is the Retired Persons Incentive Act that is implemented by the Belize Tourism Board. The program, which resembles the popular pensionado program in Panama, is designed to attract foreign retirees and foreign capital.

Known as the "qualified retired persons" (QRP) Program, the law offers significant tax incentives to those willing to become permanent residents, but not full citizens. The program is aimed primarily at residents of the U.S., Canada and the U.K., but is open to all.

A "qualified retired person" is exempted from all taxes on income from sources outside Belize. QRPs can own and operate their own international business based in Belize exempt from all local taxes. Local income earned within Belize is taxed at a graduated rate of

15% to 45% and QRPs need a work permit in order to engage in purely domestic business activities. For QRPs, import duties are waived for personal effects, household goods and for a motor vehicle or other transport, such as an airplane or boat. There is no minimum time that must be spent in Belize and QRPs can maintain their status so long as they maintain a permanent local residence, such as a small apartment or condominium.

To qualify for the QRP Program, an applicant must be 45 years of age or older and prove personal financial ability to support one-self and any dependents. A spouse and dependents (18 years old or younger) qualify along with the head of household at no extra fee. Initial fees for the program are US$700, plus US$100 for an ID card upon application approval. Minimum financial requirements include an annual income of at least US$24,000 from a pension, annuity or other sources outside Belize.

For information about the QRP Program, contact the following agencies:

Immigration and Nationality Department
Ministry of National Security and Immigration
Belmopan City, Belize
Tel.: 501-222-4620, Fax: 501-222-4056
Website: http://www.belize.gov.bz/mp.asp?mp=27
Email contact page: http://www.belize.gov.bz/sp.asp?xdurl=mail/mail.asp&mp=27

Belize Tourism Board
P.O. Box 325, 64 Regent Street, Belize City, Belize
Tel.: 011-501-227-2420 Toll free: 1-800-624-0686
Email: info@travelbelize.org
Website: http://www.travelbelize.org
See also: http://www.belizeretirement.org

In spite of British, U.S. and OECD pressures, Belize is not about to enact income or corporate taxes that would drive away foreign investors and residents. In this relatively impoverished country, the offshore sector is a needed and highly valued source of foreign capital that has strong government support. Any modifications to offshore laws are likely to be minimal and mainly window dressing to silence foreign critics.

The offshore professional sector in Belize certainly is not comparable to a highly developed nation such as Panama as an offshore haven, but it also has not sold out to outside pressures, as many of the British overseas territories have. Its laws offer a full array of offshore entities for asset protection and as investment vehicles, trusts, IBCs and limited liability companies. Its one weakness is its small banking community, but you can just as easily locate your Belize IBC bank account in Panama or London, where private banking is an art.

Contacts

Government of Belize: http://www.governmentofbelize.gov.bz

Belize Embassy
2535 Massachusetts Avenue, N.W.
Washington, D.C. 20008
Tel.: (202) 332-9636
Fax: (202) 332-6888
Website: http://www.embassyofbelize.org
Email: ebwreception@aol.com

Belize travel information office, New York, NY
Tel.: (800) 624-0686

United States Embassy

Floral Park St.
Belmopan, Cayo Belize
Tel.: + (501) 822-4011
Email: embbelize@state.gov
Website: http://belize.usembassy.gov

Recommended Bank:

The Belize Bank International Ltd.

Matalon Business Center
Coney Drive, 2nd Floor
Belize City, Belize
Tel.: (501) 227 0697
Fax: (501) 223 0986
Website: http://www.belizebankinternational.com
Shakira Tsai, Marketing Manager
Email: stsai@belizebankinternational.com

Recommended Law Firm:

Barrow & Williams

Attorneys-at-Law, 99 Albert Street, P.O. Box 617
Belize City, Belize,
Tel.: +501 227-5280
Fax: +501 227-5278
Email: attorneys@barrowandwilliams.com
Website: http://www.barrowandwilliams.com

Bermuda

This mid-Atlantic island is the world's leading place for "captive" self-insurance used by businesses and also for re-insurance; it offers excellent asset protection trusts and IBCs. Its respected banks have worldwide branches and investment services. But as a U.K. colony, Bermuda is forced to take orders from London.

The crown jewel of the Atlantic and a world-class offshore center, Bermuda is located in the mid-Atlantic, 750 miles southeast of New York City, 3,445 miles from London. The island (69,000 people, 21 square miles) has a long history as a low-tax and banking haven. In the past, this has been a world-class financial outpost, not to mention a very pleasant place to visit or live in any season. But recently the government has experienced budget deficit problems enough that Fitch Rating Service reduced its bond rating.

The islands were first settled in 1609 by shipwrecked English colonists heading for Virginia. Bermuda has remained in British hands ever since and today is a British overseas territory with internal self-government. A referendum on independence was defeated in 1995 but sporadic independence talk continues.

Bermuda enjoys the fourth-highest per capita income in the world (US$69,900), more than 50% higher than that of the U.S. Its economy is primarily based on providing financial services for international business and luxury facilities for tourists.

Because of its liberal regulatory laws, a number of U.S. re-insurance companies relocated to the island following the September 11, 2001, U.S. terror attacks and again after Hurricane Katrina in 2005, contributing to the expansion of a then growing international business sector.

Bermuda's tourism industry, 80% of its visitors from the U.S., continues to struggle but remains the island's second-largest industry. Most capital equipment and food must be imported. Bermuda's industrial sector is small, although construction continues to be important. Agriculture is limited with only 20% of the land being arable.

A self-governing British overseas territory, Bermuda is a major international financial center. In the early days, the focus was based largely on re-insurance companies. About 30% of the world's 5,000 self-insured "captive" insurance companies are domiciled in Bermuda. The insurance industry includes more than 1,400 insurance and reinsurance companies, with active companies having US$172 billion in assets and writing almost US$50 billion in annual gross premiums.

Tax-Free Business, Expensive Real Estate

Bermuda imposes no corporate income, gift, capital gains, or sales taxes. The income tax is extremely low—11% on income earned from employment in Bermuda. More than 13,000 international business corporations call Bermuda home. They are drawn by the island's friendly, tax neutral environment, established business integrity and minimal regulation. Over 60% of these companies operate as "exempted," meaning their business is conducted outside Bermuda (except for the minimal contacts needed to sustain an office on the island). Since Bermuda does not levy direct taxes, there are no double tax treaties with other jurisdictions. There is a tax treaty with the U.S. which exempts insurance premium payments from U.S. franchise taxes, and grants tax breaks to U.S. companies holding conventions in Bermuda.

Bermuda is also home to more than 600 "collective investment schemes" (mutual funds), unit trusts and limited partnerships. Under the strong protective umbrella of the U.K. Copyright Act of 1965, also applicable in Bermuda, many collective investment schemes with intellectual property and software interests use the island as a legal home port. With a statutory structure for protection, Bermuda also has become a center for offshore trust creation and management. The island offers a wide variety of trusts to meet every need, including offshore asset protection.

The "jewel of the Atlantic" is also a great place to live, but be aware of tough real estate restrictions. Demand for homes is high and supply short. In general, non-Bermudians are permitted to own only one local property. Acquisition is allowed only after careful background checks (at least one bank reference and two or more personal references). Out of 20,000 residential units on the island, only 250 detached homes and 480 condominiums qualify for non-Bermudian purchasers based on government set values.

In January 2012, the average price in Bermuda for a modest two-bedroom, single-family house without water views was $1.65 million. The average price of a condominium was above $1 million. In addition to the purchase price of a home or condominium qualified for sale to non-Bermudians, there is a 25% government upfront purchase tax on homes and 18% on condominiums. Purchase licenses are granted by the Department of Immigration and require six months or more for approval.

Bermuda Banking

Over many decades, Bermuda has achieved a global reputation as a world-class business center. It has set high standards with the best laws and infrastructure with continuing improvements based on experience. There is a spirit of cooperation between business and government in support of the offshore sector. Bermuda as an offshore financial center dates to the 1930s, but began to grow significantly after 1960, initially concentrating on Canada, the U.K. and countries in the sterling area. When Bermuda moved to the Bermuda dollar on a par with the U.S. dollar in 1970, focus shifted from the U.K. to the United States.

Such extensive worldwide finance and insurance activity requires a highly sophisticated banking system. Bermuda provides this with up-to-date services and fiber-optic connections to the world. The four local banks clear over US$3 billion daily. Under the Banking Act of 1969, no new banks can be formed or operate in Bermuda unless authorized by the legislature. The chances of that happening are slim. However, international banks may form exempted companies engaged in non-banking activities and many have done so. Perhaps the biggest local banking news in years occurred in 2003, when the world's second largest bank, HSBC, purchased control of the Bank of Bermuda.

The Bermuda dollar circulates on par with the U.S. dollar. U.S. currency is accepted everywhere. There are no exchange controls on foreigners or on exempt companies, which operate freely in any currency, except the Bermuda dollar.

Unlike Panama, the Cayman Islands or The Bahamas, Bermuda has no bank secrecy laws officially protecting privacy, but bank and government policies make it difficult to obtain information in most cases. To do so requires judicial process. A 1988 tax treaty with the U.S. allowed for governmental exchange of limited information in certain cases, but a more recent Tax Information Exchange Agreement (TIEA) with Washington opened the door to free exchange of information with the IRS. In my opinion, on a comparative 1-to-10 international banking privacy scale, Bermuda now ranks about five or less.

Bermuda currently has 21 TIEAs with the United States, Australia, the United Kingdom, New Zealand, Sweden, Norway, Finland, Denmark, Iceland, Greenland, the Faroe Islands, the Netherlands, Germany, Ireland, the Netherlands Antilles, France, Mexico, Aruba, Japan, Portugal and Bahrain.

For your personal and business purposes, a Bermuda bank account can offer a tax-free means for global financial activity and vast investment possibilities. If you have need for an offshore-based business locale, Bermuda, with its IBC creation laws and its modern digital Internet connections, may be a good bet.

Foreign Tax Evasion a Crime

Bermuda has toughened the provisions of the U.S. Bermuda tax treaty. It also upgraded anti-money laundering laws, as well as financial management laws governing the chartering and operation of banks and trust companies. These laws were seen as Bermuda's calculated response to demands from the Foreign Office in London, the OECD and FATF.

The rewrite of the 1986 U.S.-Bermuda tax agreement in 1995 toughened the existing agreement at Washington's request. It clarified and expanded the types of information that Bermuda can now give the IRS "relevant to the determination of the liability of the [U.S.] taxpayer." For the first time, Bermuda also permitted on-site inspections of records by foreign tax authorities. The Proceeds of Crime Act fiscal offenses list was broadened to include tax fraud. In effect, this meant that by proxy, American tax laws and their enforcement mechanisms were adopted by Bermuda.

Most importantly, the fraudulent evasion of foreign taxes was a made a crime, a major reversal of prior Bermuda policy and law. This made Bermuda the first major tax haven (and the first British overseas territory) to adopt such legislation. Together, these laws allow the U.S. IRS and the U.K.'s Inland Revenue (as well as other nations' tax collectors) to pursue their alleged tax-evading citizens with the assistance of Bermuda prosecutors and courts.

In 2002, Bermuda became an "approved jurisdiction" of the U.S. IRS for tax reporting purposes under the IRS Qualified Intermediary (QI) program described in Chapter 3. That means that the island's banks, investment advisors and other financial services that deal in U.S. securities agree to disclose to the IRS the names of their U.S. clients, or to impose a 30% withholding tax on investment income paid to such U.S. persons. This agreement was said to show IRS approval of Bermuda's stricter know-your-customer and suspicious activity reporting rules.

Business

Because of the large number of international companies that conduct insurance operations from Bermuda, the island does not rely as heavily on personal offshore services and banking as do most other havens. In 2011, over 15,000 international businesses maintained registration in Bermuda and over 4,000 locally. Total income generated by international companies was over US$2 billion. In the past the number of business permits surged as the island promoted itself as an e-commerce haven and opened its shores to licensed investment services providers for the first time. There is no income tax in Bermuda and international companies pay vastly reduced corporate taxes compared to the United States and Europe.

The Bermuda Stock Exchange, established in 1971, was intended as a domestic equities market. With the growth in international financial business, the exchange was restructured into a for-profit entity owned by the Bermuda banking institutions. It offers fully electronic clearing, settlement and depository services. The BSX has become the world's largest offshore fully electronic securities market offering a full range of listing and trading opportunities for global and domestic issuers of debt, equity, depository receipts, insurance securitization and derivative warrants.

Bragging Rights

Its strict laws have led the government to claim that the island is "the business leader among the British overseas territories," ready to meet and exceed international financial standards and regulation.

The British Westminster system confers an immensely important constitutional right on each U.K. overseas territory, that of declaring independence. Until 2004, most local political leaders avoided the issue of Bermuda's possible independence from the United Kingdom. But then-Prime Minister Alex Scott called for a national debate on the subject, looking towards the possibility of ending London's control over the island. Independence is a possibility, but a remote one. Nothing came of the debate, such as it was.

Too Cozy

Beginning in 2009, after Barack Obama became the U.S. president, Bermuda became the renewed target of leftist anti-tax haven American politicians led by Senator Carl Levin (D-MI). Obama as an Illinois senator had joined Levin in sponsoring anti-tax haven legislation that would have revoked long-standing U.S. corporate tax breaks. As a 2008 presidential candidate, he repeatedly denounced tax havens as places where he claimed rich Americans engaged in tax evasion.

U.S. companies who re-incorporated in Bermuda were a special target. The reason companies did this is easy to understand. Under U.S. tax law, a corporation pays 35% or more in federal and state taxes, one of the highest corporate taxes in the world. Once that company changes its corporate registration to Bermuda, its profits from foreign operations are tax-free if the funds are kept offshore outside the U.S. It's easy for U.S. politicians to demagogue this issue, rather than do the hard work of reforming tax laws and lowering U.S. corporate taxes.

In 2009, President Obama tax proposed abolition of this offshore corporate tax break, but without any compensating reduction in the U.S. 35% tax. Obama wanted to tax all income from corporations whose main operations are in the U.S. wherever the income was earned or located.

As a result of the announced legislative intentions of Obama and his congressional allies, in late 2009 a growing number of U.S. companies decide to move from Bermuda to Ireland or Switzerland as part of a search for "a more stable environment." In a sense, Bermuda was being made to pay a price for being too cozy with Washington in the past.

The Willis Group, the world's third-largest insurance broker, joined a growing list of U.S. companies putting more distance between themselves and Washington. The giant consulting firm Accenture also announced its move to Ireland from Bermuda followed by Tyco Electronics Ltd., Boston-based medical device maker Covidien and the diversified industrial company Ingersoll-Rand.

Also in 2009, some major British corporations that had previously moved their corporate headquarters from the U.K. to Bermuda began to have second thoughts. Reacting to heavy handed attacks by the U.K. Labor Party government on tax havens and concerned about what London might do, these companies moved to Switzerland where a network of over 70 double tax treaties offers a more secure tax environment

Bermuda remains a good, basic, no-tax asset protection jurisdiction for the location of offshore trusts, IBCs and it is great for insurance. Its banks are first-class. But its willingness to cooperate with tax-hungry governments in Washington and London has diminished what was formerly a policy of strict financial privacy.

Contacts

Government

Bermuda Corporation Registry
Tel.: + 441 297-7753
Website: https://www.roc.gov.bm/roc/rocweb.nsf/roc?OpenFrameSet

Bermuda Monetary Authority
BMA House 43 Victoria Street
Hamilton HM 12; Bermuda
Tel.: +441-295-5278; Email: info@bma.bm
Website: http://www.bma.bm

Official
Bermuda's interests in the U.S. are represented by the Embassy of
the United Kingdom
3100 Massachusetts Avenue, N.W., Washington, D.C. 20008
Tel.: (202) 588-6500
Website: http://www.britainusa.com

U.S. Consulate General
Crown Hill, 16 Middle Road
Devonshire DV03
Tel.: +1- 441 295-1342 or after hours: + 441 235-3828
Website: http://hamilton.usconsulate.gov
Email: HmlAmConGen@state.gov

British Virgin Islands

BVI, as it's known, has a bit more than 31,000 people — but more than 400,000 registered IBCs, second only to Hong Kong in total number. That's because the BVI specializes in creating, servicing and promoting offshore corporations for every purpose. The BVI can truthfully say, "IBCs R Us." And don't overlook their asset protection trusts, international limited partnerships and insurance. But remember: they take orders from London.

The British Virgin Islands consists of more than 60 islands, only 16 inhabited, at the eastern end of the Greater Antilles in the Caribbean, 25 minutes flying time east of Puerto Rico. Its economy is closely integrated with the nearby (to the west) U.S. Virgin Islands. The currency, since 1959, has been the U.S. dollar and there are no exchange controls. First settled by the Dutch in 1648, the islands were annexed in 1672 by the English.

The capital, Road Town, located on Tortola, is the financial center and the seat of government and courts. As a British overseas territory, the BVI has a long history of political stability with a measure of self-government, but London calls the shots. There is a ministerial system of government headed by a chief minister, with an executive council chaired by the U.K. appointed governor and a legislative council. The BVI is one of the world's most popular offshore jurisdictions for registering international companies and is a growing, but much lesser force in offshore hedge funds (currently about 2000), trust administration and captive insurance markets.

The economy, one of the most stable and prosperous in the Caribbean, is highly dependent on tourism, generating an estimated 45% of the national income. Almost one million estimated tourists, mainly from the U.S., visit the islands each year.

IBCs R Us

The BVI adopted its successful International Business Company (IBC) Act in 1984. The Act was superseded by the BVI Business Companies Act 2004, which removed the distinction between 'offshore' and 'onshore' companies. Well over 400,000 have registered by mid-2012 the government says. Hong Kong and Latin America have been the main sources of clients, which is ironic, since Hong Kong leads all jurisdictions in registration of offshore corporations. (Many of BVI's Hong Kong clients are newly rich Chinese seeking to avoid taxes on the mainland.)

The IBC Act allows quick and cheap formation of tax-free corporations to hold assets and execute offshore transactions. The IBCs are used as holding companies, for consultancies, royalty income, foreign real estate, equipment leasing and ownership of moveable assets, such as airplanes and yachts.

The BVI has significant mutual fund and captive insurance sectors. Banking activity is, by design, minor. The BVI has tried hard to exclude money laundering, mostly with success, and has a relatively good reputation.

There is no statutory duty of confidentiality or privacy under BVI laws. However, confidentiality is imposed under the British common law and also may be imposed by contract. A breach, or threatened breach, of confidence is actionable in court, which may grant an injunction or award damages for an actual breach. Several laws waive confidentiality for criminal investigations.

In the past, one of the major attractions for BVI corporate registration was that true beneficial ownership was not a matter of public record. That has now changed. Under pressure from the Labor government in London, the BVI colonial government enacted numerous laws that compromised this former strict corporate privacy.

In 2002, the BVI signed a tax information exchange agreement with the United States. In 2009, the BVI adopted the Article 26

OECD guidelines for tax information exchange. Its leaders signed 12 TIEAs and came into compliance with the international tax information exchange standards.

Anti-money laundering laws cover reporting of suspicious activities and apply know-your-customer rules. The use of bearer shares (freely transferable corporate shares with the owner designated only as "bearer") has been so restricted that they remain "bearer shares" in name only.

BVI companies still are not subject to withholding tax on receipts of interest and dividends earned from U.S. sources. There are no capital gains or asset taxes. Use of a standard domestic BVI corporation can be more profitable than an IBC, particularly if one wants to take advantage of the BVI double tax treaties in effect with Japan and Switzerland. The U.S. canceled a similar BVI tax treaty more than a decade ago.

The BVI suffers somewhat as an offshore center because of its status as a U.K. offshore territory under the control of the government in London. That's where its orders come from and it follows them.

But the colonials are growing restless. With the past attacks on tax havens coming from London, BVI folks fear their economic lifeline could disappear. The revenue from registering foreign companies has paid for a community college and a hospital. But if you need an IBC to conduct your worldwide business, the British Virgin Islands will provide it efficiently—and all the service and maintenance you will ever need. And they also offer trusts and limited partnerships.

Contacts

Government
Ministry of Finance
3rd Floor West Atrium, Central Administration Building
33 Admin Drive, Road Town, Tortola, BVI VG1110

Tel.: (284) 494-3701 ext. 2144
Email: finance@gov.vg
Website: http://www.finance.gov.vg

BVI International Finance Center
1 Haycraft Bldg., 2nd Floor
Pasea Estate, Road Town, Tortola, BVI
Tel.: 1 284 468 4335
Email: ortizs@bvifsc.vg
Website: http://www.bviifc.gov.vg

BVI Government
Central Administration Complex
Road Town, Tortola
Website: http://inotes.bvi.gov.vg/portal/home.nsf
BWI is represented in the United States by the Embassy of the
United Kingdom, 3100 Massachusetts Avenue N.W.,
Washington, D.C. 20008
Tel.: 202-462-1340
Website: http://www.britainusa.com/

The U.S. has no embassy in the BVI. The nearest is:

U.S. Embassy Barbados
Wildey Business Park,
Wildey, St. Michael
Tel.: 246-436-4950
Website: http://barbados.usembassy.gov

The U.S. Consular Agent in Antigua is closer to the BVI and can
also assist in some limited, non-emergency cases. The Consular
Agency is located at:

Suite #2, Jasmine Court, Friars Hill Road, St. John's, Antigua
Tel.: + (268) 463-6531
Cell: +(268) 726-6531
Email: ANUWndrGyal@aol.com
Mailing address: P.O. Box W-1562, St. John's, Antigua

Cayman Islands

Years ago the Cayman Islands could claim that its financial institutions stood fifth in the entire world in the total number of dollars (billions) under management. It was the jurisdiction of choice for tax free international banks and businesses that wanted (and got) ironclad secrecy guaranteed by law. But a series of highly publicized cases involving drug and other criminal money laundering, plus a major case in which a local bank was used for wholesale U.S. tax evasion, ended this haven's secrecy.

Under extreme pressure from London and Washington, this U.K. colony weakened, but did not end, its still-formidable financial secrecy laws. The Caymans remain an efficient, tax-free OFC for offshore bank accounts, trusts and international business corporations, as well as hedge and mutual funds, insurance and annuities. Its name may be a red flag for foreign tax collectors and anti-tax haven politicians everywhere but it has weathered the political storm as well as the occasional hurricane.

Let's face it: the major reason the Cayman Islands originally became a world-renowned tax-free haven was its strict bank and financial privacy — not just privacy, but near absolute secrecy. Guaranteed by law and zealously enforced by local courts, any foreigner doing business here was shielded from scrutiny — unless it was shown that he was engaged in overtly criminal acts. Even then, a lengthy judicial process often was needed to pierce this wall of secrecy. Secrecy was for sale and the Caymans sold it well.

That was the old Cayman Islands before it was forced, under orders from its colonial masters in London, to compromise its bank and financial secrecy, and instead become a potential proxy tax collector for other nations.

Many of Caymans' 52,560 residents do not agree with what has happened to them. Michael Alberga, a leading Caymans lawyer with a long list of foreign clients, accuses the world's richest nations of practicing "economic terrorism" against the Caymans. We were simply "practicing pure capitalism; few or no taxes and little regulation," he claims, asking to be left alone.

Government & History

The Cayman Islands is a parliamentary democracy with judicial, executive and legislative branches. The present 1972 constitution provides for governance as a British Dependent Overseas Territory, meaning ultimate power rests with London.

The territory consists of three islands in what was known as the British West Indies, Grand Cayman (76 sq. mi.), Little Cayman (10 sq. mi.) and Cayman Brac (14 sq. mi.). Administered by Jamaica from 1863, they remained a British dependency after 1962 when Jamaica became independent. Grand Cayman is located directly south of Cuba, approximately 500 miles south of Miami, Florida. The capital, George Town, is located on Grand Cayman and serves as the center for business and finance.

The Cayman Islands is an English-speaking, common-law jurisdiction with no direct taxation on income, profits, wealth, capital gains, sales, estates or inheritances. Described as being "one of the more mature jurisdictions ... in terms of regulatory structure and culture," the traditionally impenetrable confidentiality of the Cayman Islands ended finally in 2001, when it signed a tax information exchange treaty with the United States. Among other things, that treaty gave the U.S. Internal Revenue Service permission to examine accounts of Cayman financial institutions. (In 2012, the islands had signed 27 tax information exchange agreements and had seven agreements awaiting signature.)

Offshore Business Leader

The Cayman Islands is one of the largest offshore banking centers in the world with about 270 banks (74 of them U.S. branches) including 40 of the world's 50 largest banks with deposits reportedly worth about US$1.725 trillion. It is the second largest captive insurance base after Bermuda, with assets worth US$57.4 billion.

The Cayman Islands trust sector is thought to manage more than US$500 billion. Mutual funds are a growing sector, especially since the opening of the Cayman Islands Stock Exchange in 1997. The Cayman Islands have emerged as a predominant registration base for hedge funds;

As of 2008, there were over 10,000 hedge funds registered here with assets of more than US$600 billion. Cayman dominates offshore hedge funds with approximately a 65% world market share.

The Caymanian dollar is fixed against the US dollar at KYD1.00 to US$1.20. There are no exchange controls. Cayman is an expensive jurisdiction with an established commercial and professional infrastructure in place and a flexible approach to regulation, within a strong desire to maintain respectability. It has excellent communications facilities and extensive professional services.

The Caymans is home to over 80,000 international business corporations (IBCs), 9,705 mutual funds, 239 trust companies, 815 insurance companies, 777 captive insurance companies and thousands of closed-end funds — plus the latest financial schemes dreamed up by cutting edge lawyers and investors as the Enron scandal showed. (Enron's creative managers formed scores of IBCs that were used to conceal company debts, leading to the company's collapse and damaging the Cayman's reputation.)

Until recently, a business could only be carried on in the Cayman Islands by: 1) a CI citizen or a resident foreigner who had a Residence Certificate or; 2) a company licensed to do business or to trade within the Cayman Islands.

In 2011, a new law allows exempted companies and limited partnerships that locate in a "special economic zone" if they are registered with the Registrar of Companies for this purpose. Under the former CI law "exempted" CI companies or exempted limited partnerships could not engage in trade other than business outside the Cayman Islands. Under the 2011 "SEZ Law" this restriction remains but now even if a business has a physical presence in the CI it is legally deemed to be outside the CI for tax purposes. The SEZ law also ends in certain cases the requirement that local companies had to have 60% CI share control, beneficial ownership and at least 60% of its directors were Caymanians.

At one time, the Caymans ranked as the world's fifth-largest financial center behind New York, London, Tokyo and Hong Kong. Offshore business accounts for roughly 30% of the territory's gross domestic product of nearly US$2 billion. Many of the world's most reputable companies, including many American companies, do business through subsidiaries registered in the islands, to take advantage of the favorable, tax-free laws.

The Caymanians enjoy a standard of living comparable to that of Switzerland with a per capita GDP of US$43,800 a year.

Politics as Usual

The Caymans, even more than Bermuda, became a major punching bag for U.S. politicians, what with the defunct Enron Corporation having used it for its numerous tax avoiding subsidiaries, and Hollywood movies such as *The Firm* depicting the islands as a sinkhole of fetid corruption awash in billions of illicit cash.

Many U.S. firms have legal tax-saving subsidiaries registered in the Cayman Islands including big energy companies such as El Paso Corp., Transocean Inc. and GlobalSantaFe Corp. Most U.S. companies have corporate units offshore for strategic, financial and tax reasons and they make no attempt to hide them because, at least at this writing, they are fully legal.

On the 2008 presidential campaign trail, then-candidate Barack Obama made his hostility toward offshore jurisdictions clear. He repeatedly scored points with crowds when he said, "There's a building in the Cayman Islands that houses supposedly 12,000 U.S.-based corporations. That's either the biggest building in the world or the biggest tax scam in the world, and we know which one it is."

It made no difference to him that a similar building in Wilmington, Delaware, home of his running mate, later U.S. Vice President, Joe Biden, housed more than 50,000 American corporations as a means legally to escape state taxes in other American states. Ugland House, on South Church Street near the center of George Town, is indeed home to Cayman's largest law firm, Maples and Calder that serves a registered agent for these all those legal corporations that it represents.

The issue was injected in the 2012 presidential campaign when Democrats attacked Republican nominee Mitt Romney who had legal tax-reducing investments based in the Cayman Islands.

This sort of publicity has made the Caymans the stereotypical media "tax haven" but objective reality does not support that false image.

The truth is that Cayman has tried hard with a large number of laws to keep up with the international pressure for offshore centers to keep themselves clean, even accepting in 2001 investigation of fiscal wrong-doing when criminality is shown both internationally and in Cayman itself. But, fortunately, the prevailing attitude in Cayman is still to protect financial confidentiality in the absence of demonstrated criminality.

Although the Cayman Islands was briefly included on the FATF list of jurisdictions with inadequate defenses against money laundering, in 2001 the Cayman Islands was praised by the FATF for its substantial efforts to conform to 40 recommendations set out by the FATF in a code of good practice governing money laundering, including the issuance of money laundering regulations and amendments to the Monetary Authority Law and the Proceeds of Criminal Conduct Law. Amendments have also been made to the Banks and Trust Companies Law and the Companies Management Law; and compulsory licensing for financial firms was introduced in late 2002.

Money Laundering Crackdown

The Cayman Islands rightfully viewed themselves at the forefront of the fight against money laundering in the Caribbean. Drug money laundering was made a serious crime in 1989 and so-called "all crimes" anti-money laundering legislation took effect in 1996.

In 2000, the government issued a new code of conduct for financial institutions aimed at further curbing money laundering, supplementing the 1996 landmark law that had criminalized money laundering in all serious crimes. The new code encouraged reporting of suspicious transactions by providing a safe harbor from liability for those who reported suspected crimes.

In 2000, the government proudly announced what its politicians repeatedly had said they would never do. They had reached an agreement with the OECD on the issue of future "transparency." Thus, the government officially embraced the OECD's demand for an end to the Caymans' traditional bank and financial secrecy, guaranteeing it would provide financial information about Caymans' clients to foreign tax collecting authorities. In return for this major surrender, the OECD promised the Caymans would not appear on the OECD blacklist of tax havens allegedly engaged in "harmful tax practices" published in 2000.

Within three weeks of the FATF report, all the primary legislation necessary to address every one of the FATF's concerns was on the statute books. Within a further few weeks, more anti-money laundering rules were introduced to complete the legislative framework. The Cayman Islands now have a regime considerably tougher than that which exists in many of the FATF's 29 member countries.

The laws allow the Cayman Islands Monetary Authority to obtain information on bank deposits and bank clients without a court order and ended existing restrictions on sharing information with foreign investigators. A new provision made it a crime for bankers to fail to disclose knowledge or suspicion of money laundering. Previously, it had been a crime for financial sector workers to disclose any private financial information without a court order. The Caymans government even went so far as to guarantee that it would stop island financial services providers from "the use of aggressive marketing policies based primarily on confidentiality or secrecy."

Recommendation

Regardless of the end of financial secrecy here, enormous amounts of money have flowed through these islands over many years. That has created an impressive financial and professional community from which you and your businesses can benefit. These professionals can provide first-class investment advice, a variety of offshore legal entities, trusts and IBCs, annuities and life insurance. There are many mutual and hedge funds in which to invest.

If you value financial privacy and are considering or have financial dealings in the Cayman Islands, as with any British overseas territory haven, plan accordingly. But don't overlook what they have to offer—even if everything these days is out in the open.

Contacts

The Cayman Islands are part of the consular district administered by the U.S. Embassy in Kingston, Jamaica:

United States Embassy
142 Old Hope Road, Kingston 6, Jamaica
Tel.: + (876) 702-6000 or after hours: + (876) 702-6000
Email: opakgn@state.gov

U.S. Consular Agent in the Cayman Islands
Unit 222, Micro Center, North Sound Road
George Town, Grand Cayman
Tel.: + (345) 945-8173

Cayman Islands Department of Tourism:
Miami (305) 599-9033
New York (212) 889-9009
Houston (713) 461-1317
Chicago (630) 705-0650
Web: http://www.caymanislands.ky

Immigration Department Cayman Islands Government
P.O. Box 1098GT, Elgin Avenue
George Town, Grand Cayman, Cayman Islands
Tel.: + (345) 949-8344 or + (345) 949-8052

The Cayman Islands are represented in the United States by the
Embassy of the United Kingdom, 3100 Massachusetts Avenue
NW, Washington, D.C. 20008
Tel.: 202-462-1340
Website: http://www.britainusa.com

Cayman Islands Monetary Authority
P.O. Box 10052 APO, Elizabethan Square
Grand Cayman, Cayman Islands
Tel.: + 345-949-7089

Website: http://www.cimoney.com.ky

Recommended Attorney:

Michael Alberga, Esq.
Harbour Place, 2nd Floor, 103 South Church Street
Grand Cayman, KY1-1106, Cayman Islands
Tel.: +1 345 949 0699 Office
Email: malberga@thorpalberga.com
Website: http://www.thorpalberga.com

The Island of Nevis

While it is not that well known outside offshore financial circles, Nevis is a leading tax-free asset haven jurisdiction. It has had in place for 30 years asset protection-friendly laws allowing trusts, IBCs and limited liability companies. The government and courts have enviable records of support for offshore business. It has few banks, but you can bank elsewhere. And any legal entity you need can be set up in a matter of a few days at minimal cost.

If there is any one financial center that has all the things you need for smooth offshore operations, it's the eastern Caribbean island of Nevis (pronounced KNEE-vis). Best of all, Nevis has a no-nonsense banking and business privacy law that even the U.S. government can't crack. Its pro-offshore laws have existed for three decades — so there is plenty of experience and precedent in the local courts — and the legislative assembly keeps the applicable laws current. There are well-established service companies that can do what you want and several have U.S. branch offices for your convenience.

The two island "sovereign democratic federal state" of St. Kitts & Nevis (as its 1983 constitution ceremoniously describes it), has a governmental form and name almost larger than its population of 50,726 (July 2012 estimate) and total land area (103 sq. miles). It is part of the chain of islands known in colonial days as the British West Indies, but now known without the "British" part of that title.

But this tiny West Indies two-island nation, known to the natives as "St. Kitts-Nevis," has earned prominence in offshore financial circles. That's because Nevis has no taxes, extremely user-friendly, quick incorporation and trust laws and an official attitude of hearty welcome to foreign offshore corporations and asset protection trusts.

The islands are located 225 miles east of Puerto Rico and about

1,200 miles south of Miami. Until their 1983 declaration of independence, both were British colonies. They are still associate members of the British Commonwealth. Her Majesty, Queen Elizabeth II, as the titular head of state, still appoints the Governor General. The elected unicameral parliament sits in the capital of Basseterre on St. Kitts (population 40,000). The population of Nevis is about 10,000.

Very Independent

Nevis, the tax haven half of the federation, has its own Island Assembly and a no-nonsense strict banking and business privacy law. Its pro-offshore laws have existed for a quarter of a century—so there is plenty of experience and precedent in the local courts—and the legislative assembly keeps the applicable laws current. There are well-established offshore financial service companies to help you, and some have convenient U.S. branch offices.

The Nevis independence movement owes much of its success as the business-friendly "Delaware of the Caribbean." Over the last 25 years, the Nevis parliament has adopted and constantly updated excellent offshore corporation, trust and limited liability company laws, augmented by strong financial privacy.

There are no exchange controls and until recently there were no tax information exchange treaties with other countries. However, since 2009, the country has signed 18 TIEAs, including those with Canada and the United Kingdom, but none with the United States as yet.

Unsuccessful moves by the St. Kitts-based government to take over the Nevis financial sector have played a major role in spurring continuing calls for secession.

St. Kitts & Nevis suffer under none of the restrictions inflicted by London on British overseas territories. Their national sovereignty allows them to enact their own laws and make their own policies, free from outside pressures.

Nevis also has its own Island Assembly and retains the constitutional right of secession from St. Kitts. For years, there were heated demands for separation. Then, in 1998, defying international pleas, residents of the seven-mile-long island of Nevis voted on whether to secede from St. Kitts and become the smallest nation in the Western Hemisphere. Approval of two-thirds of the island's voters was required for secession. The vote was 2,427 for secession and 1,418 against, falling just short of two-thirds.

The vote was the culmination of a struggle that began with Britain's colonization in 1628. In 1882, Britain stripped Nevis of its legislature and wed it to St. Kitts. When the islands became independent in 1983, Nevis reluctantly joined in a federation with neighboring St. Kitts, but Nevisians insisted on a constitutional clause allowing them to break away. After years of complaining that they are treated like second-class citizens by the federal government on St. Kitts, they invoked that right with the failed referendum.

St. Kitts & Nevis is already the smallest nation in the Western Hemisphere. It retains the right to secede and proponents vow they will try again.

Offshore Corporate Home

Based on the Island Assembly's adoption of the Business Corporation Act of 1984, Nevis has an established record of catering to offshore corporations. The statute contains elements of the American State of Delaware's extremely liberal corporation laws, along with English commercial law. As a result, both U.S. attorneys and U.K. solicitors are comfortable navigating its provisions.

The corporation statute allows complete confidentiality for company officials and shareholders. There is no requirement for public disclosure of ownership, management, or financial status of a business. Although they must pay an annual fee of US$450, international business corporations are otherwise exempt from taxes — no withholding, stamps, fees, or taxes on income or foreign assets. Individually negotiated, government guaranteed tax holidays are available in writing, provided the IBC carries on no business locally. Official corporate start-up costs can be under US$1,000, including a minimum capitalization tax of US$200 and company formation fees of US$600. These low government levies compare very favorably with those imposed by other corporate-friendly havens like the high-profile, high-cost Cayman Islands.

Under OECD Pressures

There are no exchange controls and no tax treaties with other nations. In 2000, St Kitts & Nevis was named on the OECD and FATF blacklists, but was removed from both after adopting anti-money laundering laws in 2001-2003. As a matter of official policy, until 2009, the government of Nevis did not exchange tax or other information with any other foreign government. However, in 2009, St. Kitts & Nevis was placed in the G-20/OECD "gray list" of countries allegedly failing to meet international standards concerning tax information exchange.

Its officials took great offense at this listing and publicly denounced the OECD and larger nations for ganging up on small countries. Nevertheless, in 2009, it adopted a law containing the tax information exchange standard of OECD Article 26, allowing information to be provided in individual cases of alleged foreign tax evasion. It also negotiated a series of TIEAs with several nations in an effort to appease the G-20 and OECD critics.

Nevis corporate law is somewhat unique in that it contains a very modern legal provision. It allows the international "portability" or transfer of an existing foreign company from its country of origin to the island. Known as the "re-domiciling provision," this allows the smooth and instantaneous transfer of an existing corporation from any nation and retention of its original name and date of incorporation. This is all done without interruption of business activity or corporate existence. The only requirement is the amendment of existing articles of incorporation to conform to local laws. Principal corporate offices and records may be maintained by Nevis companies anywhere in the world.

New company creation and registration is fast in Nevis. It's accomplished simply by paying the capitalization tax and fees mentioned earlier. Using Nevis corporate service offices in the U.S. (see below), your corporation or limited liability company (LLC) can be registered and ready to do business within 24 to 48 hours. You can do everything by phone, fax, wire and FedEx. Your confirmation papers can be sent to you overnight from Nevis. Formal incorporation documents must be filed within 10 days of receiving the confirmation papers. Corporate service firms will assist you with ready-made paperwork.

Small wonder that in 25 years since the corporation law's original adoption, thousands of foreign corporate owners have established their companies in Charlestown, Nevis.

Contact:

Nevis Services Ltd.
545 Fifth Avenue, Suite 402
New York, New York 10017
Tel.: (212) 575-0818
Email: nevisserv@cs.com
Website: http://www.morningstarnev.com/nevis_services.htm

Asset Protection Trusts

Building on their reputation for statutory corporate cordiality, in 1994, the Island Assembly adopted the Nevis International Trust Ordinance, a comprehensive, clear and flexible asset protection trust (APT) law. This law is comparable and, in many ways superior, to that of the Cook Islands in the South Pacific, already well-known as an APT world center.

The Nevis law incorporates the best features of the Cook Islands law, but is even more flexible. Its basic aim is to permit foreign citizens to obtain asset protection by transferring property titles to an APT established in Charlestown, Nevis.

Nevis also is taking advantage of the worldwide explosion in medical, legal and professional malpractice lawsuits. Legislative and judicial imposition of no-fault personal liability on corporate officers and directors has become a nasty fact of business life, especially in the U.S. A Nevis trust places personal assets beyond the reach of foreign governments, litigious plaintiffs, creditors and contingency-fee lawyers.

Under the 1994 law, the Nevis judiciary does not recognize any non-domestic court orders regarding its own domestic APTs. This forces a foreign judgment creditor to start all over again, retrying the case in Nevis courts and with Nevis lawyers. A plaintiff who sues an APT must first post a US$25,000 bond with the government to cover court and others costs before a suit will be accepted for filing. And the statute of limitations for filing legal challenges to a Nevis APT runs out two years from the date of the trust creation. In cases of alleged fraudulent intent, the law places the burden of proof on the foreign claimant.

All these factors combine to create an atmosphere in which a claimant confronted with a Nevis APT may settle for cents on the dollar, rather than attempt to fight an entire new battle in Nevis at great cost. This is especially useful to American doctors or other health providers who can shield their personal assets in an APT and may use the trust as a substitute for high cost malpractice insurance.

Nevis APT Formation

Nevis has a small international bar and local trust experts who understand and can assist in furthering APT objectives. The APT act has proven popular and a considerable number of trusts have been registered in Nevis.

Under the statute, the Nevis government does not require the filing of trust documents. They are not a matter of public record. The only public information needed to establish an APT is a standard form or letter naming the trustee, the date of trust creation, the date of the filing and the name of the local trust company representing the APT. The fee is US$200 upon filing and an equal annual fee to maintain the filing.

Broad Trust Powers

Under the Nevis International Trust Ordinance, the same person can serve in the triple role of grantor, beneficiary and protector of the APT. This allows far greater control over assets and income than U.S. domestic law permits. Generally, American law forbids the creation of a trust for one's own benefit. The basic structure of a foreign asset protection trust differs little from an Anglo-American trust.

The grantor creates the trust by executing a formal declaration describing the purposes, then transferring assets to be administered, according to the declaration, by the named trustees. Usually, there are three trustees named, two in the grantor's country and one in Nevis, the latter known as a "protector." Named trust beneficiaries can vary according to the grantor's estate planning objectives and under Nevis law, the grantor may be the primary beneficiary.

A word of caution: from the point of view of American courts and law, it's far better that a grantor not serve as a protector or trustee. That's because U.S. law (and the IRS) view a grantor in that capacity as having such a large degree of control over the assets as to call into question the validity of the trust. In many such cases, U.S. courts have ruled the entity to be an invalid "sham trust."

Nevis requires the appointment of a "trust protector" who, as the title indicates, oversees its operation and ensures legal compliance. A protector does not manage the trust, but can sometimes veto trustee actions. Nevis also allows a beneficiary to serve in the dual role as protector.

Tax and Legal Advantages for Americans

Under U.S. tax law, foreign asset protection trusts are tax neutral, as are domestic trusts. This means income from the trust is treated by the Internal Revenue Service as the grantor's personal income and taxed accordingly. Because the grantor retains some control over the transfer of his assets to any foreign trust, including those established in Nevis, U.S. gift taxes can usually be avoided. Although Nevis has no estate taxes, U.S. estate taxes are imposed on the value of trust assets for the grantor's estate, but all existing exemptions for combined marital assets can be used.

One device that a trust grantor can use to retain some control of trust assets is to form a limited partnership, then make the Nevis trust itself a limited partner. This arrangement allows you, as trust grantor, to retain active control over the assets you transfer to the Nevis trust/limited partner. It also adds further protection to the trust from creditors and other legal assaults.

Aside from the undoubted protection offered by the Nevis International Trust Ordinance, this is a small nation, although indebted, with political stability, a highly reputable judicial system, favorable local tax laws, no language barrier and excellent international communication and financial facilities.

Nevis also has enacted comprehensive anti-money laundering laws, which are enforced. This has kept Nevis off the FATF blacklist of "dirty money" jurisdictions.

Fast Citizenship for Sale

St. Kitts & Nevis is one of two countries that offer citizenship for sale. Its passport is well-regarded internationally and the program has been carefully managed with very few passports issued. St. Kitts & Nevis citizens enjoy a passport with an excellent reputation and very good visa free travel to many nations. For visa-free travel throughout Europe, a St. Kitts & Nevis passport can be combined with a residence permit in a European Union country.

Citizens of St. Kitts & Nevis are allowed to hold dual citizenship, and the acquisition of citizenship is not reported to other countries. St. Kitts & Nevis's excellent citizenship program was established and is governed by the Citizenship Act of 1984. It offers the benefits of visa-free travel to over 120 countries and territories.

Under the 2006 changes to the citizenship-by-investment regulations, to qualify for St. Kitts & Nevis citizenship, you must invest at least US$350,000 in designated real estate plus pay considerable government and due diligence fees besides real estate purchase taxes. Or you can contribute to the Sugar Industry Diversification Foundation in the amount of US$200,000 (for a single applicant). If you are interested in obtaining this citizenship and a second passport contact:

The Nestmann Group, Ltd.,
P.O. Box 11, Juris Bldg. Main St.
Charlestown, Nevis W.I.
Fax: +1 (869) 469-4603

Contacts

Government of Saint Kitts & Nevis:
Website: http://www.gov.kn

Nevis Government Information Service:
Website: http://www.queencitynevis.com

Ministry of Finance
Nevis Offshore Financial Services, PO Box 882
Rams Complex, Stoney Grove, Nevis
Tel.: + (869) 469-0038
Email: info@nevisfinance.com
Website: http://www.nevisfinance.com

Embassy of St. Kitts & Nevis
3216 New Mexico Avenue, N.W.
Washington, D.C. 20016
Tel.: (202) 686-2636
Website: http://www.embassy.gov.kn
Email: stkittsnevis@embassy.gov.kn

There is no American embassy in St. Kitts & Nevis. The nearest
U.S. Embassy is located in Barbados:

U.S. Embassy in Bridgetown
Wildey Business Park
Wildey St. Michael, Barbados
Tel.: (246) 227-4399
Emergency after-hours telephone: (246) 227-4000
Fax: (246) 431-0179
Email: BridgetownACS@state.gov
Website: http://barbados.usembassy.gov

Saint Vincent & the Grenadines

As an offshore financial center, Saint Vincent & the Grenadines has unusual European origins and more recently some questionable banking scandals. It's a great place for a vacation, but would you want to put your money here?

Saint Vincent & the Grenadines is a group of 18 small islands with 103,507 people that is part of the Windward Islands, located 1,600 miles east of Miami, between the Caribbean Sea and Atlantic Ocean, north of Trinidad and Tobago. Included are the popular holiday islands of Mustique and Bequia. The islands average more than 200,000 tourist arrivals annually mostly to the Grenadines.

Resistance by the native Caribs prevented foreign colonization on St. Vincent until 1719. Disputed between France and the United Kingdom for most of the 18th Century, the islands were ceded to the U.K. in 1783. The country gained independence from the U.K. in 1979 and has a parliamentary and common law system.

Most Vincentians are the descendants of African slaves brought to the island to work on plantations. There also are a few white descendants of English colonists, as well as some East Indians, native Carib Indians and a sizable minority of mixed race. The country's official language is English, but a French patois may be heard on some of the Grenadine Islands.

Recent years have seen important changes in the islands' precarious economy. Previously, St. Vincent & the Grenadines depended largely on agriculture, especially bananas that replaced the main sugar crop. The government has encouraged diversification, promoting other crops and supporting the development of tourism and financial services. The islands are vulnerable to external shocks, both natural (from weather changes, such as droughts or hurricanes) and economic, from recession in the major tourism markets of the U.S. and U.K. In the 1990s, GDP growth variations ranged from a high of 8.3% to a low of 2.9%. In 2008, following two years of strong growth, the economic climate drastically deteriorated with the onset of the global financial crisis.

With jobless rates as high as 20%, persistent high unemployment has prompted many to leave the islands. In 2008, GDP amounted to $1.3 billion, with per capita GDP of $10,500. To put this in perspective, in 2003, the revenue from the local filming of the Walt Disney movie, Pirates of the Caribbean, starring Johnny Depp, surpassed that of the total income from the country's agriculture.

Questionable Banking

The country has a long tradition of international banking and finance, but its current banking reputation is questionable at best. Its first bank was set up in 1837 by Barclays out of London and the first domestic bank opened its doors in 1909.

Kingstown, the capital, on the main island of St. Vincent, is the seat of the government and also the business and finance center, including an ever-smaller offshore banking sector that claims to have adopted international banking and financial regulatory standards. In 1996, a major legislative overhaul of financial regulations was supposed to make financial services a focal point of the economy.

The twin objectives of the legislation were said to protect the right to financial privacy and for maximum asset protection. The government stated then that it would not help other countries collect taxes under the guise of "fishing expeditions" or prosecuting tax offenses. However the islands were soon embarrassed by banking scandals. In spite of what was claimed to be careful vetting, the licenses of three banks were revoked in 2005.

In 2002, the U.S. Treasury issued a formal warning to U.S. banks that the islands' banks were suspected of money laundering and the OECD Financial Action Task Force (FATF) placed them on their dirty money blacklist. The response was official adoption of an anti-money laundering law that was said to be "on a par with the highest of international standards." In 2003, FATF removed the islands from its blacklist.

The head of government of St. Vincent & the Grenadines boasted in 2008 that he had closed 34 of 40 banks since 2001, hardly a major confidence builder. In 2009, regulators took control of another island bank, Millennium Bank, which U.S. authorities linked to an alleged $68 million Ponzi scheme. As it happens, for several years I had warned people who were attracted to this bank by promises of unrealistically high gains that the bank was questionable. In 2009, questions were raised about another island bank that was accused of allowing two fraudsters based in Norway and New Zealand to use the bank to promote their Internet banking schemes.

International Offshore Center

The concept of an international financial services sector here was first introduced by Swiss and Liechtenstein lawyers in 1976, three years before independence. A host of Swiss/Liechtenstein drafted offshore laws authorize various entities including international banks, international business companies, limited duration companies, international asset protection trusts, mutual funds and international insurance companies. Exempted companies and exempted limited partnerships receive a statutory guarantee of tax-free status for 20 years. At present, there are no corporate or individual income taxes or other taxes.

Until 2002, St. Vincent's law provided for strict financial privacy under the Confidential Relationship Preservation Act of 1996. This was repealed and replaced by the Exchange of Information Act of 2002. This Act allowed for the exchange or disclosure of information between island regulators and foreign regulatory/government and tax officials.

In 2011, the government adopted the International Cooperation Tax Information Exchange Agreements Act to ensure effective information exchange as required by Article 26 of the OECD model act. The government now has signed 31 agreements, 10 double tax agreements and 21 tax information exchange agreements.

Contacts

Embassy of St. Vincent and the Grenadines
3216 New Mexico Ave. N.W.
Washington, D.C. 20016
Tel.: 202-364-6730
Email: mail@embsvg.com
Website: http://www.embsvg.com

The United States has no official presence in St. Vincent. The nearest U.S. Embassy is located in Bridgetown, Barbados,

U.S. Embassy in Bridgetown
Wildey Business Park
Wildey St. Michael, Barbados
Tel.: (246) 227-4399
Emergency after-hours telephone: (246) 227-4000
Fax: (246) 431-0179
Email: BridgetownACS@state.gov
Website: http://barbados.usembassy.gov

Turks & Caicos Islands

The Turks & Caicos Islands are an English-speaking British overseas territory that combines tax-free status, an idyllic climate and close proximity to the United States. They impose no income, corporate or estate taxes. There are no exchange controls and the U.S. dollar is the country's legal tender. There is a wide range of financial and other professional services readily available. Unfortunately, self-government has not gone well here in recent times.

In 2009, the Foreign Office in London deposed the elected head of government and the parliament for corruption. Control of the islands was temporarily placed with Her Majesty's appointed Governor General, where it remains still.

Until recently, the Turks & Caicos Islands were a British self-governing territory, a chain of more than 40 islands, only eight of which are inhabited. (Self-government was suspended by the U.K. in 2009). The inhabited islands of Providenciales, Grand Turk, North Caicos, Middle Caicos, South Caicos, Parrot Cay and Pine Cay long have attracted those who love pristine beaches, as well as shrewd investors. The Islands are located in the Atlantic Ocean 575 miles southeast of Miami at the southern end of The Bahamas chain. They have non-stop air services from Miami, New York, Boston, Charlotte, Atlanta, Philadelphia, Toronto and London.

The Turks & Caicos are called the "Isles of Perpetual June" because they enjoy a year-round comfortable climate cooled by trade winds, but with lots of sunshine. They have 230 miles of sandy beaches and have become a major stop for eco-tourists and divers who discover some of the finest coral reefs in the world. In recent times, celebrities such as movie actor Bruce Willis and author Jay McInerny have taken up residence.

In 1512, Europeans first visited these islands but no settlement resulted. In the late 17th Century, British settlers from Bermuda came in search of salt. Gradually the area was settled by U.S. planters and their slaves, but with the local abolition of slavery in 1838, the planters left. Until 1848, the Islands were under the jurisdiction of The Bahamas. In 1873, they became a dependency of Jamaica and remained so until 1959. In 1962, Jamaica gained independence and the Turks & Caicos became a British Crown colony. Although independence was agreed upon for 1982, the policy was reversed and the islands remain a British overseas territory. Since 1976, it has had local autonomy, until it was suspended in 2009.

There has been a continuing political struggle between the islands on one hand and the colonial governors and the Foreign Office in London on the other. This was partially due to a strong pro-independence movement, but also because of alleged drug smuggling in the TCI. A low-key, but persistent movement has been afoot for years seeking to have Canada annex the Turks & Caicos and is still alive today. Some members of the Canadian House of Commons even have championed annexation. Despite having adherents in both jurisdictions, this unusual proposal hasn't gained any serious support. The TCI legal system is based upon English common law, as well as a number of laws from both Jamaica and The Bahamas.

Economy

The economy is based on tourism, fishing and offshore financial services. Most capital goods and food for domestic consumption are imported. The U.S. is the leading source of tourism—accounting for more than half of the 175,000 visitors per year. Major sources of government revenue include fees from offshore financial activities and customs receipts. Most tourist facilities are located on Providenciales (known as "Provo") and Grand Turk Islands. Provo is the tourist hub and scene of major developments including a Carnival Cruise ship dock, a Ritz-Carlton resort and numerous large condominium developments.

The offshore financial services sector began in 1981 with the adoption of the TCI Companies Ordinance, an innovative law that provides for formation of exempted companies (IBCs), as well as of local domestic companies, foreign companies, non-profit organizations and limited life companies. Companies can be formed by a local agent within 24 hours at a low cost between US$1,000-2,500 plus an annual maintenance fee of US$300 for exempt companies. A 20-year guarantee of tax exemption is available.

Offshore activity contributes 7% of GDP and ranks second to tourism as the main source of income. Since 2005, the government has conducted a sustained publicity campaign in the U.S., U.K. and other nations to attract offshore financial activities and investments.

The government encourages tourism, which pulls in nearly 175,000 visitors in some recent years. It has also created TCInvest (see below), to encourage inward investment with incentives. Financial services developed rapidly in the 1990s, and there are more than 20,000 offshore enterprises, mostly using the International Business (Exempt) Company form. The key offshore sectors are banking, insurance and trust management. The Islands have a popular yacht registry and also a registry for aviation ownership. There is a reasonable level of professional expertise on the Islands and costs are low by comparison with many jurisdictions.

No Taxes

The Turks & Caicos is a zero-tax jurisdiction. Government revenues come from various user fees, levies and duties on imported goods and services. Investors in approved projects get duty concessions, which are more generous in the lesser developed islands. The

U.S. dollar is the local currency. There is no central bank or monetary authority and no restrictions on movement of funds in or out of the territory. The financial sector generates up to $20 million each year, or about 10% of all government income.

There are five licensed banks with combined assets of about $900 million, 20 trust companies and about 3,000 insurance companies. The TCI has developed a niche market for captive insurance companies known as credit life or "producer owned reinsurance companies" (PORCS). These companies are typically owned by U.S. retailers and provide reinsurance for credit life and product warranty insurance.

If maximum financial privacy is important to you, keep in mind that the TCI are a British overseas territory and, ultimately, under the policing and political control of the Labor government of the United Kingdom. Banking confidentiality and secrecy were governed by the Confidential Relationships Ordinance 1979, which provided for penalties and terms of imprisonment for professionals, including government officials, who make unauthorized disclosure of confidential information. The Companies Ordinance 1981 contains similar provisions in relation to exempted companies. Additionally, the common law also imposes civil liability for breaches of professional privilege.

In 2009, the Turks and Caicos were on the G-20 OECD "gray list" of tax havens judged to be deficient in tax information exchange policies. Now that the U.K. government has taken control of the islands government it will no doubt apply Article 26 OECD guidelines for tax information exchange. In 2008, British Prime Minister Gordon Brown had sent a letter ordering the TCI to sign TIEAs to share tax information with the U.K. and with other governments or face sanctions.

Colonialism Returns?

In 2009, the British government took control of the Turks & Caicos Islands after a report pointed to widespread corruption in the territory, a move the islands' premier Michael Miscik, called "draconian." The "clear signs of political amorality and immaturity and of the general administrative incompetence, have demonstrated a need for urgent suspension in whole or in part of the constitution," a special investigator found.

The House of Commons in London approved handing over control to the Queen's appointed Governor General of the islands. At the center of the corruption claims was Michael Misick, who resigned as premier in 2009. He is alleged to have built up a multi-million-dollar fortune since his election in part by corrupt acts. The 43-year-old London-educated lawyer and realty broker was elected in 2003 to lead the islands after eight years in the opposition. In 2007, he was sworn in for a second four-year term after leading his party to a sweeping victory, capturing all but two of 15 parliamentary seats.

The U.K. Foreign Office denied any colonial ambitions. "This would not be direct rule, nor would it be indefinite. It would be a smart, targeted, intervention for an interim period by the governor whose responsibilities not only include representing the Crown in the islands, but also the interests of the people of the Turks & Caicos Islands."

Contacts

Official

TCInvest, Turks & Caicos Investment Agency
P.O. Box 105, Hon. Headley Durham Bldg.
Church Folly, Grand Turk, Turks and Caicos Islands BWI
Tel.: 649 946-2058/2852.
Website: http://www.tcinvest.tc
Email: tcinvest@tciway.tc

For information on the Turks & Caicos, contact the British Embassy, 3100 Massachusetts Ave N.W., Washington, D.C. 20008 Website: http://www.britain-info.org.

There is no U.S. embassy or consular agency in the Turks & Caicos. The U.S. Embassy in Nassau, The Bahamas, has consular responsibilities over the territory.

U.S. Embassy
42 Queen Street, Nassau, The Bahamas
Tel.: + (242) 322-1181 or after hours: + (242) 328-2206;
Email: embnas@state.gov
Website: http://nassau.usembassy.gov

Turks & Caicos Islands Tourist Board
81 Rumsey Road, Toronto, ON M4G 1P1 Canada
Tel.: 416-642-9771 Toll Free: 866-413-8875
Cell: 416-819-4319
Email: rwilson.tcitourism@allstream.net
Website: www.turksandcaicostourism.com

Mrs. Pamela Ewing, Manager
5 Applewood Dr., HC1 Box B8
Swiftwater, PA 18370 USA
Tel.: 800-241-0824
Email: pewing@tcigny.com

Stubbs Diamond Plaza
Providenciales, Turks & Caicos Islands.
Tel.: 649-946-4970
Email: info@turksandcaicostourism.com

A Last Word about London

This is a point at which to repeat what was stated at the beginning of this chapter: it is important to realize that all British overseas territories with significant offshore sectors have the same or very similar Westminster system constitutional status as the TCI. That includes Anguilla, Bermuda, the British Virgin Islands, the Cayman Islands, and Gibraltar.

In all of these territories, the British government can and, on occasion, has imposed its designated policies on the inhabitants over the head of the locally elected legislature.

As I have noted, in recent years, Britain has "encouraged" its overseas territories to sign Tax Information Exchange Agreements with high-tax countries. These agreements require the territories to release financial information on clients of banks and trust companies upon request to tax officials in the signatory countries.

For many investors there's a comfort knowing that Britain stands behind its overseas territories. Yet this comes at a price of diminished democratic rule and financial privacy. Before you invest or do business in any of these jurisdictions, be aware of the political powers with which you ultimately will be dealing so there are no surprises.

United States Virgin Islands

It's not well known, but under a unique special U.S. federal income tax arrangement applying only to the U.S. Territory of the Virgin Islands, it is possible for U.S. nationals and others who make the islands their main residence to enjoy substantial personal and business tax benefits. These lower taxes make the islands an offshore tax haven option for very wealthy U.S. citizens, entrepreneurs and foreign nationals seeking U.S. citizenship.

The Virgin Islands of the United States, as their name is officially styled, constitutionally are "an unincorporated territory" of the U.S.

With the Caribbean Sea to the south and the Atlantic Ocean to the north, the Virgin Islands offer a variety of deep sea and coastal fishing. Their tropical climate and minimal industrial development assure an abundance of unspoiled reefs for divers and snorkelers, with sandy beaches ringing deep coves. The large number of isolated, secure anchorages in the U.S. Virgin Islands and the British Virgin Islands just to the east has made the chain a center for yachting. A thriving charter-boat industry in the Virgin Islands draws tens of thousands of visitors annually for crewed sailing adventures.

After their discovery by Columbus in 1493, the islands passed through control by the Dutch, English and French. In 1666, St. Thomas was occupied by Denmark, which, five years later, founded a Danish colony there to supply the mother country with sugar, cotton, indigo, and other products. By the early 17th Century, Danish influence and control were established and the islands became known as the Danish West Indies. That political status continued until Denmark sold the islands to the U.S. for US$25 million in 1917.

The islands — St. Croix, St. Thomas and St. John — have a strategic value for the U.S. since they command the Anegada Passage from the Atlantic Ocean into the Caribbean Sea as well as the approach to the Panama Canal. U.S. citizenship status was conferred on the V.I. inhabitants in 1927. Although they do not vote in U.S. presidential elections, residents are represented by a non-voting delegate in the U.S. House of Representatives.

Little-Known U.S. Low-Tax Paradise

The United States Virgin Islands (USVI) lie 1,100 miles southeast of Miami, Florida—and it's one of the most impoverished jurisdictions under the American flag. But most Americans only know the islands as a vacation venue with beautiful resort hotels, white sandy beaches and blue lagoons.

The four principal islands —St. Croix, St. John, St. Thomas, and Water Island—have a population of about 110,000. Per capita income in the territory is only US$14,600. That's less than half the average in the continental United States and $10,000 less than in Mississippi, the poorest state.

In addition to poverty, the USVI has another unusual distinction. They have been, until now, America's very own "offshore" tax haven. So much so, that the low-tax hating OECD denounced the USVI as the U.S. version of "unfair tax competition." What upset the OECD was the territory's prohibition against U.S. and local ownership of USVI "exempt companies," although this was required by the U.S. Congress in the U.S. Internal Revenue Code. The USVI was removed from the OECD "unfair tax" black list in 2002, but the OECD continued to criticize the islands for being America's own tax haven.

In 2009, when the G-20/OECD issued its list of tax havens allegedly deficient in tax information exchange, not surprisingly, the USVI appeared on the "white list" of "good" offshore financial centers. No surprise, because the United States, led by President Barack Obama, led the G-20 attack on all tax havens. More importantly, the U.S. finances most of the budget of the OECD black list writers.

The islands—St. Croix, St. Thomas, St. John, and Water Island—have been territorial possessions of the United States since they were purchased from Denmark in 1917. They are overseen by the U.S. Department of the Interior. The Naval Services Appropriation Act of 1922 (Title 48 U.S.C. § 1397) provides in part: "The income tax laws in force in the United States of America ... shall be held to be likewise in force in the Virgin Islands of the United States, except that the proceeds of such taxes shall be paid to the treasuries of said islands."

USVI residents and corporations pay their federal taxes on their worldwide income to the Virgin Islands Bureau of Internal Revenue (BIR), not the U.S. IRS. Persons who are born in the USVI or those who become naturalized U.S. citizens in the USVI, for purposes of U.S. federal gift and estate taxes, are treated as nonresidents of the U.S. Since the USVI has no estate or gift taxes, this means that upon death the estates of such persons owe zero U.S. or territorial estate or gift taxes as long as they are domiciled in the USVI at the time of death or at the time of making a gift and have no U.S. assets. (Like any other nonresidents of the U.S. for gift and estate tax purposes, assets located in the U.S. are subject to federal estate and gift tax.)

Generous Package

To attract outside investment, the USVI Economic Development Commission (EDC) grants generous tax relief packages that include a 90 percent credit against U.S. federal income taxes. This tax grant package, which is offered for a period of 10 to 30 years depending on the business location within the USVI (with possible 10-year and then five-year extensions), is available to USVI chartered corporations, partnerships and limited liability companies. The tax credit applies to income from USVI sources, such as fees for services performed in the USVI, and certain related income, such as sales of inventory and dividends and interest from non-U.S. sources received by banking and finance companies based in the USVI.

For many years, a few U.S. investors with business activities ranging from petroleum production, aluminum processing, hotel and other tourism activities, to transportation, shopping centers, and financial services, have taken advantage of USVI tax laws and enjoyed income with very little taxes. As a result of the EDC marketing campaign to attract corporations, about 100 companies qualified for the program in between 2002 and 2004, and employing nearly 3,100 people.

The tax benefit program began paying dividends almost immediately after hedge fund managers started moving to the USVI in 1995. The islands' tax revenue doubled from US$400 million to US$800 million in a five-year period ending in 2005. The increase effectively erased a US$287.6 million deficit for the territory in 1999. The EDC program was worth about US$100 million annually to the local economy. A USVI government spokesperson said that the EDC was crucial in lifting the territory from a dire financial crisis seven years ago to a 2007 projection of a fiscal year surplus in excess of US$50 million.

Paradise Lost

All went well until the early 2000s when the IRS noticed a rapid increase in the number of high net worth individuals moving to the USVI—based on the increasing amount of taxes that the BIR counted as tax-exempt income the USVI. The IRS then received copies of what it perceived to be "marketing materials" from various EDC beneficiaries seeking additional investors—the federal and local statutes did not limit the number of investors to one beneficiary.

In 2003, the IRS raided a financial services firm, Kapok Management, in St. Croix, accusing the firm of sheltering income for dozens of partners who were living on the U.S. mainland, not in the USVI. In 2004, a Massachusetts life insurance executive who used this ruse, pled guilty to federal tax evasion in St. Croix, although as of late 2007 he still had not been sentenced. But in 2009, after a two-month trial in the USVI federal district court, the IRS lost a big case when a jury acquitted the defendants of conspiracy, attempted tax evasion and fraud charges. The original indictment accused Kapok of fraudulently using the Virgin Islands' economic development program designed to promote local economic development and employment through the use of tax credits.

Strict Six-Month Residency Requirement

In 2004, U.S. Senator Charles Grassley (R-Iowa) drafted legislation to impose a strict six-month residency requirement and limited the territory's tax benefits only to income earned exclusively within the islands. (The 1986 legislation had provided that the territory's tax benefits applied to USVI and income connected with a USVI trade or business—but directed the IRS to issue special regulations to define "source" and "effectively connected income" for this purpose. But the diligent IRS went 18 years with no regulations.)

Grassley slipped his changes into a major tax bill without any hearings, and with no notice to the USVI delegate to Congress, the governor, or the U.S. Interior Department, all of whom were stunned to learn what had happened. This major change was imposed without any testimony, territorial input, and certainly without any consideration or understanding of the critical importance of the territory's Economic Development Program to its impoverished economy. The Congressional Joint Committee on Taxation estimated in a wild guess that Grassley's legislation would increase federal revenue by US$400 million over a 10-year period.

IRS Terror

In a reign of tax terror after the 2004 insurance executive case, the IRS opened about 250 audits on individuals who filed as USVI residents and on businesses that were beneficiaries of the economic development program. Many of these individual audits were of persons who had no economic development credits and made no tax exemption claims on their returns. The IRS and the U.S. Department of Justice also brought the Kapok case mentioned above. At that point everyone who lived in the USVI had to wrestle with the six-month residency requirements whether they were being audited or not. Since the 2004 changes were adopted, about 50 hedge funds managers and other financial services companies either halted activities temporarily or withdrew from the islands.

The islands' finance sector boom withered, crushed by the IRS and Grassley with a combination punch of the law and subsequent IRS rules that are still unclear with regard to income eligible for tax credits.

Residence Rules

The old, pre-Grassley rules required a person to be a bona fide USVI resident on the last day of the tax year, "looking to all the facts and circumstances," similar to the "domicile" test for estate and gift tax purposes. There was no "number of days" test and no requirement that a person be a resident for all or most of the year to file as a resident for that year.

The rules now require a resident to be present physically in the USVI at least 183 days, or roughly six months, every year. The IRS did set up four alternative ways to meet the physical presence test of the new residency requirement: 1) spend no more than 90 days in the United States during a taxable year; 2) spend more days in the USVI than in the U.S. and don't have more than $3,000 in earned income from the U.S.; 3) average 183 days a year over a rolling three-year period, or; 4) meet a "no significant connection" test. This last test means no house, no spouse, no minor kids, and no voting registration in the United States—and no days counting requirement.

The residency rules also require a "bona fide resident" to have a "closer connection" to the USVI than anywhere else—looking to where you vote, what address you use, where the closet is in which most of your clothes hang, where you have homes, where you bank, and where your family lives. Finally "a bona fide resident" must have a tax home in the USVI—which is usually your principal place of business.

The IRS claims authority to go back as far as it wanted and examine tax years without regard to the usual three-year statute of limitations. The number of financial firms and other service businesses that make the USVI their corporate home now has fallen to fewer than 40 from more than 80 several years ago.

The IRS also drafted an intrusive form for island residents it says is needed to prove valid residency. Form 8898 requires those who stop filing tax returns with the IRS, in order to file them in the USVI, to list where their immediate family lives, where their cars are registered and where they hold driver's licenses.

The former chief executive officer of the EDC has said, "In the States, they definitely see that they are losing taxes when some of their taxpayers move elsewhere. All of the people everywhere are competing for the same business. What's wrong with the Virgin Islands attracting some of those people?"

In fact, the betrayal of the USVI by the federal government, assures only one thing—that Americans seeking legal tax breaks will instead find them in secure tax havens such as Panama, Belize, the Channel Islands, Singapore and Hong Kong.

Something for Everyone

Notwithstanding all of the above, tax breaks could still be

yours—but it is an absolute necessity that a person actually live and make their main residence in the USVI.

The USVI offers two types of benefit programs that are either fully or partially exempt from USVI taxes and U.S. federal income taxes as well.

One type is a USVI corporation (or partnership or LLC) that qualifies for the benefits of the Economic Development Program for its USVI business activities. Most beneficiaries of this program are in one of three areas—hotels, manufacturing, and service businesses serving clients outside the USVI. But benefits are also available for businesses engaged in transportation, marinas, large retail complexes, medical facilities, and recreation businesses. Most of the service businesses that have obtained benefits are engaged in fund management, general management, and financial services activities.

The beneficiaries that do qualify are fully exempt from most local taxes including the gross receipts tax (otherwise four percent), property taxes (otherwise .75%) and excise taxes on raw materials and building materials. Beneficiaries also get a 90% credit against their USVI income taxes (although for C corporations the credit is equal to 89% of taxes). Beneficiaries also enjoy a special customs duty rate of one percent. They are exempt from U.S. federal income taxes on their USVI operations. The 90% credit also applies to dividends or allocations to a beneficiary's USVI bona fide resident owners—which is why it is so critical to meet the residency requirements.

Strict Requirements

To get these great benefits, a business must employ at least 10 people full-time (32 hours a week) and must make a minimum capital investment of $100,000 (or more). Beneficiaries must also provide health and life insurance and a retirement plan to employees and must purchase goods and services locally, if possible.

For non-U.S. foreign persons, generous exemptions are available through the use of the second type of tax-free entity, a USVI exempt company. The USVI is the only jurisdiction in the world where a non-U.S. person can establish a tax-free entity under the U.S. flag. These exempt companies are used as holding companies for portfolio investments, for the ownership of aircraft that are registered with the U.S. Federal Aviation Administration, or as captive insurance companies. There are a number of other offshore tax-planning structures that can take advantage of USVI exempt companies. Up to 10 percent of the shares of an exempt company can be owned by U.S. residents and up to 10 percent can be owned by USVI residents.

The USVI also has a research and technology park at the University of the Virgin Islands, and technology businesses can also benefit from world-class connectivity through Global Crossing, AT&T's underwater cables on St. Croix.

Close By

Moving your residence to the USVI is no more difficult than moving from one U.S. state to another. The USVI has a well-developed infrastructure. The legal system is subject to the U.S. Constitution and is part of the Third Circuit Court of Appeals. The U.S. court system, postal service, currency, and customs and immigration agencies serve the islands. There is no restriction against maintaining a second home elsewhere inside or outside of the United States, as long as you maintain your principal residence in the USVI.

This American tax haven is limited, but certainly worth considering for any high net-worth foreign person considering U.S. naturalization, or any current U.S. citizen willing to relocate to a warmer climate to legally avoid burdensome taxes. The benefits are particularly beneficial for businesses with a global, rather than a U.S., focus because certain foreign source (but not U.S.) dividends and interest are treated as effectively connected income for tax credit purposes and owners of such a business do not have to spend 183 days in the USVI as long as they are in the United States for no more than 90 days and have a closer connection to the USVI and a USVI tax home.

Obviously, the USVI tax exemptions are unique in that they require a foreign or U.S. person to reorder their personal and business lives in a major way. It means moving and establishing a personal residence and/or business headquarters in the USVI. However, this is a comparatively small price to pay to gain the substantial tax savings that can result from such a move.

Contacts

U.S. Virgin Islands: Website: http://www.usvi.net/usvi/

U.S. Virgin Islands Economic Development Authority: http://www.usvieda.org

U.S. Virgin Islands Taxes: http://www.usvi.net/usvi/tax.html

V.I. Bureau of Internal Revenue
9601 Estate Thomas
Charlotte Amalie, St. Thomas, V.I. 00802
Tel.: (340) 715-1040
Website: http://www.viirb.com/

Recommended Attorney:

Marjorie Rawls Roberts, PC, LLB, JD, AB
P.O. Box 6347, St. Thomas, U.S.V.I. 00804
Tel.: +340-776-7235
Email: jorie@marjorierobertspc.com
Website: http://marjorierobertspc.com

Chapter Ten

Emigrate to Canada, Leave Taxes Behind

Canada is not an offshore tax or asset haven. But in combination with several other factors, Canadian law offers the possibility of an American dream—the end to paying U.S. income and other taxes for the rest of your life. The process called "expatriation" can be considered drastic—even extreme—but it accomplishes this tax freedom for Americans.

Here, the U.S. expatriation process is explained, as well as how Canadian law can complement that process. Expatriation requires professional advice, considerable preparation and careful planning. It also requires determination, will and a lot of courage. But it can lead to tax freedom. Read on.

First, I apologize for some of the overly lawyer-like words and phrases in this chapter. (It gets even worse in Chapter 11 because that chapter covers U.S. tax laws.)

Some of what you will read here may seem rather dry and legalistic. But that's because the process described must be done very carefully and thoroughly in accordance with the laws of two different nations. I am going to walk you through all the steps so that you understand exactly what must be done and how to do it.

As you go, keep in mind an absolute must—you must obtain competent professional advice to guide you every step of the way, both U.S. and Canadian. Check the end of this chapter for the names of professionals who can help you.

Expatriate to Canada

A land of vast distances and rich natural resources, Canada became an independent, self-governing dominion in 1867 while retaining ties to the British Crown. It is the second-largest country in the world (after Russia) with 3,855,100 square miles covering 6.7% of the earth.

Canada is also one of the premier nations in the world for allowing others to exercise the most effective wealth protection strategy—expatriation. But for a U.S. citizen (or anyone else), expatriation means eventually terminating U.S. or other national citizenship, then becoming a foreign national—becoming a Canadian. Eh?

Radical? You bet.

Expatriation is an extreme measure meant for those who have the most to lose by continuing to pay high taxes in their home country.

First, understand that Canada is not a tax haven comparable to many offshore financial centers described in these pages. Except in the specific programs designed to entice new immigrants to Canada, which I will explain, it doesn't offer tax breaks to foreigners. But these foreign investor programs can be very important for you in saving, instead of paying, taxes.

Wealthy Americans stand to lose billions to the IRS. President "Fair Share" Obama has pledged that for anyone who earns $250,000 or more annually, taxes will go up—and up. At this writing an Obama second term is in question, but whatever the 2012 election outcome, what you read here still applies.

Without good estate planning, U.S. government death taxes could take up to 55% of the assets you wish to leave to your heirs when you pass on—and that final tax insult comes after having paid up to 40% of your earnings in federal income taxes every year—all your working life. Throw in state and local income and sales taxes and you stand to lose well over half your earnings during your lifetime in taxes. For those with estates worth millions, the prospect of having their money enrich the bloated coffers of the IRS should be enough to force them to take drastic avoidance measures.

Especially for younger Americans, entrepreneurs and those with a realistic prospect of future wealth, expatriation should be considered as an option to be exercised sooner rather than later.

Wealthy Americans are increasingly turning to expatriation. Perhaps surprisingly, many are expatriating to America's friendly northern neighbor, Canada. Some types of immigrants are welcomed in Canada more than others for a variety of reasons—and you may be just the type of new citizen Canada welcomes with open arms.

Expatriation is a drastic measure, but it may be the only escape for the wealthy. This is definitely not a strategy for everyone, but it may make sense for you. There are certain trade-offs involved, each of which must be researched and carefully considered. Most importantly, to ensure the process runs smoothly, always get qualified professional help.

Why Canada?

Canada and the United States have long been staunch, if somewhat uneasy, allies. As one Canadian put it, "How would you feel if you were forced to sleep in a bed with an elephant next to you?" These friendly neighbors share the largest undefended border in the world, although post 9/11 anti-terrorist measures have made border crossing slower and more cumbersome. Random U.S. aerial surveillance drones now fly overhead. These days, citizens and residents of both nations must have official passports or equivalent documents in order to cross the border, even for a day trip of a few hours.

Every day, many thousands of people from all parts of the world choose Canada as an excellent place to visit, do business, even to live—and with good reason.

Economists at the United Nations researched the best nations in which to live and work. They judged Canada number one. Japan came in second, the United States only sixth and the United Kingdom tenth. Canada has a high standard of living, minimal social class divisions, a low crime rate, a clean environment, beautiful scenery, economic opportunities, government support services, extensive infrastructure, comprehensive shopping and sports facilities, affordable housing and the generous hospitality of the Canadian people.

A distinct advantage that comes with this Canadian citizenship is the international official acceptance of the country's passport, one of the most respected in the world. And as citizens of a member nation of the British Commonwealth, Canadians are allowed to enter Britain without obtaining a prior visa, and entry to Britain allows travel access to all the nations of the European Union. It also allows visa-free travel to scores of British Commonwealth countries.

The Canadian downside includes long harsh winters and continuing English-French political and ethnic differences in the Province of Quebec.

But the major reason to choose Canada is because its laws allow its new citizens, those who have a certain level of wealth, eventually to legally escape Canadian income and estate taxes.

Immigration

The virtues of Canada as the place to live are known around the world. Recent immigration figures attest to that fact. In recent years, Canada's population of 34.3 million has increased annually by over 200,000 immigrants. Citizenship and Immigration Canada proudly announced a record number of permanent and temporary residents had been admitted from 2007 through 2011; the new permanent resident total exceeded 1,065,000. From 2007 through 2011 also admitted were 898,000 temporary foreign workers and over 430,000 foreign students.

A modern nation built by European settlers, Canada has increased its inflow of immigrants by three-fold in the last two decades. The top immigrant sources were the United States, India, Vietnam, Poland, the United Kingdom, the Philippines, Guyana and El Salvador. Those increasing numbers also included many wealthy Asians, especially residents of Hong Kong who came before Hong Kong was returned to Communist Chinese by the British in 1995. (Many of those new Canadians have since returned to Hong Kong as dual citizens.)

About Canadian Taxes

Before I get to the good news—the big tax breaks for new immigrants—you should know that the Canadian tax system is tough and comprehensive. Combined Canadian federal and provincial personal income taxes range from 45% to 54%, depending on the province. And the heavy Canadian tax burden has been a direct result of capital flight, which is relatively unrestricted, although there is an exit tax for those citizens intending to leave permanently, as there is in the United States.

Unlike America, Canada's taxation system is based on physical or constructive residence. Residents of Canada are subject to taxation on their worldwide income, while non-residents are only subject to taxation on certain types of Canadian source income. When an individual ceases to be a resident, the provisions of the Canadian Income Tax Act attempts to tax the individual on all his or her income earned up to the date that residence terminates (called the "date of departure"), especially the income that will not be taxable once the individual becomes a non-resident. This tax is referred to as the "departure tax."

The departure tax is a tax on the capital gains which would have arisen if the emigrant had sold his assets when he left Canada ("deemed disposition"), subject to exceptions. However, in Canada, unlike the U.S., the capital gain is generally based on the difference between the market value on the date of arrival in Canada or later acquisition and the market value on the date of departure.

Canadian taxes are "territorial"—meaning taxes are levied for the most part only on earnings from within the country, not on offshore income. Although residents are hit with stiff taxes, unlike the U.S., Canada does not tax the worldwide income or foreign assets of its nonresident citizens. Canada taxes only the worldwide income of its resident citizens and resident aliens who live in Canada at any time during the calendar year. "Residents," by law, include individuals, corporations and trusts located in Canada. Recent tax court decisions have upheld taxes on Canadian controlled offshore corporations and trusts when facts show management is in and from Canada.

Tax-Free New Resident Loophole

However tough taxes may be for the average Canadian citizen, wealthy new immigrants can take advantage of a huge loophole available only to them. This major tax saving was deliberately written into law in order to encourage wealthy new arrivals. This preference for new citizens with substantial investment capital can translate into huge tax savings and far-reaching financial gains for you and your business.

High net worth immigrants who come to Canada have some useful and attractive options. Here are a few:

1. A qualified immigrant accepted for eventual Canadian citizenship is eligible for a complete personal income tax moratorium for the first five calendar years of residence in Canada—you

pay no taxes if the source of your income is a previously existing offshore, non-Canadian trust (known as an "immigrant trust") or an offshore corporation. Because of the costs of setting up and administering such a trust, it generally is only beneficial for immigrants who have in excess of C$1 million (US$1,023,439) in assets that they can put into the offshore trust.

An offshore trust can be created in any of the many offshore havens described in this book before you move to Canada and become a citizen. The Bahamas, Barbados, Anguilla, Cayman Islands, Bermuda, Cook Islands, Isle of Man or the Channel Islands of Jersey or Guernsey all are appropriate. These havens all have little or no taxes, have British common law legal systems compatible with Canada and that accommodate this type of trust planning with suitable financial institutions that can act as trustees.

As a general rule, Canada has a three-year residence requirement after immigrant admission before citizenship is granted, but a five-year residence is required in order to be eligible for this very special tax break.

2. Canadian citizens and resident aliens employed by certain "international financial centers" have a 50% exemption on income taxes.

3. Canada has abolished all national death (estate) taxes (but the provinces do have such taxes).

4. After living three to five years tax-free in Canada as a new citizen, you can move your residence (and your tax domicile) to another country and afterwards you pay taxes only on income earned or paid from within Canada. You pay no taxes on your worldwide income. But there is an exit tax paid after filing a notice of intent to live abroad.

5. If an individual, who has never resided in Canada and never plans to reside in Canada, creates a trust in an offshore jurisdiction for the benefit of Canadian resident beneficiaries, such a trust (known as a "Granny Trust") may never be taxable in Canada. A "Granny Trust" can be tax free in perpetuity for the trust's Canadian tax resident beneficiaries.

But beware: a naturalized Canadian citizen who lives 10 consecutive years or more outside Canada can be stripped of citizenship at the discretion of the government, although this is very rare and usually done for cause.

Stop Paying U.S. Taxes

Let's suppose you, as an American citizen (or U.S. resident alien), wish to sell an established business, or convert fixed assets into liquid cash for investment or other purposes.

Depending on how long you have held the property and how the liquidation deal is structured, you may face U.S. capital gains taxes at the current maximum rate of 15% (or more, since on January 1, 2013 many taxes increase unless Congress acts to continue current levels. President Obama also has advocates increasing the CGT). Depending on your tax bracket, income taxes can amount to 40% or more. In either case, a major part of the cash proceeds from the sale or conversion will be devoured by the U.S. Internal Revenue Service and state tax authorities—before you ever see a dime.

How can you avoid enormous tax burdens such as this?

What if you transfer the title of the U.S. business to a foreign trust (with the property owner—you—as the beneficiary) or to a corporation you control, conveniently located in a low- or no-tax offshore jurisdiction?

And what if, after the trust or corporation receives title to your former property, you apply for and receive Canadian citizenship, later voluntarily end your U.S. citizenship, as you have a right to do, and become a legal resident of Canada for at least five years?

As a new Canadian, that previously created offshore trust or corporation can pay you benefits and income for five years — tax-free — if you carefully follow the regulations that govern this incredible tax break. You can be a free spirit with absolutely no income or capital gains tax liability in either the U.S. or Canada.

Think it sounds too good to be true? Read on.

Testing the Waters

Maybe you would like to test the northern waters before making any major decisions about a future in Canada. Fortunately, Americans thinking about emigrating can explore life north of the border for an extended period. The U.S.-Canadian Free Trade Agreement allows reciprocal extended stays for workers of up to one year, with no requirement to obtain a special visa. Plus, the number of one-year extensions is unlimited. Tourists are allowed to stay for at least 90 days without special permission for a maximum of 180 days.

Americans employed in certain occupations can enter, live and work in Canada without a work permit and without prior approval. Those welcome to work in Canada include Americans involved in research and designing, purchasing, sales and contract negotiation, customs brokering, financial services, public relations and advertising, tourism and market research, as well as professionals paid by U.S. sources.

Open Door for Immigrant Investors

Before obtaining Canadian citizenship, you should first explore any past family ties you might have had in the country. The Canadian government will help you learn if you are eligible for citizenship based on ancestry. Canadian consulates will provide a personal history information form to be completed and submitted with copies

Border Crossing

Since the 9/11 terrorist attacks, entry into Canada has tightened and now is solely determined by Canadian Border Services Agency (CBSA) officials in accordance with Canadian law, see http://www.cbsa.gc.ca for details.

Canadian law requires that all persons entering Canada must carry both proof of citizenship and identity. A valid U.S. passport or NEXUS card satisfies these requirements for U.S. citizens. The NEXUS program allows pre-screened travelers expedited processing by U.S. and Canadian officials at dedicated processing lanes at designated northern border ports of entry, at NEXUS kiosks at Canadian preclearance airports, and at marine reporting locations.

If U.S. citizen travelers to Canada do not have a passport or approved alternate document such as a NEXUS card, they must show a government-issued photo ID (driver's license) and proof of U.S. citizenship such as a U.S. birth certificate, naturalization certificate, or expired U.S. passport. Children under 16 need only present proof of U.S. citizenship.

U.S. citizens entering Canada from a third country must have a valid U.S. passport. A visa is not required for U.S. citizens to visit Canada for up to 180 days. Anyone seeking to enter Canada for any purpose besides a visit (to work, study or immigrate) must qualify for the appropriate entry status, and should contact the Canadian Embassy or nearest consulate and see the Canadian immigration website at http://www.cic.gc.ca/english/index.asp.

Anyone with a criminal record (including even misdemeanors or driving while impaired [DWI]) may be barred from entering Canada and must qualify for a special waiver well in advance of any planned travel for further processing, which may take some time.

For information on entry requirements, contact the Canadian Embassy at 501 Pennsylvania Avenue N.W., Washington, D.C. 20001; Tel.: (202) 682-1740 or the Canadian consulates in Atlanta, Boston, Buffalo, Chicago, Dallas, Detroit, Los Angeles, Miami, Minneapolis, New York, San Juan or Seattle. The Canadian Embassy's website is http://www.canadianembassy.org/.

of relevant birth records to the Registrar of Canadian Citizenship in the capital city of Ottawa. A "Certificate of Canadian Citizenship" is automatically issued to anyone who qualifies for citizenship by family descent. If you are lucky enough to qualify, this is the least complicated basis on which to establish a new legal residence in Canada.

Independent applicants for permanent residence are rated on a point system that takes into account age, education, fluency in English and French, financial standing, occupational or professional experience, local demand for certain types of workers, geographic destination and a personal assessment of the applicant. These factors comprise a 100-point scale; 70 points and over is passing.

Completely separate from the point system for admissions, Canadian law favors a special independent class of preferred immigrants, including investors, entrepreneurs, the self-employed and those who will add to the "cultural and artistic life" of the nation. With minor variations in each of the provinces, investor-immigrants generally must have a net worth in excess of C$500,000 (US$511,483) and be willing to invest at least C$250,000 (US$255,740) in some Canadian business for a minimum three- to five-year period (conversion figures based on July 2012 rates). Purchase of a residence usually does not qualify as an investment, although it may if you work from home.

With proof of sufficient assets and an attractive business plan (especially one creating new jobs for Canadians) your permanent resident status and eventual citizenship is almost assured. Government loan guarantees and other assistance may be available for immigrants willing to invest larger sums of C$750,000 (US$767,184) or more.

For potential investor visa applicants, the government rolls out the proverbial red carpet, officially known as the "Business Migration Program." Business experience, marketing skills, contacts within Canada, an adequate credit rating and available funds all greatly increase your chance of success. Applicants are usually required to submit detailed business proposals or general business plans, which must accompany the application for permanent residence. Such plans must detail the nature of the business, operating procedures, key personnel (which may just be the applicant), a marketing plan and a financial strategy.

While Canada's national immigration laws facilitate the entry of certain foreign corporations and their key staff, the provinces offer their own investors and skills immigration programs. In British Columbia, for example, the province has a "Provincial Nominee Program" that offers expedited immigration solutions for international investors wanting to immigrate to Canada and who wish to settle in that province.

Canadian Immigration Process

The immigration process begins with a visit to the Canadian Embassy located at 501 Pennsylvania Avenue N.W., Washington, D.C. 20001; Tel.: (202) 682-1740; Website: http://canadaembassy.org/ You can also try at one of the many Canadian consulates located in New York and other major U.S. cities.

There you can get an "Immigration Questionnaire" requiring basic personal information about you, your spouse and family. Within a few weeks, a more detailed questionnaire is sent to acceptable applicants. After this second document is reviewed, a personal interview and medical examinations are required.

If all goes well, you will shortly receive a visa for entry into Canada as what is known as a "landed immigrant" — "Welcome, Bienvenue à Canada."

It is worth noting that Canada recognizes the principle of dual nationality. They allow successful applicants for citizenship to retain their nationality of origin. For reasons that will become obvious in a moment, that choice is not a viable option for a future ex-American expatriating to Canada who wants to end U.S. tax obligations.

The Big Change—U.S. Expatriation

The potential immigrant from America will eventually have to surrender United States citizenship in order to formally end his or her U.S. tax obligations. You should review my comments in Chapter 2 concerning the U.S. "exit tax" that is now in effect to see if you come within the exit tax definition of a "covered person." If you are a covered person, depending on your net worth and other factors, the financial impact of the exit tax on you may outweigh any benefits to be gained by immigration to Canada.

Under the U.S. exit tax law, a person who is a "covered individual" falls within the clutches of the expatriation provisions if, on the date of expatriation or termination of U.S. residency:

(i) the individual's average annual net U.S. income tax liability for the five-year period preceding that date is US$145,000 or more (to be adjusted for inflation);

(ii) the individual's net worth as of that date is US$2 million or more; or

(iii) the individual fails to certify under penalties of perjury that he or she has complied with all U.S. federal tax obligations for the preceding five years.

Of course, if you're lucky and don't come within these definitions, the law may offer a very real opportunity to escape U.S. taxes, especially if you have a good prospect of becoming more prosperous in the future. You can leave now and escape the tax.

Do it the Right Way

Here's how to expatriate from the U.S. and avoid pitfalls along the way:

First, it is necessary to obtain proper legal advice on expatriation in order to be effective in surrendering citizenship. The worst outcome is to wind up with ambiguous dual nationality status. In that case, you go through an extended period retaining not only U.S. citizenship, but citizenship in another country as well. You may then find yourself within the potential grasp of two governmental taxing authorities.

Generally, an ex-American who properly surrenders citizenship is treated by U.S. law as a nonresident alien and taxed at a flat 30% rate on certain types of passive income derived from U.S. sources and on net profits from the sale of a U.S. trade or business at regular graduated rates. Expatriates can safely spend only about 122 days a year in the United States. After that, they expose themselves to IRS claims for full U.S. taxation based on having alien residence status.

Another strict caution: You must be certain to obtain valid foreign citizenship before you surrender your U.S. citizenship—if you fail to do so, you could become a "stateless" person, the proverbial "man without a country." A person without a passport and a nationality is legally lost in this world of national borders and bureaucratic customs officials and as such is not entitled to the legal protection of any government.

Valid surrender must be an unequivocal act in which a person manifests an unqualified intention to relinquish U.S. citizenship. In order for the surrender to be effective, all of the conditions of the U.S. statute must be met; the person must appear in person and sign an oath before a U.S. consular or diplomatic officer, usually at an American Embassy or Consulate abroad. Because of the way in which the law is written and interpreted, Americans cannot effectively renounce their citizenship by mail, through an agent, or while physically within the United States. In recent years, it has taken many months to obtain an expatriation appointment at U.S. embassies in many foreign countries, including Canada, so plan ahead.

Once the surrender is accomplished before an American diplomatic or consular officer abroad, all documents are referred to the U.S. Department of State. The Office of Overseas Citizens Services reviews them to ensure that all criteria under the law are met, but the State Department has no discretion to refuse a proper surrender of citizenship. This personal right is absolute. (If you do surrender your U.S. citizenship, in theory you could get it back, but only through a long and complicated process that any new U.S. immigrant applicant must undergo. And that takes years and involves attorneys and other costs.)

Long before such a drastic final step is taken towards ending U.S. citizenship, the new Canadian immigrant should have his or her official Canadian citizenship in order, papers in hand and an established residence in their new homeland. This will most likely be in the metropolitan areas of Montreal, Toronto, or Vancouver, where the vast majority of immigrants decide to live.

Canadian Potential

One of the foremost benefits of becoming a Canadian citizen is the ability to take advantage of what is often called an "immigrant offshore trust."

The key to eligibility for this unusual tax-free "window of opportunity" is found in section 94(1) of Canada's Income Tax Act of 1952. This law ensures that an immigrant who has never been a Canadian resident can move to Canada and earn tax-free foreign source income from a nonresident trust or affiliated corporation for the first five calendar years of his new Canadian residency. But before you surrender U.S. citizenship, you must have already attained citizenship in Canada. As I said, this requires fulfillment of at least the first three of your five-year exemption period. As a U.S. citizen, during that time you are still subject to taxation on your worldwide income, including the trust income.

Beneficiaries

To qualify for this big tax break, the arrangement must include an immigrant residing in Canada plus either: 1) a foreign corporation or a trust with which the immigrant is "closely tied;" or 2) a foreign affiliate corporation controlled by a person resident in Canada. The essential factor is that the nonresident trust must have one or more beneficiaries who are Canadian residents, or the offshore corporation must be "closely tied" in some manner to one or more Canadian residents. The beneficiaries likely will be your family members and can include yourself. The foreign trustee will follow your instructions on how the trust assets should be invested and income disbursed.

A "beneficial interest" in a nonresident trust is defined as belonging to a person or partnership that holds any right—immediate or future, absolute or contingent, conditional or otherwise—to receive any of the income or principal capital of the trust, either directly or indirectly. It would be difficult to find a broader definition of "beneficial entitlement" than this—and the implications for tax avoidance are obvious and potentially huge.

Canadian tax officials and court cases have repeatedly stated that such immigration trusts and related businesses, when properly created and managed abroad, are not an abuse of the tax laws. That's because section 94 clearly is designed as a vehicle for exempting new immigrants from taxation for the stated period of five years. In the case of almost every other tax avoidance scheme, the Canada Revenue Agency would pounce. Here, the law does more than permit tax avoidance, it approves and encourages it.

Only a change in Canadian law by Parliament could remove this generous tax break and there is no current talk of removing the provision that has been so successful in attracting much-needed capital and business to the nation.

Trust Property Sources

In order for a nonresident trust or a nonresident corporation to qualify as a "controlled foreign affiliate," and to receive section 94 tax-free treatment, it must have acquired its property from a person who meets all of the following requirements:

- the donor must be the trust or affiliate corporation beneficiary, or related to the beneficiary (spouse, child, parent), or be the uncle, aunt, nephew, or niece of the beneficiary;

- the donor must have been resident in Canada at any time in an 18-month period before the end of the trust's first taxation year or before his or her death; and

- if the trust property came from an individual, the individual donor eventually must be a resident in Canada for a period or periods totaling more than 60 months.

Section 94 applies regardless of the method by which the nonresident trust or corporation acquires its property including purchase, gift, bequest, inheritance or, exercise of a power of appointment by or from an individual. The law treats all such transfers as if you had transferred your property to the trust or corporation.

You must be careful to follow a few rules when donating assets to such a trust or corporation. You cannot retain any reversion right or power to designate beneficiaries after the trust is created. This is what is known in both U.S. and Canadian law as an irrevocable living trust. You cannot retain any control over how the trust property will be disbursed during your lifetime, nor can you retain more than 10% equity ownership in an offshore corporation to which you donate.

As a general rule, a trust donor should transfer only cash and title to intangible assets to an offshore trust. Portable assets, such as gold coins or diamonds, also can be used. Title to real estate or a business located in Canada or the United States definitely should not be made part of the trust property. Transfer of tangible property physically located in either nation does nothing to keep those assets away from Canadian or American creditors or tax authorities. Such action could even subject the trust to the jurisdiction of a Canadian court. By holding title to assets within Canada, the offshore trust could be deemed liable for Canadian taxes.

Foreign Control a Must

In order to determine if an offshore trust is "nonresident" from a tax perspective, the Canada Revenue Agency looks at who controls it and its ownership.

The residence of a trust is determined by where the managing trustees or the persons who control the trust assets actually reside. It is therefore important that the offshore trust have a majority of trustees living in the foreign jurisdiction where the trust is registered and where its operation is located. This requirement for majority offshore control does not diminish the ability of a trust beneficiary to serve as a trustee and to live in Canada. Neither status jeopardizes the offshore, and therefore tax-free, status of the trust.

The requirement for offshore control of a trust to qualify for tax exemption was restated in 2012 in the case *Fundy Settlement v. Canada* in which the Supreme Court of Canada held that the "central management and control" test used to determine residence of corporations for tax purposes also applies to the determination of the residence of trusts.

Canadian tax law specifically allows offshore immigration trusts to receive tax-free income from investment business conducted by a resident Canadian citizen during the five-year residency period.

Thus, the new Canadian investor-citizen is free to roam the world by email, phone, fax, telex, wire, courier, or letter, using his capital and ability to produce profits for the trust and its beneficiaries. To maximize tax avoidance, the trust should not carry on other active business in Canada or invest in property located in Canada. Income from these sources may subject the trust to certain domestic taxes because of the Canadian source or location.

Creating an Offshore Trust

So where should you establish such an offshore trust? You could

Case Study: Let's say you have C$3 million (US$3.075 million) you wish to invest. Like any reasonable person, you want to avoid Canadian taxes on the income produced from your investment. The following strategy can help natural-born Canadian citizens and wealthy new immigrants.

First, you need a nonresident of Canada — a friend or relative — to act as manager of your offshore investment corporation. You also need a trust registered in an established asset haven. For this example, let's say you choose to set one up in Panama. You can't do it yourself, since the new Canadian immigrant must live in Canada for five years.

You transfer the C$3 million (US$3.075million) to the Panama-registered trust, also administered by your friend as trustee, probably in the same Panama office. The trust manager invests that money in Canadian government treasury bills or public company stocks. The interest income this produces can be paid to you, your children, or any other named beneficiaries tax-free. At current interest rates, that means a savings of about C$100,000 (US$102,500) per year in taxes.

While this tax haven structure might be expensive to establish, the arrangement qualifies under section 94 for five years of tax-free income for trust beneficiaries. Even after the five-year period ends, this arrangement can continue to shield the Canadian beneficiary from taxes, so long as it is controlled by non-Canadians.

conceivably set up shop anywhere in the world.

To do so effectively, you must look abroad for a friendly national jurisdiction in which to locate your assets. The host government must impose little or no taxes on foreign investors. Elsewhere in these pages, I describe several offshore financial centers, some of them located in the warm waters of the Caribbean, not too far from the U.S. or Canada. One nation favored by Canadians is Barbados because it has a double taxation avoidance treaty with Canada.

As explained in Chapter 2, an offshore asset protection trust (APT) located in a tax haven is proven and effective for offshore financial planning. The APT is the safety vehicle that places personal assets beyond the reach of many irritants: your home country tax authorities, potential litigation plaintiffs and claims, an irate spouse, or unreasonable creditors—wherever such opponents may be located.

Even though an offshore immigration trust can guarantee five tax-free years for new Canadian immigrants, the non-tax benefits are also important. The trust allows Canadians asset protection, a high degree of financial privacy, flexible estate planning and the ability to make internationally diversified investments unrestricted by domestic Canadian law.

A Need for Caution

The objective of an offshore tax haven is the legal reduction of your tax obligations. Keep in mind that it will do you no good to suffer the bother and cost of restructuring your financial life, only to find yourself embroiled in years of complex and expensive court battles with the Canada Revenue Agency—or worse, facing criminal charges for tax evasion or a variety of other possible tax crimes.

Reasonable caution places a premium on pursuing the correct path from the very beginning. This means the assistance of competent tax experts (see the list at the end of this chapter) from the very start. Cutting corners will only leave you and your financial advisors in deep trouble.

Mechanics of Offshore Business

The country in which your Canadian immigration trust and the managing trustee are located should be, for obvious reasons, a nation with strong financial privacy laws. As I have said, most offshore financial centers countries do guarantee statutory privacy rights but they also enforce tax information exchange agreements.

The ideal places for establishing asset preservation or tax avoidance trusts are OFCs such as Panama, Nevis, the Isle of Man, the Channel Islands or the Cook Islands. These are all countries with statutes tailored to asset protection needs.

Tougher Offshore Reporting

Creating an offshore immigration trust will affect your personal tax return, in that a taxpayer must disclose the existence of an offshore trust on his or her annual Canadian federal tax return. Generally, foreign trustees are not required to divulge information about assets held by a trust. They usually cannot be forced by Canadian courts to turn over trust assets. The Canada Revenue Agency and other creditors must first go through the host country's judicial system at great expense.

Reporting laws require that all resident Canadian taxpayers must report the existence of their offshore assets that exceed the aggregate of C$100,000 (US$102,500). This includes offshore bank accounts, securities holdings and rental properties and interests in foreign trusts, partnerships, corporations, or any other offshore entities. Prior law required payment of taxes on offshore income by Canadian residents, but did not mandate a listing of assets as the new law does.

Commenting on the reporting law, a leading Canadian financial management company gave this opinion: "Revenue Canada seems to be following the U.S. Internal Revenue Service with respect to offshore entities and transactions. Some of the new reporting is tougher than the IRS, some less, but the intent is the same; the government wants to know everything."

Nevertheless creditors must get a court to order you to reveal your tax return and the existence of the trust in any civil action. That takes time. If they do discover the trust's offshore location and file a collection suit in the haven country, local laws are hostile to nonresident creditors and the trustee can shift the trust and its assets to another country and another trustee in an emergency. Then, pursuing creditors must begin the process all over again.

Trust Advantage

This protection in a civil suit gives trusts a distinct privacy advantage over corporations.

In most tax and asset haven countries, at least one person involved in organizing a corporation must be listed on the public record, along with the name and address of the corporation. In many countries, the directors must be listed on the original charter. In a few maximum privacy countries, only the organizing lawyer is listed, but even that reference gives privacy invaders a starting point for nosey investigators.

With a trust, nothing more than its existence is required to be registered in an asset haven nation—and often not even that. The trust agreement and the parties involved do not have to be disclosed and there is little or nothing on the public record. In privacy-conscious countries, the trustee is allowed to reveal information about the trust only in very limited circumstances.

The country chosen for such a trust must have local trust experts who can assist you in achieving your objectives. The foreign local attorney who creates your trust must be familiar with all applicable laws and tax consequences.

In its simplest form, the offshore immigration trust can be a trust account in a foreign bank. Many well-established multinational Canadian banks can provide trustees for such arrangements and are experienced in such matters. As an extra level of insulation from government pressure, however, use a non-Canadian bank. We have special arrangements with Royal Bank of Canada (RBC) for Sovereign Society members. Contact information is available at the end of this chapter.

With today's instant communications and international banking facilities, it is just as convenient to hold assets and accounts overseas as it is in another Canadian or U.S. city. Most international banks offer Canadian and U.S. dollar-denominated accounts, which often have better interest rates than Canadian institutions.

International Business Corporation

The offshore corporation is best suited for the needs of Canadian business owners who seriously desire to run a legitimate international business. Establishing your corporation offshore can lower your taxes and increase profits immensely. Under section 94, income from "affiliated" offshore corporations qualifies for the five-year tax exemption. The company can also be for tax avoidance after the five-year moratorium ends, as I explain below.

But foreign corporations, as Canada Revenue Agency demands, must be more than a mere sham. A full-scale company, complete with working offices, staff, international fax and telecommunications facilities, bank accounts, a registered agent, board of directors, a local attorney and an accountant can cost upwards of US$50,000 annually.

Members of your board of directors and associates of the local tax specialists who help you form the company, may be paid about

Example: Because it is a legitimate business with established foreign transactions, your Canadian company can incorporate an offshore affiliate in, say, Barbados. Like Canada, Barbados is a member of the British Commonwealth. More importantly, it is a place where qualifying international companies pay only 2.5% corporate income tax and benefit from credits and inducements for foreign-owned businesses. Compare that to Canada's 26% corporate tax.

You can set up your affiliate with offices in the capital, Bridgetown (population 8,000). It has eight major international banks including branches of the Royal Bank of Canada, the Canadian Imperial Bank of Commerce, Chase Manhattan and Barclays. Regular air service is offered by Air Canada, British Airways, American and other major carriers.

Your Bridgetown affiliate will handle all foreign sales and international marketing for your Canadian company. For these services, it will charge a 15% mark-up on the value of the goods it sells. This will amount to about US$750,000 a year at your current export levels.

What you have done is legally transfer the profits from your Canadian company to an offshore affiliate where taxes are much lower — 2.5% vs. 45%! After gladly paying US$18,750 in local corporate income taxes, the rest of the money, US$731,250, can be sent back to Canada as a dividend from exempt surplus income. This is paid to your company — tax-free! During the first five years of your citizenship, you personally can share in that corporate income — again, tax-free!

Even after your five-year tax-free period ends, Canadian taxes on the income can be deferred indefinitely. You can do so until the parent company's shareholders need the money for their own use, or until they sell the business. If the shareholders want payment immediately, it can be paid out as dividends. Dividends are taxed at 36%, well below the personal income tax rate of over 50%.

US$2,500 a year. There will be annual taxes to pay and reports to be filed with the local government and with Canada.

As the Canadian owner, you will want to visit your company offices once or twice a year, a pleasant enough activity if you locate your business in one of the tropical venues specializing in such corporate arrangements. January is an excellent month for Canadians to head south for a visit.

Investment Potential

The Barbados affiliate could also serve as an investment arm for your parent company. In this capacity, it can actively make international investments. All the earned income from such investments — dividends, interest and capital gains — will go to your Bridgetown affiliate. This will be taxed at the 2.5% rate that applies to offshore corporations. Investment profits can also be sent to the parent company tax-free. In order to follow this course successfully, all corporate investment decisions must originate with your Bridgetown money manager. The money manager must run your affiliate on a daily basis (i.e., you cannot dictate every move by phone from Montreal or Ottawa). As an added consideration, those with experience say that in order to be successful in using foreign affiliates for investment purposes, a minimum of US$1 million in capital will be needed to start.

In theory, this all sounds grand, but there are practical problems associated with an offshore corporation.

First of all, just as in establishing a domestic corporation, legal formalities must be strictly observed. The Canada Revenue Agency will check this carefully. Moreover, the cost of starting up can be considerable. You will need a local legal counsel who knows the law and understands your business and tax objectives. Corporations anywhere are rule-bound creatures requiring separate books and records, meetings, minutes and corporate authorizing resolutions, which make it less flexible than many other arrangements.

But you can pay for a whole lot of recordkeeping with the money you will save in taxes.

When the Five Years End

After five, tax-free years, it won't be easy to face the Canada Revenue Agency. Your offshore trust can either be converted to a domestic Canadian trust (by passing majority control to trustees who reside in Canada), or its affairs can be terminated and the assets distributed to the beneficiaries. In this case, the beneficiaries will owe Canadian capital gains taxes on the fair market value at the time of distribution.

This is especially worrisome when you compare the outrageously high Canadian tax rates with those imposed in foreign tax havens. Luckily, prudent Canadians can take advantage of this wide international tax disparity by establishing an offshore tax shelter that can easily double after-tax disposable income.

This can be accomplished in full compliance with federal law. If you follow the rules, the Canada Revenue Agency will not be able to mount a successful challenge, despite their recent efforts to go after anything they consider to be an "overly aggressive tax strategy."

Aggressive Tax Enforcement

The most dangerous attitude one can adopt when dealing with the establishment of offshore business arrangements is the cavalier approach—the stupid idea that "white collar" crimes are somehow less serious than violent crimes, or that the federal government is less concerned about financial offenses than they are about other civil wrongs.

Canadian courts display a stiff attitude towards tax scofflaws and the long arm reaches across oceans. For example, the Canadian Supreme Court held that the former manager of the Freeport branch of the Canadian Royal Bank could be forced to give testimony at a tax evasion trial in Canada, even though doing so would be a breach of the Bahamian bank secrecy law.

Powerful laws aimed at preventing tax evasion have aided the federal government's vigorous international enforcement efforts. By law, there is no statute of limitations on tax evasion, but a Canada Revenue Agency audit can only cover three prior years. The CRA has the power to obtain "foreign-based information or documents," and elaborate annual corporate reporting requirements were imposed on inter-company transactions between Canadians and any offshore entities. Failure to report, or false statements concerning such transactions, can result in fines of up to US$24,605.

The Canada Revenue Agency keeps an eagle eye on the tax shelter industry. Before the adoption of the new offshore reporting requirements, Revenue Canada officials tracked the offshore business activity of individual Canadians as best they could. Now they have powerful new tools that place personal responsibility to report squarely on taxpayers.

In spite of these tough federal policies and an array of laws with sharp teeth, there are still many opportunities for profitable offshore financial activities. Offshore tax havens are legal and in selective circumstances, nonresident owned international investment and business structures can be used to reduce taxes.

Conclusion

There you have it. It may seem a difficult road to travel, but becoming a Canadian citizen investor can save a former U.S. citizen millions of dollars that would otherwise go directly to the IRS.

Yes, these savings are predicated on major life and financial changes you must be willing to make, including surrender of your U.S. citizenship. You must relocate yourself, your family and your business to Canada and possibly to another country later on. Despite these drawbacks, the true bottom line measured in dollar savings can be enormous.

Contacts

Federal Government of Canada: http://www.canada.gc.ca/home.html

Canada Revenue: http://www.cra-arc.gc.ca/menu-eng.html

Citizenship & Immigration Canada: http://www.cic.gc.ca/english/
Immigration: http://www.cic.gc.ca/english/immigrate/index.asp
Citizenship: http://www.cic.gc.ca/english/citizenship/index.asp
Visas: http://www.cic.gc.ca/english/visit/index.asp

Embassy of Canada
501 Pennsylvania Avenue, N.W.
Washington, D.C. 20001
Tel.: (202) 682-1740
Website: http://canadaembassy.org/

United States Embassy
490 Sussex Drive
K1N-1G8 Ottawa, Ontario
Tel.: + (613) 238-5335; Fax: + (613) 688-3082
Website: http://www.usembassycanada.gov

Royal Bank of Canada (RBC)
Robert (Bob) Spicer
Investment & Retirement Planning, Royal Bank of Canada
1 Westmount Square, Westmount, Quebec, H3Z 2P9 Canada

Tel.: 514-874-5523
Email: bob.spicer@rbc.com
Websites: www.rbc.com
https://financialplanning.rbcinvestments.com/bob.spicer

Specialist in Immigration Law:

Joel S. Guberman, Esq.
Guberman, Garson
130 Adelaide St. West, Suite 1920
Toronto, Ontario M5H 3P5
Tel.: (416) 363-1234
Email: immlaw@ggilaw.com
Website: http://www.gubermangarson.com/

Business and Commercial Law:

Douglas Hendler, Esq.
Blaney McMurtry, LLP
2 Queen Street East, Suite 1500
Toronto, Ontario.
Tel.: (416) 596.2888
Email: http://www.blaney.com/lawyers/douglas-hendler#
Website: http://www.blaney.com/lawyers/douglas-hendler

See Appendix for recommended U.S. attorneys.

Notice: As we went to press, the Canadian government announced a suspension until January 1, 2013 or later of the immigrant investor program and some other programs in order to reform them. For information on the status of these programs, contact the office of Joel Guberman listed above.

CHAPTER ELEVEN

The United States as an Offshore Tax Haven

Unbeknownst to most Americans, the complex tax laws of the United States make America one of the world's leading offshore tax havens—not for Americans, but rather almost exclusively for foreign citizens who invest in America. There are ways that U.S. persons can also get reduced taxes from U.S. tax laws that benefit foreigners, but those ways are highly complex, requiring costly professional advice and constant tax management.

In this chapter, the intricacies of the U.S. Internal Revenue Code are explained, so forgive me once again for the legalistic approach. It is much more complex than Chapter 10 on Canada and expatriation. But again, I urge you—get competent professional advice and realistic cost estimates before you embark on any plans this chapter may inspire you to attempt.

Tax Haven America

Few hard-pressed American taxpayers realize it, but the United States is considered a major tax haven for foreign investors.

There are a whole host of laws that provide liberal U.S. tax breaks that apply only to foreigners. While Americans struggle to pay combined taxes that can rob them of more than 50% of their total incomes, careful foreign investors can and do make lots of money in the United States—all tax-free.

The fact that the United States itself is a major tax haven exposes the rank hypocrisy of American politicians who rail against "offshore tax havens." That includes President Obama, who has made a major political and legislative issue out of the legal use of offshore tax havens by U.S. individuals and corporations, as described in Chapter 3.

These demagogic attacks portray Americans' legal use of tax havens as unpatriotic and akin to tax evasion. But these same politicians have no problem when foreigners use the U.S. as their offshore tax haven — because they welcome the billions of dollars they bring into the U.S. every year.

Foreigners have more than US$4 trillion in passive investments in the form of bank accounts or brokerage accounts in the United States, according to U.S. Treasury figures. The U.S. government does not tax foreign persons on what the IRS calls "portfolio interest" income or on passive capital gains earned in America. The government gives huge tax breaks to foreigners because the government wants and needs their money and their capital investments to keep the faltering U.S. economy afloat.

However, foreign corporations operating within the U.S. do pay corporate income taxes on some of their U.S. earnings and, often, they pay plenty.

A haphazard array of complex provisions in the U.S. Internal Revenue Code (IRC), coupled with a host of international tax treaties, provide rich opportunities for the astute foreign investor. Assisting these investors is an elite group of high-priced American tax lawyers and accountants known as "inbound specialists." Their specialty is structuring business transactions so as to minimize taxes and maximize profits for

The U.S. Treasury and the politicians need this foreign capital to bolster the national economy, to finance huge government deficit spending, and to refinance the enormous national debt — as of this writing nearly US$16 trillion, a figure that exceeds the gross domestic product of America. With an estimated population of the United States at 314 million, each citizen's share of this debt exceeds US$50,000. Since over 50% of U.S. people pay no income tax that means that those of us who do pay are stuck for a debt of over $140,000 each.

A large portion of foreign investment goes directly into short and long-term U.S. Treasury securities. This enormous cash inflow keeps the U.S. government afloat from day to day. (The debt has increased by an estimated $4 billion each day since September 28, 2007!) Billions of dollars of the much talked-about "national debt" is owed directly to European and Asian investors. The communist government of the People's Republic of China is one of America's largest individual creditors by virtue of their investments in U.S. government debt securities. The old saying about government debt that "we owe it to ourselves" doesn't apply anymore—if it ever did.

Another scary fact is that the annual interest paid on the US$16 trillion government debt is now nearly a trillion dollars annually, a figure that exceeds all other federal budget program costs except that of the Defense Department. Some 15% of the entire budget is for interest payments alone, and much of it goes to foreign investors.

So we're talking very big money here!

As a consequence, these foreign investors have a lot of power over America and Americans.

When the U.S. Congress imposed a 30% withholding tax on all interest payments to foreign residents and corporations doing business in the U.S., foreign investors bluntly let it be known they would take their money elsewhere if the withholding tax remained. Not surprisingly, the IRC is now riddled with exceptions to the 30% tax.

The biggest U.S. tax break for many foreigners comes from a combined impact of domestic IRC provisions and the tax laws of the investor's own country. As Americans are painfully aware, the United States taxes its citizens and residents on their worldwide income. But non-citizens and nonresidents are allowed by their own domestic laws to earn certain types of income from within the U.S. tax-free. As you can guess, droves of smart foreign investors take advantage of this situation.

Foreign direct investment (FDI) in the United States declined sharply after 2000, when a record US$300 billion was invested in U.S. businesses and real estate. In 2008, the peak year, foreign direct investment in the U.S. was $328 billion. In 2010, it had fallen to $194 billion, a reflection of the global recession. The U. S. defines foreign direct investment as the ownership or control, directly or indirectly, by one foreign person (individual, branch, partnership, association, government, etc.) of 10% or more of the voting securities of an incorporated U.S. business enterprise or an equivalent interest in an unincorporated U.S. business enterprise.

Where There's a Will

In a qualified, but highly circuitous way, and under the right circumstances, a U.S. citizen or resident alien also can benefit from this U.S. tax-free income that makes so many foreign investors wealthy. The qualifying process is complex, but the U.S. Tax Code does offer possibilities.

It is possible for an American to establish an offshore corporation to invest tax-free in U.S. securities and other property. Nevertheless, unfortunate things can happen if you don't structure these backdoor, offshore arrangements properly, due to the morass of IRS rules designed to keep Americans from benefiting from this reverse offshore tax avoidance route.

Offshore Corporation Loophole

Years ago, a U.S. person could pay a pleasant, tax-deductible business visit to a tax haven nation, say, The Bahamas, and form an IBC there.

You could then transfer some cash to the new company and have it put that money into selected U.S. investments. If you picked right and this triangle shot paid off, all the corporate income was tax-free. As long as your foreign corporation did not have an office in the U.S., the IRS treated it as a "nonresident foreign corporation" and most of its income was not taxed. As an owner, the company could pay your legitimate business-related expenses, and no income tax was imposed until you decided to pay yourself dividends. Meanwhile, assuming good management, profits could be deferred, ploughed back, and allowed to increase in value.

Part of that happy scenario remains true today.

As long as a foreign corporation does not maintain a U.S. office, or have sufficient contacts with the U.S. that would make it "effectively connected" to this country, the IRS considers it a "nonresident foreign corporation." Under the law, it can avoid taxes on certain U.S. source income as defined by law.

The very big difference today is that the U.S. shareholder in an offshore corporation is taxed like a partner in a partnership. This means a controlling U.S. shareholder of a foreign corporation must pay annual income taxes on his or her pro-rata share of certain types of the foreign corporation's income when it is earned, even if that income is not distributed as dividends or in any other form, and even if the corporation retains these profits.

No longer can the profits sit offshore out of the IRS tax collector's grasp. As you can guess, this has substantially reduced the incentive for Americans to create offshore corporations as a tax avoidance mechanism. If you abide by the law, most of the tax avoidance is gone.

Except — and there's always an exception when it comes to U.S. tax laws — for two remaining loopholes that still might allow tax-free investment possibilities for Americans using offshore corporations. You need to execute these strategies very carefully, with professional help, to make them both legal and effective.

But first, a little background history and some definitions that hopefully will broaden your understanding of what's going on here.

Controlled Foreign Corporations

The basic purpose of the complex rules governing controlled foreign corporations (CFCs) is to prevent U.S. taxpayers from avoiding or deferring taxes through the use of such offshore companies. Keep in mind as you read this that the object is to avoid having your offshore corporation being tagged by the IRS as a CFC because that status means higher taxes.

These rules can be found in IRC sections 951 through 964. Essentially, if a foreign corporation is controlled by U.S. taxpayers, those who own 10% or more of the corporation must report their respective share of the CFC income on their annual personal income tax return (IRS Form 1040). The effect is similar to the flow-through tax treatment of a domestic U.S. partnership or subchapter S corporation, but much more complicated.

The great ingenuity of the American lawyers and accountants who are inbound specialist tax advisors has produced numerous loopholes used to circumvent early versions of the CFC tax laws. Over time, the IRS and Congress have repeatedly revised the law, trying to close these loopholes. Undaunted, the tax experts found new loopholes, the IRS reacted, and Congress changed the laws again. The foreign tax area has become an ongoing battle of wits between the international tax experts and the IRS. Much of the Enron scandal came from the too-imaginative use of these offshore tax shelters.

We tell you this because no prudent investor or businessperson should venture into this offshore tax arena without being fully prepared. You need to be ready to cope with uncertainty and highly complex tax rules that are always in a state of flux. And don't forget the potential cost in accounting and legal fees required just to keep up with constant change. Unless the tax savings are significant, the cost of these arrangements may not be worth it.

Just so you understand how complex this area of tax law can be, I readily admit that most of what I explain in this chapter is an over-simplification, a crude condensation of thousands of pages of IRS regulations, rulings and tax court cases. But persevere, for there's a potential for big profits, along with light at the end of the tunnel.

U.S. Shareholders

First test, only a "U.S. shareholder" is affected by CFC tax rules.

A U.S. shareholder is defined as a U.S. person (including any legal entity), that owns 10% or more of the total voting power of the stock of a foreign corporation. This can mean a citizen or resident of the U.S., a domestic partnership or corporation, or a U.S. estate or trust that is not a foreign estate or trust. However, if a foreign trust is a grantor trust, or has U.S. beneficiaries, the U.S. grantor or beneficiary is treated as a shareholder of the foreign corporation.

In the case of a foreign estate, if a U.S. person is a beneficiary, then that beneficiary is considered a shareholder of the foreign corporation. In each instance, the IRS looks through the legal tangle and focuses on U.S. citizens receiving, directly or indirectly, income from a foreign corporation.

But there's another caveat: unless the corporation qualifies as a CFC under the second test described below, the U.S. shareholders are not required to report their share of the corporate income on their personal tax return unless the corporation is also a passive foreign investment company (PFIC—pronounced pee-fik).

Second Test

A foreign corporation is considered a CFC only if more than 50% of the total voting power or the total value of the stock is owned by U.S. shareholders having a 10% or greater stock interest on any day during the tax year. (Different rules apply to insurance companies.) If foreign persons (or entities) own 50% or more of the corporation stock, then it is not considered to be a CFC.

However, if a U.S. person is related to the foreign person or entity, then the U.S. shareholder is deemed to be a shareholder of the foreign corporation under the constructive ownership rules in IRC, section 318 (also called the attribution of ownership rules). These rules apply with respect to U.S. persons and foreign entities, but not to foreign individuals. Section 318(b) refers to section 958(b) with respect to the attribution rules for a CFC. IRC 958(b)(1) provides an exception to the constructive ownership rules in IRC 318. Thus, if a foreign relative (parent, child, grandchild, grandparent, or spouse) owns 50% or more of a foreign corporation, the U.S. owners are not subject to the CFC tax rules.

Third Test

If a corporation qualifies as a CFC for an uninterrupted period of 30 days or more during any tax year, then every U.S. shareholder (as defined above) who owns stock in such corporation on the last day of the tax year in which it qualified as a CFC must report as personal gross income, his or her pro-rata share of the CFC income.

Fourth Test

If the corporation is a CFC, its U.S. shareholders are required to report any CFC income that meets the definition of what is called Subpart F income. This includes most kinds of foreign source investment income, and foreign income derived from those related parties we just mentioned, but not income earned in the U.S.

The related parties means anyone who owns or controls (directly or indirectly) more than 50% of the stock of a foreign corporation, or one who is controlled by the foreign corporation, or a person (entity) who is, in fact, in a brother-sister affiliated corporate relationship. The related party can be individuals, corporations, partnerships, trusts, or an estate. These rules apply even though true ownership is masked by a long chain of interrelated controls. The IRS wants to know who controls the income source, and who gets the payoff. All of this legal jargon is laid out in IRC section 954(d)(3).

Subpart F income does not include any income earned in the U.S. because this income is taxable for the foreign corporation, just as it is for a domestic U.S. company. Thus, if a foreign company's domestic income is taxed by the IRS, it's not foreign-source income and is not subject to the CFC rules.

Generally, subpart F income does not include any income derived from doing business in a foreign country, so long as the buyer or supplier is not a related person. In plain language, the CFC rules are aimed at foreign corporations that buy or sell goods or services in a "sweetheart deal" from their related U.S. entities at a presumably favorable price. These underhanded firms then resell their goods or services abroad at a normal market price, thereby shifting the profit into the foreign entity.

Having said all this, we must point out that the specific rules applicable to subpart F income do not require that there be any actual shifting of profits to the foreign corporation in order for the IRS to rule that CFC status exists.

Additionally, where the foreign corporation is primarily an investment company that invests in foreign stocks, bonds or other passive income investments (as distinguished from an active trade or business), all of that investment income is treated as subpart F income. Also, note that the related party rules are not applicable to investment income.

Tried but Not True

Now that I've tried to explain what a CFC and a U.S. person

are in the tax context, let's look at some related schemes that the IRS has rejected.

Formally assigning title to half the offshore corporation's shares of stock to your offshore attorney, with his or her agreement to vote the shares as you instruct, will not avoid a CFC determination. The IRS looks at the reality of the situation, and easily sees through facades that use "straw man" ownership. The use of a foreign corporation with bearer shares that are held by any unrelated party on behalf of the real owner is treated the same as when an attorney holds the shares on behalf of the taxpayer.

Some slick offshore advisors will try to convince potential clients that a chain of legal entities putting lots of paperwork between you and your offshore corporation will fool the IRS into thinking there is no CFC. Of course, the more entities you set up, the more the cost and the more a promoter is paid.

Forget it! An interlocking chain of offshore trusts and corporations, usually with a trust holding the operating corporation's stock, is a dead giveaway to the IRS. It may even provide strong evidence of tax fraud, which is a criminal act. The IRS is likely to conclude that since the person who is ultimately responsible for creating the entities in the chain, is the beneficial owner of the stock. The only remotely attractive feature of this kind of tinker-toy legal arrangement is that it might be difficult for the IRS to uncover it. Once exposed, however, the sheer complexity would be seen as evidence of deliberate fraud. Don't do it!

What Does Work

Now let's examine some ways to avoid having your investment ruled a controlled foreign corporation. In other words, let's explore a few strategies to help minimize your tax burden. (By the way, you'll often hear a non-CFC called a "decontrolled foreign corporation" — they're the same thing.)

One way is to make certain that no U.S. citizen or resident alien owns more than 10% of the corporation.

Here's why: for purposes of the CFC rules, if any five or fewer U.S. persons or U.S. residents own 10% or more of an offshore corporation's voting stock, it's a CFC.

Suppose you and at least 10 of your associates (folks unrelated to you—see below) plan to divide ownership interests in an offshore investment company. Divide 100% by 11, and you get a 9.09% share for each U.S. shareholder. Your offshore corporation is not a CFC, because no one U.S. person owns 10% or more of the voting stock. Your group can invest its capital within the United States with little or no tax cost, just as a foreign citizen does. The income can compound tax-free until you decide to pay yourselves dividends, which then become taxable personal income.

One caveat: Beware of the attribution of ownership rules mentioned above; if related U.S. persons are offshore corporate share-holders, they will be considered as constructive joint owners. Their shares will be added together for purposes of the CFC control test. Don't choose 10 associates who are your family members, and don't use your U.S. entities as owners. If you do, the offshore corporation probably will be ruled to be a CFC.

If you establish an offshore company with one U.S. person owning more than 50% of the voting stock, and other U.S. persons with less than 10% each, a CFC does exist because of the 50% U.S. shareholder. However, here's a twist; only the 50% shareholder is taxed on his pro rata share of the corporation's earned income each year. Because they have less than 10% of the voting shares each, the other U.S. persons are treated as though the company is a decontrolled corporation. They don't have to report their company income share annually, and are liable for taxes only when they actually do receive dividends or other corporate distributions. If a CFC also qualifies as a PFIC, then all U.S. shareholders are liable for their share of taxes on the income of the PFIC.

Real Foreign Partners

Another way to guarantee your offshore company will qualify as decontrolled is to invest along with one or more truly unrelated foreign partners. If the foreign person(s) own 50% or more of the voting power shares, the corporation is decontrolled. It then enjoys tax-free investments in the United States as a nonresident alien. Even though you are a partial American owner, you are taxed only as you withdraw money from the corporation, not each year. The foreign person can be a relative of the U.S. owner or owners.

Of course, the foreign persons must be the true owners of the stock. This sort of 50-50 ownership arrangement is particularly popular when foreign investors are from a country with similar tax rules, such as Germany. There have been many U.S.-German tax saving joint ventures in real estate that allow both halves to avoid a CFC designation by their respective national tax agencies.

What Kind of Income?

There's another way around the CFC designation, and that depends on the type of income the offshore corporation takes in; only subpart F income is counted as taxable and treated as though it passes through to U.S. shareholders. Non-subpart F income is not reportable annually on a pro rata basis. That income can accumulate and compound tax-free in the corporation until it is taken out as dividends.

Here are the types of income that are counted as subpart F income and are taxable for U.S. shareholders on a pro rata basis annually:

Foreign personal holding company income: All interest, dividends, royalties, and gains on securities, plus rents from related parties, are taxable. In other words, just about every kind of usual investment income is included in subpart F income. One exception is rent derived from the active conduct of a trade or business is not included, unless the rental income is received from a related party.

Example: suppose your foreign corporation owns an office building in The Bahamas. You occupy 15% for your own business, and your paid staff leases the remainder to unrelated parties and provides maintenance and other services. This would be considered the active conduct of a rental business in a foreign country, and rental income is not subpart F income.

Or, suppose your foreign corporation owns an oil drilling company in a foreign nation. When your equipment is idle, it is leased to other oil drilling companies. The rental from the leases is not considered subpart F income and can be accumulated in an offshore corporation. (Because there are special IRS rules for banking, insurance, shipping, or oil services income earned offshore, if that's your type of business, consult with an experienced international tax advisor who knows these rules.)

The IRS is so generous with the rent income exception because it knows that many tax haven countries prohibit nonresidents from owning land, so not many will be able to qualify for this rental income tax break.

Foreign-based company sales income: This is essentially income from the purchase of property from a related person, or the sale of property to anyone on behalf of a related person. Caveat: to avoid having this kind of income treated as subpart F income, you must purchase your goods or services from unrelated parties, and not sell your goods to a related party.

Foreign-based company service income: This is income from consulting services (legal, accounting, engineering, architectural, or management services) performed for, or on behalf of, a related person, but outside the country in which the foreign corporation is organized. Note: if your offshore corporation performs services for unrelated parties outside the U.S., that service income is not subpart F income.

De Minimis Test Games

Yet another way to avoid offshore company subpart F income is to take advantage of the IRS' so-called *de minimis* rule. Here's the rule: If the sum total of the foreign-based company's service income, plus the gross insurance income, does not exceed 5% of the CFC's total income, or US$1 million (whichever is smaller), none of the income is considered foreign-based company income or insurance income.

For example, suppose that your offshore corporation buys some condominiums in Panama. You rent the condominiums to tourists who are unrelated to any corporation owners. Since rental income from unrelated persons is not subpart F income, this will not be passed through pro rata and taxed to U.S. shareholders. In addition, if the rental income makes up at least 95% of the offshore corporation's total income, it will keep the subpart F income from being passed through to the U.S. shareholders under the *de minimis* rule. (Get it? Five percent is considered as *de minimis*, an amount so small it gets you out from under the CFC taxes.)

If you have U.S.-based manufacturing or personal consulting services that can be moved offshore, you might be able to use non-subpart F income generated by these operations to shelter investments in the United States. Any importing and exporting of tangible products through a foreign corporation would escape the subpart F rules, so long as the products are not bought from or sold to a related party. In addition, offshore manufacturing and consulting income probably will not be subpart F income, so it is also sheltered from tax in the offshore corporation.

But be careful. There's a flip side, what might be called the reverse de minimis rule: if 70% or more of the offshore corporation's income is defined as subpart F income, then all income is treated as such. In that case, you really are stuck tax-wise. You can see how important the type of the income can be.

For clarity's sake (I hope), let's consider another example:

Suppose that your offshore business sells a product with very high production costs and low mark-up. Assume the product costs 90% of its selling price. As we know, investment income is considered subpart F income, but under the rules, if the gross income from the investment measures less than 5% of the gross product sales, then the offshore corporation won't be considered a CFC.

To make it more specific: If the offshore foreign corporation sells US$10 million of widgets, it can make up to US$526,500 of gross investment income without becoming a CFC (US$10,526,500 x 5% = US$526,325). However, in this example, the profit on the US$10 million of widget sales would be US$1 million, while the profit on the gross investment income might be close to US$500,000.

Now you know why foreign corporations need such good lawyers and accountants.

Watch Out For...

There's a trap that must be avoided when using the *de minimis* rule as a CFC designation avoidance tactic.

The rules say that if 50% or more of the foreign company's total asset value is used to produce passive income, or if 50% of those assets are being held for the production of passive income, the foreign corporation is treated as a passive foreign investment company (PFIC), which is discussed further below.

Take it from the experts: as a practical matter, it requires more assets to produce a 5% return in the form of passive investment income than to produce the same amount of net income from a business activity. A business might typically generate a return of 15% to 20% on its net assets, and about 10% to 15% on its total assets. Thus, in the example above, if the foreign corporation needs US$10 million in assets to produce US$1 million in gross profits from widgets sales, it cannot exceed a maximum of US$10 million in passive assets held to produce investment income. If it does, it is considered a PFIC. If the return on those investment assets is 5%, the example given above would work—but just barely.

Before venturing into PFIC territory, we'll reiterate the obvious: subpart F income rules offer many possible avenues of tax avoidance. But after reading this, we don't have to tell you the rules are very complicated and riddled with exceptions. Even more discouraging, most of them were not even mentioned here. As always, consult an experienced U.S. international tax advisor before launching your offshore corporate career.

The PFIC (Pee-fik)

In yet another skirmish between offshore tax specialists and the IRS, Congress attempted to plug even more foreign corporate loopholes with the Tax Reform Act of 1986. This law established the concept of the *passive foreign investment company* (PFIC), and authorized the rules that govern such entities.

First, a definition: passive income is generally considered earnings from interest, dividends, capital gains, royalties, and a few other non-sales or service income types. The PFIC rules that apply to passive income are generally more difficult to avoid than other rules we already discussed.

Under the law, a PFIC is any foreign corporation that makes 75% or more of gross income from passive income sources. A corporation will also be considered a PFIC if at least 50% of the value of its assets produce passive income, or are being held for production of passive income. Unlike a CFC, there is no control test for a PFIC. Any offshore corporation that has the minimum amount of passive income, even if its ownership is only 1% American, qualifies as a PFIC.

Owning PFIC shares can be fairly costly. You may face a tax penalty or a loss of your tax deferral. Here are the two possible punishments:

1. You pay an interest charge on the value of the deferred tax either when you sell the PFIC shares, or when you receive an excess distribution. The interest charge assumes that the undistributed PFIC income and gains were actually paid to you annually, but that you didn't report the income and pay taxes owed on it each year. As penalty for your tardiness, you must pay the original tax owed plus interest based on the number of years you held the PFIC shares without paying the taxes. The shares of a PFIC are deemed to be sold at the date of your death, and your estate will be liable for the deferred taxes.

2. The other option is to set up your PFIC as a qualified electing fund corporation (QEF) from the very beginning (the IRS has a name for everything). That means you report your pro-rata shares of the PFIC's income and gains annually, just as you would with a U.S.-based mutual fund. In other words, you lose any benefit that comes with tax deferral and compounding of profits. In order to make this election, the PFIC must be willing to provide you with annual information on your share of its income. Unless U.S. owners control the PFIC, this is not likely to happen. Another option is to use the mark-to-market election to compute your gains (or losses) each year based on the difference in the market value of the shares at the end of each year. However, this election is limited to widely-held foreign fund shares sold through major exchanges.

You also can avoid PFIC interest charge by electing "mark-to-market" treatment in some cases. My colleague Mark Nestmann informed me as follows:

"A shareholder of a PFIC may also elect each year to recognize gain or loss on the shares as if he/she/it had sold the PFIC shares at fair market value. Such election is available only for shares the market value of which is readily determinable (e.g., regularly traded shares). Shares subject to this election are not subject to the tax and interest regime. Also, this election is independent of prior PFIC elections (i.e. QEF or Sect 1291 election), for example: If stock X was purchased in 2007 for $100, has a FMV on 12/31/11 of $120, and no PFIC forms were filed until 2011 (when Sect 1296 mark-to-market election was made), no PFIC filings would be needed for the prior years as long distributions were less than 125% and no capital gains occurred. For the current year, 8621 would be filed using mark to market and the ordinary income would be $20. See Section 1.1296-1 3 b.iii.

Your foreign corporation can avoid the PFIC trap by reducing the percentage of the offshore corporation's gross income that is passive. On the other hand, you could increase the amount of the assets used to produce active business income. If the corporation is a PFIC because more than 75% of its gross income is passive income, then it's only necessary to change the percentage by generating more active business income, or less passive investment income. If the corporation is a PFIC because of the 50% asset test, then you can increase assets to produce more active business income, or you can reduce passive investment assets. To qualify, it's necessary to meet both of these tests. Failure to qualify on either ground could subject shareholders to the adverse tax treatment of a PFIC.

Another option is to combine the investment activities of an offshore corporation with an actual operating business. If you have manufacturing or consulting operations overseas, these can be used to avoid the PFIC penalty.

Another potential trap is the foreign *personal holding company* rules. In most cases, if you can avoid the CFC rules, or qualify as a decontrolled offshore corporation, you can also avoid the foreign personal holding company rules.

Offshore Corporations Operating in the United States

Once your offshore corporation has done everything necessary to gain a favorable foreign business tax status under IRS rules, it is free to invest in the United States and reap the benefits of tax-free income just as a foreign citizen would.

But what you cannot do as a foreign corporation is "engage in a U.S. trade or business" as defined under U.S. tax law. Here are the guidelines to follow:

- No physical office or agent in the United States

- Books and records must be maintained outside the U.S.

- Actual management and control must be exercised elsewhere

- Directors' and shareholders' meetings must be held outside the U.S.

- The corporation cannot have a business located within the U.S.

Once your offshore corporation secures its status as a foreign business, some of the immediate benefits include no obligation to pay U.S. taxes on interest from U.S. Treasury securities or bank deposits, and no tax on capital gains earned on U.S. stocks and bonds. Although there could be tax liability for some dividends paid by American stock shares, these taxes often can be reduced or avoided by locating the offshore corporation in a country with a favorable U.S. tax treaty. Some bilateral U.S.-foreign tax treaties provide for a greatly reduced U.S. withholding tax rate on dividends paid to foreign corporations.

A good example of this dividend tax avoidance advantage became known during the so-called "junk bond" mess and the widespread collapse of insurance companies and savings and loan debacle in the 1980s. When these faltering American companies tried to sell assets, many foreign corporations or partnerships submitted the best bids for their portfolios of junk bonds and shares. While potential U.S. bond buyers faced taxes on interest and capital gains, foreign inves-

Warning — *The Per* Se List

For U.S. persons who control the shares in a foreign corporation, there are major limitations on U.S. tax benefits that would otherwise be available to a corporation formed in the United States. That is because the foreign corporation may be on what is known as the IRS *"per se"* list of foreign corporations, which appears in IRS regulations, section 301.7701-2(b)(8)(i).

The listed *per se* corporations are barred from numerous U.S. tax benefits. This means that U.S. persons cannot file an IRS Form 8832 electing to treat the corporation as a "disregarded entity" or a foreign partnership, either of which is given much more favorable tax treatment.

Under IRS rules, the foreign corporation that engages in passive investments is considered a "controlled foreign corporation," which requires the filing of IRS Form 5471 describing its operations. U.S. persons also must file IRS Form 926 reporting transfers of cash or assets to the corporation.

A U.S. person who controls a foreign financial account of any nature that has in it $10,000 or more at any time during a calendar year must report this to the IRS on Form TD F 90-22.1. There are serious fines and penalties for failure to file these IRS returns and criminal charges can also be filed. As a general rule, U.S. persons can be guilty of the crime of "falsifying a federal income tax return" by failing to report offshore corporate holdings.

Any eventual capital gains an IRS-listed per se corporation may make are not taxed in the U.S. under the more favorable capital gains tax rate of 15%, but rather as ordinary income for the corporate owners, which can be much higher. There is also the possibility of double taxation if the foreign corporation makes investments in the U.S., in which case there is a 30% U.S. withholding tax on the investment income. Under U.S. tax rules, no annual losses can be taken on corporate investments, which must be deferred by the U.S. owners until the foreign corporation is liquidated.

However, compared to these IRS restrictions, there may be

offsetting considerations, such as complete exemption from foreign taxes, which may be more important in your financial planning. Therefore, it is extremely important that U.S. persons obtain an authoritative review of the tax implications before forming a foreign corporation for any purpose, including holding title to personal or business real estate.

tors, facing no U.S. taxes, could offer bids 10% or more above those of U.S. competitors. If these offshore companies were incorporated in tax-free havens like Panama or Nevis, they escaped dividend and interest taxes on these "fire sale" stock buys completely.

U.S. Real Estate a Tax Bargain

Investing in U.S. real estate used to be an easy avenue to tax-free income and gains for foreign citizens. However, the real estate tax rules were changed in 1980, and profits earned by foreign owners are no longer tax-free. Still, investment in U.S. real estate through a decontrolled offshore corporation can result in lower taxes on profits if the transaction is structured properly.

In the complicated and rapidly changing area of tax law, an offshore company should be incorporated in a country that has a favorable tax treaty with the United States. The offshore company then creates a subsidiary U.S. corporation, which buys the real estate. Sometimes, it makes sense to have one U.S. company hold title to the real estate, while another is created to receive property management fees.

Don't forget that foreign investors can also enjoy U.S. stock market trading profits entirely tax-free. This applies whether or not their home country has a double tax treaty with the U.S. The IRS periodically issues revenue rulings attacking current schemes, so obtain up-to-date advice from an experienced U.S. tax advisor.

There is a 10% withholding tax imposed on the gross proceeds from the sale of a U.S. real estate property interest by a foreign person. This term includes an interest in the form of corporate stock, partnerships, trusts, etc. In a case where there is no depreciation taken, a gain on U.S. real estate of 67% of the gross sales price would be subject to a 15% tax, resulting in a tax equal to 10% of the gross sales proceeds. Where the gain is less than 67%, the foreign investor would be paying too much tax with a 10% rate of withholding. Where the property is subject to depreciation, the accelerated depreciation is subject to a 25% rate of tax instead of 15%. This is an extremely complicated subject and one that I have not gone into in any real depth.

It's possible for a non-resident investor to file a U.S. tax return and get back some or all of the tax withheld in certain circumstances.

Summary

The major points you should remember are those that apply to the offshore ownership structure (decontrolled corporation vs. CFC), and the type of income to be earned (either subpart F or not).

In evaluating any offshore tax planning proposal, be especially wary of:

- schemes involving chains of foreign entities, all of which ultimately are controlled by the same person;

- foreign-based agents who offer to act as accommodation agents to establish proxy control of a foreign entity;

- any plan that depends on secrecy, non-reporting and hindrance of IRS oversight;

- poorly capitalized, low asset corporations. The IRS and the courts often simply ignore such corporations when determining tax liabilities on any specific transaction. They view them as dummy or sham corporations with no continuing business purpose, set up mainly to avoid taxes.

This information overload is not meant to deter you, but to educate you about the risks of haphazard planning. The most disturbing aspect of studying offshore foreign corporations is the large number of Americans who are unaware of the tax saving possibilities that do exist. If you take the next step and explore these strategies, you won't regret it as long as you are careful to play by the rules.

Also, have an expert on costs "run the numbers" before you create a foreign corporation. It takes a net profit of about US$100,000 in a foreign-based business to justify the added operating expenses with the potential tax savings. Each foreign venture will involve different facts and costs, so that each one will need to be evaluated in terms of whether the potential tax savings is worth the cost and the complexity of operating offshore.

If you want to establish any offshore trust or corporation, your financial future will be determined in large part by attorneys and accountants and their professional abilities. It is vitally important that these professionals be both qualified and experienced in practical offshore business and legal operations.

New IRS Rule Affects Foreign Investors

In 2012, President Obama's IRS finally adopted a controversial regulation first proposed by in 2001 by President Bill Clinton. The regulation requires all U.S. banks to report annually to the IRS all interest they pay to nonresident alien individuals, so that the IRS can pass on this information to the tax collectors in the many countries with which the U.S. has tax treaties.

The IRS rule was advanced at the specific request of the tax hungry European Union, led by high-taxing France and Germany.

As noted, unlike the U.S., which taxes the worldwide income of its citizens and residents aliens, most other countries have a territorial system of taxation that only taxes income earned within that country or when foreign income is repatriated back to the country. Thus, so long as earnings from dividends, interest and capital gains remain outside these countries, there is no tax liability.

Of course, Europe's welfare states want to know what their citizens are earning offshore, how they spend their cash, all the better for EU tax collectors to squeeze out every last dollar or euro they can find. The noted offshore lawyer, Marshall Langer, argues that this IRS rule will would cause major harm to the American economy by diverting billions in needed capital away from America.

Earlier in this chapter, I noted the trillions of investment dollars have flowed into the U.S., much from Europe, especially from France and Germany, where taxation and regulation are especially onerous. This capital flow has enabled U.S. businesses to expand plant and equipment, increase productivity, and create new and higher paying jobs, and enjoy higher rates of economic growth than in Europe, even during our own major recession.

At a time when the U.S. economy is struggling to climb out a five-year recession, the last thing needed is a major policy change that will seriously hurt capital investment and jobs.

During the eight years under the administration of President George W. Bush, this proposal was put aside and never finally approved because of the economic damage it can do.

However, the anti-tax haven President Obama has demanded that foreign governments assist the IRS in obtaining information about all Americans who bank or do business offshore. He and Democratic legislators in Congress have pushed all sorts of increased reporting and restrictions that harm Americans who dare to invest and do business offshore. The prime example is the "Foreign Account Tax Compliance Act" (FATCA).

Taken together the new IRS rules requiring reporting to foreign governments of foreigners' American income and FATCA opens a two-way avenue for U.S. and foreign tax collectors, working in tandem, to wring every last penny from taxpayers.

It remains to be seen how this will affect foreign investment in America at a time when it is badly needed.

APPENDIX I

Recommended Attorneys

Josh N. Bennett, JD

440 North Andrews Avenue, Fort Lauderdale, Florida 33301

Tel.: (954) 779-1661

Email: josh@joshbennett.com

Website: www.joshbennett.com

Josh Bennett has more than 25 years' experience in law with extensive work in all aspects of international tax, estate, and gift tax planning for U.S. citizens, resident aliens, and non-resident aliens.

Michael Chatzky, JD

Chatzky & Associates

6540 Lusk Boulevard, Suite C121, San Diego, California 92121

Tel.: (858) 457-1000

Email: mgchatzky@aol.com

Michael Chatzky specializes in U.S. and international taxation and wealth protection with an emphasis on business, estate and asset protection planning. For 36 years Michael has helped clients establish a variety of wealth preservation structures.

Gideon Rothschild, JD, CPA, CFP

Partner, Moses & Singer LLP,

405 Lexington Avenue, New York, NY 10174

Tel.: (212) 554-7806

Email: grothschild@mosessinger.com

Website: www.mosessinger.com

Gideon Rothschild is a nationally recognized authority on offshore trusts and other planning techniques for wealth preservation. He is an

Adjunct Professor at the University of Miami School of Law Graduate Program, and a Fellow of The American College of Trust and Estates Counsel.

Recommended Consultant on Residence and Citizenship

Mark Nestmann
The Nestmann Group, Ltd.,
2303 N. 44th St. #14-1025
Phoenix, AZ 85008 USA Tel./Fax: +1 (602) 604-1524
Website: http://www.nestmann.com

Henley & Partners AG
Klosbachstrasse 110
8024 Zurich, Switzerland
Tel.: +41 44 266 22 22
Website: www.henleyglobal.com
Contact: Chris Kalin
Email: christian.kalin@henleyglobal.com

William M. Sharp, Sr.
Sharp Kemm International Tax Law
4890 W. Kennedy Blvd., Suite 900
Tampa, FL 33609-1850
Tel.: + 1 (813) 286-4199
Email: wsharp@sharptaxlaw.com
Web: http://www.sharptaxlaw.com
Bahnhofstrasse 98
CH-8001 Zürich, Switzerland
Tel.: +41 (44) 218 12 81
101 California Street, Suite 2940
San Francisco, CA 94111
Tel.: + 1 (415) 677-9877

APPENDIX 2

Legal and Investment Glossary

A

acceptance: unconditional agreement by one party (the offeree) to the terms of an offer made by a second party (the offeror). Agreement results in a valid, binding contract.

accredited investor: A term used by the U.S. SEC to define financially sophisticated investors that can purchase hedge funds and other exempt securities for lower minimums than other investors. In the U.S., individual accredited investors must have a liquid net worth of $1 million or earn income of $200,000 in each of the previous two years or earn a combined $300,000 income in conjunction with their spouse.

alternative asset class: non-traditional assets (versus traditional assets like stocks, bonds and cash) such as hedge funds, managed futures, real estate, private equity and collectibles (such as art, coins, wine, etc.). The diversification benefits of adding alternative investments to traditional portfolios are due to the low correlation of alternative investments to traditional investments

arbitrage: the simultaneous buying and selling of a security or currency in different markets to take advantage of the price differential.

assets: items that have earning power or other value to their owner. Fixed assets (also known as long-term assets) are things that have a useful life of more than one year, for example buildings and machinery; there are also intangible fixed assets, like the good reputation ("goodwill") of a company or brand.

asset allocation: investment process whereby the total portfolio assets are divided among traditional assets (stocks, bonds and cash) and alternative assets (hedge funds, managed futures, real estate, private equity and collectibles) in an effort to reduce overall portfolio risk and improve risk-adjusted returns through portfolio diversification.

asset protection trust (APT): an offshore trust which holds title to, and protects the grantor's property from, claims, judgments, and creditors, especially because it is located in a country other than the grantor's home country.

attachment: the post-judicial civil procedure by which personal property is taken from its owner pursuant to a judgment or other court order.

B

basis: the original cost of an asset, later used to measure increased value for tax purposes at the time of sale or disposition.

basis point: one-hundredth of one percentage point, or 0.01%. Therefore 1.0% equals 100 basis points. Basis points are an easy way to state small differences in yield. For example, a return of 6.0% is 50 basis points greater than a return of 5.5%.

bear market: a prolonged decline in the prices in stocks, bonds, commodities or any other asset class usually brought on by declining or poor market fundamentals. In a bear market, prices trend downwards and investors, anticipating losses, tend to sell. This creates a self-sustaining downward spiral.

bearer share/stocks: a negotiable stock certificate made out only to "Bearer" without designating the shareowner by name. Such shares are unregistered with the issuing company and dividends are claimed by "clipping coupons" attached to the shares and presenting them for payment. Bearer shares are illegal in most countries.

bench mark: a standard against which the performance of a fund or investment can be measured.

beneficiary: individual designated to receive income from a trust or estate; a person named in an insurance policy to receive proceeds or benefits.

bequest: a gift of personal property by will; also called a legacy.

bond: a debt security, or, more simply, an IOU. The bond states when a loan must be repaid and what interest the borrower (issuer) must pay to the holder. Banks and investors buy and trade bonds.

bull market: a sustained rise in the prices in stocks, bonds, commodities or any other asset class usually brought on by improving or positive market fundamentals when prices are generally rising and investor confidence is high.

C

CTA (commodities trading advisor): professional managed futures managers also referred to as CPOs (commodity pool operators).

call option: an option contract that gives its holder the right (but not the obligation) to purchase a specified number of shares of the underlying stock at the given strike price, on or before the expiration date of the contract.

capital: wealth (cash or other assets) used to fuel the creation of more wealth; within companies, often characterized as working capital or fixed capital.

capital gain: the amount of profit earned from the sale or exchange of property, measured against the original cost basis.

captive insurance company: a wholly owned subsidiary company established by a non-insurance parent company to spread insured risks among the parent and other associated companies. Bermuda is the leading jurisdiction where such entities are registered.

carry trade (currency): investment position involving the borrowing of funds or investments at a relatively low interest rate and the simultaneous purchase of an offsetting position earning a higher yield. Also the borrowing of currency at a low interest rate, converting it to a currency with a high interest rate, and then lending it. The element of risk is in the fluctuations in the currency market.

civil suit: a non-criminal legal action between parties relating to a dispute or injury seeking remedies for a violation of contractual or other personal rights.

civil forfeiture: laws that allow the U.S. and state governments to seize private property allegedly involved with a crime without charging anyone with the crime; the burden is on the property owner to disprove the alleged criminal association.

Chapter 11: a term from U.S. bankruptcy law that describes court-supervised postponement of a company's obligations to its creditors, giving it time to reorganize its debts or sell parts of the business.

closed fund: a fund that is closed to new investment but may be available on a secondary market.

closed-end fund: a fund that issues a set number of shares and trades on a stock exchange with daily liquidity at market price. Unlike more traditional open-end funds, transactions in shares of closed-end funds are based on their market price as determined by the forces of supply and demand in the marketplace. The market price of a closed-end fund may be above (premium) or below (discount) the value of its underlying portfolio (or net asset value).

collateralized debt obligations (CDOs): financial structure that groups individual loans, bonds or assets in a portfolio, which can then be traded.

contrarian: investment strategy that invests contrary to prevailing market trends.

commercial paper: unsecured, short-term loans issued by companies; funds that are typically used for working capital, rather than fixed assets, such as a new building.

commodities: products such as agricultural products or iron ore that, in their basic forms, have a market price and are bought, traded and sold. See also futures.

common law: the body of law developed in England from judicial decisions based on customs and precedent, constituting the basis of the present English, British Commonwealth, and U.S. legal systems. See also equity.

community property: in certain states in the U.S., property acquired during marriage jointly owned by both spouses, each with an undivided one-half interest.

contract: a binding agreement between two or more parties; also, the written or oral evidence of an agreement.

corporation: a business, professional or other entity recognized in law to act as a single legal person, although composed of one or more natural persons, endowed by law with various rights and duties including the right of succession.

corpus: property owned by a fund, trust or estate; also called the principal.

creator: See grantor.

credit default swap: a swap designed to transfer credit risk, in effect a form of financial insurance. The buyer of the swap makes periodic payments to the seller in return for protection in the event of a default on a loan.

creditor: one to whom a debtor owes money or other valuable consideration.

currency: official, government issued paper and coined money; hard currency describes a national currency sufficiently sound so as to be generally acceptable in international dealings.

custodian: person or institution entrusted with the safekeeping of a client's securities; one appointed to take charge of the affairs of another.

cyclicals: cyclical stocks rise and fall in sync with the economic cycle.

D

dead cat bounce: a phrase long used on trading floors to describe a short-lived recovery of share prices in a bear market.

debtor: one who owes another (the creditor) money or other valuable consideration, especially one who has neglected payments due.

decedent: a term used in estate and probate law to describe a deceased person.

declaration: a formal statement in writing of any kind, often signed and notarized, especially a document establishing a trust; also called an indenture or trust agreement.

deed: a formal written document signed by the owner conveying title to real estate to another party.

deflation: the downward price movement of goods and services.

derivatives: investments that are short of full ownership but are "derived" from something else; options are derivatives because the option has an underlying stock, commodity or other asset on which its price is based. Futures, forwards and options are the most common types of derivatives, which are used to generate returns and/or hedge against certain risks.

distressed securities: debt, equity or "trade claims" of companies that are bankrupt or in financial trouble. Until these firms are restructured or other remedial action has been taken, their securities often trade significantly below par value and attract distressed securities managers anxious to benefit from a turn-around they expect can be realized.

dividends: a payment by a company to its shareholders, usually linked to its profits.

diversification: strategy that seeks to minimize overall portfolio volatility or risk by spreading investments across multiple securities and various asset classes; the basic premise behind Modern Portfolio Theory.

domicile: a person's permanent legal home, as compared to a place that may be only a temporary residence. Domicile determines what law applies to the person for purposes of marriage, divorce, succession of estate at death and taxation.

Dow Jones Industrial Average (DJIA): price-weighted average of 30 actively traded blue-chip stocks, primarily industrials including stocks that trade on the New York Stock Exchange. The Dow is a barometer of how shares of largest U.S. companies are performing.

due process: the regular administration of the law, according to which no citizen may be denied his or her legal rights and all laws must conform to fundamental, accepted legal principles.

due diligence: the quantitative and qualitative investigation process conducted prior to making an investment decision by a prudent person exercising reasonable care; investigation and background check into individuals prior to agreeing to do business

E

emerging markets: strategy focused on investing in securities of companies from emerging or developing countries; may involve volatility, currency risk, political and liquidity risk.

equity: a body of judicial rules developed under the common law used to enlarge and protect legal rights and enforce duties while seeking to avoid unjust constraints and narrowness of statutory law; also, the unrealized property value of a person's investment or ownership, as in a trust beneficiary's equitable interest; also, the risk sharing part of a company's capital, referred to as ordinary shares.

equal protection: the guarantee under the 14th Amendment to the

U.S. Constitution that a state must treat an individual or class of individuals the same as it treats other individuals or classes in like circumstances.

estate: any of various kinds or types of ownership a person may have in real or personal property; often used to describe all property of a deceased person, meaning the assets and liabilities remaining after death.

estate tax: taxes imposed at death by the U.S. on assets of a decedent. On and after January 1, 2011, the estate tax rate will be 55% unless the law is changed before that date.

executor: a person who manages the estate of a decedent; also called an executrix if a female, personal representative, administrator or administratrix.

exemption: a tax law, a statutorily defined right to avoid imposition of part or all of certain taxes; also, the statutory right granted to a debtor in bankruptcy to retain a portion of his or her real or personal property free from creditors' claims.

expatriation: the transfer of one's legal residence and citizenship from one's home country to another country, often in anticipation of government financial restrictions or taxes.

F

family partnership (also, family limited partnership): a legal business relationship created by agreement among two or more family members for a common purpose, often used as a means to transfer and/or equalize income and assets among family members so as to limit individual personal liability and taxes. See partnership and limited partnership.

FATCA: "Foreign Account Tax Compliance Act," U.S. Public Law 111-147, seeks to require all foreign financial institutions to report to IRS information on U.S. clients.

FATF: a subgroup of the OECD that claims to establish international anti-money laundering standards. See also OECD and G-20.

FBAR: "Report of Foreign Bank and Financial Accounts," U.S. Treasury Form U.S. persons with offshore accounts with a value of $10,000 or more must file annually by June 30th.

fee-based accounts: accounts with low and steady annual fees with little or no transaction costs; financial advisor compensation is related to the size of the assets rather than the level of trading activity; popular with fee-sensitive clients.

Federal Reserve: (informally called "The Fed") is the quasi-public, quasi-private central banking system of the United States created in 1913.

fiduciary: A person holding title to property in trust for the benefit of another, as does a trustee, guardian or executor of an estate.

FinCEN: Financial Crimes Enforcement Network: a law enforcement agency of the U.S. Treasury Department responsible for establishing and implementing policies to detect money laundering.

flight capital: movement of large sums of money across national borders, often in response to investment opportunities or to escape high taxes or pending political or social unrest; also called hot money.

front-end load: a charge levied on a fund at the time it is purchased.

FTSE-100: an index of the 100 companies listed on the London Stock Exchange with the largest market capitalization; the share price multiplied by the number of shares. The index is revised every three months.

fundamentals: a company's assets, debt, revenue, earnings and growth. Fundamentals determine a company, currency or security's value.

fund of hedge funds: a fund invested in a number of hedge funds and hedge fund strategies generally uncorrelated to each other usually with at least 20 separate funds.

futures: an agreement to buy or sell a commodity at a predetermined date and price. It could be used to hedge or to speculate on the price of the commodity.

future interest: an interest in property, usually real estate, possession and enjoyment of which is delayed until some future time or event; also, futures, securities or goods bought or sold for future delivery, often keyed to price changes before delivery.

G

G-20: a formal association of 19 of the world's largest national economies, plus the European Union (EU). Collectively, the G-20 economies comprise 85% of global gross national product, 80% of world trade and two-thirds of the world population. Member countries are Argentina, Australia, Brazil, Canada, China, France, Germany, India, Indonesia, Italy, Japan, Mexico, Russia, Saudi Arabia, South Africa, South Korea, Turkey, United Kingdom and United States.

GDP: gross domestic product. A measure of economic activity in a country of all the services and goods produced in a year. There are three main ways of calculating GDP—through output, through income and through expenditure.

gift tax: U.S. tax imposed on any gift made by one person to another person annually in excess of $13,000 (2009 exempted amount).

grantor: a person who conveys real property by deed; a person who creates a trust; also called a trust creator or settlor.

grantor trust: in U.S. tax law, an offshore trust, the income of which is taxed by the IRS as the personal income of the grantor.

gross estate: the total value for estate tax purposes of all a decedent's assets, as compared to net estate, the amount remaining after all permitted exemptions, deductions, taxes and debts owed.

growth stocks: stocks with higher-than-market earnings gains that are expected to continue to show high earnings growth; they typically have a higher price/earnings ratio and often pay no dividends

guardianship: a power conferred on a person, the guardian, usually by judicial decree, giving them the right and duty to provide personal supervision, care, and control over another person who is unable to care for himself because of some physical or mental disability or because of minority age status.

H

haven or haven nation: a country where banking, tax, trust, and corporation laws are specially designed to attract foreign persons wishing to avoid taxes or protect assets.

hedge fund: a private investment fund with a large, unregulated pool of capital said to be managed by experienced investors using a range of sophisticated strategies to maximize returns including hedging, leveraging and derivatives trading.

hedging: making an investment to reduce the risk of price fluctuations to the value of an asset; for example, when one owns a stock and then sells a futures contract agreeing to sell that stock on a particular date at a set price. A fall in price causes no loss nor would there be a benefit from any rise.

I

indices of ownership: factors indicating a person's control over, therefore ownership, especially of trust property, including the power of revocability.

income beneficiary: the life tenant in a trust.

incorporation: the official government registration and qualification process by which a corporation is formed under law.

indemnity: an agreement by which one promises to protect another from any loss or damage, usually describing the role of the insurer in insurance law.

inflation: the upward price movement of goods and services.

inheritance tax: a tax imposed by government on the amount a person receives from a decedent's estate, rather than on the estate itself; also known as death tax.

insider dealing: selling or purchasing corporate shares for personal benefit based on confidential information about a company's status unknown to the general public.

interest: a right, title, or legal property share; also, a charge for borrowed money, usually a percentage of the total amount borrowed.

international business corporation (IBC): a term used to describe a variety of offshore corporate structures, characterized by having all or most of its business activity outside the nation of incorporation, maximum privacy, flexibility, low or no taxes on operations, broad powers, and minimal filing and reporting requirements.

interbank rate of exchange: the interest rate which banks charge each other in their dealings. See also LIBOR.

insurance: a contract or policy under which a corporation (an insurer) undertakes to indemnify or pay a person (the insured) for a specified future loss in return for the insured's payment of an established sum of money (the premium).

IPOs (initial public offerings): initial public sale of stock by a private company usually smaller firms who need capital from external shareholders to expand operations; IPOs are risky because share value on first trading day can be extremely volatile.

irrevocable trust: a trust which, once established by the grantor, cannot be ended or terminated by the grantor.

J

junk bond: a bond (or loan to a company) with a high interest rate to reward the lender for a high risk of default.

joint tenancy: a form of property co-ownership in which parties hold equal title with the right of survivorship; a tenancy by the entireties is a similar tenancy reserved to husband and wife in some American states.

judgment: an official and authenticated decision of a court.

jurisdiction: the statutory authority a court exercises; also, the geographic area or subject matter over which a government or court has power.

K

Keynesian economics: economic theories of the late John Maynard Keynes; belief that government can directly stimulate demand in a stagnating economy by borrowing money to spend on public works projects such as roads, schools and hospitals (aka economic stimulus).

L

large-cap securities: stocks with a market capitalization of $1 billion or more.

last will and testament: a written document in which a person directs the post-mortem distribution of his or her property. In the U.S., state law governs the specific requirements for a valid will.

legal capacity: the competency or ability of parties to make a valid contract, including being of majority age (18 years old) and of sound mind.

leverage: borrowing money to invest in the hopes of earning a greater rate of return than the rate at which the money was borrowed.

liability: a financial obligation, debt or payment that must be made at a specific time to satisfy contractual terms of the obligation; also an obligation arising out of damage to a person or property.

LIBOR: the London Inter Bank Offered Rate; the rate at which banks in the U.K. and many other countries lend money to each other.

life insurance trust: an irrevocable living trust that holds title to a policy on the grantor's life, proceeds from which are not part of the grantor's estate.

life estate: the use and enjoyment of property granted by the owner to another during the owner's life, or during the life of another, at the termination of which, title passes to another known as the remainderman.

limited liability company (LLC): a flexible legal entity for conducting business that blends elements of partnership and corporate structures.

limited partnership: a partnership in which individuals known as limited partners have no management role, but receive periodic income and are personally liable for partnership debts only to the extent of their individual investment.

M

macroeconomics: analysis of big-picture trends in global markets and major currencies and other large-scale economic factors.

managed futures: globally oriented investment strategy that trades in listed financial, currency and commodity futures markets. A managed futures funds includes futures and forward contracts representing a wide range from agricultural products and livestock to gold, silver, interest rates and stock indexes.

margin call: a demand for payment a brokerage firm makes when a client's position that was established using borrowed funds declines in value past a certain point; the client must either deposit additional funds into the account or sell part of the position.

market capitalization: total market value of a company or a stock calculated by multiplying the number of outstanding shares by their current market price. Investors generally divide equity markets into three basic market caps: large-cap, mid-cap and small-cap.

marital deduction: the right of the surviving spouse under U.S. law to inherit, free of estate taxes, all property owned at death by the deceased spouse.

mark-to-market: recording the value of an asset on a daily basis according to current market prices; also called marked-to-market.

marriage: the legal and religious institution whereby a man and woman join in a binding contract for the purpose of founding and maintaining a family.

mid-cap securities: stocks with a market capitalization of approximately $250 million to $1 billion

modern portfolio theory: portfolio management theory that seeks to maximize risk-adjusted returns and optimize worth through security valuation, diversification, and asset allocation strategies.

money laundering: the process of concealing the criminal origins or uses of cash so that it appears the funds involved are from legitimate sources; a crime in most nations.

MSCI (Morgan Stanley Capital International) World Index: index that tracks the stocks of approximately 1,300 companies representing stock markets of 22 countries.

mutual fund: a fund consisting of a group of investors pooled money with investments in a diversified portfolio of equities, bonds, or other securities. Each mutual fund has a specific stated investment objective and must operate within the investment parameters outlined in a legal offering document called a prospectus.

mutual legal assistance treaty (MLAT): bilateral treaties between nations governing cooperation in international investigations of alleged criminal conduct.

N

NASDAQ (National Association of Securities Dealers Automatic Quotation System): an indexed electronic system providing price quotations to market participants about leading companies in all areas of business including technology, retail, communications, financial services, transportation, media and biotechnology industries. About 3,300 companies trade on the NASDAQ.

numbered bank account: any account in a financial institution that is identified not by the account holder's name, but a number, supposedly concealing the beneficial owner. In the past, associated with Swiss banking, such accounts no longer exist since under current rules the true account owner must be known to the bank.

nationalization: the act of bringing an industry, banks or other private assets such as land and property under state control.

negative equity: a situation in which the current value of one's house or other mortgaged real estate is below the amount of the mortgage that remains unpaid.

O

OECD: the Organization for Economic Cooperation and Development, an international research group financed by the G-20 that has led attacks on tax havens. See FATF and G-20.

offer: a written or verbal promise by one person (the offeror) to another (the offeree), to do, or not to do, some future act, usually in exchange for a mutual promise or payment (consideration). See acceptance and contract.

offshore: refers to jurisdictions that specialize in providing low taxes, guaranteed privacy, banking, finance, asset protection, insurance, annuities and investments.

offshore fund: a fund that is managed and domiciled in a foreign country.

offshore financial center (OFC): currently politically correct term to describe a jurisdiction used to be called a "tax haven"

option: a contract provision allowing one to purchase property at a set price within a certain time period.

P

partnership: an association of two or more persons formed to conduct business for mutual profit. See also limited partnership.

passive foreign investment company (PFIC): A foreign-based corporation that has one of the following attributes: 1) at least 75% of the corporation's income is considered "passive", which is based on investments rather than standard operating business; 2) at least 50% of the company's assets are investments that produce interest, dividends and/or capital gains. PFICs include foreign-based mutual funds, partnerships and other pooled investment vehicles that have at least one U.S. shareholder.

policy: in insurance law, the contract between insurer and insured. See also insurance.

Ponzi scheme: similar to a pyramid scheme, an enterprise in which, instead of genuine profits, funds from new investors are used to pay high returns to current investors. Named after the Italian-American fraudster Charles Ponzi, such schemes are destined to collapse as soon as new investment decreases or significant numbers of investors simultaneously seek to withdraw funds.

power of attorney: a written instrument allowing one to act as agent on behalf of another, the scope of agency power indicated by the terms, known as general or limited powers.

preservation trust: any trust designed to limit a beneficiary's access to income and principal.

primary residence: especially in tax law, a home place, as compared to a vacation or second home. See also domicile.

prime rate: a term used in North America to describe the standard lending rate of banks to most customers. The prime rate is usually the same across all banks, and higher rates are often described as "x percentage points above prime."

private equity: equity capital offered to private investors rather than being offered publicly on an exchange.

probate: a series of judicial proceedings, usually in a special court, initially determining the validity of a last will and testament, then supervising the administration or execution of the terms of the will and the decedent's estate.

property: anything of value capable of being owned, including land (real property) and personal property, both tangible and intangible.

protector: under the laws of some offshore haven nations, an appointed person who has the duty of overseeing the activities of an offshore trust and its trustee.

put options: an option contract giving the owner the right, but not the obligation, to sell a specific amount of an underlying security at a certain price within a given time.

Q

quit claim deed: a deed transferring any interest a grantor may have in real property without guarantees of title, if in fact any interest does exist.

R

rate of return: percentage gain or loss of a security over a particular period.

real estate: land and anything growing or erected thereon or permanently attached thereto.

real estate investment trust (REIT): an investment fund in trust form that owns and operates real estate for shareholding investors who are the beneficiaries.

recession: a period of negative economic growth technically defined as two consecutive quarters of negative economic growth when real output falls. In the U.S., many factors are taken into account, such as job creation and manufacturing activity but this usually means that it can be defined only when it is well along or already over.

remainder: in testamentary law, the balance of an estate after payment of legacies; in property law, an interest in land or a trust estate distributed at the termination of a life estate. The person with a right to such an estate is the remainderman.

rescind: cancellation or annulment of an otherwise binding contract by one of the parties.

revocable trust: a living trust in which the grantor retains the power to revoke or terminate the trust during his or her lifetime, returning the assets to themselves.

right of survivorship: an attribute of a joint tenancy that automatically transfers ownership of the share of a deceased joint tenant to surviving joint tenants without the necessity of probate.

S

search and seizure: examination of a person's property by law enforcement officials investigating a crime and the taking of items as potential evidence; the 4th Amendment to the U.S. Constitution forbids unreasonable searches and seizures but has been greatly weakened by court decisions and unconstitutional executive and police policies.

securitization: a process by which existing debt such as mortgages with their interest and principal payments are combined and converted into financial instruments backed by the cash flows from a portfolio or pool of mortgages or other assets. Securitization allows for an organization (such as a bank) to transfer risk from its own balance sheet to the debt capital markets through the sale of bonds. The cash raised is then used to issue new mortgages allowing the mortgage bank to increase its operational leverage. This type of securitization is known as a "mortgage backed security" (MBS). This type of activity was a major contributor to the global banking melt down in 2008-2009 because buyers ultimately had no way of assessing the value of these debt instruments, which came to be known collectively as "toxic debt."

settlor: the common law name for the person who creates a trust, also called grantor or creator.

short selling: a technique used by investors who think the price of an asset, such as shares, currencies or oil contracts, will fall. They borrow the asset from another investor and then sell it in the relevant market. The aim is to buy back the asset at a lower price and return it to its owner, pocketing the difference; also called shorting.

small cap securities: stocks with a market capitalization of less than $250 million.

spend thrift trust: a restricted trust created to pay income to a beneficiary judged by the trust grantor to be too improvident to handle his or her own personal economic affairs.

stagflation: the dreaded combination of inflation and stagnation; an economy that is not growing while prices continue to rise.

stop loss measures: a system designed to limit trading losses by automatically selling a position when a certain price is reached.

subchapter S corporation: under U.S. tax law, a small business corporation that elects to have the undistributed taxable income of the corporation taxed as personal income for the shareholders, thus avoiding payment of corporate income tax.

sub-prime mortgages: a mortgage with a higher risk to the lender (and therefore they tend to be at higher interest rates) because they are offered to people who have had financial problems or who have low or unpredictable incomes.

swap: an exchange of securities between two parties. For example, if a firm in one country has a lower fixed interest rate and one in another country has a lower floating interest rate, an interest rate swap could be mutually beneficial.

T

tax information exchange agreement: also known as a TIEA, a formal bilateral agreement between two countries governing tax treatment of its nationals by the other country; also providing methods of information exchange upon request.

technical analysis (technicals): analysis and selection of stocks based on analyzing statistics generated by market activity, such as prices and volume. The security's intrinsic value is of no consequence to the technical trader.

territorial tax system: a national system of taxation that only taxes financial and economic activity within its borders and exempts such activities by its residents when conducted offshore.

toxic debt: debts that are unlikely to be recovered from borrowers. Most lenders expect that some customers cannot repay; toxic debt describes a package of loans that are unlikely to be repaid. See also securitization.

trust: a legal device allowing title to and possession of property to be held, used, and/or managed by one person, the trustee, for the benefit of others, the beneficiaries.

unit trust: in the U.K. and in Commonwealth nations, the equivalent of the investment fund known in the U.S. as a mutual fund.

U

"U.S. person:" for U.S. tax purposes, any individual who is a U.S. citizen or a U.S. resident alien (green card holder) deemed to be a permanent resident; also refers to a U.S. domiciled corporation, partnership, estate or trust.

W

warrants (plural): documents entitling the bearer to receive shares, usually at a stated price; also a warrant is a judge-issued document based on probable cause directing police to arrest a named person or search a place or for named objects.

Y

yield: The percentage rate of return paid on a stock in the form of dividends, or the effective rate of interest paid on a bond.

Z

zero interest: the lowest percentage of owed principal that a central bank can set. In monetary policy, the use of a 0% nominal interest rate means that the central bank can no longer reduce the interest rate to encourage economic growth. As the interest rate approaches zero, the effectiveness of government monetary policy is reduced as a macroeconomic tool.

zero-tax haven: an offshore financial center that impose no taxes on foreign investments or business under a territorial tax system.

THE
SOVEREIGN
SOCIETY
Feel the Freedom of Total Wealth